ANOUCHKA JENNINGS

A distinguished biographer, Caroline Moorehead writes for *The New York Review of Books, The Times Literary Supplement, The Spectator,* and *Index on Censorship.* She has worked directly with African refugees in Cairo, as a founder of a legal advice office, in addition to raising funds for a range of educational projects. She is the author of *Gellhorn* and lives in London.

ALSO BY CAROLINE MOOREHEAD

The Collected Letters of Martha Gellhorn (editor)

Gellhorn: A Twentieth-Century Life

Iris Origo: Marchesa of Val d'Orcia

Dunant's Dream: War, Switzerland and the History of the Red Cross

The Lost Treasures of Troy

Bertrand Russell: A Life

Betrayed: Children in Today's World (editor)

Troublesome People

Beyond the Rim of the World: The Letters of Freya Stark (editor)

Freya Stark: A Biography

Sidney Bernstein: A Biography

Fortune's Hostages

HUMAN CARGO

HUMAN CARGO

A JOURNEY AMONG REFUGEES

CAROLINE MOOREHEAD

PICADOR

HENRY HOLT AND COMPANY

NEW YORK

www.picadorusa.com

Picador® is a registered trademark and is used by Henry Holt and Company
under license from Pan Books Limited.

For information on Picador Reading Group Guides, as well as ordering,
please contact Picador.
Phone: 646-307-5629
Fax: 212-253-9627
E-mail: readinggroupguides@picadorusa.com

The author would like to thank Eva Hoffman for permission to quote from *The New
Nomads*; Mandla Langa for permission to quote from *The Naked Song*; and Random House
for permission to quote from Giuseppe Lampedusa's *The Leopard*.
Parts of the prologue are based on an article that appeared in
The New York Review of Books in 2001.

Designed by Victoria Hartman

LIBRARY OF CONGRESS CATALOGING-IN-PUBLICATION DATA

Moorehead, Caroline.
    Human cargo : a journey among refugees / Caroline Moorehead.
        p.   cm.
    Includes bibliographical references and index.
    ISBN 0-312-42561-9
    EAN 978-0-312-42561-6
    1. Refugees. I. Title.

HV640.M66   2005
305.9'06914—dc22

2004054239

First published in the United States by Henry Holt and Company, New York

First Picador Paperback Edition: April 2006

10 9 8 7 6 5 4 3 2 1

To

Lyndall

CONTENTS

A Refugee Story   1

Prologue: The Lost Boys of Cairo   3

Part One: A View of History
————

1. The Homeless and the Rightless   31

Part Two: Leaving
————

2. *Gli Extracomunitari:* Sicily's Boat People   57

3. The Fence: The Migrants of San Diego and Tijuana   83

Part Three: Arriving
————

4. Fair Go: Australia and the Policy of
Mandatory Detention   115

5. Newcastle and the Politics of Dispersal   156

6. Little Better than Cockroaches:
Guinea's Long-term Camps   187

7. The Corridors of Memory:
The Naqba and the Palestinians of Lebanon   220

8. The Illness of Exile   257

Part Four: Afterward
_____

9. Going Home: Afghanistan   291

10. Dead Dreams: The Dinkas of Oulu   328

Epilogue: A Mode of Being   349

Sources   373

Acknowledgments   379

Index   381

HUMAN CARGO

NORTHERN HEMISPHERE

SOUTHERN HEMISPHERE

SIERRA
LEONE
LIBERIA

IVORY
COAST

CHILE

N

A REFUGEE STORY

One day a man in a country in Africa was arrested and accused of belonging to an illegal opposition group. He was sent to prison and tortured. In his cell was a very small window. By standing up very straight, in the far corner of the room, he could just see a field outside. From time to time, cows came to graze in it. As the weeks passed, he grew to recognize their shapes and colors. One in particular pleased him, and he gave her a name. From that day on, whenever she passed his window, he talked to her. He told her about his wife and children who had disappeared, about his house and his parents, and about the village where he grew up.

The day came when he was freed. He left his African country and went into exile, taking his cow with him. In his new country, he was offered an appointment with a doctor, to talk through his experiences. On the first day, he arrived in good time, leading his cow behind him. When the receptionist ushered him into the consulting room, he made sure the cow had plenty of room to follow him. Week after week, the man and his cow attended sessions together.

Several months went by. One day, the doctor suggested that the moment had come for the man to bid farewell to his cow. He replied that it was too soon. Several more months passed. Then the morning came when the man accepted that he could keep his cow with him no longer. That day, he was extremely sad. He brought the cow with him, as usual, and then, crying, told her that the time had come for her to go home. Saying good-bye to his cow made him weep more than he had wept for many years.

PROLOGUE

The Lost Boys of Cairo

Refugees live in a divided world, between countries in which they cannot live, and countries which they may not enter.

— ELIE WIESEL

When Musa Sherif arrived at the house of his friend, a tailor from Sierra Leone, early in February 2000, he found no one there. He was surprised, because his friend was nearly always at home, waiting for him with his supper, but he reasoned that the tailor might have had to make a long journey to the other side of Cairo for a fitting with a client. The room looked unusually neat and empty, but his place was laid, and there was dinner in a pot on the stove. On the table sat a brown paper parcel, tied with string. Musa sat and waited. When some time had passed, he began to grow anxious. He needed to eat and leave, so that he could find somewhere to sleep that night; as a Liberian asylum seeker in Egypt he had no money for a place of his own. And, this being his only meal of the day, he was hungry. Finally, he ate, sitting uneasily at a corner of the table. Then he waited some more.

It was now that he suddenly noticed that the brown packet had his name on it. He opened it. Inside were a newly made pair of trousers, a shirt, and a tie, folded neatly, with a letter on top. "Dear Musa," it said. "Here is a present for you. Forgive me. I have wanted to tell you every day for many weeks now, but I have been too cowardly. I was chosen for resettlement in Canada. Today I am leaving." Musa took the clothes his friend had made for him, put them on, threw away the frayed and filthy ones that he had been wearing for many months, and went back to the streets.

Musa is one of the lost boys of Africa. Though the phrase has come to be used for the young Sudanese separated from their families during their flight from the civil war of the 1990s, who grouped together and eventually made their way to the United States, Cairo is full of lost boys, though most are no longer boys now, but young men, from Sierra Leone and Liberia, Ethiopia and Eritrea, Sudan, Guinea, the Ivory Coast, Rwanda, and Burundi. Over the last ten years they have come to Cairo by a hundred different paths, on foot, by ferry, in airplanes, on trucks and trains, by camel and horseback, believing that, for all its horror, life was still worth living, that Egypt would be the gateway to a future, and that their past, as victims of the savagery of civil war and modern conflict, was somehow their passport to that future. If the lost boys have something in common, beyond a look of stunned and mistrustful defeat, a sort of hooded inwardness, it is that they have all witnessed acts of unconscionable cruelty, which they alone, out of their large families, have inexplicably survived. Fate—luck—has a particular meaning for them.

. . .

I MET MUSA Sherif for the first time in the late afternoon of February 5, 2000, shortly after his friend's departure for the United States. It was my first day in Cairo. I wouldn't have noticed him, for he was one of fifty-six young Liberians gathered in the office of the African Studies department of the American University in Cairo, had it not been for his pressed, almost starched new trousers. He was also the only young man in a tie. Later, I would see him in very clean denim dungarees, and in a baggy green suit of trousers and bomber jacket, in a fashionable military color, with striking emerald green leather sneakers: clothes, for Musa, as for many of the young men, were a symbol of possibility, of belief that there was some order in a profoundly disordered world, and still some hope of being able to make an impression on it.

On this afternoon in early February, Musa had followed the other young men to a meeting called by Barbara Harrell-Bond, who, as emeritas professor in refugee studies at the American University, long a defender and protector of refugees, had become a point of reference for asylum seekers in Cairo. They were sitting on the floor, pressed closely together because the office was too small for such gatherings, in a room of faded elegance, with ornate latticed doors and decorated tiles, remnants of Cairo's earlier grandeur. Musa was one of the young men who spoke. His English was good and his voice clear and precise. With his shirt and tie, and his overly big glasses with their round frames, he had the look of a bookish, eager accountant or librarian. What I didn't then know was that Musa had been a schoolteacher until the nightmare of his current life overtook him, and that, as the brightest and most promising in a large family of sons, he had been selected by his father as the one to study and make his way in a world beyond their farm and village. Nor did I know then that peculiar-looking little Abdullai, with his bright pink woman's quilted jacket and children's furry earmuffs, to which were attached wire antennae, which quivered as he moved his head, was not yet fifteen, and living in a derelict car abandoned beyond the airport, and that he was often hungry; or that Abdularam, sitting cross-legged in the front row and asking a stream of highly technical questions about the Refugee Convention,* spoke such unfathomable English because he had no back teeth on either side, from years of violence and neglect. Later, all these Liberians would become real people to me, as I carried their stories around with me

---

* The Convention Relating to the Status of Refugees was adopted in 1951 to provide international protection for refugees. Under the Convention, the Office of the United Nations High Commissioner for Refugees is charged with supervising its application by collecting information about refugees, reporting on their status, and working to find durable solutions to their problems.

in my head, stories of murdered parents and burned-out homes, tales of terror and flight, and as I slowly pieced together, fragment by fragment, from meetings or calls late at night from public telephone boxes and offered tentatively as bits in a vast, uncompleted jigsaw, the map of each one's particular odyssey. In the same way, later, Liberia itself would become a real place for me, a country of rivers and mountains and towns, but also a place of war and violence, with its military commanders, its rebel checkpoints, and its random, hideous brutality. Unschooled, for the most part on the run and lost for several years, these young men turned out to be keen historians of the civil wars that had destroyed their families and their childhoods.

●　●　●

THAT LATE AFTERNOON in February, as the winter sun went down, and the light in the small cramped room faded, and the noises from the narrow street of car repair shops and spare parts outside began to grow faint, the Liberians talked on and on, about themselves and their fears about what was happening to them. It marked a particular moment in the lives of these fifty-two young men and four young women. Until that afternoon, these young people had been drifting along the margins of Cairo's immense refugee population in search of help, teaming up sometimes, like Musa, with another asylum seeker from another African country, but for the most part totally alone. After this time, they would become a band, with the rivalries and animosities inevitable among people so anxious and so destitute, but a band nonetheless, looking after the interests of the others, so that when Abudu was the first to be accepted for resettlement in the United States, and Amr went to prison on obscure charges of spying for Israel, these events would be personal in the life of each of them.

●　●　●

IT WAS ON that late February afternoon in Cairo that I started to keep notes and that this book began. I wanted it to be about those whose stories I had been hearing for over twenty years of writing about human rights: refugees and asylum seekers, both those who travel to flee torture and persecution and those who move to escape poverty and failed lives. It would be, I hoped, a record of what happens to people when their lives spiral out of control into horror and loss, of the lengths they will go to in order to survive, of the extraordinary resilience of ordinary men and women and children who must accept the unacceptable, and also an account of how the modern world is dealing with exoduses that far exceed in complexity and distance anything the world has known before. And as the months went by and I got to know the Liberians, and then traveled to other places in search of other refugees, this account grew to take in their journeys and their expectations, their former lives, their destinations, and the experiences of those working with them and struggling to formulate coherent policies for the future. I would start with no preconceived ideas, beyond a recognition that among the asylum seekers there are those who lay claim to a history of persecution they do not possess. Without attempting either to cover all parts of the world or all facets of the subject, I would listen to their stories and follow wherever they led, over the whole journey of exile from flight to resettlement or return home, describing only what I saw and heard.

. . .

AMONG THE YOUNG Liberians, Musa is remarkable only for the remorselessness of the horrors that overtook him. His father was a prosperous Mende farmer in Grand Capemount County, with four wives. Musa, the brightest boy in the family, was sent away to Sierra Leone to train to become a teacher. He was a studious boy and he learned good English and Arabic. When he was seventeen, he went home to teach in the local school and prepare to succeed his father as village elder. In a photograph taken at the time, which he has carried with him all these years, he looks absurdly small and young. He is a short, stocky young man, with a very round face and an almost jaunty manner. Musa was at home, in the large family compound, with his pregnant new wife, sixteen-year-old Zainab, when in 1997 Charles Taylor's second wave of civil war brought marauding killers to Grand Capemount County. Taylor's soldiers wanted no elders and no educated Mendes in the new Liberia. The killing was slow and deliberate. First the women and the girls, after raping them; then the elders, using machetes to chop off arms and legs; then the young men, shot with Kalashnikovs. Musa, in a line with four of his brothers, was the last. By the time the soldiers reached him, an officer had arrived. The killing was stopped. His brothers were all dead, along with his mother, father, and sisters. Musa was alive.

· · ·

HE FLED. THREE days later, at the border with Sierra Leone, he found Zainab; she had been raped twice but had not lost the baby. They crossed the frontier and wandered in the bush, eating grass and roots, with Zainab's mother and a little girl of five, found abandoned along the way, whose parents had been murdered in front of her. One day rebels—bands of soldiers roamed both sides of the border—caught Musa's mother-in-law as she was gathering berries; they raped and mutilated her, and, in great pain, she died. Then Musa was captured, slapped about, scarred with the blade of a bayonet. But Zainab hid in the bushes with the little girl; Zainab's baby, a boy, was born under a tree soon afterward and survived. Musa escaped and found them and they pressed on, hiding in the undergrowth, begging food from villagers. At last they reached a refugee camp, but they were turned away: it was full, and those who ran it by now feared that all young Liberian men might be killers with tribal scores to settle.

So they wandered on, stopping from time to time to rest, until one day, on the outskirts of Liberia's capital, Monrovia, they met a friend of Musa's father, a Lebanese trader. The friend, knowing that Musa could not survive for long in a country run by Charles Taylor's men—who were then hunting down all they suspected of being rebel fighters—brought him a plane ticket and a visa for Egypt. Zainab, their son, their adopted daughter, and a new second baby found refuge with an aunt. Musa was now twenty-two. In Egypt, he believed that he would find asylum; the United Nations High Commissioner for Refugees—UNHCR—would surely grant him refugee status and bring his wife and children to join him. He flew to Cairo, expectant, exhausted by months of fear, frantic with worry about his family.

.   .   .

THAT WAS IN 1999. By the time I reached Cairo in February 2000, Musa was still alone, stateless, without papers, work, a home, or his family. UNHCR had neither interviewed him nor recognized his claim to be a refugee. He had lost touch with Zainab and the children; he believed they had fled over the border into Guinea, where the camps for those who escape Liberia's continuing carnage are renowned for rape and casual murder. The politics of the modern refugee world are not on Musa's side, chiefly because he arrived in Egypt too late. By 1999, all Africa seemed to be on the move, running from the civil wars that to this day consume the continent, while many other desperate people had been drawn north by Egypt's open-door policy, not knowing that the country had neither the means of looking after those they so hospitably allowed in, nor any intention of doing so, and that the rest of the world had few plans to give them refuge, either.

Over the next three years, shocked by what he felt to be betrayal, Musa slowly shed his hopes. He accepted that he had nowhere to sleep, but had to move from week to week to the floors of other refugees' rooms, always hiding, knowing that if he was picked up by the police without papers he might be deported or imprisoned. He had understood that he would still have to wait, perhaps for years, for UNHCR to decide whether what he witnessed and endured amounted to the "justified fear of persecution" that would alone grant him refugee status and the possibility of resettlement in the West. He had accepted that he would find no work other than occasional day labor in the black economy, for as an asylum seeker with no papers he could not officially work. He concentrated only on one thing: finding his wife and children and bringing them to live with him on the streets of Cairo. (It was not until much later, when I went to the border between Liberia, Sierra Leone, and Guinea, that I really understood why the young Liberians had known that they had to flee.) Among the small community of Liberian lost boys, he was seen as a loner; he preferred to put his energy into his dreams, alongside which Cairo, with its overcrowding and its incessant noise, its poverty and racism, its bullying police and indifferent aid workers, was a passing nightmare. The boyhood image he had of himself as a teacher and future village elder remained as real to him as it had ever been; he could not and would not give it up, just as he would not learn Egyptian Arabic, for to do so meant that he had accepted that he would never leave. And so he preferred not to seek out the company of the other Liberians, with similar pasts, young men like Abdula, who made jokes in an American accent learned from the tourists who used to come to Egypt before the specter of terrorism destroyed the holiday market, and who saw rebel soldiers burn his father over an open fire before hacking him into little pieces, or Mohamed, a tall boy with a moonlike face and frightened eyes, who watched as his godmother's head was kicked about like a football, or Abu, the boy soldier, whose rite of passage included the slitting open of a pregnant woman's stomach. What these lost boys had seen and been forced to do is not something others cared to hear about.

. . .

IN AUTUMN, THE early mornings in Cairo are almost cool. The pollution, which normally hangs over the streets like a heavy yellow blanket, is light and at this hour the city is still and quiet. Long before it is properly day, the asylum seekers gather at the gates of the offices of UNHCR. There are the Dinkas from Sudan with their very long legs, and the elegant high-cheekboned Somalis; some of the Sierra Leoneans have no arms or hands, the rebels there having decided that mutilating civilians was an effective way of terrorizing those who might be tempted to support the government. Then there are the Ethiopians, whose ancient allegiance to Haile Selassie has branded them as traitors to their country's new regime; men and women from Rwanda and Burundi, where massacres became a way of life; other Sudanese, dissident survivors of torture in Khartoum's security headquarters. They come at dawn to wait, in the hope that their names may feature on the new lists of those called for interview, to hand in documents, to jostle for a slip of paper with a date on which they can collect a form that will allow them to apply for an interview, many months, even years, into the future. Documents of any kind, even scraps of paper with a number on them, are infinitely precious: they suggest identity, a possible existence. Tattered high school certificates, old driver's licenses, envelopes with addresses on them, preserved against all odds during flight, are guarded and produced with pride. At UNHCR's gates all fear that they may learn that their appeal has failed and their file is closed, so that the future contains only statelessness or deportation. "Closed File," the terrible phrase that signifies the end of this particular road, is written in large black capital letters.

. . .

SINCE THE MIDDLE of the 1980s, Egypt—along with forty other countries—has opted for the solution of having UNHCR interview its asylum seekers in order to decide how well founded is their fear of persecution. The result is that the UN body, once revered for its mandate of protecting refugees, is, in Egypt, both prosecution and defense, an anomalous and uneasy position it occupies today with growing prickliness and suspicion. In 2000, 3,057 refugees left Cairo for new lives in the United States, Canada, and Australia (nearly all go to the United States). But after September 11, 2001, President George W. Bush declined to fix a quota for that year's intake, thereby closing the door not only to the refugees who hoped to win places, but also to all those who had already been accepted but had not yet left and have now been told they need to be vetted again for possible terrorist links. No one really thinks that the United States will ever again be very welcoming to those persecuted in other lands.

Inside UNHCR's offices, where only those called for interview ever penetrate, there is an embattled air. It is not easy to be a gate-keeper to the future of so many desperate people; nor is it easy to keep in mind the intricacies of civil war and political repression across much of the African continent. Not all the young Egyptians employed to vet cases enjoy pronouncing on whether the violence suffered and remembered constitutes a degree of persecution ex-treme enough to make return too dangerous. In this daily listening for the nuances of deceit, the little lies that will mark a claim as false, something of UNHCR's noble mandate is being lost, but it is per-haps wrong to blame those who listen, hour after hour, to these tales of bloodshed and torture. There are too many cases, too much suf-fering, too little time. What is happening in Cairo today is happen-ing all over the world; as the funds are cut and the number of asylum seekers keeps on growing, as the West becomes more fearful and more isolated, those who man the gates in Cairo are under pressure to search ever more keenly for lies and inconsistencies, while refugees despair.

· · ·

FEAR, MEMORY, AND expectations endlessly deferred rule in the quicksands of Cairo's refugee world. Psychiatrists say that it is im-portant for peace of mind to live in the present, to come to terms with daily existence, and to neither brood about the past nor attach too much meaning to the future; but the refugees trapped in Cairo today, haunted by terrifying memories of loss and savagery, seduced by a longing for a world they perceive as stable and fulfilling, cannot accept the present. Cairo is a prison sentence, to be endured because there is no option. They simply wait. "The problem for refugees here," a young man told a church worker not long ago, "is that they have no real existence: they live in their head." Like Musa, no African will consider learning more than the few words of Arabic he needs to live: it is too potent a symbol of failure. The few lucky enough to have the desperately desired blue refugee card are not al-ways the happiest. Gone are the terrors of sudden arrest, but reset-tlement is never automatic and it can take many years; the waiting becomes almost too painful. The image of the West becomes more glorious month by month. There have been suicides, people unable to wait any longer; they have no courage left, having used it up on their torturers and the long, frightening journeys to safety. When the refugees decide to die, some do so by jumping from the balconies of Cairo's tall buildings; a ten-year-old-boy killed himself this way shortly before my last visit.

Cairo is not just one of the most polluted cities in the world. It is dirty, intensely overcrowded, broken down, and full of rubble, with roads built up on legs above other roads in an attempt to ease the traffic jams that paralyze the city for all of the day and most of the night. Occasionally, between the brick and the cement, you catch glimpses of filigreed minarets, delicately carved porticoes and arcades, stately facades and the traces of sumptuous courtyards, earlier Cairos of the Islamic master craftsmen and Coptic merchants, when the city was a splendid place of pleasure gardens and cool palaces, and civil servants in their red fezzes strolled along tree-lined avenues where visitors drank sherbet in famous tea rooms. It is the utterly derelict nature of the city today that partly makes possible its absorption of so many refugees—200,000? 500,000? No one can say for sure. Around the city's edges, entrepreneurs keep constructing identical cinder-block buildings in ever widening circles, always leaving the top floor unfinished, so that more floors can be added year by year. From the top of the buildings along the Nile, on the rare moments when the smog evaporates and the setting sun lights up the horizon, you can see the Pyramids in Giza, framed by the jagged edges of unfinished blocks. Wherever the buildings are most derelict, the electricity supplies most sporadic, the water least reliable, there the refugees live.

Donzo is another young Liberian, an almost jaunty good-looking Mandingo with deep regular gashes along both his cheeks. He was one of the first of the young men to bring me his testimony, for me to turn into a formal application for refugee status with UNHCR. When he was sixteen, Donzo was caught by Charles Taylor's men. They didn't want him for a boy soldier, but they wanted informa-

tion about the Mandingos. He had none to give. Before letting him
go, a soldier took out his knife and, getting his companions to hold
the boy still, carved slits across both sides of his face. Six years later,
having lost his grandparents, both parents, seven brothers and sisters, several aunts and uncles, and many cousins, he fled to Cairo
and went to live with eleven other young Africans on the seventh
floor of what must once have been a fine apartment block. This was
soon after the meeting in the offices of the African Studies department at the American University in February 2000, when the young
Liberians took to living in groups, and I started visiting them at
home, so that they could show me, with a mixture of pride and embarrassment, how they were coping with their lives.

In two high-ceilinged rooms with cornices and the remains of
parquet floors, these eleven young men have two broken beds, two
chairs, three blankets, a lightbulb, and a very old, erratic television
set. The glass in the windows up the staircase has long since broken,
leaving a few splintered edges. An elevator, its mahogany doors
wrenched off, dangles from one rusting pulley. Rubbish fills every
corner; down the wide marble stairs, chipped and blackened by filth,
trickles an open sewer. The bannisters have gone. It is almost completely dark. Donzo and his companions live on $40 a month, the al-
lowance received from UNHCR by the one Sierra Leonean
recognized as an official refugee. At the beginning of the month,
when the money comes, Donzo tells me, they eat rice and some vegetables cooked in oil; by the end they are down to just bread. They
seldom leave the building, for fear of arrest, preferring to spend the
months of waiting in the semi-dark, almost comatose with boredom
and inertia. Izako, Donzo's friend and a former customs officer, had
left a wife and two children in Monrovia, after he had been tortured
and raped by Charles Taylor's soldiers: he worries, during the long
empty days, over whether they are still alive. If UNHCR acceptance
rates remain the same, I write in my notebook after this first visit to
their rooms, seven of these eleven boys will never leave Cairo.

Asylum seekers with families, like the thousands of Sudanese
who have arrived since the war intensified in southern Sudan in the

late 1990s, prefer to live in shantytowns on the outskirts, where women, whose husbands have been killed, share rooms without light or water. Tuberculosis among these families is endemic; the children have open sores and scabies; they cough and scratch constantly. They do not go to school, for school is not available to asylum seekers, and a whole generation is growing up illiterate. When the Sudanese women find work as maids, they lock their children for safety into the almost empty, dusty, boxlike rooms, where they lie on blankets on the dirt floor. Apart from the shafts of light that filter through cracks in the door, it is dark; they stay there all day. At Arba Nos, where the desert begins, three hundred Sudanese families live and wait.

. . .

IN THE NEXT three years, between the spring of 2000 and late 2003, I went back to Cairo four times, with Lyndall Passerini, a writer friend. We returned to help set up a legal advice center for asylum seekers to prepare their submissions and their testimonies for their interviews with UNHCR, and, with money from friends, to start a number of small educational projects among people for whom schooling is often the only symbol of a possible better future. We found the money to provide teachers for classes of young Somalis, held in the homes of those fortunate enough to have homes; to fund a nursery school at Arba Nos for Sudanese children up to the age of four, giving them food and medical care and somewhere to spend the days, so that their mothers when going out to work did not have to leave them; and to support English classes for adult Sudanese who, hoping for eventual resettlement in Australia, Canada, or the United States, knew that speaking English was a first step to getting there. But it was the Liberians who, day after day, brought us their stories and proved the most engaging and demanding students.

By the spring of 2001, exactly a year after my first visit to Cairo, a flat had been rented in one of Cairo's poorest and most distant suburbs, two classes formed with blackboards and plastic chairs, maps of Africa pinned to the walls, and books brought out from England. A teacher had been found, and Mohamed Bafalie, a tall, responsible young man who had been a teacher in Monrovia before having to flee Charles Taylor's men, was appointed director of the school. Bafalie's wife, Khalidatou, who had followed him to Cairo after being persecuted by soldiers, had been forced to leave their small son and daughter behind with her mother. From the first day the young Liberians were absolutely clear about their school: they wanted to learn everything. Asked to make lists of what they wished to be taught, they wrote down: engineering, psychiatry, car maintenance, political science, economics, media studies, philosophy, law, history, medicine, creative writing. Most could read and write, but very few had completed more than a couple of years of elementary school. They accepted with good grace when offered English grammar, literature, and a little modern history and politics. Given their fares by bus to this distant flat, they came assiduously, though their journeys—they were the only black people in crowds of often hostile Cairenes—were frightening. Mohamed, the moonfaced boy, was attacked one day on a bus by a group of teenage boys, who beat him about the head with a stick with a nail in it. Early gatherings were polite, subdued; as the months passed, as they felt safer, the young men began to challenge and argue. They began to want things. They were always polite, but they were now also firm. In class, they asked questions, they demanded tests; they wanted, always, more: more homework, more classes, more information. They wanted the Internet and new computers, they wanted certificates, they wanted assurances that they would not be abandoned.

And, slowly, they advanced up the uncertain and interminable queue at UNHCR. By the time of my third visit, in the spring of 2002, all fifty-six had had their first interview, and five had been accepted for resettlement in the West. Their pleasure, their excitement at such good fortune, spread through the group: it had happened to five, it could happen to them all. Though they were still living on the edge of destitution and subject to casual racist attacks, the mood within the group became lighter. They gave out a sense that the future had opened again. Now, e-mailing me when I was back in London, they tentatively asked for things, impossibly ambitious often, but a sign that they imagined a life in which they might really become engineers and lawyers. Kabineh, a short, very young-looking boy with cropped hair and a childish grin, wrote: "I am sleeping from place to place with a lot of disturbance. 2 books I really wished you could send for me: (1) mass communication, (2) Business Management." Bility, who always wore a brown woolly hat, whatever the heat, wondered whether he could have a shortwave radio, to listen to the news from Liberia. All longed for computers.

In the autumn of 2002, something happened that changed the Liberian story. One of the young men, Amr, was arrested. For a while, no one could discover why. It became known that he had been taken to the Mogamma, a vast, ugly government building that faces Cairo's fine Museum of Antiquities in Tahir Square, with cells for those Egypt is planning to deport. There were rumors that he had been tortured. At a first court appearance, he was seen to have bruises on his face and neck, and he appeared confused and fragile. Then it transpired that the security police had spotted him outside the Israeli embassy, decided that he had been spying for Israel, and further suspected that he was involved in a money-laundering operation. The charges were absurd; but in the precarious world in which Cairo's asylum seekers exist, they were terrifying. If the Egyptian police could really imagine that a Muslim Liberian was helping the Israeli secret police, then which one of them might not be a target next?

Other arrests followed. One of the first was Kono, a short, thickset, phlegmatic young man of twenty, one of the group's only two Christians. He was solid, slow moving, and very sad. I knew Kono from my first visit to Cairo, when he came to my flat one day and described his childhood. He was the only son of parents who had both worked for Samuel Doe, president of Liberia until ousted by the rebels; when the rebels closed in on the presidential palace, they arrested everyone they found with any connection to the dead president, and killed both his parents. Kono had then gone to live with a much-loved uncle and aunt, who brought him up as their son, until the day that his aunt went to the market and was captured by rebels and raped before being killed. His uncle survived for a while longer, but then he, too, died in one of the frequent outbreaks of violence that consumed Monrovia in the 1990s. Kono was then twelve.

In Cairo, awaiting news of his UNHCR interview, Kono had decided, for reasons he was never able to explain to anyone, to accept an offer made to young Muslims from Africa to study at Al Azhar, Cairo's Islamic university, and to take a place in the dormitory they provided for homeless students. He did not, of course, tell them that he was a Christian. However, someone informed on him. He was immediately arrested by the university's guards and turned over to the police, who announced that he would be deported. Unusually, he was left in a corridor while arrangements were being made to take him to a prison; he escaped, and made his way to the offices of UNHCR, where an outraged young Egyptian interviewer told him that she wanted nothing more to do with him, as, having lied to Al Azhar, he was clearly a liar, and as such ineligible for any kind of UNHCR assistance. Kono disappeared into hiding.

The next to go was a wiry, bookish boy called Mustafa Kromer. Mustafa had once explained to me that as the youngest son of a man with many wives and many children, he had never been quite sure how many of the boys and girls who thronged the family compound in Liberia were his full brothers and sisters. His own mother died when he was seven, and he had been cared for by a grandmother. Mustafa was out fishing when the rebels came to Grand Capemount County in 1991. His grandmother, fearing the advance of the soldiers, took him to hide in the bush, but life was very hard and she was elderly. She died. Returning to his village, Mustafa found his father; with him and other children he moved from village to village across northwestern Liberia in search of safety. He was eleven when he saw his first killing, a cousin beaten to death in front of him for failing to answer questions from rebel soldiers. Because the rebels now advancing through Grand Capemount County toward Monrovia were led by a man called Alhaji G. V. Kromah, anyone bearing the name Kromah or Kromer was suspect in the eyes of the government forces sent out to confront them. One by one, members of Mustafa's large

family were captured and killed. Mustafa himself was picked up with
two of his brothers and taken to an army camp, where he was beaten
and questioned. My record of his testimony, given to me over several
weeks, runs to many pages: it is a slow, sad story of flight, violence,
and the gradual destruction of a once happy and united family, as
adults and children disappeared, were killed, or simply died from
hunger and exhaustion. By September 1998 Mustafa was the only
survivor. A family friend, finding him wandering on the streets of
Monrovia, smuggled him to Cairo. He was seventeen.

Mustafa spent three weeks in an Egyptian cell behind a police
station in the spring of 2002. My notes say that his friends, who had
been allowed to see him, told me that he was given only water for
the first five days and kept permanently blindfolded. He was not allowed to use the lavatory. He was also slapped and kicked, something he made little of, being accustomed to physical brutality. In
Cairo, prisoners give the name of "freezer" to the room set aside in
prisons and police stations for questioning and physical brutality.
Mustafa was not subjected to the electric shocks given to many
taken into detention, but when they took off his blindfold after five
days they put him into a small cell and left him there. It was not
empty; on the contrary, it held about fifty people. There was no
room for the prisoners to do anything but stand. They took turns
sitting down.

Mustafa was eventually released; he was not told why he had
been arrested. By now, however, there was a rumor going around
the Liberian community that they were being singled out for persecution by the Egyptian police because Charles Taylor, who was then
the president of Liberia, had publicly announced his support for Israeli prime minister Ariel Sharon. It was now widely said that the
Liberian boys were suspected of being spies for Israel.

As more arrests took place, as more of the young men were taken
in for questioning, slapped about, held overnight, threatened with
deportation and indefinite detention in one of Egypt's infamous
jails, where prisoners remain for years without charge or trial, as
Amr remained inside and, it was learned, had been tortured again, as

Kono disappeared altogether, so fear began to spread among the Liberians. The fact that Amr had been an accepted refugee, with his blue card from UNHCR and the possibility of being resettled before too long in the West, and yet was still not safe from police brutality, added to the tension. UNHCR, whose mandate of protection for refugees should in theory have saved Amr from torture and arbitrary detention, was able to do nothing. Edgy and fearful, the young Liberians began to fall out among themselves, accusing one another of absurd and random misdemeanors, watching over their shoulders for betrayal. A feeling of panic seized the group. Musa, who had avoided all overtures of friendship, suddenly disappeared from Cairo. He was reported to have returned to Liberia to look for his wife and children, but a rumor started going around that he had become a spy for the Egyptian secret service in return for food and a place to sleep. He was said to have been sighted talking to a stranger near the Mogamma. His ticket to Monrovia was said to have cost $650, and the fact he could find such a sum was proof, said the others, of his guilt. I had last seen him walking along the towpath by the Nile, in his emerald green sneakers, talking feverishly about his rejection by the group, like an animal expelled from a pack. He was defiant and agitated.

Toward the end of July 2002, a month when temperatures in Cairo rise to over a hundred degrees and the normally frenetic city is stunned into inertia, six more Liberians lost their nerve. Approaching one of the foreign smugglers and traffickers who prey on refugees and asylum seekers everywhere, they were directed to catch a bus to Nueba, a resort on the Red Sea. The plan was for them to cross by night into Israel, something of an irony given the suspicions of their spying. Before they were able to slip across, as they were leaving their hotel in the dark, the Egyptian security police arrived and arrested them. Two of the group were married, a young couple called Gedaweh and Mahmada, who had been forced to leave behind their two children in Liberia when fleeing from Charles Taylor's men in 1999. Gedaweh and Mahmada were both recognized refugees, but they had already waited over three years for their promised resettlement in the West, from where they would be able to have their children join them, and they were now afraid that if arrested they might never see their children again. Gedaweh, like Musa, was a teacher. He later told a friend what happened to them in Nueba. They were just leaving their rooms in the hotel when the security men arrived. Mahmada was pushed back into the room and onto the bed, with such force that she fell to the floor. The Liberians were then taken to the local police station, and next morning they were interrogated. "They asked us," Gedaweh told his friend, "what we were doing in Nueba. We said that we were tourists. They insisted that we were spies for Israel. When we asked for some water to drink, because it was very hot and we were very thirsty, they gave us seawater. For three days, all we were given to drink was salt water." Later, Gedaweh heard one of the policemen say to his superior officer: "Captain, you're wasting your time with these people. If it was me, I would open fire on them, and that would be the end of it." The six were freed.

By the time I returned to Cairo in November 2002, Gedaweh and Mahmada had gone. The trafficker had found a better route across the Sinai and they were in hiding in Tel Aviv, paying off the smuggler's fee in hard labor, laying a new water pipeline for the settlements. They were living, word reached Cairo, in a disused hangar, under guard, and working twelve-hour days. They were said to be hungry. They had taken with them Fumbe, the soccer player, who had cleaned our kitchen meticulously during our first visit to Cairo in 2000; and also a shy and gentle boy called Mamadu, with a rather small head and close-cropped hair, who had been badly slapped about by the police on their first attempt at escape. Mamadu was one of the Liberians I knew best. He was among the first who came to talk to me, and having come once, he came back again and again, adding details to his original testimony that he had been at first too ashamed and too afraid to recall. Mamadu had been a boy soldier. A small, myopic child, he had seen his parents and his three younger siblings dragged out of their house in Monrovia and killed in front of him, his mother and father shot, the children battered to death. At least, he said, he hadn't actually seen this happen, because the rebels had pulled him behind their jeep; but he had heard it, the shots and the sounds of bodies being hit and the cries. He was then eleven. The rebels took him back with them to their camp, to join the other children they intended to turn into soldiers. What happened to him next was something I only slowly pieced together later, when I had got to know him well and he trusted me, and when I had finally understood how very shortsighted he was and taken him to an eye doctor, who told me that he could barely see across a room.

For a while, the rebels left Mamadu with the girls they had captured on earlier raids. These children prepared food for the rebel leaders, fetched wood, and washed clothes. But the day came when Mamadu was ordered to follow the soldiers on a raid, and a day soon after when he was given a Kalashnikov and told to shoot a captive, a terrified woman with a small child clinging to her. Mamadu refused. He was beaten, slapped, denied food. Later, he was again taken on a raid and given a gun. He was told that if he refused to shoot, he would be killed. The captives, this time, were all men. Mamadu shut his eyes and fired. He never asked whether he had killed anyone; he didn't want to know. He suspects that he did. The raids went on. Mamadu spent his days planning his escape. At last the day came when he was trusted sufficiently to be sent to a nearby village in search of food. When he got there he found a woman in the market and begged for help. She took him in, hid him, and later helped him to make his way to Monrovia. Behind the fragility, the shortsighted stare, the gentle manners, lay an absolute will to survive. In Cairo, this became a desperate need to be educated, as if only an education could redeem the horror of the past. Education was all he wanted to talk about when I saw him on my visits to the rented Liberian classrooms. He was one of the most eager and dedicated students, attending every session, whatever it was about. Now, having heard that he had been taken by the smugglers to Tel Aviv, I tried to find him. I could only imagine how frightened he must have been, how very close to the edge of endurance, to have made the decision to flee. His last e-mail from Cairo had been sad, but then I had not known what he was planning. "We do promise to never forget about you. Especially me, Mamadu. You know it's just such kind of cruel juke [*sic*] of nature to suddenly surprise us with such big and ugly separation." In Israel, friends tried to trace him. He seemed to have disappeared.

In November 2002 I started to keep a proper diary. Eleven Liberians were by now in Israel, among them probably Donzo, the boy with the scars across his face. Two had left for resettlement in the States. Two had vanished, rumored to have been deported to Liberia. Musa was still missing. Abdula, the charming, jaunty boy with an American accent and spiky hair, who had watched his father burned very slowly to death over an open fire, was in the hospital, seriously ill with tuberculosis and pneumonia. "The Liberians are frightened," I wrote in my notebook. "Amr is in prison, Kono in hiding, Mamadu has fled. No one feels safe." The Liberian apartment had been closed down, after the security police called in the teachers for questioning. The classes had been transferred to a room in the American University, but only half the Liberians were now attending, and when they came they were anxious and distracted. The others were staying at home, not daring to be seen on the streets. At UNHCR, in the wake of September 11, the refugees said that the emphasis during interviews was on lies, how best to catch out the asylum seekers, find holes in their testimonies so that they could be turned down. I learned that a new stamp had been devised—"LOC," for "lack of credibility"—and that it was now stamped onto most of the files as a reason for rejection. "But who is to say what is credible," I wrote in my diary, "when you have been shot at by rebels, when you have seen your mother raped and your brothers and sisters burnt to death in your house, when your father has disappeared and you are now alone in the world? When you are ashamed to describe to the young woman sitting across the desk from you with her tapping pencil and her inquisitive eyes what the soldiers did to you and how you are afraid that you may have AIDS from being raped by the guards and how you ache for news of your family whom you really know perfectly well that you will never see again? How do you explain that the journey from your village in Africa to Cairo took everything you had in terms of money, and more than money, courage, imagination, and hope? That if the woman sitting at the desk turns you down, you have no idea what you will do next, and that your reserves of hope have gone? That though you look tidy, well turned out, this is because you have spent the money you borrowed on soap with which to wash yourself and your clothes for this interview, and that you are absolutely terrified that you may not be saying the right things?"

I wanted to see Amr, still in a police lockup on the edge of Cairo. There was talk that he would soon be released, after almost a year in prison, for lack of evidence. One morning, I had a call from Fofana, the best-educated of the young Liberians, with a degree in law, completed at Al Azhar after arriving in Cairo. Fofana had recently been told that his resettlement application for the United States had gone through. With his serious, even ponderous manner, he had become something of a legal spokesman for the group. He would, he said, take me to the police lockup, where we would at least be able to call to Amr through a fence.

Later, I wrote: "Amr's name is called. I see his fingers first, clutching at the top of a black-painted iron gate covered with thick wire netting, where there is an eighteen-inch gap between the gate and the ceiling. After his fingers, the top of his head appears, and then his eyes, as he pulls himself up by his arms, helped by other prisoners below. We call out to each other. I have brought him a belt, to hold up his trousers, because his own has been taken away from him, and some food. It is passed from hand to hand, from guard to guard, and then given to Amr, whose arm can just squeeze through the gap. Since I can only see the top of his face, I cannot tell how he is." Going back into Cairo by bus, we passed the City of the Dead, Cairo's great array of mausoleums and mosques built to house the bodies and spirits of the departed. Konoba told me that it now has six million live people living in it, a figure I find almost impossible to believe.

· · ·

SIX MONTHS LATER, in the spring of 2003, I was back in Cairo. Amr had been released. A Spanish woman, Ana Liria-Franch, had been appointed to head UNHCR's Cairo office and with her had come more generous policies toward the asylum seekers. Some groups were now being accepted de facto as refugees under the 1951 Convention, not by virtue of their individual fears of persecution but because of the continuing turmoil inside their home countries. First interviews had speeded up considerably; by now, all the Liberians were through that stage, and some were on their way to resettlement in the West. Those destined for the United States were full of excited dreams, and had taken to carrying American comics and magazines around with them. For those who remained in Cairo, better things were promised. Liria-Franch and her colleagues were trying to make plans—"durable solutions" in the language of the UN—for those whose cases were not strong enough to win them full refugee status under the 1951 Convention but who nonetheless were unable to go home. Among the Liberians—now down to thirty-four—the other twenty-two were scattered among Israel, the United States, Canada, and Liberia—the mood was buoyant. "Group very depleted," I wrote. "Most of those who remain are excited, talkative. But some are still worried. Bility, in his brown woolly hat, says that he can't talk about English grammar any longer when he has nowhere proper to live and often nothing to eat." Bility told me that he had been buying chicken carcasses from restaurants, on which the wings are usually left, and that he made soup from them.

But for the most part the young Liberians were reclaiming their lives. All, that is, except for those who had fled across the desert and into Israel and who now found themselves in limbo. After many months, news had reached the group in Cairo that those in Israel had worked off their smugglers' fees and were now free. Accorded the lowest rung of recognition by the Israelis, they were safe to stay, but they still had no proper papers and no right to travel, and their prospects for an education were very poor. Gedaweh and Mahmada had not seen their children for almost four years now, and there was no possibility of bringing them to Israel. Like Fumbe, the young soccer player, they felt most bitterly about the fact that, had they stayed in Cairo, they would by now have been on their way to the United States, Australia, or Canada, with Kono and Mohamed, to be resettled in new lives. It was from Mamadu, the shortsighted boy soldier, from whom I had heard nothing in almost a year, that I had the saddest news.

Having twice tried and eventually succeeded in reaching Tel Aviv, Mamadu was still working off his smuggler's fee in a cement factory. His health was poor, and made considerably worse by the dust; he had lost many days of work through illness. He wheezed constantly. He was sleeping on the floor of a disused warehouse; he seldom had enough to eat. "I feel myself growing older and do not know anything," he wrote. When I sent him money, partly for a doctor to treat a rash that had spread across his face, he wrote again, about "repairing wounds from my face . . . There is no way I can pay you back for everything that you've done for me, you are a special credited person from the deepest part of my heart and someday I believe you will be proud of me . . . hopefully I will be fine as long as I know myself." A few months later, he e-mailed me to say that he had found work washing up in a hotel. "Am quite sure some day things are going to be much better with lots of fun and joye. A day that one does not have to always worry about how life is going to be tomorrow. Pretty soon that day will arrive." This was soon after his twentieth birthday. He had been alone for nine years. His dream was to become a mathematician.

• • •

THE REFUGEES ARE not absolutely without help in Cairo. There is something in the utter desolation and loss of the refugee existence, the courage of the stories of endurance, that strikes a chord among those drawn to work in human rights. Lawyers, doctors, teachers, and a few social workers, both Egyptian and foreign, struggle to respond to a situation that appears more intractable with every passing week. In shabby offices in various parts of the city, I discovered people helping the asylum seekers with their testimonies so that no opportunity would be lost when the date for an interview with UNHCR finally arrived; doctors who, in their spare time, treated those who have been tortured the worst and who worried about increasing alcoholism among the men and about how to alleviate the profound depression that afflicted so many refugees; priests who collected money and unwanted clothes to give to the most destitute; church workers who ran small feeding programs. Like charitable endeavors everywhere, all this touched only the very edges of what was wrong. Lying at a crossroads for the flows of Africa's displaced people, Cairo is a staging post for refugees, a step on a journey that should, but seldom does, move from terror to safety. Neither the beginning nor the end of their odyssey, Cairo is where the policies and the resolutions succeed or fail, where all that is expected of UNHCR is most visibly exposed. In the great international debate about the future of asylum, the trading in quotas, the many arguments about mandate and responsibilities, the haggling over economic migrants, the seminars about "irregular movers" and the internally displaced, Cairo provides one view of the collapse of this ideal.

. . .

NOT LONG AGO a Sudanese man, carrying a small girl in his arms, managed to get past the guards at UNHCR and into the office of a member of the staff. The child was crying loudly. The man was also crying. Arriving before the interviewer's desk, he drew back the skirt of the girl's dress and pointed to her legs: they were covered in open, bleeding, infected sores. "Help me," he said to the woman. "Help me to do something, help me to go to a doctor." The woman, it seems, sat frozen, speechless. The man grew more agitated and insistent. Still she did nothing. At last, in despair beyond endurance, he pulled from his pocket the blue refugee card he had fought so long and so hard to obtain, and tore it in shreds. "Now," he cried out, trying to explain an act so symbolic and so momentous in words that nothing could make strong enough, "I am ashamed to be a refugee."

PART ONE

A VIEW
OF HISTORY

THE HOMELESS AND THE RIGHTLESS

Displacement is like death. One thinks it happens only to
other people.

— MOURID BARGHOUTI

When Henri Dunant arrived home from the battle of Solferino in
June 1859, full of disgust and pity at the treatment of wounded soldiers, Geneva was a small, pious, scholarly city, where people lived
modestly and regarded themselves as enlightened conservatives. In
the narrow streets of the fine old town, up and down the Grande
Rue where the rich, long-established families lived, they had long
felt pride not only in the number and variety of their philanthropic
endeavors, but also in the welcome they extended to the people they
called aliens, the foreigners and political refugees like Voltaire and
Jean-Jacques Rousseau who had come to settle along the shores of
their lake, and whom they regarded as assets and not as liabilities.
For all their instinctive misgivings about Dunant's impetuousness
and touches of vanity, the Genevois quickly perceived that there was
much luster to be gained for their city in his impassioned pleas for
humane action in the conduct of war. Soon, committees were meeting to draft articles on the laws of war, on the care of wounded soldiers, and on injuries caused by particular kinds of weapons. They
were not the first proposals for the regulation of warfare, but they

were more ambitious than most that had gone before, and the timing was right. In 1863, the Red Cross movement was born and the next year the first Geneva Convention was drafted and presented for signature to the nations of the world. The Genevois took immense pleasure in their new initiative, though by now Dunant himself was an outcast, victim of a foolish financial speculation, consigned to obscurity until unexpectedly awarded the first Nobel Peace Prize as an old man nearly forty years later.

Geneva's credentials for the new humanitarian movement were excellent. Switzerland was strategically placed at the heart of Europe, its absolute neutrality sanctioned by the Peace of Westphalia in 1648 and again by the Treaty of Vienna in 1815, since when it had welcomed a steady flow of people at times of European unrest. It was prosperous and it was pacifist. Not surprising, then, that when millions of people were made stateless by the dismantling of the multiethnic Austro-Hungarian and Ottoman empires and the collapse of tsarist Russia, it was to Geneva that the world looked for the creation of an organization to care for those fleeing chaos, famine, and persecution. By then the League of Nations had been set up in the Palais des Nations, not far from the lake. For the International Committee of the Red Cross, just up the road, deeply involved in refugee matters and enjoying considerable international prestige as a result of its work during World War I, it was an obvious step to put pressure on the new League to care for refugees.

In 1921, the League persuaded the Norwegian explorer Fridtjof Nansen—he was sixty and would have preferred to pursue his scientific interests—to take the job of negotiating the repatriation of some 500,000 Russian prisoners of war; the following year, he was appointed the League's first High Commissioner for Refugees. Nansen received little funding, but he possessed a great deal of passion and energy. He persuaded governments to recognize travel documents for stateless Russians—the "Nansen passport"—and then turned his attention to helping the hundreds of thousands of Bulgarians, Romanians, Magyars, and Armenians—the latter, survivors of the Turkish massacres—all now wandering around Europe, repeatedly turned away at borders. "Once they had left their homeland," wrote Hannah Arendt in the 1950s, "they remained homeless; once they had left their state, they became stateless; once they had been deprived of their rights, they became rightless, the scum of the earth."

Nansen worked extremely hard all through the 1920s. By his death in 1930, he had almost single-handedly helped a large number of people and established a principle of moral responsibility for the displaced; but that principle had as yet very little bite, and could do little to help the Jews who by the early 1930s were already looking for safety from Nazi rule and finding the doors of western states closed against them. In 1933, the League of Nations set up a High Commissioner for Refugees from Germany, but so anxious was it not to offend the German government, still at this point a member of the League, that it agreed to regard the treatment of Jews solely as an internal affair and to confine its attentions to emigration and travel documents, with no questions asked about domestic conditions and the causes for flight. An outspoken early commissioner, James G. McDonald, resigned in despair in 1936. Two years later, the Germans left the League, but even so the Western governments remained reluctant to offend them. When it came to human lives, McDonald urged bitterly but without effect, "considerations of diplomatic correctness must yield to those of common humanity."

The economic depression that spread across North America and Europe in the 1930s did much to set back the refugee cause. National interests, governments argued, would be best served by imposing tough limits on immigration. In country after country, ever more restrictive laws, aimed at keeping out all but carefully selected groups, were passed. Only under considerable pressure from Jewish associations did President Roosevelt agree, in 1938, to call an international conference at Evian, at which to discuss ways to resettle the Jews now trying to escape Austria and Germany. Evian is a shameful milestone in the history of refugee affairs. Delegates from most of the major Western powers rose to talk about their own national levels of unemployment and to argue that the movement of so many

Jewish refugees could only be "disturbing to the general economy." Evian offered no lifeline to the Jews of Europe. All it achieved was the creation of a feeble intergovernmental committee on refugees, unable either to persuade Germany to allow its Jewish citizens to emigrate with money or possessions, or to convince Great Britain not to curtail the immigration of Jews into Palestine. Germany, encouraged by the world's evident indifference to the suffering of the Jews as well as to the other unwanted members of its population, set about stepping up its own punishments and restrictions. Nansen's dream of a world that took responsibility for the fate of those who fell victim to human rights abuses and were forced to flee their homes lay in ruins.

· · ·

BY EARLY 1945, there were more than 40 million people drifting about Europe, stateless, displaced, lost. There were Germans, trying to go home; there were the survivors of the concentration camps of occupied Europe; there were the people whose countries and homes had been swallowed up when borders had been redrawn and territory changed hands. Many of these people, Russians and Czechs, Poles and Hungarians, Ukrainians and Romanians, found themselves in Germany, where almost everything—houses, roads, railway lines, water supplies, industry, agriculture—had collapsed.

The Western powers had been preparing for this moment. In November 1943, meetings had been held by the Allies to discuss what relief measures would be necessary when the Axis countries were at last defeated. Mindful of their lack of generosity in the prewar years and appalled by the knowledge now emerging from the occupied countries of the German atrocities, forty-four states agreed to donate large sums to assist and repatriate the displaced. Between the autumn of 1943 and the summer of 1947, a UN Relief and Rehabilitation Administration, employing at its peak more than 27,000 people, spent $3.6 billion, the bulk of it given by the United States. One of UNRRA's many tasks, debated at some length at both the Yalta and the Potsdam conferences, was how to repatriate as quickly and as efficiently as possible all those wanting to return home at the end of hostilities. Unlike its predecessors, UNRRA proved effective. In the first five months of peace, three quarters of the displaced went home.

However, it soon became apparent that not everyone actually wanted to go home, particularly as news began reaching the West that Stalin was sending many of those who returned straight to the gulags. By 1946 repatriation had all but stopped, and a million people were still in Europe's refugee camps. Unlike earlier refugees, who had fled their countries in the 1920s and 1930s and could not go home because they were not wanted, these were people who were wanted—if only for reasons of revenge—but who were themselves unwilling to go home.

It was in New York and Washington, rather than in Geneva, that the next step in the refugee story took place. At the heart of the postwar sessions debating the new United Nations, and among those drafting the Universal Declaration of Human Rights 1948, the talk was all about the rights of people, their right to flee from oppression, to express their own views, to practice their own faiths, and to choose for themselves where they wanted to live. Refugees, lacking state protection, became people of international concern and subject to international protection. And their problems were no longer understood simply as a matter of groups of people, fleeing and assisted together, but of individuals, with their own cases, their own choices and fears and anxieties. According to Article 14 of the Universal Declaration, every individual was to have the "right to seek and to enjoy in other countries asylum from persecution."

UNRRA had been established to deal with repatriations. As its chief funder, America now decided to wind up its activities. In the face of bitter opposition from the Eastern Bloc, which continued to call on its former citizens to come home, the United States voted to create a new body, the International Refugee Organization. The IRO's mandate was subtly different: to "resettle" people uprooted by war. The Soviets refused to join, accusing the West of turning refugee camps into centers of anticommunist propaganda and using them to recruit the forced labor needed to rebuild western Europe's shattered countries. But an important step had been taken. Under IRO's mandate fell a vital new element: the protection not merely of groups but of individuals with valid objections to being repatriated. During the four and a half years of IRO's existence, barely 50,000 people returned to their former homes in central or eastern Europe.

The question now was what to do with those who remained in the camps for displaced people. The fit and healthy were soon recruited for the very labor schemes so condemned by the Russians. In return for volunteering to build roads, or work in the mines, industry, and agriculture in the United States, Canada, and Australia and across Europe, refugees could apply for citizenship in the countries that offered them work. No one, however, wanted the sick or the elderly, and as the Cold War dragged on, 400,000 "hardcore" cases lingered on in the camps. Before finally shutting down its operations—which, at $428.5 million, had proved expensive—IRO officials warned that what once had seemed a temporary phenomenon would in time turn out to be a very permanent one.

• • •

IT WAS NOW 1950. The United States, having spent many millions of dollars on refugees in Europe, decided that the problem was no longer theirs to deal with, particularly as they were now helping European countries directly through the Marshall Plan, which in turn would, they argued, benefit the refugees as well. What neither they, nor it seems anyone else, envisaged was a world in which refugees would keep on coming, as the IRO had warned. War, famine, violence, and poverty would send people fleeing across borders, and as fighting broke out in Korea and Palestine and starvation spread across China, it became plain that yet another measure would be needed to counter these new flows of displaced people. In the United Nations, talks began about the setting up of a new body, an Office of the UN High Commissioner for Refugees (UNHCR), and a new convention that would spell out their rights. Louis Henkin was a young lawyer at the U.S. State Department, interested in international law, when he was invited by his boss, Dean Rusk, to sit with the U.S. team negotiating what became the 1951 Convention Relating to the Status of Refugees. With him were delegates from twenty-six countries. Professor Henkin, a courteous, upright man with a bony face and rather large ears, is now in his late eighties and the only member of the committee still alive. He remembers many hours devoted to wrangling over the meaning of the word "refugee," and a general ill-defined feeling that the topic did not have great significance for the modern world. There was much talk about whether there should be a "right" to asylum, or only the right to "seek" it. The all-important Article 33, about *nonrefoulement*—the not sending back of refugees to countries where they faced persecution—was pushed through by the French, who reminded the others of the fate of the Jews trying to flee the Nazis. The nations of eastern Europe declined to attend the sessions, saying that in their view the refugees left in the camps in Europe were all traitors, and the United States argued strongly that the new organization's mandate should be one of protection only, not of assistance or relief, and that its budget should be limited. The meetings, Professor Henkin recalls, which took place in Washington and on the shores of Lake Geneva, were on the whole good-tempered, but not without argument, for the British wanted host states to bear responsibility for the refugees on their territory (and had very few) while the French (who had many) wanted other countries to share the burden. Germany, Austria, and Italy, all of which were overwhelmed by the large numbers of refugees still living in camps, had no voice at the table.

The document that emerged—in a surprisingly short space of time, little more than six weeks—was a simple reflection of the immediate postwar world. The terms it came up with remain in use to this day. The definition of a refugee, according to Article 1 of the Convention, revolved around the idea of persecution, "a well-founded fear of persecution on account of race, religion, nationality, membership in a particular social group, or political opinion." The phrase "asylum seeker" would apply to someone seeking refugee status. The persecutors, it was tacitly agreed, were the totalitarian

Communist regimes, and the refugees were therefore, by definition, "good." "Bad" refugees lay well into the future. In the 1950s, "good" refugees were seen to be useful pawns in Cold War diplomacy. "Migrants," it was spelled out, were people who could go home; "refugees" were those who could not. That there would soon be people fleeing in great numbers from poverty, generalized violence, or lives without bearable futures, was not foreseen. The "durable solutions" to the lives of refugees, which UNHCR undertook to explore, included resettlement in another country, integration nearby, or (only if the refugee wished it) repatriation. In 2004, the Refugee Convention, together with the 1967 Protocol that extended its scope beyond Europe to take in the rest of the world, remains the most important international document on refugee protection. It is the foundation of EU policy toward refugees, and ratification is a condition of European Union membership.

In 1951, however, it reflected the concerns of the day. The decision was taken not to include the 458,000 exiled Palestinians who, for political reasons, were to be assisted by the United Nations Relief and Rehabilitation Administration, with the result that there would be no international organization to protect them. And there was much discussion about what groups UNHCR should concern itself with. "Internally displaced" people—later called IDPs—who had not crossed an international border in their flight, were eventually excluded. Sovereignty was not challenged. While the new agency could assist or at least protect refugees once they had fled over a border, it was not invited to concern itself with what had led them to leave home in the first place. UNHCR, opening its doors for business in Geneva, not far from the Palais des Nations and in the company of a growing number of aid agencies and international organizations now clustering together in Switzerland, was given a very small budget, an emergency fund to be used only in dire necessity, a few rooms, and a handful of staff.

In 2001, UNHCR celebrated its fiftieth birthday. No international organization, argues Gil Loescher, the author of a comprehensive and authoritative evaluation of its achievements, has ever had such an inauspicious beginning, or been born of such inherent paradoxes. Apolitical, UNHCR acts as chief advocate for the refugee cause. Forbidden to challenge governments over their internal affairs, it has a mandate to protect those whom governments persecute. The world it looked out on in 1951 was divided, deeply respectful of the sovereign right of states, and little interested either in refugees or their futures. The United States, from the beginning, was so suspicious of entrusting responsibility to a United Nations body that it immediately set up an International Office for Migration to ensure that its influence remained strong in the world of displacement and the movement of people. What UNHCR had not been given was power. The question was: how far could it get with persuasion?

. . .

THE FIRST HIGH Commissioner for Refugees was Gerrit Jan van Heuven Goedhart, a shrewd, modest, likable man who was admired for his eloquence and who had spent the war in the Dutch resistance. Goedhart liked to say that he had been a refugee himself. The United States, which had wanted an American commissioner, showed its irritation by marginalizing the agency while he remained in office. The original International Refugee Organization was also annoyed by having its position usurped. Goedhart further alienated some of the donors by his determination to include relief in his mandate, and he had considerable trouble raising the necessary funds until bailed out by the Ford Foundation. Goedhart died suddenly in 1956 of a heart attack, but even his critics reluctantly admitted that he had managed to make much of the Western World aware that it owed a measure of responsibility for refugees.

The next few years were crucial. The second High Commissioner, Auguste Lindt, was a Swiss diplomat, popular with the Americans and a personal friend of Dag Hammarskjold. He and his successor, another Swiss diplomat called Félix Schnyder, negotiating their way delicately through the minefields of the Hungarian revolution and the Algerian war of independence, cleverly turned

UNHCR into the genuine focal point in the refugee world, while shifting its concerns away from Europe and toward Africa, where one country after another was in postcolonial turmoil. UNHCR, declared Schnyder, needed a "universal character." This was not quite enough for the nascent African states, however, who complained that UNHCR's tight definition of a refugee failed to reflect the reality of conditions on their continent. In 1964, the Organization of African Unity appointed a commission that in time drew up its own convention with a more generous definition of the word "refugee," to take in not solely those fearful of individual persecution, but all who were driven to flee their homes because of war and civil conflict. Wars, violence, ethnic fighting would all now enter the refugee debate, as qualifying people to be recognized as refugees—though not by Europe and North America—when in 1984 ten Central American states signed the Cartagena Declaration on Refugees.

The fourth High Commissioner was the second son of the hereditary imam of the Ismaili sect of Shiism. Suave and gregarious, Prince Sadruddin Aga Khan had once shared a room with Edward Kennedy at Harvard, where he attended lectures by Henry Kissinger. He spoke perfect French and English, had excellent contacts in the developing world, and was determined to make UNHCR a major international political player. He had not long stepped down, after ten generally well-regarded years, yielding his place to the former Danish prime minister, Poul Hartling, a clergyman with progressive views, when the flight of people from Vietnam, Laos, and Cambodia, which had begun in 1975, sharply intensified. Under Hartling, who ran the agency more democratically than the somewhat cliquish Aga Khan, more than 2 million refugees, the boat people of Indochina, were resettled in the West. It was during Hartling's tenure, too, that there was a global surge in refugee numbers. Vast camps were set up in Africa and Asia, later to prove hard to dismantle. "Refugee warriors," operating from camps across borders, became players in regional struggles for power. During the 1980s, the number of refugees worldwide rose from 10 million to 17 million; contributions from reluctant donors failed to keep up with their needs.

Something else was also happening. As more and more refugees, driven by violence and human rights violations, left their homes in the developing world, they began to travel farther afield, arriving in ever greater numbers in European countries to claim asylum. Until now, requests for asylum had been few and confined to dissident scientists and ballet dancers from the Eastern Bloc whose defections made headlines in national newspapers. The political upheavals across Africa, Asia, and the Middle East produced a surge of arrivals by plane, truck, and boat, people who bypassed normal channels, often with the help of newcomers on the refugee scene: traffickers and smugglers of illegal travelers. The refugees came from Ethiopia, from what was then Rhodesia, from Sri Lanka, Iran, Iraq, and then Somalia. In 1976, 20,000 people had asked for asylum in western Europe; by 1981 the figure had reached 158,500, and UNHCR was beginning to struggle to keep its position as main arbiter over asylum policy.

Right through the 1970s and early 1980s, European bureaucracy coped well with immigration. In the face of the immense numbers of unexpected arrivals, the system crumbled. Waiting times for decisions became longer, and appeals backed up. There were growing doubts about the nature of the asylum claims, questions about the extent to which the newcomers were valid refugees under the 1951 Convention. The idea emerged of the "bad" refugee, a person not so much in flight from persecution but actively in search of work and a better life, using the asylum route as his way into Europe. The phrase "economic migrant" entered the jargon of refugee affairs. UNHCR in Geneva kept urging European governments to be generous, arguing that even if some of the claimants were not, strictly speaking, Convention refugees, there was still too much danger at home for them to risk returning; states responded by drafting ever tighter restrictions. By the mid-1980s, most European countries, agreeing that the best way to stem the flow was to prevent people from arriving in the first place, were drawing up measures to deter them. Soon, with the advent of the European Union, an outer European perimeter was defined and barricaded against newcomers. Financial support was withdrawn from asylum seekers who were deemed not to meet the criteria; detentions and deportations began. When UNHCR complained, Western governments paid no attention and concentrated on their own refugee policies. No one listened when Hartling pleaded that those who sought asylum should be seen as victims, not abusers.

By the late 1980s, UNHCR had reached a low point, excluded from many of the main worldwide refugee debates. In any case, donors seeing the political upheavals and natural disasters of the day wanted to fund relief operations, not refugee protection, particularly when relief kept vast numbers of refugees from arriving at their doors. And, under the next High Commissioner, Jean-Pierre Hocké, they went some way to establish and fund these operations. Hocké had been head of operations for the International Committee of the Red Cross at the time of the Biafra crisis, in 1967; he knew all about the logistics of relief.* He was decisive, even authoritarian, and he wanted to see an end to the long-term camps that had by now become endemic in the refugee world. These camps, said Hocké, with considerable reason but ahead of his time, crushed "human dignity" and reduced the "human capacity for hope and regeneration"; what the West should be doing was not keeping them afloat, but attacking the root causes for the exoduses. Hocké also longed to revise the 1951 Convention, to bring its definition of a refugee into line with that of the Organization for African Unity, in order to take in all those affected by the wars and civil conflicts now chronic in many places. But Hocké was too dictatorial and his style of leadership offended people. In any case, Cold War politics continued to dominate the regional conflicts of Africa and Asia. Shortly into his second term, in 1989, he resigned, after a bruising scandal over his expenses. Few were sad to see him go.

Hocké's departure coincided with another event that trans-

---

* In 1967, intertribal conflict in Nigeria led to the secession of the eastern region, which became the Republic of Biafra. Never widely recognized, the new nation collapsed in 1970, and the area was reincorporated into Nigeria.

formed the refugee world. With the coming down of the Berlin Wall, the very nature of the refugee question altered. Gone were all the old Cold War certainties about the "good" refugees fleeing communism. In their place came a decade of unprecedented violence, ethnic conflict, environmental disaster, and spreading poverty. The 1990s saw war in Iraq and Chechnya, ethnic cleansing in the Balkans, genocide in Rwanda, the collapse of Sierra Leone and Liberia, the disintegration of Somalia, the transformation of the Great Lakes of Africa into an area of barbarity and anarchy, and the targeting of civilians and later of aid workers. In Rwanda, almost all girls past puberty were raped, and many were then murdered. Of twenty-seven major conflicts in 1992, only two were actually between states. By now, around 90 percent of the casualties of war were civilians. Hocké's successor, Thorvald Stoltenberg, a Norwegian former minister of defense, stayed in office just a year. He was replaced by Sadako Ogata, a small, determined, elderly Japanese professor of international relations, the first woman and the first Asian to hold the post. Japan was recognized as an important funder and Ogata's American education and academic background were seen as useful. She was also hardworking, politically astute, and keen to avoid confrontations, arguing that over such prickly matters as asylum policy it was better to be tactful than morally superior. "The real problem," she announced, "is saving lives. We can't protect dead people."

Faced with the killings in Rwanda, Somalia, and the Balkans, watching refugees flowing in rivers across borders, or trapped in desolate no-man's-lands, hungry, desperate, and confused, Ogata turned to relief operations. Relief, she announced, *is* protection. Bosnia, in 1992, transformed UNHCR into the world's largest emergency relief agency, at its peak delivering food, tents, and medicines to more than a million and a half "war-affected" people—almost the entire population, along with returnees, the internally displaced, and refugees. Repatriation, long considered a sensitive subject, became another of Ogata's goals. During her time in office tens of thousands of people went home to Ethiopia, Eritrea, Angola, Cambodia, Mozambique, and Namibia.

Building on Hocké's logistical skills, Ogata now made the agency into a more broadly based humanitarian organization, helping not only the traditional Convention refugees, who had been able to cross borders, but the internally displaced, who had remained within their own countries. Donors liked Ogata. Giving money to relief was preferable to being forced to address the root causes of the emergencies that drove people into becoming refugees, or to consider too closely the ethics of their increasingly restrictive asylum policies. The media liked her, too. They welcomed her open manner and her obvious desire to attract their attention. Within the UN, UNHCR became the most admired of all the agencies, and, at the height of the Yugoslav refugee crisis, the one with the biggest budget.

Ogata's interests matched the mood of the times. In 1992, the Secretary General of the UN, Boutros Boutros-Ghali, announced that the "time of absolute and exclusive sovereignty" was over, and that intervention against repressive regimes was a necessary component of international politics. For the first time, collective interventionist policies were seen as a legitimate way to prevent refugee flows. For Ogata, intervention, which she welcomed, would take the form of diplomacy and the pressing of human rights concerns, with a view to making it easier for the victims of war to remain at home. But it was not always easy; moral choices arose, about whether, in effect, to collaborate in ethnic cleansing by helping people leave their countries, or to abandon the defenseless to die. Ogata acted decisively. She would help people survive, whatever the implications. She would even work with the military, if she had to, especially after aid workers began to be targeted. As she had said, she could do nothing for the dead. But neither could she always do much for the living. Rwanda proved a bitter failure for many UN agencies, UNHCR among them. Neither were the *génocidaires* halted as they killed, nor were the camps housing survivors later prevented from being militarized. The question before Ogata and her colleagues was painful: to what extent does relief make things worse by prolonging conflict?

Not everyone was sad to see Ogata leave. People had liked her personally and found her style of leadership friendly. But she had stayed a little long. By the end of the 1990s, the mood was again changing. Protection for refugees was felt to have suffered during her tenure, when so much emphasis had been placed on relief. In Kosovo, which saw the largest mass refugee movement in Europe since World War II, UNHCR was accused of having been poorly prepared and having acted too slowly. For its part, the agency felt itself to have been sidelined by states and forced to stand by while basic standards were violated and competing actors followed their own agendas. Donors moved away, preferring to invest funds directly or give to nongovernmental organizations. UNHCR was not the only agency to suffer, but between 1992 and 1997, its budget dropped by 21 percent. The principal loser, as ever, was Africa, where by 1999 UNHCR was spending just one tenth of what it spent in the Balkans. And by now Africa, with 12 percent of the world's population, had nearly half of its displaced people.

·   ·   ·

IN JANUARY 2001, Ruud Lubbers, a former Dutch prime minister, became the ninth High Commissioner for Refugees. With political stature and confidence enabling him to meet world leaders on equal terms, Lubbers was perceived as a man able to confront Western governments over their ungenerous asylum policies and their reluctance to honor their refugee commitments; at the same time, he was decisive and clearheaded enough to reform a large and unwieldy office that had grown unaccountable during the years of major relief operations. It was hoped that he would persuade more countries to provide UNHCR's funds, 94 percent of which still came from the United States, Japan, and the European Union, and which had fallen from $1.25 billion in 1996 to $911.6 million in 1999. In recent years, donors have taken to reneging on their promised contributions. And, what was possibly even more important than all these things, Lubbers was known to be determined to restore to UNHCR its primary function as a protector of refugees,

rather than see that work sunk further in all-consuming relief operations. Hocké's reign, say the experts, was flawed by his manner and
his mistakes, but he had been right in his insistence on protection.
Ogata, though admired for the tenacity with which she put the
agency at the very front of the humanitarian world and kept it there,
had made a fundamental mistake in letting slip the commitment to
protection, so that success came to be measured in terms of how
much relief could be delivered how quickly. To fill the vacuum, the
many nongovernmental organizations now working with refugees
had themselves begun to move into protection.

The new millennium contains huge challenges. Though refugee
numbers are actually down, from a peak in the early 1990s of 19 million, to around 12 million today, and though the number of asylum
claims in Europe has dropped to its lowest point in four years, global
attitudes toward refugees have degenerated into chaos and panic.*
Governments, having allowed asylum seekers to become scapegoats,
have effectively marginalized them and made it harder for them to
integrate. Though refugee protection, drawing on many different
strands of international law, is now embedded in a broad field of human rights and humanitarian treaties and agreements, restriction,
not generosity, has become the order of the day. The talk is all of
"humanitarian pragmatism." Refugees, accused of using scarce resources at times of high unemployment, have been exploited by
xenophobic politicians. International humanitarian action to prevent mass exoduses has never seemed so severely limited by lack of
political will or money.

About half of the world's refugees today are under the age of
eighteen, and almost 5 percent of these are unaccompanied minors,
traveling the world on their own. Like adults, they are obliged to
prove that they can meet the definition of a refugee under the 1951
Convention, whose adult-centered approach to asylum fails to take

---

* In 2002, there were 587,400 applications for asylum to thirty-seven countries, down 5.4
percent from 2001. The decline was highest in Australia (-50 percent), followed by the
United States (-11 percent).

into account the fact that some abuses of our times are aimed specifically at children. Child soldiers have no special claims. Child refugees are to be found in prisons and detention centers in many parts of the world, including Australia and the United States.

As Jeff Crisp, an Englishman who for a while ran UNHCR's evaluation and policy unit, sees it, UNHCR itself has become "profoundly dysfunctional," failing to provide protection to all those most in need of it and condoning discriminatory practices that ensure that only people with access to considerable amounts of money can hope to escape from unstable countries (by paying smugglers). Large sums are spent on keeping small numbers of refugees out, and small sums on protecting large numbers of refugees in distant camps. Never, Crisp believes, has there been so much hypocrisy. Countries happy to profess their support for the 1951 Convention at meetings at home do all they can to obstruct the arrival of the asylum seekers whose rights they have just upheld. UNHCR, once regarded as a teacher and keeper of refugee standards, has lost much of its former credibility. There has been some talk about the need for UNHCR to be more accountable, and much debate across the aid world generally about how to incorporate the protection of human rights into the wide sweep of humanitarian work. The Refugee Convention is in the odd position of being the only major human rights treaty that is not externally supervised; all other key UN human rights accords have some mechanism to ensure that states are held accountable for what they have agreed to.

Not the least of Lubbers's challenges is what to do about all those who have fled their homes but not crossed international borders, either because they have not been able to or because they do not want to. There have always been people displaced within their own countries by war, disaster, and poverty. But they came late to international attention, and it was not until 1992 that the UN Secretary General appointed a former Sudanese diplomat, Francis Deng, as his representative on internally displaced persons (IDPs). In 1998, Deng presented the UN with a definition—someone forced to flee on account of armed conflict, violence, violation of human rights, or natural or manmade disasters, but who has not crossed a recognized state border—and a set of guiding principles. But there is still no treaty on IDPs, and though UNHCR is not mandated to take responsibility for them, no other agency has been willing to step forward, so in practice it frequently falls to UNHCR to fill the gap. In January 2000, the then U.S. ambassador to the UN, Richard Holbrooke, declared that to use initials to talk about any one group of people was unhealthy, and urged the world to stop distinguishing between victims in such an arbitrary way; in 2001 the UN set up a special unit to better coordinate assistance, but the internally displaced remain the poor relations of the refugee world.

According to the Global IDP Database, run by the Norwegian Refugee Council in Geneva, there are 25 million IDPs in the world today, scattered across fifty countries. Over half of them—some 13 million people—are to be found in Africa, in camps, on the edges of cities, in shantytowns and condemned buildings; here they have become indistinguishable from the urban poor, victims of violence and civil conflict, of floods and tropical storms, droughts, famines, and deforestation, epidemics of measles and cholera and AIDS.

Though funds have not actually grown under Lubbers, they have at least stabilized. He has proved good at attracting small new sources: in 2003, Russia gave $1 million, its first donation, and Kuwait $2 million. However, refugee crises today attract a huge, uncoordinated mixture of multilateral, national, and nongovernmental initiatives and organizations, each raising money separately, and large sums are spent every year both on special units to address specific groups and concerns—women, children, or the environment—and on UNHCR itself. Refugee emergencies and long-term camps continue to eat most available money, making it hard for the High Commissioner to practice the ideal of protection he has consistently championed since his arrival. Few people inside UNHCR today question the need for more staff and better training in protection matters and human rights education, or for the kind of programs that will reduce the need for people to flee. But UNHCR is under constant pressure from governments, from its executive committee, and from the UN itself, and its position is being seriously weakened by a growing perception that refugees are a threatening and destabilizing force. The whole notion of security, once seen as a matter of keeping refugees safe—during flight, in camps, while waiting for the outcome of their asylum applications—has shifted. Now it is the refugees themselves who are seen to pose the danger, particularly in the wake of September 11. Since those attacks, human smuggling routes are increasingly referred to as routes for international terrorists.

Nowhere, however, is the challenge to UNHCR's authority more visible than over current asylum policy. Asylum has always posed difficulties—not least of definition—but while numbers were small and posed little threat, and the asylum seekers were "good" refugees fleeing communism, the issue assumed little importance. But as requests for asylum in Europe, North America, Australia, and Japan rose through the 1980s—to reach around 700,000 in the European Union in 1992, the same year UNHCR recorded a peak of 19 million refugees throughout the world—so Western states intensified their efforts to prevent the refugees from arriving, investing millions in complicated entry rules, which in turn led to backlogs. Pressure grew to make asylum unattractive. Barriers that had been erected to keep out those in search of work—the so-called economic migrants—became barriers to those fleeing persecution. As states fought to appear in control of their borders, visa requirements were introduced, then made stricter. Airlines transporting illegal immigrants became liable for fines. The industrialized world, country by country, closed its doors to asylum seekers, leaving no legal way for them to enter. Migrants and asylum seekers alike were now using the same routes, so that stories arose about "bogus" refugees and hostility to all refugees grew, whatever their origins and whatever their reasons for flight.

Today there is no alternative but to enter the European Union illegally, a fact that has played into the hands of smugglers, whose business is flourishing as never before, with strong links to the criminal underworld of drug smuggling and the trafficking of women and children for prostitution. Eight hundred thousand people are said today to be transported each year across international borders, at a turnover of some $10 billion. In 2000, two UN protocols to the Convention on Transnational Crime were drafted, declaring that those "trafficked" for clearly sexual purposes were to be considered victims and entitled to assistance, while those who paid to be "smuggled" were deemed only to require "humane treatment." To this day, there is virtually nothing to protect asylum seekers who use smugglers, though in practice they are often drawn into a web of exploitative relationships in order to pay off their debts.

Not surprisingly, then, untruths surround refugees. As hostility has increased toward those who arrive without documents, so anti-immigration campaigners have manipulated statistics to paint a picture of the West under siege by greedy migrants, and so the asylum seekers themselves have resorted to embellishing their pasts, the better to merit acceptance. It is not easy, for people who have fled violence, or persecution, or even just poverty, to handle truth, so anxious are they to convince their listeners, and so aware that what they say may be misunderstood or manipulated. A story is often told about the Vietnamese boat people who arrived in their thousands in Hong Kong and Bangkok in the late 1980s. UNHCR staff were sent out to interview them, in order to decide whether their fear of persecution at home was such that they were entitled to refugee status and resettlement in the West. The screening of the boat people became the largest and most expensive of UNHCR's operations at the time.

Among the boat people were many unaccompanied children, some as young as six or seven. UNHCR staff quickly realized that the story these children told was always the same. Their parents were dead. Word, it seemed, had reached Vietnam that orphans would be quickly resettled and could become an anchor for their siblings and eventually for their parents, who would in fact turn out not to be dead at all and who would rejoin them in the West. In practice, only a quarter of these children were accepted; the rest were sent home. UNHCR staff working in the camps at the time remember how hard they tried to get close to the children, to explain to them that their parents had sent them off on the boats not because they did not love them, but because they were to be the family's passports to a future.

Women of a certain age arrived in the company of the small children, claiming to be their grandmothers. They had been told, it seemed, that their chances of resettlement were far better if they had small children in their care. When it became clear that it made no difference to their chances, they reappeared at the registration offices to say that the children were not theirs after all, and that they would prefer not to be burdened by having to look after them.

. . .

IN GENEVA, IN London and Washington, in circles where refugee policy is made and discussed, the mood is one of despondency and confusion, fed by the anti-immigration lobby, which in turn feeds growing xenophobia. The gap between reality and Western rhetoric has never been wider; the need for coherent EU and global asylum policies, for burden sharing, for generous yet realistic measures has never been greater. Fewer than half of all people applying for asylum get it, leading governments to conclude that the majority are economic migrants, not in need of protection, who are abusing the process. No European country has proved able to establish fair, fast, and efficient systems to determine refugee status, and their inability to send failed asylum seekers home has undermined their credibility. Deportation is expensive and almost impossible to enforce, particularly now that decisions can take several years to reach, by which time the asylum seeker has laid down roots. Overstayers, those who fail to leave when their visas or papers run out, are simply tolerated, making it possible for the public to argue that governments are incompetent. The situation also encourages asylum seekers to regard their journeys as worthwhile, given that deportation may never happen. In any case, airlines are reluctant to accept deportees, who may refuse to board unless handcuffed, and ordinary travelers object strongly to becoming witnesses to forcible deportations.

Some $10 billion is being spent annually by governments to deal
with a relatively small number of asylum seekers*—807,000 people
applied for asylum in 141 countries in 2003—while humanitarian
organizations find it impossible to raise a fraction of that money for
the considerably larger number who remain in camps in the developing world. This $10 billion is about twelve times what UNHCR
receives to look after more than 17 million refugees, displaced
people, and others "of concern" to them around the world. Whether
in Europe or North America, large sums go each year to patrolling
borders: Canada takes in 13,000 refugees each year, but spends $300
million controlling its borders—ten times what it contributes to
UNHCR. Today it is the world's poorest countries, in Asia, Africa,
and the Middle East, that bear the burden for receiving the displaced: 90 percent of refugees in fact stay in their own regions. In
2000, when the countries of western Europe were complaining most
loudly about the sacrifices they were making and the money they
were spending on asylum seekers, the top receiving countries for
refugees were in fact Iran, Pakistan, and Tanzania. In 2003, the
Ivory Coast, Guinea, Liberia, Tanzania, Yemen, Burundi, and
Sierra Leone all reported the arrival of substantial numbers of
refugees.

Confronted by the global spirit of intolerance and unease, mindful of the ways in which Western states have taken to manipulating
the definition of a refugee to suit themselves, Lubbers has launched
a series of new initiatives intended to make governments reaffirm
their commitment to UNHCR's original mandate and to pay a
fairer share of the costs for helping the world's refugees. In the wake
of criticisms about UNHCR's failure to assess and analyze its own
performance, its embroilment in scandals involving the sexual exploitation of people in camps, and its apparent reluctance to con-

---

* In 2003–2004, the cost of handling asylum seekers in the UK was estimated to be £835
million, the equivalent of £34 for every household in the country. The UK also contributed 5 percent of UNHCR's budget.

template institutional change, there has been much talk about improving and strengthening the implementation of the Convention, through monitoring bodies or special rapporteurs.

As of 2004, only about 145 countries of the world's 190 have signed the 1951 Convention, and even those violate its articles every day.

· PART TWO ·

LEAVING

GLI EXTRACOMUNITARI

Sicily's Boat People

We are old, Chevalley, very old. For over twenty-five
centuries we've been bearing the weight of superb and
heterogenous civilisations, all from outside, none made
by ourselves, none that we could call our own.

—GIUSEPPE DI LAMPEDUSA,
THE LEOPARD

Nene and Vera Sciortino were watching television when the storm
broke. It started abruptly, a sudden torrential downpour, and by
midnight a great gale had risen and hail began to fall—solid balls the
size of potatoes, as Nene would later tell visitors when he showed
them the holes in the table on his terrace. The noise these hailstones
made on the plastic terrace roof was so loud that the Sciortinos were
obliged to raise the volume on their television, so it was some time
before they heard the cries coming from the beach. At first, Nene
thought these shouts were all part of the game show that he and
Vera usually watched on a Saturday night. Nene is an actor, a singer
of Sicilian folk songs, a ruddy-faced friendly man in his mid-thirties;
when he is not traveling around Sicily talking to conferences and
seminars about the need to preserve the Sicilian language and popu-

lar culture, he and Vera put on theatrical sketches for schoolchildren in the Greek temples at Agrigento and Selinunte.

As the cries and shouts continued, Nene got up and went to the window that looks out of their sitting room directly onto the long sandy beach at Realmonte, not far from Agrigento, on Sicily's southern coast. Peering out into the utter darkness, he could make out only the white crests of the waves breaking over the sand. But then he saw some people running along the water's edge. How absurd, he said to Vera, to go swimming on a night like this. The hail was still crashing down, and there was also lightning and thunder. But then more people came running; now Nene saw that they were gathering in a circle just in front of La Playa, a new bar on Capo Rossello, where on summer evenings foreign tourists come to dance to a small band. This being a Saturday in the middle of September, the dance floor was crowded, and when he and Vera put on their rubber boots and found an umbrella and trudged through the wet sand, they discovered the dancers standing at the water's edge, in the pouring rain, pulling from the sea a number of gasping, sodden, half-naked young Africans, their clothes hanging in rags about them, their teeth chattering from the cold. As it happened, one of the members of the band spoke some English, and when the strangers had stopped panting and shaking and were able to speak, they explained in that language that they were asylum seekers and that their boat had struck the rock that juts out above the reef just offshore, not a hundred meters from La Playa. There were, said the young Africans, gesticulating frantically toward the sea, still many others on board, and the boat was sinking. They had reached the shore because they were swimmers. They didn't think anyone else on board could swim. Some said they had sisters and brothers on the boat; one said that his wife was there.

The onlookers peering into the darkness could see nothing, though by now the hail was no longer crashing down, as Nene explains when he talks about the long night of the *naufragio*, the shipwreck. On that night, Saturday, September 14, 2002, a boat carrying 150 Liberian asylum seekers, *extracomunitari*, went down off Realmonte's popular beach. As Nene says, the night's weather was cata-strophic, a freak storm the likes of which he had not experienced in all his twelve years in his beach house, and the unfortunate Liberians were *disgraziati*, uniquely afflicted, to have chanced to try to come ashore that very night.

When the dancers at last understood what had happened, when the terrified Liberians had told them, again and again, the story of what had befallen them and it had been translated into Italian, the police were called. Soon the beach was covered in police cars, and carabinieri and marines arrived from the Guardia Costiera stationed not far away at Porto Empedocle. The fishing boats pulled up on Realmonte's beach were too small to make any headway against the surf, and when a lot of calls had been made over the walkie-talkies and the mobile phones, it was found that there wasn't a working rub-ber dinghy with a big enough outboard along the whole of the Sicil-ian coastline. By now, it was nearly three o'clock in the morning. A powerful searchlight was at last produced by the police; when its beam was cast toward the rock, not only could the boat itself be seen, tipped far over on its side and half underneath the water, but, to the horror of the onlookers, people could be spotted clinging to the rock.

As Nene watched, first one, and then another, slipped beneath the waves. The thunder had stopped, and in the lulls between the crashing waves, he could hear cries coming from the reef. The Vice Questore from Agrigento appeared, took off his clothes, and swam out in his undershirt and pants to the wreck. When he returned to shore, he was able to tell the crowd that help was needed for at least a hundred people. Boats from the various naval services stationed at Porto Empedocle at last came in sight, and it was not long before other sodden, bedraggled, gasping Liberians were being helped into La Playa and given hot tea and blankets. Almost none of them would take off their sneakers, even though they were full of water, because it was there that they kept their money, saved up with such painful slowness for this one, illegal, dangerous journey to the shores of Eu-rope. Their eyes, Nene remembers, were very red, bloodshot, al-most like fire.

The only one to take off his shoes was a portly, fair-skinned man with a large inflatable life jacket, whose pockets rather than his shoes were found to be bulging with dollar bills. He was assumed to be the *scafisto*, the trafficker, and the police led him to one side, where he sat in silence, refusing to answer any questions. Eventually taken to prison and repeatedly questioned, he began to talk, but then abruptly fell silent again and has remained silent ever since, because, say the police, he had been got at by the Mafia, who are known to run the network of *scafisti* along the shores of Tunisia. Some say he was Egyptian, others Libyan. Early on, he told a policeman that he was Palestinian, from Gaza, but when they questioned him about Gaza, he was vague.

As for the *extracomunitari*, they were happy to talk, but only about the horrors of the shipwreck, the hours of pitching at sea, the fear, the lack of water and food, the nightmare moment when the boat hit the rock and began to sink; on the question of where they came from, and who owned the boat, and where they were going, they would say nothing at all. By six o'clock on Sunday morning, there was very little left for anyone to see. The boat had by now partly sunk to the bottom of the shallow bay. Realmonte returned to the closing days of its long hot summer.

Early on Monday, the partly submerged boat was pulled to shore and a body was found on board. The police banged on the Sciortinos' door and asked whether they had any plastic bags to cover it with. Vera was disgusted. She gave them a sheet, and the Sciortinos were upset to find that the police planned to leave the body there all day, lying in the sand just in front of the terrace, until the proper authorities could be persuaded to come to collect it later in the afternoon.

But the episode was still not quite all over for Nene and Vera. At ten o'clock on Wednesday morning, a fine calm day when the tourists were all back on the beach, Vera saw a body floating in the water about twenty yards from the shore in front of the house. She called Nene, and together they stood at the water's edge. A second body bobbed to the surface, not far from the first, and then a third. Over the next two hours, as they stood watching with horrified fascination, nine other bodies, bloated and purple, the skin flayed away by the sharp volcanic rock, shot like corks to the surface of the flat sea. From a distance the Sciortinos thought they looked rather like the tourists peacefully floating in the warm, still water. By then, the shore was once again crowded with onlookers, and the police sent frogmen to bring in the bodies and look for others. This was the worst part of the whole *naufragio*, and for several days neither one of them could sleep for the horror of what they had seen.

For a few weeks, fragments of clothes were washed up at the water's edge and even part of a torn life jacket, but the people who collect Realmonte's rubbish eventually took them away, when it was felt that they made a bad impression on the tourists. Though no one was ever able to establish precisely how many people had been wedged into the Liberians' *carretta di mare*—a "sea cart, some ten to twelve meters long, and open but for a very small cabin"—ninety-five had been saved. At least thirty-five were known to have drowned. One body was that of a girl the police doctor thought was no older than fifteen. Most of the dead had no names, the survivors being unable or unwilling to say who they were. One or two, taken to identify the bodies, hesitated, then said nothing.

By Christmas, Nene had been able to put it all behind him. It had helped when Father Giuseppe, Realmonte's parish priest, held a mass on the beach, exactly a month after the shipwreck, and the villagers threw flowers into the water where the boat had gone down. It helped, too, that journalists and tourists curious about the *naufragio* came by and banged on the Sciortinos' door and Nene was able to talk about it with them, though he was very angry when a cartoon appeared in the scurrilous local *La Sicilia*, showing a pedal-boat with two tourists' corpses floating alongside, captioned "*Turismo macabro.*" In the end, Vera had decided that she could no longer eat fish, not knowing what flesh they might have fed on; when Nene goes out fishing in the small, red-bottomed wooden boat he keeps pulled up outside their house, Vera will cook his catch but she will not put it in her mouth. She says that she will never eat fish again.

. . .

FOR THE YOUNG Liberians, whose savings had gone into this journey to a new life, whose families had sold their houses and lands and animals to pay smugglers to take them to a continent where they would not be persecuted and where they would be safe and prosperous, this last lap, on a boat carrying ten times the number of people it was built to carry, had been a time of terror.

For Mercy, Happy, and Roland, two sisters and a brother from a town called Maryland, not far from Monrovia, the journey had started many weeks before, on a truck that carried them to the coast, then on a first ship, which paused after five days, they do not know where, to transfer them to a second boat, which itself paused, some four days later, far out at sea, to transfer them to yet another boat, this time the small, open wooden boat on which they had been standing and crouching for almost five days, thirsty and very hungry, when the storm arose. Clinging to the boat's wooden rim, too closely packed and too frightened to move, as the storm gathered strength and the hailstorms—the likes of which they had never seen or imagined—pounded them, they could see the lights from La Playa, and, between the gusts of wind and the thunder, they could just hear snatches of music from the dance floor. Mercy, clinging to her sister on the boat, remembers the moment of impact with the rock, when the small boat, with a sudden shuddering lurch, crashed against something hard. Those on board were flung violently to one side, and she saw some of her companions lose their hold and slip over the side and into the darkness. Almost at once, she lost sight of Happy, and in the jostling, crying, flailing crowd, found herself pushed to the very edge of the boat. As it began to tilt and sink, she started to slip over the side herself.

Mercy cannot swim. When I went to find her, she was still living in Realmonte, some 300 yards from the beach of Capo Rossello. She told me that she could remember the water seeming to draw her down, and then feeling a sharp edge of rock just under the surface. She reached out and grasped it with all her strength, as those around her slipped past and disappeared. She is short and slight and does not look very strong. But because she was young, just twenty, and because she simply could not bear for all the months of skimping and saving and planning and indecision and longing to be lost so casually, in a single moment of disaster, she went on clinging to her small piece of rock. She was still there four hours later, when the rescue boats from Porto Empedocle arrived. The sailors pulled her up and on board and took her to land, where ambulances were waiting with blankets and hot sweet coffee. What she did not know then was that she was two months pregnant. The father of her baby was a boy from Maryland whom she had planned to marry, but who had not got together enough money for the journey by the time she and Happy and Roland set out to make their new lives in Europe.

For Happy, the *naufragio* was the end of that dream. Mercy never saw her again after that moment when, clinging to each other, the two sisters felt the terrible crash against the rock. Roland did see her once more: it was when he was taken to a mortuary in Porto Empedocle and asked to look at the dead Liberian refugees, lying side by side in their torn clothes. Happy's was the first body he saw. She was twenty-two.

Later, after my visit to Mercy and Roland, driving back along the superstrada toward Agrigento—a city built, as Plato noted, as if its people would never die, while they ate as if they had not an hour to live—I was directed to the wrecker's yard where, as the Italians put it, a "cemetery" had been created for the boats that carry the *extracomunitari*. There, among smashed Fiats and BMWs, lay the Liberians' boat, wedged at an angle between two other similar, wrecked boats, scraps of netting still hanging from their sides, what remained of their decks littered with empty plastic water bottles, a couple of torn jackets, a dirty blanket. Happy's boat looked absurdly small to have carried so many people, and almost festive, with its bold stripes of blue, yellow, and red paint, and its name, a flourish of Arabic lettering along one side; it was not easy to imagine it at sea, tossed around in the dark and the hail, with 150 terrified people clutching the sides and each other. Salvaged by the coastal police when the fine weather resumed and taken to the wrecker's yard to await any subsequent inquiry into the shipwreck, the boat sits with some dozen others, a few smaller, one or two larger, wrecks, condemned as unseaworthy long before their final journeys, gaudy and infinitely sad. Beyond the yard lies a meadow, which in spring is bright with yellow daisies and the deep red of the wild clover that covers this part of southern Sicily, while above rises a rocky escarpment that leads, not half a mile away, to the ridge on which stands the Doric Temple of Concord, which held out against the Carthaginians for eight months. It is perfect against the clear sky.

· · ·

EVEN DON GIUSEPPE, the priest of Realmonte, feels that there was something demonic in the fury of the storm that hit his parish on the night of the *naufragio*. He has lived in and around Agrigento for many years, but he has known no weather as terrible or as ferocious as that night's. Don Giuseppe has been proud of the way that his parishioners behaved at the time, the way they hastened to the shore when they heard about the shipwreck, carrying with them blankets and coats, and he admires the insistence with which they pressed him to find a house not only for Roland and Mercy, but for Daniel and Adrean, the only married couple among the survivors, who were expecting a baby. In Sicily, he says, "we are used to strangers. We've had Arabs, we've had the Spanish, we've had the Greeks, we've even had the Americans. And now we have Liberians." Realmonte is very poor. Though the people do not go hungry, unemployment is as high here as in all parts of Sicily, and there is very little luxury to be had. As it happens, Realmonte has within its commune a salt mine, and a second, smaller mine of malachite, which could give work to a number of the villagers; but some years ago a dispute broke out between an industrialist from the north, who wanted to buy them, and the Italian authorities, who refused to let him begin mining until favorable terms were worked out for profit sharing. The mines have stayed closed ever since.

When the living had been sorted out from the dead, and the single young men sent off to a hostel in nearby Racalmuto, the Misericordia, Italy's voluntary ambulance service, decided to give the two couples the use of a flat off Realmonte's main square. Francesco di Salvo was on duty with the ambulance that night, and saw the bodies lacerated by the sharp rocks. As he sees it, they must have been truly desperate to risk so much. He is haunted by the memory of a very young girl, rescued from the water too late to be resuscitated, who was brought to shore already dead, clinging so tightly to her sole possession, a small handbag, that her fingers could not be prized loose from its handle.

By the time Mercy realized that she was pregnant, not long after the shipwreck, Adrean was about to give birth. When her little girl was born prematurely in January 2003, and had to stay on in the hospital for several weeks, Realmonte's women took it in turns visiting her and helping her plan the baby's return to the village. Mercy's baby, Angela, arrived in April, after a Caesarean birth, and when Mercy brought her home the women again visited to show the young mother how to care for her child, though they worried that she seemed curiously inept at feeding the baby, and less attached to her than they expected her to be. As Mercy and Roland are Christians, Angela was baptized by Father Giuseppe in Realmonte's church. All through the autumn and winter, neighbors dropped by with vegetables from their plots of land outside the village, with baby clothes and toys and even a baby carriage.

Roland is as reluctant as all the survivors to go into details of his escape from Liberia, but he is eager to talk about the conditions that drove him and his two sisters to flee—the marauding bands of rebels that descended on Maryland; his fears of being forcibly recruited as a soldier; the collapse of his business selling building materials—and about the terror and cold of the long journey at sea, with too little food and water and no idea where the boat was heading. Like many of the young Liberians in Cairo, Roland and his sister are Mandingo, among the most persecuted of the various ethnic groups. Since his rescue, though he is not yet officially recognized as a refugee and so not, in theory, permitted to work, Roland has been able to do casual work in Realmonte's supermarket, the villagers feeling only too conscious of his need for money, being so constantly in need of it themselves. However, he still cannot bring himself to write to tell his widowed mother, who stayed behind in Maryland with a cousin while her three children set out for their new life one hot August morning, of Happy's death. He thinks she would prefer not to know.

. . .

IT IS QUITE possible that the Liberians' boat was not heading for Sicily's southern shore at all. Roland told me that the first he knew that his destination was not another African country was when, swimming to shore after the shipwreck, he saw that the people on the beach were white. This is a joke repeated with pleasure by Sicilians: Not long ago, a young Senegalese man was brought by a smuggler to within a hundred yards of shore, pushed overboard, and told to swim. He climbed out of the water on the beach and approached a fisherman working nearby. "Wo ist der Bahnhof?" he asked, having been assured by the trafficker that he was being landed in Germany. The same joke is told, with equal pleasure, by the inhabitants of Capri, off the coast of Naples.

More likely, Dr. Moscat of Agrigento's Prefetura explains, Roland and Mercy's boat was destined for the island of Lampedusa, a hundred miles farther south, and it was here that I went next, looking for other refugees from Africa's civil wars. Though none of the Liberians in Cairo had traveled this way, some had made long sea journeys, terrifying and bewildering experiences that themselves had become a kind of passport. Unlike the documents they shed along the shore and in the sea, this one conferred dignity and promise. Very few of the refugees coming from the landlocked parts of Africa have ever seen the sea and few can swim, which makes the prospect of crossing these great expanses of often rough water horrific.

In 2002, eight thousand *extracomunitari* arrived on Lampedusa from Turkey, Malta, and the ports and beaches of North Africa, where they had collected and waited until enough were assembled to make up a boat. Sfax, a known gathering point for the Tunisian smugglers, lies barely seventy miles from Lampedusa, and it is here that the would-be asylum seekers learn how much their journey will cost them and what their destination might be. It is the traffickers, said to operate in Mafia-like associations, who tell the asylum seekers to give away as little as possible when they land, to get rid of all their documents so that they can lie about where they have come from and so cannot then be sent home or the traffickers themselves traced. In the tangled process that seems to govern southern Italy's response to the asylum seekers and migrants who flock to its shores, in which the coast guard, carabinieri, harbor police, immigration authorities, and the *scafisti* themselves all play their interlocking parts, Lampedusa has taken on a vital role. Lampedusa is Europe's southernmost tip, the first toehold in the climb toward northern Europe.

A spit of barren, flat, rocky land, the island looks, on the map, like the skull of a primitive, long-jawed creature, its nose tapering to a thin wedge. The property of the feudal princes who founded Palma, on Sicily's southern coast, in the early seventeenth century, the island is bare, baked hard and dry for many months of the year into a uniform stony whiteness. Lampedusa is neither pretty nor, with its jagged, limestone cliffs, hospitable. The author of *The Leopard*, last in the line of Lampedusas, never even visited it, though the family retained a rampant *gattopardo*—the word is more properly translated as "ocelot"—on their coat of arms. According to legend, the founder of the Lampedusas was Tomasso, "the Leopard," commander of the Imperial Guard of the sixth-century Byzantine emperor Tiberius, whose daughter Irene he married; the island was a gift in recognition of services rendered.

Lampedusa was once thickly wooded. Today, the dozen or so stunted pines that are its sole trees lie almost parallel to the ground, bowed by the winds that blow from the west. In the autumn, hunters come from Sicily and the mainland to slaughter the protected hoopoes and golden orioles migrating to winter in Africa, and leave their spent cartridges scattered between the rocks and wild herbs on the low hills; but otherwise Lampedusa is popular mainly with scuba divers, fishermen, and tourists in search of sun, heat, and the deep and unpolluted waters that surround the island. Once a NATO base, it was discovered by Italians overnight, in the summer of 1986, after Colonel Muammar Qaddafi fired two missiles toward Italy. They landed a dozen miles off the coast, bringing journalists to the island and in their wake several thousand tourists, who slept on mattresses on the ground until enough rooms and hotels could be built to absorb them. Dry stone walls, demarcating plots of land long since abandoned to stones and wildflowers, stretch away from the single small town, where the uncontrolled building of summer shacks has made the island resemble the rest of Italy's ruined coast.

Lampedusa is where Italy ends and Africa begins. Spring and summer, on the long calm days, the refugees arrive almost daily, in their battered and crumbling boats, frightened, unsure, expectant. Experts in asylum matters, who study the flows of refugees and their journeys to the north, call the way to Lampedusa the blue route after the blue waters of the Mediterranean; and it enjoys a lucrative share of the estimated $5 to $7 billion revenue of the world's traffic in smuggled people. Gangs reported often to belong to the same Mafia as those that traffic in drugs run complex shipping networks that involve large boats carrying 600 or more *clandestini*, illegal arrivals, for the first part of long journeys, transferring them to small, ancient, unseaworthy craft for the final stretch to shore. Since arrivals seem to mesh neatly with available space in Lampedusa's single reception center, it is said that there is a *basista*, a spy or lookout, for Tunisia's Mafia, who phones to say when Lampedusa is ready to absorb more newcomers.

On Lampedusa, I looked for people to tell me about their clandestine boat journeys from Africa, and I found Alex. Alex is a twenty-three-year-old Liberian who, having lost his family in the civil war, spent eleven years with his sisters as a refugee in Côte d'Ivoire before deciding to escape the constant fear of being picked up by rebels and forced to become a soldier. He described a journey that began in Monrovia with twenty others, hidden on a large ship and not being told its destination by their trafficker, to whom they had each paid $200. For four days, while the vessel was still tied up in port, without food or water, the young men hid in different corners. After it set sail, they were gathered together, then transferred, far out at sea, to a smaller boat. This took them to Turkey, where three of them were dropped off on a remote beach. They made their way to the nearest town and found some "black brothers" who put them in touch with a new set of smugglers. They paid over $1,000 each, then went into hiding. A few nights later, they were led back to the coast, put onto a small boat, and taken out to a larger one. On board were eighty-five other *extracomunitari*, all Africans, from Nigeria, Ghana, Sudan, and Tunisia; all but four were men, reflecting the fact that most of the asylum seekers who make these hazardous journeys are men in their twenties and thirties, while the refugee camps across Asia and Africa are full of women and children for whom the journeys are too difficult.

The asylum seekers had been told to bring food and water for eight days. The weather was very bad, the seas were rough, and the boat developed engine trouble. It drifted without power for two days, sprang a leak, and began to sink. A fishing boat appeared. It came alongside and was able to take eleven people off—Alex among them—before the boat went under, drowning all the rest, including the four women. Alex, who could not swim, broke his hand when being pulled on board; his two friends were drowned. The fishing boat was extremely crowded, but it took them into Lampedusa; Alex was taken to a hospital and his hand treated. He still had $800, the rest of his life's savings, hidden in his shoes. "They asked me a lot of questions," he says, "but I didn't really have much to tell them. I had planned for my life to be secure, and I wanted a place with peace of mind." The Italians have given Alex a humanitarian permit to remain, a halfway measure that ensures him protection for a year and permission to work, if he can find work; the permit is renewable. But he has changed his mind about escape, for he has not found the life of an exile what he imagined it would be. "I want to go home to my sisters and my farm," he says. "I don't want to be alone."

Rarely, in fact, do those arriving at Lampedusa make it to shore on their own steam. More often, their boats are spotted by the helicopters that patrol these coasts, or are picked up on the radar screens of the coast guard, who go out to meet them as they near land. The coast guard hopes both to net a *scafisto*, bringing his cargo into land, and to help a sinking craft, by taking its passengers on board, in order to conduct them into a secluded corner of Lampedusa's large natural port, far from the eyes of tourists who might be offended by the spectacle of such bedraggled and confused new visitors.

Comandante Rino Gagliano is the captain of one of the Italian coast guard's middle-sized motor launches that patrol Lampedusa, though the more exciting tours of duty for the coastal police are farther north, along the Albanian coast. An Italian-Albanian agreement to try to stem the flow of migrant workers escaping the extreme poverty of Albania has succeeded in diminishing the numbers who manage to get out. Off the Albanian coast, says the comandante, he chases traffickers who have taken to putting four powerful engines on their fast rubber dinghies, with which they can easily outmaneuver the slower police launches. But the comandante is not really after excitement. His wife taught history at Lampedusa's one secondary school until her early death not long ago, and he has a particular fondness for the island's low white houses and its stark shoreline. He talks with sympathy about the desperate people he regularly fishes from the water, and the cups of good Italian coffee he takes pleasure in giving them: like all Sicilians, he is baffled by the idea of countries where coffee is not a staple of life. He says that rescuing boats about to sink takes priority, as it does under all the laws that have governed seafaring for many generations, over arresting *scafisti* as they hasten back toward international waters. Like all the sailors and coast guards who work these parts, he tells stories of asylum seekers flung into the sea at gunpoint so that the trafficker can get away faster, of boats so old and ailing and crowded that even small waves can sink them, of headless bodies found floating at sea. What haunts him is those he never sees: the refugees who are known to have drowned in these stretches of water, whose names are never recorded and whose bodies are never found. The *"canale di Sicilia,"* he says, has become a cemetery. Of the 3,000 known deaths recorded by human rights groups of people trying to enter Europe in the last ten years, many are those who drowned in the waters that separate Italy and Spain from North Africa.

The comandante, like the majority of the islanders, feels mostly sympathy for those so desperate that they will risk their lives in this way. To suffer so much is to merit recognition, assistance: the more the suffering, the swifter and more just the recompense. The tales of these travelers have come to fascinate the local people, for whom shipwrecks and endurance are part of the fabric of their history, something that reflects well on the strength and vigor of their island, its robustness in withstanding cycles of invaders and newcomers and in providing pioneers for new worlds elsewhere. The fact that the *extracomunitari* arrive with nothing, sometimes virtually naked, having shed or lost their clothes in rough seas, shorn, as it were, of their pasts, makes them appealing. There is pride in being the first to show off Europe, to vaunt all that it has to offer, as if to reassure the survivors of such terrors and hardships that the journeys have been worth it. The past is truly another country, and their hosts intend to make it so.

In Italy, a country renowned, with exasperation and affection, for the confusion and corruption of its bureaucracy, the operation to corral and process asylum seekers appears almost streamlined. On Lampedusa, the *extracomunitari* are marched off into a Centro di Permanenza Temporanea, a Permanent Temporary Center, the absurdity of its name belying a system that those who run it claim is both humane and practical, but that in recent months has been cracking under the strain of growing numbers. Here, in a former military barracks, new arrivals are briefly interviewed, provided with clothes and a few necessities, and given cigarettes and permission to use a telephone. There is a sense of pride among the island's year-long residents that they have responded so calmly and generously to their unexpected visitors. Father Francesco, Lampedusa's young and eager second priest, who for three months last year became acting director for the island's CPT, speaks of a larder always kept full in anticipation of new refugees, of doctors on duty to care for those who have been at sea for many weeks, of having to fend off journalists after a sudden influx of boats. Though few of the asylum seekers described their reception so glowingly, Father Francesco talks about his permanent temporary visitors indulgently and says that they are given forks, but no knives, and no razors (they enjoy the services of the local barber), though there have been no attempted suicides on the island. Macaroni with meat sauce, he volunteers, is their preferred dish. Some arrive with scabies, others with malaria and heart disease, and many of the women are pregnant, but all are treated kindly, and those few who have died while he has been on Lampedusa have been given a corner of the town's cemetery, where they lie together, under plain wooden crosses, in earth covered with geraniums and wildflowers.

. . .

BECAUSE OF ITS geographic position, at the southern edge of Europe, and its long coastline—over 4,500 miles—Italy has now become the first country of arrival for more asylum seekers than any of its European Union partners. A few go overland from the former Yugoslavia, but most arrive by sea, making the boat people of Italy—18,000 arrived in 2002 on Sicily alone; 20,000 in 2003—the seafaring refugees of our times. And of all times: Europe's earliest migrants came by sea to Sicily, perhaps as early as 20,000 B.C., from east and west, and later by sea and land came Greeks, Carthaginians, Phoenicians, Romans, Saracens, Normans, Hohenstaufens, Angevins, Aragonese, Castillians, Austrians, Piedmontese, and the Neapolitan Bourbons. Over the centuries, Sicily has been conquered, abandoned, colonized, and recolonized by tyrants, kings, mercenaries, dukes, plenipotentiaries, and emperors. There is probably less Italian blood, so Sicilians say, in their veins than there is Greek, Arab, Norman, or Spanish. Positioned on the east–west and north–south routes in the Mediterranean, the island is fertile, with excellent natural harbors, but Goethe, on his travels at the end of the eighteenth century, described it as a morose place, though this was long before Palermo's vast palazzi had crumbled, the fortunes of their families eaten up by feuds and generations of squabbling and idleness.

Yet right up until the 1980s, Italy, particularly its impoverished south, was associated more with emigration than immigration. Between unification in 1861 and the end of the twentieth century, about 26 million Italians are said to have left home for the New World, driven abroad by the neglect and plunder of rich absentee-landowner families, so that as early as 1827 de Tocqueville, traveling around the island, described its interior as almost entirely devoid of human habitation. By World War I, some villages had lost most of their male population, and one out of eight Italian emigrants was a Sicilian. Though part of the new united and unified Italy, Sicily remained its most neglected area, and not until after World War II was it granted regional autonomy and its own Parliament.

At first, influxes of migrants into Italy were treated as single emergencies and approached with leniency. In 1990, the then minister of justice, Martelli, annulled Italy's existing reservation to the 1951 Refugee Convention—the reservation allowed refugee status only to European asylum seekers—and set up a single procedure for deciding refugee status, under a commission based in Rome. The decision procedure was to take no longer than forty-five days, during which the applicants would be housed and fed. But then came a large number of landings—Albanians in 1990 and 1991, Yugoslavs in 1992, more Albanians in 1997, Kurds in 1998—each dealt with under measures of temporary protection. Though Italy is a signatory to Europe's various immigration treaties, it was only with the Napolitano Bill of 1998—which Italians regard as their first attempt at formulating a proper asylum policy—that rules were drawn up to govern procedures and the deportation of those deemed not to be bona fide asylum seekers. In many ways, even the Napolitano law was regarded as generous, since its right to asylum was broadened to include people suffering discrimination at home by virtue of their sex and their membership in particular persecuted ethnic groups.

With Silvio Berlusconi's 2001 election much of the leniency has vanished. Migrants seeking to work in Italy can no longer simply arrive and then look for jobs; they must apply for work permits first at the Italian consulate in their own countries, and once their contract is over, they must return home. Under the Bossi-Fini law, passed in 2003, those who arrive illegally on Italy's shores may now be held for sixty days in a CPT for processing, after which those identified in preliminary hearings as coming from "safe" countries—hence the reluctance of asylum seekers to say too much about where they come from—or judged criminal or too blatantly in search of work, are given deportation orders. It was Umberto Bossi of the Lega Nord who declared that cannons should be set up on Italy's coasts to deter would-be asylum seekers. Only around 10 percent—compared, say, with Sweden's 50 percent or the UK's 40 percent plus—of all who enter Italy illegally are said to be ultimately recognized as genuine refugees and given that status under the Convention. While they wait to be processed, they are released, like Roland and Mercy, to cope as well as they can, until summoned before a commission in Rome to put their case for asylum. However, since this process can now take up to a year or more, many have left their designated addresses long before the summons, to disappear into Italy's vast black economy, or to drift northward illegally into other European countries. Only 20 percent of those who apply for asylum are reported to turn up in Rome for their interview with the commission.

As of 2001, Italy was said to have over 1.5 million legal migrants and as many as 1 million illegal ones. On average, 75,000 of the latter are deported each year. (Only Greece expels more.) Over a third of Italy's prison population is now said to be foreign. In 2002, it was reported that only 16 percent of the nation's 50,000 to 70,000 prostitutes were in fact Italian; the rest came mainly from Albania, followed by Yugoslavia, Nigeria, and South America. The word *extracomunitari* has come to have distinctly racist connotations, and violent attacks on refugees, Jews, Gypsies, and especially on African and black immigrants, attacks previously almost unknown in Italy, have become widespread. Officially, Italy has no Maghrebini—people from Algeria, Tunisia, or Morocco—because the North Africans have earned the reputation of being involved in drugs and crime and so tend to fail the first screening process. After September 11, there was a sharp increase in the number of negative decisions handed down to asylum seekers.

The Permanent Temporary Centers have attracted considerable hostility among Italy's liberals, who fear that the secrecy and high walls, the rolls of barbed wire and hangarlike structures, conceal deprivation and ill-treatment. Sixty days, they argue, is a frighteningly long period to spend locked up, in total idleness, not knowing what will become of you. Migrants emerging from the CPTs complain of inedible food, extreme discomfort, and a pervasive despair and anxiety. Not long ago, Médecins Sans Frontières carried out research into Italy's sixteen CPTs. They found that in some of them, the refugees were kept in small enclosures, freezing in winter, boiling in summer; that the guards were sometimes brutal; that there was excessive use of antidepressants and tranquilizers; and that self-mutilation was endemic. A politician of the left, Calogero Micciche, amid considerable publicity, insisted on being allowed into Agrigento's CPT, which is housed in a former factory in one of the town's newer concrete suburbs. Conditions inside, he told waiting reporters when he emerged, flustered by having his video camera confiscated, were appalling, with excrement all over the walls, and women detainees offering their services as prostitutes.

After the fuss died down, those who are allowed to visit the centers officially, the priests, doctors, and welfare officers, expressed astonishment at his words, insisting that the CPTs, though indeed charmless since most are housed in former barracks and factories, behave honorably and generously toward the asylum seekers. "The paradox," says Daniela D'Amico, who recently helped set up a new voluntary organization dealing with issues of migration in Agrigento, "is that all these new laws which are designed to stop arrivals in fact make no difference. Migration, asylum, these are a social phenomenon of our time. We have lost the memory of our history. Immigrants are the myth of our particular culture." The truth is that many Sicilians have mixed feelings about the asylum seekers: they are at least partly proud of the hospitality they accord their unexpected and unwanted visitors, remembering that the Italians, out of all the people of Europe, most softened the Nazi persecution of the Jews, so that of 60,000 Jewish Italians a third survived the war. They are also pleased with their apparent efficiency at dealing with such large numbers, and they are understandably reluctant to see in these detention centers anything but humane holding operations for a fair and just refugee policy. Sicilians regard themselves as rather apart from the people of the mainland, and with some reason: Cavour, the prime minister who achieved unification in 1860, and who had personally never been farther south than Florence, once said in Parliament that he thought Sicilians spoke Arabic.

A third of the migrant inmates have served prison sentences in Italy, for a variety of criminal acts, and are sent to the CPTs to await deportation. Those from Sicily may be incarcerated there or on the mainland, for as one center fills up, newcomers are shunted to those that currently have space. *Clandestini, extracomunitari*, illegal migrants, refugees, asylum seekers: nowhere is the muddle that surrounds migration more apparent than on the shores of Sicily, and nowhere is the line that separates those judged worthy to enter from those turned away more gray.

· · ·

THE SHIPWRECK THAT killed Happy and landed Mercy and her unborn child on the beach at Capo Rossello has had ripples all along Sicily's southern shores. Something about the intensity of the freak storm, the extraordinary size of the hailstones, and the way that the survivors clung for so long to the lacerating volcanic rocks touched a chord with Sicilians more accustomed to tourists enjoying the tranquillity of their beaches. In the days that followed the accident, as journalists and television reporters flocked from all over Italy, people from miles around Realmonte arrived with offers of clothes and food. Dr. Palumbo is the village physician for San Biagio Platani, some twenty-five miles up into the mountains above Agrigento. He was having lunch, at three o'clock on a sunny afternoon, after a long morning with his patients, when I found him at home, surrounded by wisteria and orange trees. It was after his wife read about the bereaved Liberians in Realmonte, he explained, that he went to the prefect in Agrigento and offered to help. Dr. Palumbo knows all about the *clandestini:* he is the chairman of his local branch of the Misericordia, and the director of social services for the CPT in Agrigento.

After Dr. Palumbo's intervention, fifteen young Liberians, five of them women, moved to San Biagio, a small town set among high summer pastures, where the inhabitants were quick to come forward with offers of help. Like Father Giuseppe in Realmonte, Dr. Palumbo was proud of his patients' generosity toward their visitors. His wife, a teacher, soon borrowed a room in a neighbor's house and fashioned a classroom with a borrowed blackboard and chairs and books scrounged from the local school; she began giving lessons in Italian. One of the young Liberian girls found work as an occasional maid; several of the boys were invited to help out the local builders. Though none could be officially employed, it was tacitly understood that they should be paid like everyone else while they were waiting for their claims for asylum to be heard, and that they should not stay idle and penniless. When one of the young women was found to be pregnant, and had her baby, the Italian woman who had become close to her offered to adopt and care for both mother and child.

But soon, the warm relationship between the Sicilians and their Liberian guests seemed to turn a little sour. As Dr. Pa everyone understood that at first the Africans would be ᴏ talk much about who they were and where they came from. But everyone assumed that their reticence would evaporate once they felt secure and appreciated. But it didn't; if anything, it grew stronger. It was as if word had reached them that they should give away absolutely nothing about themselves, not even their real names. They began changing their names, and then their ages, and any details that they had previously let slip about their journeys. After he overheard two of the young men speaking French to each other, Dr. Palumbo began to wonder whether some were not in fact Sierra Leoneans or Guineans; he thought that they might have been primed by the smuggler to give as their home Liberia, a country so bedeviled by constant civil war that refugees believe that no European nation would feel able to return refugees to it. Several of the young women turned out to be pregnant; when one gave her age first as eighteen, and then as twenty-five, and then as twenty-two, Dr. Palumbo was at first amused, and then mildly irritated, and he begged her to find an age and stick to it, if only for the sake of convenience.

In the early autumn of 2002, when the group first settled in San Biagio, several of the young men had gone willingly to the local bars in the evening, to play pool and listen to music. But as the weeks passed, they went less and less, preferring to sit in the rooms lent to them by the villagers, watching television and talking to one another in the Liberian English outsiders find so hard to follow.

The inhabitants of San Biagio, and down the mountain, those of Realmonte, where much the same thing was happening with Roland and Mercy, were perplexed. They could not quite see why people on whom they had lavished genuine concern and affection, whose futures they felt personally involved with, did not appear to trust them enough to confide their true stories in return. They began to feel a little resentful when the young Liberians simply smiled when asked to talk about the terrifying boat ride, or looked vague when questioned about their families and their past lives. Even a few confidences, as Dr. Palumbo says, would have made a difference. There would have been something in return for all the fruit and clothes and attention; it wasn't that his patients—or Father Giuseppe's parishioners—wanted to be thanked, but they would have appreciated, enjoyed, a little recognition; the absence of it rankled. In Realmonte, the local people now hesitated before taking around fruit or presents for the babies. Because of the increasingly taciturn replies, the blank looks, which could seem at times almost like hostility, the cutting short of any conversation leading to a question, they were soon not quite sure whom to believe when Roland went on saying that Mercy was his sister, or when the local midwife let it be known that Mercy was having sex with someone right up until the day her baby was born.

And in San Biagio, as autumn turned into winter, and freezing winds blew through the high mountains, the Africans clearly began to suspect that the life of a remote Sicilian town, safe as it was, might not be so desirable after all. Security was all very well, but what of the new life that Europe had seemed to promise? What of the affluence, the comfort, the good things they had seen on their televisions back at home? At least, that is what Dr. Palumbo assumes they thought, for the young people themselves said nothing. After a few weeks' halfhearted appearance at Signora Palumbo's Italian classes, one by one they stopped attending. The day came when San Biagio woke to find three of the Liberians gone, departed on the early bus for Palermo. A few days later, another five had vanished. By January, there were none left. Even the girl with her new baby had disappeared. Not one said good-bye to anyone. "It wasn't that we wanted thanks," said Dr. Palumbo again. "We didn't help them for gratitude. But to leave saying nothing? It made us feel foolish, used." It also made them feel sad, thinking about these wandering young Africans, slipping quietly into the night, to scatter and vanish into Europe, to lives as uncertain as those that they had left behind them. No one imagines that they will ever see their Liberian guests again.

Not everyone, of course, was able to leave so quickly. Traveling with a premature baby, or while heavily pregnant, even in Italy, in dead of winter and with no papers, no money, and nowhere to go, is not simple. In Realmonte, the four young Liberians and their two little girls felt that they had no choice but to wait out the weeks until their summons from the commission in Rome. Because they are Liberians, or at least appear to be Liberians, from a country still not settled, because they are survivors of a shipwreck and the parents of babies, they do not anticipate problems with their refugee status. But as the months have passed, their irritation with Realmonte has grown. They are not content. It is as if the long wait to reach Europe has once again been extended; and this last wait, until they can set out for a life somewhere better, more interesting, more promising, more like the Europe they had imagined, is almost unbearable. Realmonte has become just another limbo.

Before leaving southern Sicily, I went back to Realmonte, to the ground-floor flat with its tile floors and television set, and the furniture and the baby things provided by the Misericordia. I wanted to see Daniel and Adrean, the young married couple, who had been away in Palermo on my first visit, taking their premature daughter for a checkup with a pediatrician. I wanted to ask Adrean to tell me about her journey from her village in Liberia to Monrovia, and about the boat that finally sank, leaving her, like Mercy, clutching a rock, and about what it had been like to be pregnant and frightened and not to know where the child would be born, or whether it would survive the hours she spent in the sea. When I knocked on the shutters of the flat, I found the kitchen unexpectedly full of people, young men from Ghana and Sierra Leone, and other arrivals from Liberia. Some had been in Italy for almost twenty years, part of earlier migrant waves, and were now possessors of legal work and residence permits. The authorities had complained agitatedly about parties and noise made by the two Liberian couples, about brawls and shouting matches, but this was a muted gathering, though not a very friendly one. It was my first and almost only encounter with the rougher side of migration. Among the young men gathered in the room, there was little pretense about their reasons for coming to Europe: they were in search of better lives, and they were resentful and angry that Italy seemed to offer them so little.

There was, it was immediately made clear, no question of talking to the women. Daniel, who was rather suspicious about my visit, told me that the women were looking after the babies, and that in any case they were ill. What, he asked, was there in my visit that would help him? What would I do for him if he answered my questions? Wasn't it true that reporters paid for information? He could tell me nothing about the boat, he said: he had spent the whole time belowdecks, and since he possessed no watch he had no idea how long they were at sea. He had not noticed who was in charge. He had no idea whether anyone had been seasick or what food they had been given. The only thing that he could say was that he had been aware of a lot of running up and down on deck just before the boat hit the rock. As it happened, I knew that the boat had no proper cabin, and that, with up to 150 people on board, wedged immovable together, there would have been no running anywhere. He soon drove me away with the truculence of his manner and his anger against the people of Realmonte. Was it true, he asked, that in Germany, at least, refugees were treated really well, given houses and money and cars, not forced to work?

.   .   .

TO THE EMBARRASSMENT of Realmonte's inhabitants, the parish had a cemetery too small and too crowded to accommodate the coffins of the thirty-five drowned Liberians. After the bodies had lain in the graveyard of Porto Empedocle for several days and the smell of decomposition was so bad they had to lock the gates, the priests and mayors from nearby towns and villages were invited to provide burial plots for the dead *clandestini*. Agrigento, whose lemon groves, fish ponds, and bird pavilions had been the marvel of the ancient Greek world, had no room to spare. The most generous offer, to take fifteen, came from Canicatti, a bustling, rapidly growing town some twenty miles inland, where the cemetery, once standing isolated in the lee of the mountains, is now surrounded by factories and the hideous, tall, square boxes that are Italy's answer to cheap housing. Sicily's destiny, Lampedusa once said, had been set by a combination of the cruelty of its climate and twenty-five centuries of "foreign invasion and indigenous folly"; the conquerors landing from every direction had among them destroyed most of the paradise that the island had once been, though even so the warped grandeur of its chaotic towns and eroded hillsides still shone brighter than the drabness of the industrial north.

It was to Canicatti that Happy had been taken. I wanted to find her before I left.

The custodian of Canicatti's cemetery, a slight man in a pea-green jacket and with a bad squint in one eye, was just locking the iron gates when I finally located his cemetery. I was very lucky to find him, he said, taking the key out again, for he would normally have closed long before, but he had decided to have a shower before going home that night, though the sun had set long before. He did indeed know where Realmonte's Liberians were buried, because he had gone to Porto Empedocle with Canicatti's mayor when the coast guard was bringing in the bodies, but for his own part, he thought the whole event had been tragically mishandled.

There is a brand-new wall just inside his cemetery, with some sixty new graves, not yet used or even promised but waiting for any arrivals, and it was here, he says, that the *povere creature* should have been put, all together, and not separated and scattered all over the place in different cemeteries, so that even the fifteen in Canicatti are not together, but slotted away in ones and twos, wherever a wall had a place still to fill in. Even in death, he said, they had been given no dignity.

And there she was, Happy, three graves up, in the middle of a wall: "Cittadina Liberiana, Naufraga a Porto Empedocle, 15 Settembre 2002." Her surname, on the piece of cardboard that identifies the grave, is wrongly listed as Roland, her brother's first name. Not far from her, in another row, high up on an identical wall, among the plastic flowers and the chiseled saints, shaded by the ancient cypresses for which Italian cemeteries are famous, lies Joy, another Cittadina Liberiana, the youngest of the drowned, said the custodian; and not far from the two girls, three other Liberians, all young men, only these have no identities, and below the words Cittadino Liberiano there is only a single bold, black letter to distinguish one from the others, for there was no one among the survivors able or willing to give these bodies a name. Happy and Joy, and three nameless Liberian boys, come to lie under the cypresses of a continent they dreamed would make their lives.

THE FENCE

The Migrants of San Diego and Tijuana

Man is, of all sorts of luggage, the most difficult to be transported.

—ADAM SMITH

One night in October 2003, when cold winds and low temperatures had already come to the bare mountains along the border between northernmost Mexico and southern California, a thirty-eight-year-old Mexican woman arrived at a refuge for migrant women in Tijuana. She was very thin and very poor. With her were her children, two girls aged twelve and nine; they too were small and underfed. They came, the woman told Sister Hema, the missionary nun who runs the refuge, from Guadalajara in the south, where they had been working on a ranch until the job ended. They planned now to go north, to cross into California, where they had been told there was work in the fields and on farms, and even modest fortunes to be made. The woman's husband was with them, but because Sister Hema does not take men into her refuge, he had gone to sleep two doors away, in the Casa del Migrante, which is run by Father Luis from the same missionary order of San Carlos.

Sister Hema never saw the husband, but she looked after his wife and small daughters for fifteen days, trying to build up their strength with hot, nourishing food. Like their mother, she says, the little girls were remarkably fair-skinned, and with their blond hair and pale eyes could have passed for white North Americans. The family said little, but Sister Hema kept thinking how frail and vulnerable they seemed, with their light shoes and cotton clothes and their air of uncertainty and apprehension. In her cupboards, she found thick clothes for them to wear, and sturdy shoes for the long walk ahead. In the evenings, when the girls were asleep, Sister Hema would warn their mother about the journey across the border, which has been closed by a fence that runs intermittently for sixty-four miles toward Arizona; even the open stretches of mountain and desert are thickly covered in sensor wires and floodlights and regularly patrolled by U.S. border agents. She talked, too, about the *coyotes*—as the human-smugglers are called—who, for $1,000 a head, will guide groups of migrants through the wilder mountain areas or across the canals and waterways that separate Mexico from California. The woman would listen but say only that they had to cross, there was no going back, the family had no money and no land and the job on the ranch was over, and that she had elderly parents who had to be looked after; and that the *coyotes* and their extortions and abandonments were nothing to her, as she did not have dollars to pay them. They would be crossing on their own.

Very early one morning, when Sister Hema came down to breakfast, the woman and her daughters had gone. From Father Luis came word that the husband had also disappeared. Sister Hema waited, hoping for news. Often, she says, people who have successfully crossed into the States telephone from California to let her know that they are safe. A few days later, Father Luis heard that the husband had been caught in the mountains by the U.S. Border Patrol, after he had fainted and been found lying by a track. After a short spell in the hospital, he had been returned to Tijuana, and had made his way back to the Casa del Migrante. Of his wife and daughters, there was no news. A few days later, the man disappeared again. This time, he did not come back.

Sister Hema waited, but she heard nothing. The thin woman and her fair-haired little girls did not come back and have not sent word. She thinks about them, wandering across the cold mountains in the dark, following a route they must have planned during the two weeks they lived with her; Sister Hema wonders whether the bands of smugglers and robbers who prey on migrants caught them, or whether they were picked up by the Border Patrol and are now in detention somewhere. Or even whether, since the husband fainted from exposure and cold, they never reached the other side, but lost their way and died in their attempts to reach America. She worries about whether she did enough for them; whether the clothes she gave them were sufficiently thick and warm.

When Sister Hema first came to Tijuana, no one had yet put up the triangular signs along the freeways that stretch away from the border and into southern California: these picture a man, a woman, and two children, running, rather like the signs you see in rural areas warning of deer or cattle crossing. These signs, telling drivers to slow down lest they hit migrants as they run across the freeways to escape the Border Patrol, are everywhere now. But when Sister Hema arrived ten years ago, Tijuana was only just becoming one of the most frequented jumping-off spots for people crossing illegally. And that was before the migrants took to making their dashes for freedom across the five-lane freeways, where cars travel at well above the limit of sixty-five miles an hour, and where the light is dim and the headlights confusing at dusk. What Sister Hema thought, seeing all the women and children hanging around the streets of Tijuana, waiting for darkness to fall, bewildered, hungry, all that they possessed left far behind in southern Mexico with parents and friends, was that she could provide a small measure of safety in the hours before the crossing. A sister of the order of San Carlos, which works with migrants across much of Latin America, Sister Hema had started her mission as a teacher in her native Brazil, before spending six years in the mother house in Rome. "Wherever there are migrants," she says, in her mixture of Spanish and Italian, "there we will go."

It was Father Luis, of the same missionary order, who first called Sister Hema to Tijuana from Rome. She arrived in the spring of 1994, to find his Casa del Migrante recently opened on one of the steep hills that overlooks the city, with beds for eighty men, who, as Father Luis puts it, had "lost their way" somewhere on their journey north, had run out of money or been robbed of it, or had simply been caught by the U.S. Border Patrol and sent back. The Casa del Migrante was for men only, so Sister Hema opened a second refuge, which she keeps spartan and spotless but not unfriendly, with a large courtyard of orange and fig trees, where the hummingbirds come to feed and where, on warm days, the women sit and their children play. Sister Hema is in her sixties, an energetic, kindly woman of great warmth and shrewdness. She wears large spectacles and her face is creased with the lines that come from laughter and smiling. She grows fond of the young women in her care, who treat her with respect and consideration, and she tries hard to provide them with the kind of guidance that will make them question the decision to make the perilous journey across the border. But she knows, even if not all of her visitors tell her so, that they have little choice: if they have gotten as far as her refuge in Tijuana, it is because they have nothing left to hope for at home.

I had started my research along the border in the autumn of 2003, when forest fires were burning all down the coast of California, fanned by a strong Santa Ana wind. I wanted to see the fence and to meet migrants whose reasons for crossing had to do with poverty and not flight from persecution—the so-called economic migrants—so I went to visit Father Luis, a purposeful man whose concern for the migrants who pass through his refuge is more than matched by a crusading determination to see the current border situation, with its deaths and ambiguities, reformed and clarified. Father Luis sees no sanity in a border so guarded, against people so desperate that they are only driven away from the safer areas to cross farther into the rocky and arid mountains. For him, the distinction between economic migrant and asylum seeker has little meaning, when people are driven to the margins by need: "Do people have to die in order to work? Something has to be wrong." Since 2001, Father Luis has watched the border grow more impenetrable, as new technology is invented and installed and ever larger numbers of border guards are taken on; he has also watched the numbers of those trying to cross grow. "There are a lot of families," he says, "who have lost their men." The men using his tidy dormitories and his generous canteen have attempted the crossing again and again, only to be caught and sent back; many of them have crossed successfully only on a fourth or fifth attempt, gone on to spend months or even years in California, then returned to see their families; now they are heading north once again. The Casa del Migrante is a waiting room in which to gather strength and courage and to exchange news on the state of the border. It is also, though Father Luis does not say so, a place where the migrants can learn where a *coyote* might be contacted, with whom to seal a deal for a safer crossing north.

In Father Luis's courtyard, with its tiers of balconies rising several stories high, where the men gather as night falls to sit on benches and exchange information and make plans, the air is full of expectation. They are permitted to stay in the refuge no more than fifteen days, so the pressure to be gone is strong. Visitors are young, mostly under thirty-five; old people, as Father Luis explains, do not migrate. They have neither the strength nor the desire. Sitting on their benches around the courtyard, the men, dark and stocky and watchful, talk of Atlanta and San Francisco and Houston, of farms where cousins and brothers have found work, of the dollars they will send home and the sadness of leaving behind wives and small children; of the dangers of the canal at Mexicali, where the current is strong and the Americans have built slopes into the water, so that the migrants who swim across cannot find purchase and climb out on the California side. The Mexicali canal is famous for its deaths. Their stories, recounted as night falls, in quiet soft voices and with a touch of bravado, are of chases in the desert, and accidents to friends, of the venality of *coyotes* and the huge hopes they have for better futures. Nowhere was I as struck by the ambiguities of refugee and migrant life, by how asylum and migration overlap and complement each other, and how slender the distinctions can be. As with some of Sicily's boat people, the reasons for these men's flight were complicated; some at least were driven by determination to find a better life. It was the women whose stories I found sadder; in Sister Hema's courtyard, the mood was not so buoyant. San Diego's forest fires, not far away, were still burning, and the sun had turned into a small, intensely red marble, glowing eerily in the yellowish light, as ash drifted out of the sky. Fears of the uncertainty and the unknown, the risks of the crossing and the dangers for their children, prey on the minds of the women who wait.

When I went in search of Sister Hema, Luisa had been with her for just a day. Sister Hema was pleased that she was there, for Luisa would be able to tell me, she said, a story that she heard again and again from women who came to her refuge. Like the fair-skinned woman and her daughters, Luisa is from Guadalajara in southern Mexico, and she has stayed with the mission before. Four years ago, when she was twenty-five, she and her husband, Pedro, and their five-year-old daughter, Dolores, traveled to Tijuana in order to cross to seek work in the States. Their family at home—the two sets of grandparents, brothers, several sisters, many children—had a house in which to live, and a little land, but there was never quite enough to eat and the family kept growing. One of Pedro's brothers had made the crossing into California earlier, and had prospered working in a factory in Houston; and the stories he sent back of his new life, and the dollars that came with them, made the young couple decide that they should follow in his steps. At night, around the table, there were long discussions about the wisdom of such an undertaking, especially with a small child, but they were adamant that they would not leave her behind, however much the grandmothers pleaded. And the day came when they packed a very small bag, with one change of clothes each, and took a bus for Tijuana.

Just down the road in the Casa del Migrante, beyond the church where the missionaries and the migrants congregate, Luisa's husband soon learned of a route through the mountains where the Border Patrol seldom went. He discussed it with Luisa and they decided that she and Dolores should remain with Sister Hema while he went ahead to explore the journey and find work in California. Soon, word came that he had made the crossing in less than a day, and that though he had seen the patrol, he had managed to hide in the bushes until they passed. He was in Hollywood, where his brother had found him a job in a restaurant. As for her own crossing, and that of their daughter, he urged them to wait while he raised the money to pay a *coyote* who would find them a safer and less arduous route across the mountains.

Luisa and Dolores waited. The day came when $1,700 arrived from Pedro, and with it instructions from a *coyote* network whose trustworthiness was known and tested. The route to be taken by Luisa was settled; but Dolores, said the unknown visitor who came to give her the details of their journey, was to be entrusted to a Mexican woman who had a daughter of much the same age. Dolores's name would be substituted for hers on the legal documents held by this woman, and the two would then cross the border at San Ysidro, where San Diego meets Tijuana, perfectly normally, and Dolores would be returned to Luisa on the other side. The whole experience, says Luisa now, was terrifying: all migrants know stories of children handed over to *coyotes* in this way and never seen again, and she hesitated before letting Dolores go. But the ruse was successful. Late one night, Luisa delivered her daughter into the hands of a total stranger who came to collect her from the refuge, promising to bring her to a safe house on the California side. Luisa then set off with a *coyote*. On the way to the mountains, they collected another woman with a little girl some years older than Dolores, and two men. The party spent a few hours in a safe house just inside Mexico, and when the time was judged right by the *coyote*, set off on foot with a young boy as guide. Children are now the *coyotes'* preferred guides across the border, since if caught they are not detained by the patrol. For several hours, they scrambled as fast and as silently as they could over the rough terrain, dodging behind bushes and rocks, stopping briefly from time to time to rest. Pausing, lying low, stopping and starting, they took almost two days to reach the safe house on the

California side. Twice, they saw, in the distance, a Border Patrol car, but the officers did not see them. Once, they came across another party of crossers, flitting silently by in the near dark. Luisa's group had cookies with them, and some bottles of water. The travelers did not talk to one another. It was as if each traveled alone. Two days later, Luisa was reunited with Dolores.

But California did not work out well for the family. Luisa found a job in a factory but soon realized that she was pregnant; after the birth of a little girl, she found herself pregnant again, and this time a son was born. Her husband's job in the restaurant was followed by a better one in a factory making toy bones for dogs, but the $285 he brought home each week was not enough to feed, clothe, and house his growing family, particularly as, being illegal migrants, they lived on the very margins of American life. For a while, they sent money home. But there was never enough even for themselves. They began to run up debts, small at first, but the debts grew, making them sad and anxious.

The day I met Luisa and her three children with Sister Hema, Dolores was a leggy, darting child of nine, with fashionable American clothes and bulky, flashing sneakers, and the family was on its way home. Dolores spoke fluent, rapid English, interpreting for her mother who, in four years in Hollywood, had never found the need to learn. Luisa longed to go home: she missed her family in Guadalajara. The crossing back from California to Mexico had been easy: a bus to the border, a short walk across at San Ysidro, past the cars queuing for inspection, the border police taking no interest in their lack of papers. They were Mexicans, after all, going home. It was the next stage in their lives that would be hard. They had come back to nothing—no prospect of work, no savings. The afternoon I sat talking to Luisa under the fruit trees, with Sister Hema hovering in the background and the smaller children playing with a torn teddy bear in the courtyard, Pedro was out in Tijuana, trying to find work to pay for the bus fare south. It was his fourth day of looking, and there was nothing to be found.

. . .

NOT FAR FROM Sister Hema and the Casa del Migrante lies Tijuana's wide and white sandy beach. Here, even on a calm day, the Pacific breaks in slow, heavy waves over the shore, and Mexicans with their children come to paddle and picnic and, on bright autumn and winter days, to stroll and smell the strong sea air. Behind, above, along the rocks, is some of Tijuana's most derelict housing, faded and crumbling cheap seaside hotels, a shantytown of plywood and unfaced brick, dwarfed by the enormous stadium housing the bullring. The view of sand and brushwood and rough pebbles stretches as far as the eye can see—except, that is, where it is broken by the fence, the great divide, part physical, part psychological, that separates Mexico from California.

San Diego and Tijuana could be a single city, running more or less without a break along the coast, from the far northern suburbs of San Diego's La Jolla and Del Mar, to Tijuana's last shantytowns to the far south. Between the two lies the fence, erected and fortified over the last twenty years to keep out the successive waves of Mexicans who have longed to make California their home. Along much of the border between the two cities, the fence is tidy, well patrolled, and floodlit. On the beach, it is rusty, a chaotic structure of iron panels and concrete poles, a curtain of ridged iron that rises straight up out of the sand. There are gaps, even holes large enough for a slim man to slip through. Far out into the sea stretches its extension, a wall of solid, circular iron railings. Two worlds, a tamed California wilderness on one side, with eucalyptus and cactus and bougainvillea, and horses grazing in fields; a place of impoverished Mexican families on the other. They are separated by a single, rusty, crumbling fence. It seems too small a structure, too insignificant, to mean so much.

Every day, migrants gather on Tijuana's sandy beach. They come to look at the fence, to measure its height, to assess how far they will have to run on the other side before they reach the cover of trees, to observe the U.S. Border Patrol in its four-wheel drives parked on the bluffs, to calculate when the tall floodlights will be least revealing. There is no mistaking those waiting to cross. Almost all are young men, traveling alone, parking their small bag or backpack on the sand as they wander up and down, looking, wondering. They test the toeholds in the fence, look through the holes at the emptiness of California, and then sit quietly, waiting for dusk. Many have made the journey before, and many will make it again.

After talking to Sister Hema, I went down to the beach. It was windy, with a faint misty sun now, and the light, still yellow and odd from the fires, was beginning to fade. On the sand, among the families with their children and their dogs, running for balls, sat silent young men, waiting. One, with the help of a friend, was testing the fence for the best place to climb; finding a gap, he slipped quickly through and, neatly, using a stick, wrote "*Passato*," "Crossed," in tidy, clear letters in the new wet sand, before slipping back, pleased with his work. He was going to make his break as soon as dark fell, he said, when the patrol changed and the fading light made figures indistinct. He intended to run very fast, along the sand toward the trees. It was his first crossing, and he had friends waiting on the other side, on the freeway leading up to the center of San Diego.

A little higher up the sand, crouching on their heels, talking in whispers to one another, were four young Chinese men. They had nothing with them, no baggage or belongings of any kind. They looked neat and rather smart, and one wore a cotton suit. They, too, were waiting for dusk. I wanted to ask them where they had come from, why they had chosen the beach at Tijuana, what their journey from China had been like, but we had no language in common, or perhaps they did not want to talk to anyone. Perhaps they were computer programmers, who are now said to be using the Mexico–California route in growing numbers, having been smuggled from Fujian at $60,000 a head.

Somewhere toward the middle of the fence, between the sea and the rocks that rise sharply toward the houses, is a large circle made of barbed wire, like a spider's web against the rusty iron. It is a memorial, according to a crude wooden plaque roughly tacked to it, to those who have died in their attempts to reach California. Beyond, also fastened to the iron panels, are a number of large wooden letters, some five or six feet tall, all that is left of a slogan once written boldly by human rights activists wanting to draw attention to the fence. ALT, they read; and then there is a gap; and then again, DIA. No one on the beach that day knew what the letters stood for. But later, people told me that they once read "Alto Operacion Guardian," "Halt Operation Gatekeeper," "Gatekeeper" being the name given to the most determined assault on the migrants, which took place early in the 1990s.

On each letter, in the years since, an artist has carefully drawn a number of skulls, very white against the fading yellow paint; and on each skull is the name of someone who has drowned swimming around the outer perimeter toward California, tossed back onshore by the waves or sucked below by the undertow that flows dangerously along this coast. There are several Josés, and many Pedros; there is a Moise and a Jaime; but most of the skulls contain just two words: "No Identificado."

. . .

THE STORY OF California's fence is the story of migration. Just as Europeans live with legends of departure, so Americans have legends of arrival. Of all U.S. residents, nearly one in ten—26 million people—is now said to be an immigrant. The fence is part of the legend. It is about a poor country looking across a border and seeing money and opportunities—all the lures that enticed the first European settlers—and wanting a share in them. It is about how, ever since anyone can remember, poor Mexicans have migrated north in search of the American dream, which for them has meant jobs in agriculture, factories, construction, and the service industries; about how they have been welcomed and discouraged by turns and have simply kept on coming, even during times of determined and brutal rejection; about how the Americans have feared being swamped and losing their own identities and livelihoods. It is the old and simple story of exclusion.

There have always been fences and walls. Clearly delineated and militarized frontiers have been known since antiquity. China began to build its Great Wall in the third century B.C., to keep out nomadic invaders, and in 120 A.D. Hadrian began his wall in Britain, from the Solway Firth to the Tyne. Medieval European cities were fortified and walled. But the idea behind the walls and fences slowly changed. With the nineteenth century, and the broad acceptance of national sovereignty, came a new vision of frontiers and border controls, with the understanding that states had the legitimate authority to dictate what took place on their own territory. To do so, they needed to control their borders. No longer were walls a means of keeping out military foes; now they blocked unwanted people from coming in, along lines that often lie like geological faults between the world's rich and the world's poor.

It has become fashionable, at the turn of the twenty-first century, to discuss borders as archaic and irrelevant in the new age of globalization and the Internet. Among free-market liberals, the talk is all of the "borderless" world brought about by developments in communication technology, along with world market forces; the peaceful interdependence of states, it is said, must lead to a further erosion of borders. In practice, of course, there is no peaceful interdependence of states, and the borderlessness of the world is all about trade, not about people. As economic borders come down in successive waves of economic liberalization, so geographical frontiers are actually being strengthened, to keep out trespassers. Increased freedom of exit has not been matched by increased freedom of entry: people today face formidable barriers if they try to cross from one country to another. Reconciling this paradox—how to make cross-border economic exchanges easier, while enforcing border controls for would-be immigrants—is perceived as one of the most delicate and challenging political tasks of our time, a task made harder by the image peddled everywhere of the huddled masses battering on the doors of the affluent world. The image, as it happens, is false. Most people today, as in the past, are not mobile. Somewhere between 2 and 3 percent of the world's population can be counted as international migrants, a fact seldom cited; the proportion is no higher and no lower than at any time in the last fifty years.

The border between Mexico and the United States is just over two thousand miles long. Ten million people today live in the twelve major border cities, which among them have forty-four ports of entry. Around 300,000 Mexicans cross *legally* every day to work in the United States. Cross-border trade has doubled in ten years. Tijuana in Mexico and San Diego in California, a single urban sprawl straddling the frontier at San Ysidro, currently have a population of around 4 million, and it is rising sharply all the time. Some 60 million people and 20 million cars cross from Tijuana into San Diego every year, making it one of the busiest frontiers in the modern world.

Migration across this long border, both legal and illegal, goes back a very long way. All through the nineteenth century, people moved back and forth more or less freely; the first American attempt to restrict entry was aimed not at the Mexicans but at the Chinese, who were landing by boat at the ports of Ensenada, Guaymas, and Mazatlán and paying traffickers $40 to take them into California. The first officers appointed to catch illegal crossers were known as Chinese inspectors. In the 1920s, when the United States imposed restrictions on European migration, the Mexico–U.S. border became a back door for Europeans and when, in 1924, the U.S. Border Patrol was created, the primary targets for its 450 officers were European and Asian migrants. Mexicans, meanwhile, continued to cross as they had always done, informally, in response to the demand for cheap labor in the expanding agricultural businesses. Deported when the Depression hit the United States, they were welcomed back to make up for the labor shortages of World War II.

Between 1942 and 1964, the "bracero" guest worker arrangement provided continuing cheap labor for the new agrobusinesses. By now, the presence of Mexicans in the United States was enshrined in a vast and complicated web of needs and agreements and when, in the 1960s, the bracero program ended, the system simply moved underground; the Mexicans' freedom of exit was guaranteed by the Mexican constitution, and they were undeterred by the largely symbolic presence of a small number of border agents. The migrants joined large Mexican communities all over America, for the most part leaving their families at home in Mexico. The Immigration Reform and Control Act of 1986, which legalized some 2 million Mexicans already working in the United States (while at the same time tightening border controls), stimulated a desire among more Mexicans to enter the United States in the hopes of receiving a similar amnesty. By 1996, more than 7 million Mexicans were living in the United States, most of them illegally. On the wall of the briefing room in San Diego's Border Patrol headquarters hangs an extraordinary photograph. Taken around the end of the 1980s, it shows a hillside on the Mexican side of the border, somewhere on the edge of Tijuana. The entire hill is covered with men, perhaps five or six hundred of them, all facing forward, toward the camera, as if watching a football match. Caught on film by a photographer on the California side, they are migrants, waiting for night to fall and the great race toward the border to begin. Facing them, not seen, are a few Border Patrol vehicles, poised to arrest as many as they can.

On a busy night, back then, Agent Angel Santa Ana of the Border Patrol told me when he showed me this photograph and explained its significance, there would be as many as three thousand arrests. It was unnerving to be an agent back in the 1980s, he said, waiting lonely and apprehensive for dark to fall, bracing yourself to hold back the surge of people as they came racing down the hillside toward you; but you soon learned that if you took a very tough line with one member of a group, the rest would fall into line and go quietly. "Even now when it is all tougher," he said, "Mexicans are not hard to catch: they are easily cowed by authority and they are fearful of men with guns." They are, as he puts it, "docile." In those days, he went on, the men crossing sometimes dug holes under parts of the fence for women and children to crawl through, while they, being men, insisted on climbing over. Agent Santa Ana is a good-looking and agreeable man in his thirties, attuned to the nuances of border affairs, and he wears cowboy boots under his green uniform. A second-generation Mexican Californian, he grew up in Texas and plans to return there.

In 1993, the newly inaugurated President Clinton, facing a recession in California and the rise of anti-immigration groups claiming that by mid-2050 only half the population of the United States would be white, launched a program to "regain control" of the country's southwestern border.* The border—particularly the most popular crossing area, around San Diego, with its few stretches of weak fencing—had long been perceived as loose but adequate: it was now seen as dangerously porous. While California became a center of anti-immigration rhetoric, Washington hardened its approach to illegal immigrants. Generous new funds were poured into the Immigration and Naturalization Service, the INS, and with the money came more guns, more agents, more equipment. Some helicopters arrived. An electronic identification system known as IDENT, which stores the fingerprints and photographs of those caught trying to cross, was introduced at border points, and the military, bringing with it sheets of corrugated-steel landing mats, sent army reservists to build a ten-foot-high fence along fourteen miles of the most vulnerable crossing points. The idea behind the Clinton administration's new commitment to curb illegal migrants was simple: "prevention through deterrence." The Border Patrol concentrated large resources of staff and technology on the relatively short stretches of border traditionally most used by illegal crossers, rather than taking the other possible course, which would have been to appoint large numbers of inspectors to mop up migrants once they were in.

It was under Clinton's presidency that the first coordinated assault to frustrate Mexican immigrants was launched along the Rio Grande in Texas, where a police chief called Silvestre Reyes de-

---

* This was not the first such program: Operation Wetback, launched in June 1954 to stop immigration by undocumented Mexicans, sent 750 patrol agents to the Southwest.

ployed closely spaced border control vehicles along a number of popular crossing points. Operation Blockade—renamed Operation Hold the Line after the Mexican government protested—was declared successful and was soon followed by Operation Gatekeeper in San Diego. Then came an extension of Operation Hold the Line, ten more miles of enforcement west into New Mexico. In 1999 came Operation Safeguard, to improve control along 300 miles of the Arizona–Mexico border. Everywhere, underground sensors, infrared scopes, huge portable floodlights, and many new agents arrived to carry out the program. It has become, say its critics, like a futuristic film, full of gadgets; only the proposal to electrify the fence has actually been defeated, after human rights groups protested. Even devices designed to save lives, like watering stations, are wired with infrared sensors that betray that they have been used.

At first, Clinton's aggressive border policies looked highly successful. The crackdown was reported widely and with approval. Silvestre Reyes announced that arrests along his stretch of the border had dropped by a dramatic 76 percent, which suggested to him— though not to many others—that those migrants were now staying at home. Reyes left to pursue a successful career in Washington.

It was true that the arrests were dropping wherever the border was now effectively enforced by patrols and equipment. But it rapidly became obvious that the numbers of those crossing had not dropped; they had simply shifted elsewhere. Squeezed away from the regular routes, migrants were resorting to *coyotes*, whose activities became more efficient and more professional, and who began to charge ever higher fees. Heretofore, the *coyotes* had operated informally; now they began to group themselves into highly effective syndicates, with agents all around Mexico, sophisticated processes for forging and selling documents, arranging safe houses and journeys by train, plane, and truck, and with carefully worked out ways of collecting fees for successful crossings. What was once a relatively simple and straightforward illegal practice has now become a complex underground web, connected to, though not the same as, the drug trade, whose members use the same routes.

And, of course, the routes the migrants were now driven to use were more dangerous. They passed through the desert, with its immense surges and drops in temperature. Or they swam: across the treacherous twenty-one-foot-deep All American Canal, in some places as wide as a football field, with undercurrents too powerful for all but the strongest swimmer, or the New River, said to be the most polluted stretch of water in the world, carrying typhoid, cholera, and hepatitis. It is down this river that many of the crossers now float, holding their breaths under submerged bridges and along a twenty-foot culvert. As Wayne Cornelius, director of the Center for Comparative Immigration Studies at the University of California at San Diego, sees it, there is something deeply immoral in a policy that deliberately puts people in harm's way. Like Father Luis in Tijuana, he is angry about the casualties. When he talks at seminars and conferences about the border, he tells his audiences about the 1,700 migrants who died trying to cross between 1994 and 2001, and the many others who have lost their lives unreported in the mountains and the desert. He shows his students slides of the Berlin Wall, and tells them that only 239 people in all lost their lives during the forty-three years of the wall's existence, stating that this is a tenth of the number who have died on the Mexico–California border. Cornelius makes another point. Increased enforcement has altered the composition of those who cross: fewer women, children, and older people now attempt the journey.

While half of Mexico lives in poverty, and Americans depend on cheap Mexican labor, economic agreements between the two countries continue to favor the migration of goods and not people—the crucial 1993 North American Free Trade Agreement, at U.S. insistence, omitted all mention of labor migration. The border remains patchily and symbolically controlled, with great shows of strength in some places and an absence of all legal authority in others, so the migrants will keep on coming, drawn by the promise of dollars that lie just within reach, confused but not deterred by the ambivalence with which Americans view their arrival. Not deterred either, it seems, by the vigilantes spawned by this particular mixture of official encouragement and restriction: in Arizona and Texas, ranchers turned cowboys, carrying machine guns and two-way radios, now regularly patrol the border. The Web site of Ranch Rescue offers the slogan "Private property first, foremost, and always," advertises weapons and combat gear, and recruits volunteers for Operations Foxbat, Jaguar, and Thunderbird. It quotes Cicero on the moral rightness of self-protection. Ranch Rescue is for people who "believe that when government fails or refuses to act, individual Citizens are obligated to act on their own" and for whom "socialism in all its forms" as well as "Environmentalist measures" are just for "liars and fools of the very worst kind." It was the vigilantes who first used a new weapon being investigated by the Border Patrol, a drone that flies along border areas and beams back photographs of people attempting to cross. The vigilantes are acting in total violation of federal and state laws, but they appear to escape prosecution.

The migrants are not put off by the penalties they face if caught. Despite the Illegal Immigration Reform and Immigrant Responsibility Act of 1996, which increased penalties for illegal entry and people-smuggling, in practice very little happens to the migrant who is arrested. So overloaded is the system all along the border that only recidivists whose fingerprints have been recorded are actually prosecuted. All others are simply returned across the border, in a "humane and orderly" fashion, as demanded by the human rights organizations active in the region and as subscribed to by the Border Patrol. Agent Angel is proud of his district and his work. Along the border as a whole, half a million crossers are said to be apprehended each year, but no U.S. border state has the resources to prosecute more than a tiny fraction of them. A migrant today is said to have just one chance in eight of being prosecuted.

It would be wrong to say that the fence dominates the border, or even that it is particularly noticeable. On the contrary, it is almost invisible. In the minds of most San Diegans, says Wayne Cornelius, the fence is an abstraction, a place where from time to time politicians make speeches, seeking votes by taking a stand against the dangers of illegal immigration, and where members of various churches gather to honor those who die in their attempts to reach America. Ordinary San Diegans, he says, do not know about the fence, and they do not care.

It is, of course, possible that a semiclosed border is precisely what suits most people. The United States needs Mexican labor. Mexicans need U.S. jobs, which enable them to send $7 billion home each year to their families in remittances. An open and free border—as advocated by some Wall Street liberal economists—would result in an unregulated surge of new arrivals, which the United States cannot handle and which would rapidly lead to an even larger anti-immigrant backlash. In any case, the events of September 11 have introduced the specter of terrorists using the migrant route, and there is something comforting about the idea of a fence, a barricade against the nightmare of a world out of control. The United States must therefore be seen to be attempting to prevent illegal immigration, with showy displays of border controls, while at the same time allowing enough people through to feed the market for cheap labor.

Seen like this, the fence and the activities that surround it become like an elaborate childhood game, in which, as darkness falls each night, the two opposing sides line up, the migrants waiting to cross, the border patrols waiting to catch enough of them to appear efficient and in control. The light grows dim, the whistle goes, the migrants begin their race toward the new world. Only, of course, it is a game with a very dark side, one in which only the fittest survive; and among the casualties are many of the women and children for whom the new rules are, quite simply, too tough.

・ ・ ・

WHAT DREW ME to San Diego's fence initially was a chance remark made one day by Jeff Crisp at UNHCR in Geneva. The fence, Crisp said, was fascinating because it was such a naked, unapologetic example of the lengths the West is willing to go to in order to keep unwanted people out. And he was right: there is something extraordinarily crude, even ridiculous, about these long stretches of wire and concrete, which look so small and insignificant against the large landscape and arid and stony mountains of the border areas. The fence does not look as if it could really keep anything out. But it was fascinating also, Crisp went on, because the people who come across every day are not all Mexicans. Among them are Turkish Kurds and Iraqis, Sri Lankans and Nigerians, and even Chinese, like the four young men I tried to talk to on the beach at Tijuana. And indeed, when I got to San Diego, I learned that, in 2003, researchers gathering material on the nationalities of those trying to cross the border illegally discovered people from seventy-three different countries in a single period of three months.

The numbers, compared to those of the Mexicans who cross, are very small: perhaps no more than 4 or 5 percent of the total. But they are enough to make an important point about modern migration: like the birds that circle the world in vast sweeps, covering thousands of miles every spring and autumn, refugees and migrants today will make extraordinary journeys in search of work and safety. But unlike the swallows' routes, which are the same year after year, the journeys made by refugees can last several years, as they wander, apparently without reason, from continent to continent. In offices where people study migration, there are maps charting the most used paths to freedom, with distance covered and time taken. The longest recorded journeys begin in China and end in Surinam, some 15,200 miles on the road, taking between six months and a year and costing between $25,000 and $50,000; Thailand to New York, at 13,500 miles, is not far behind.

Wanting to hear about these travels, wanting to understand the routes and the dangers, wanting to ask how the refugees decided which route to take, and what it was like traveling without possessions and with only a dim idea of the future to shape their days, guided not by their own instincts but by those of unknown traffickers whose honor they could not know to trust, I asked human rights lawyers in San Diego who work with asylum seekers if they would introduce me to some of their clients who had crossed into California from Mexico. The world of these long-distance crossers, as they are known—people who are not Mexican—who travel from all over the world to cross into the States along this border, is completely different. Unlike the Mexicans, most have come to California not so much in search of work as to escape persecution at home; they were not the economic migrants I originally came to find, but the asylum seekers I knew well from Europe and Africa, people so desperate that any journey, however long and arduous, however dangerous and financially ruinous, is better than likely captivity and torture at home. There are said to be about 11,000 of them in San Diego at any one time, at various stages of the asylum process.

It was from a church group in El Cajon, west of San Diego, that I heard about the Chaldeans. San Diego, like Detroit, Phoenix, and Chicago, is home to a large community of these Iraqi Catholics—descendants of Sennacherib and of Sargon the Akkadian, who ruled Mesopotamia with Babylon as their capital. Modern Chaldeans use the Aramaic language and follow the teachings of Rome. They did not fare well under Saddam Hussein. They were merchants and well educated and, since their religion did not forbid it, ran liquor stores. All were harassed; thousands were arrested, imprisoned, tortured. In El Cajon, grouped into two congregations, are hundreds of Chaldeans who have fled Iraq since the early 1980s and, granted asylum, have settled legally along its freeways and in its suburbs. They say that southern California, with its dry air and sandy soil, reminds them of their native Iraq, and that they are happy here, though many have left relations behind. In their still oddly Middle Eastern living rooms, with sofas and chairs all around the walls, and large floral carpets in the middle, they have placed enormous television sets, on which they watch the news from Iraq. When I went to the Chaldean churches, I found Iraqis who had taken remarkable routes to reach the safety of California, who had walked and driven and taken buses and ships and planes, who had spent all their savings and left behind people they loved, people whom they mourn because they are too old, or too poor, or too frail to follow them to safety. But no journey I heard about was more dramatic than

Salaam's; his story alone shows what people will do in order to escape persecution.

Salaam is twenty-nine and a doctor, a tall, spare, genial man with glasses and the gestures of someone who has always been at ease with his own life. His dark brown hair is cropped short, and his manner is generous and open. Already, in some indefinable way, after only a few months in America, he looks American; his English has a Californian drawl. Salaam was working as a doctor in Baghdad in the spring of 1999 when his turn came to serve as prison doctor for a month in Abu Ghraib, the vast jail in the suburbs of Baghdad now known throughout the world as the place where U.S. reservists and private military contractors housed and maltreated their Iraqi prisoners. As Salaam was talking, I remembered hearing about Abu Ghraib in the 1980s, when Saddam Hussein tortured his opponents in its dungeons, and something of the horror in the voices of its victims, who were confined in flooded underground cells—horror brought to the West's notice by dissidents who had finally escaped Saddam Hussein's executioners—has always stayed in my mind.

When he reported for work, Salaam knew little about conditions inside Abu Ghraib. That wasn't something you talked about in Baghdad in the 1990s. What he saw revolted him; he observed, but he said nothing. But then one day seventy-two prisoners rebelled against the atrocities being committed every day around them. The prison governor ordered that as punishment they should be locked together in a single inner room, some four yards by five, as Salaam remembers it. The prisoners stood, or sat, in total darkness. On the second day, two died; on the third, thirteen. On the fourth, Salaam was ordered to visit the survivors. "I couldn't get into the room because there was no air. The people inside had become like animals. The floor was sodden with urine and excrement and sweat." Salaam did what he could: he dragged out twenty unconscious or semiconscious people and gave them oxygen.

The next day, the governor summoned him. Salaam could no longer hold back his hatred and outrage. The conversation did not go well. Salaam was informed that he, too, would now be punished, and that his next medical job would be to extract the eyeballs of newly executed prisoners, so that the corneas could be removed for transplants. "I was ordered to attend the executions, so that the extraction could take place immediately. I refused. The governor called in a guard, and had me put into a cell." There Salaam stayed for three and a half months. Because his parents had some influence and his sister was able to put up bail, he was released. "After that, I had to leave Iraq as quickly as I could. I was marked, as a Chaldean and as a dissident."

As it happened, Salaam's sister, Rania, was now marked as well. There was no choice but to flee. Rania left directly for Jordan, on forged papers; she was accompanied by their father, since as a woman she could not travel alone. Their relatively well-off parents bought Salaam a ticket and visa to travel to Turkey.

Now the long journey into exile began, eventually to bring not only brother and sister but also their parents and remaining sisters to California. Salaam and Rania knew where they wanted to go: San Diego's Chaldean community is well known to Iraqis; furthermore, an older brother, Iman, was already settled in El Cajon. The question was how, with no genuine passports or visas, to get there.

From Turkey, Salaam traveled, by bus and car, to Turkestan, where he bought another visa, a forged passport, and a plane ticket to Amman. After several weeks, he was reunited with Rania, and the two now found a smuggler willing to traffic them to Mexico, via Guatemala, for $10,000 each. This involved living for a while in a safe house, catching a plane for Guatemala City, and making their way, in the company of a guide and four other Iraqis, up Guatemala's western coast toward the border with Mexico. The last part was through jungle. At daybreak they reached the frontier, which lay along a river. The water was high and fast flowing. Their guide directed them to the shallowest point and Salaam and Rania, hand in hand, holding tightly to each other, set out, the water swirling around their shoulders. Several times they lost their footing and thought that they would be swept away. But they reached the other side and were taken to a safe house to rest. They had now been traveling for thirteen days since leaving Jordan, and had nothing but the clothes they stood up in.

In Mexico City, the smugglers abandoned them, but they had tickets for a plane to Tijuana. When the party disembarked, only Salaam and Rania managed to get through the immigration controls; the other four were taken into custody.

Salaam and Rania now took a room in a hotel. Their brother, Iman, arrived, having crossed the border at San Ysidro on his legitimate asylum seeker papers, bringing with him a further $2,000 for each of them to pay a smuggler to get them into California. Very early one morning, Salaam and Rania were driven to the crossing at San Ysidro and told to walk, without looking right or left or pausing for anything, through the checkpoint, past the lines of cars waiting for border inspection, past the immigration controls. It had all been arranged with bribes. They didn't believe it, but it worked. They found themselves in California, in a parking lot near the border, where a smuggler was waiting with a taxi to drive them to their brother. The next day, they asked for asylum. In the months that followed, their parents and two sisters also reached San Diego. Rania has since married and works as a pharmacist; Salaam is studying American medicine for the qualifications he needs to practice as a doctor in the United States.

What Salaam remembers most about the journey is the sense of responsibility he felt for Rania. The worst moment was crossing the river, with the current pulling at their legs, and the Mexican and Guatemalan soldiers standing on the bridge, within sight, with their guns, but fortunately looking the other way. That was bad, just as it was bad leaving Jordan on a forged passport, knowing that if it was discovered he would be deported to Iraq. The journey was hard for him, but far harder for his sister, who had no knowledge or experience of danger and hardship. As for him, what he witnessed and went through in Abu Ghraib had hardened him, and in comparison, his travels do not strike Salaam as very interesting. It is the past that preoccupies him.

. . .

FROM PRO BONO lawyers who handle the cases of asylum seekers, I heard about the extent to which "aliens" have been swept off the streets since September 11, 2001. Immigrants and visitors to the United States now face an array of legal and bureaucratic hurdles.* Shortly after the attacks, on the orders of Attorney General John Ashcroft, the U.S. resettlement program, which in recent years had seen some 70,000 asylum seekers granted new lives in America, was frozen. As I had seen among the Liberians in Cairo, people whose immigration had already been approved were put back into the system for new checks. Families split between different parts of the world pending reunification in the States remained in limbo. The infrastructure of organizations caring for them, such as the International Rescue Committee, began to crumble, as their funding is calculated according to the number of new arrivals. Then arrests of "suspect aliens" started, beginning with Muslims and Arabs. At first, the number of detainees was conscientiously published each week. But when, before many weeks had passed, the figure reached a thousand, the bulletins stopped. All that was known was that foreigners working or studying in the United States, many of whom had been there for many years and had families and children, suddenly found themselves picked up and charged with technical violations of immigration law, such as failing to notify the authorities of a change in their university major. On the pretext that this was the simplest way of holding in custody and interrogating possible terrorists, some of these people have been held for months before being deported. Others have been caught under an ex post facto law, making immigrants who came to the United States lawfully subject to deportation for acts—such as

---

* There are today four main categories of immigrant in the United States: relatives of U.S. residents (69 percent); those who come for specific jobs (13 percent); refugees and asylum seekers (8 percent); and those who take part in the lottery, which is open to countries that sent fewer than 50,000 people over the previous five years (6 percent).

traffic offenses—that were not grounds for deportation when they committed them.

Another Ashcroft proposal enacted in the wake of September 11 requires visitors from twenty-five predominantly Muslim countries to register and submit to fingerprinting immediately on arrival, and then report back to the authorities after forty days in the United States. Some forgot; others misunderstood or did not take the ruling seriously. In a little less than two years, at least five thousand people are believed to have been arrested and taken into custody, of whom just four were eventually charged in connection with terrorism, and just one actually convicted of "support of unsuspected terrorism." In this context, what first took place at Guantánamo Bay in Cuba can be seen as an extreme version of the current U.S. hostility toward noncitizens: 650 men and boys—some as young as thirteen—were held incommunicado, without access to counsel, and with no hearing at which to determine whether or not they are in fact "enemy combatants" in the first place.

The attacks launched by George W. Bush and John Ashcroft and approved by Congress on America's vast immigrant population have not gone unchallenged by liberals among both the Republicans and the Democrats, who regard them as frightening harbingers of an ever greater erosion of civil liberties. As the journalist Anthony Lewis noted in the *New York Review of Books* in the autumn of 2003, paraphrasing Martin Niemöller, the outspoken anti-Nazi German pastor, what is happening today to refugees and immigrants, the "aliens," could very well happen tomorrow to American citizens, and the fact that there is so little real protest only makes future action against citizens that much more thinkable. The USA Patriot Act has already given government agents the power to subpoena any individual's records, including a U.S. citizen's, with a university, library, or telephone company. While people wait for more terrorist attacks and for yet more repressive measures taken in their wake, the emphasis is shifting all the time, away from openness and tolerance and accountability, toward secrecy and obfuscation. Prejudices on the part of certain judges hearing immigration appeals grow more marked; postponements and adjournments become the order of the day, as do layers of investigation by one government agency after another; the appeals system becomes more meaningless; nothing is as clear as it once was; and human rights lawyers learn of changes in policy not in directives but by reading between the lines of speeches. Nuances have taken on new power.

. . .

THE DETENTION OF asylum seekers has a long history in the United States. Introduced along with the first immigration controls in the late nineteenth century, it was abandoned in the 1950s, only to be revived in the 1980s in response to the influx first of Haitians and then of Cubans. They were incarcerated in camps and federal prisons in an attempt to deter too many others from following. To this day, the rule of limited parole for pregnant women, juveniles, and other vulnerable people, and blanket detention for the rest remains in place for all those reaching the United States without valid entry documents. Once they pass a screening interview, and provided they satisfy certain criteria, they are in theory eligible to be paroled, but many continue to be detained just the same. Though not criminals, they can be—and often are—held indefinitely: for six or seven months before they come before a judge, then for the two or more years before the appeal, then many more months while the law winds its convoluted course, only then to be denied bail and not told when they will be released. The conditions in which many are kept are both inhuman and degrading. They can be stripped, searched, shackled, manacled, chained, and denied access to lawyers and to their families. Though in theory the conditions of detention of asylum seekers are regulated by UNHCR, of whose executive committee the United States is a member, these rules are routinely breached, and, since September 11, increasingly so.

The numbers of detained asylum seekers keep on growing. People are held in state and local jails, in federal prisons, in private contract facilities, and in "servicing processing centers." Most are places singularly unsuited to long stays. Frequently denied access to interpreters or the help of nongovernmental organizations, shunted from prison to prison without explanation or warning, many of those detained are reported to be falling ill, the trauma of what they have fled exacerbated by the fresh trauma of uncertainty and hostility. Lawyers visiting their clients report a sense of growing helplessness and confusion and say that the women detainees in particular suffer acutely from fear, loneliness, and an inability to understand what is happening to them. Physicians for Human Rights and the Bellevue/NYU Program for Survivors of Torture not long ago carried out a series of interviews with detainees who had been held between one month and four and a half years. They found that 86 percent of them were suffering from measurable levels of depression and half were diagnosed as having post-traumatic stress disorder. Even when bail and parole are recommended, many asylum seekers cannot meet their requirements; so they remain in detention.

A number of the detainees are unaccompanied children: that is, they are under the age of eighteen and have traveled the world alone, without other members of their families. Like adults, they are obliged to prove that they can meet the definition of a refugee under the 1951 Convention. Under several different international rulings, including the 1989 UN Convention on the Rights of the Child, children should be imprisoned only under exceptional circumstances, and then for the shortest time necessary. Yet the number of unaccompanied children detained in the United States doubled between 1997 and 2001. And although the United States has sought to draw up humane rules for these wandering children, none are in fact binding. Not long ago the care, custody, and placement of unaccompanied minors was transferred to the Office of Refugee Resettlement, an agency within the Department of Health and Human Services (HHS has a long history of dealing with refugee children). Guidelines were drawn up for newly arrived children traveling on their own, drawing heavily on the liberal spirit of the Convention on the Rights of the Child. In practice, however, a third of these children wind up in secure jail-like facilities, originally designed for young offenders, where they can spend months or even years.

Amnesty International, in a 2003 report on children in immigration detention, *Why Am I Here?*, found widespread human rights violations across the country: children spent long periods in solitary confinement and were subjected to physical and verbal abuse, strip searches, and the use of shackles.

"I am tired of seeing so many depressed people," an immigration judge told the director of one of the detention centers not long ago. "You should do something about it."

· PART THREE ·

ARRIVING

FAIR GO

Australia and the Policy of Mandatory Detention

We have to remind ourselves that geographically we
are Oriental, we are not European. We are an island
just off the south-east coast of Asia, and are part of the
Oriental world. There our fate is set. . . . The decision
we must make as Australians is this: are we going to look
after our coloured future or our cultural future? . . . I
could imagine a much finer race existing in Australia in a
hundred years if their colour was the colour that so many
Australians seek to attain on the beaches.

THE RIGHT REVEREND E. H. BURGMANN,
ANGLICAN BISHOP OF GOULBURN, JANUARY 1946

In the summer of 1966, when I had just left university in London,
my father took me and my younger brother, Richard, to Australia. It
was, in some sense, to take us home. Born in Melbourne soon before
the First World War, the eldest son of a writer and journalist, my father had left Australia for Europe in 1937, to catch and report on the
last days of the Spanish Civil War. What he wanted to do was join
the other young writers and painters drawn so powerfully abroad by
a longing for a culture and history that they felt Australia lacked.
Europe, thought my father, would be fun; it would be where he

would learn about life and music and writing. His first real story, filed for the *Daily Express*, whose staff he had just joined, was about the refugees streaming across the Spanish border into France, the loyalist soldiers and their families escaping Franco's reprisals.

All his life, my father would retain a feeling of ambivalence about the country in which he was born. He loved its smells, the color of the light, and the constant heat, and wherever he went he remarked on eucalyptus trees; and later, when he came to build his own house in Italy, he surrounded the terrace with them. We grew up on what he called chop picnics: fires made on the beaches of Greece and Italy, over which he grilled the lamb chops of his boyhood journeys into the bush; but he felt trapped, whenever he went back to Melbourne, by the sense of loss of people and ideas. Australia remained both home and not home; he would return again and again, at first a little resentfully, later, after he became ill, with growing pleasure and recognition. His ambivalence about Australia, his longings and his rejection, colored the constant moves of our childhood.

We sailed for Perth from Naples, early in July, on board the *Leonardo da Vinci*, pride of the Italian shipping lines, making its last journey to Australia. Air travel had put the long sea voyages out of business. On board were 1,700 migrants, people who had accepted Australia's generous invitation of citizenship and a new life. The scenes of farewell on the docks at Naples were noisy and tearful and the *Leonardo da Vinci* sailed out of harbor festooned in paper streamers spinning in the wind, to the sounds of a brass band playing jauntily on the quay. Far out at sea, sad people continued to wave from the upper decks. The journey was very quick, by the standard of most crossings: fourteen days, with a single stop in Aden. The only episode to mar the boisterous feeling on the lower decks was when the captain announced, over the loud speaker system, that it had just been decided in Canberra that the draft for Vietnam would henceforth apply to new settlers. A mutiny threatened, but it was quieted, if I remember rightly, by an assurance that military service could also be deferred.

The migrants were, of course, all white. Most of them were Italians, in the late 1960s still among the most numerous of Australia's postwar settlers, the destination for migrants from the south and Sicily having long shifted from the United States to the suburbs of Melbourne and Sydney. "Italians," read a government poster of 1951, "make good Australians." There were some British, a few central and eastern Europeans, a handful of Spaniards; but no Asians, no one from the Middle East, and certainly no Africans. There was no sign of the small number of "distinguished non-Europeans" the government had said it was keen to welcome.

In Perth, our first port of call, the passersby were conspicuous by their whiteness. In the middle of the nineteenth century, significant numbers of Chinese coolies had been allowed in to work the Victorian gold fields, followed by Afghan camel drivers and Japanese pearl divers. But since 1901 a White Australia policy, an unashamedly racist process of selection among immigrants, had been in place to keep out "all peoples whose presence was, in the opinion of Australians, injurious to the general welfare"—people who were not, in other words, white. In the language of the day, the 7,500 Jews who found safety in Australia soon after the shameful Evian Conference of 1938—at which world governments declined to accept all but a very small number of Jews fleeing the Nazis—became "reffos" (refugees), as did the other "aliens," the Balts, Czechs, Slavs, and Poles whom Australia agreed to take in the postwar years of displacement and labor shortages. But still no yellows or blacks. As T. W. White, the Australian delegate to the Evian Conference, had said, Australia had no racial problem and "we are not desirous of importing one."

And the reffos did not always have much of a life, the young men living in strict, segregated camps, many having just come from the displaced persons camps of occupied Europe. They tended to be regarded little more favorably than the Aboriginals, whose harsh treatment continued to be widely disregarded even by contemporary historians, whose settler forebears had chosen to recognize only an empty continent, waiting to be claimed and redeemed by early British settlers. And it was now that the idea of the "good refugee" was born: the one who, fleeing Communist persecution, waited patiently in a camp far away to be selected as "genuine" and invited to Australia.

When Gough Whitlam, Australia's first postwar Labor prime minister, finally brought to an end the White Australia policy in 1973—six years after my visit—declaring that the country needed to "turn a decent face to the world," it was with two important provisos. One was that Canberra's politicians, be they from the right or left, would tacitly agree not to play the race card in their electioneering by appealing to voters' fear of refugees; the other that the new nonwhite Australians would be selected with the greatest care. The late 1970s were the years of the Vietnamese boat people, and Australia's immigration officials chose their settlers directly from the refugee holding camps of Malaysia, Indonesia, and China with a keen eye for their suitability. In the ten years that followed the fall of Saigon, Australia took 95,000 boat people, all but 5,000 of them arriving in the approved orderly manner, having been selected and processed. Australia was no longer white, but a neat and cautious system was in place. "We are all," declared successive ministers with pride, extolling their own ancestral roots among the early British settlers, "immigrants, each and every one of us." The prior existence of the Aborigines was seldom mentioned.

If the United States nurtured an idea of itself as a country opening its arms to Europe's huddled masses, and Britain chose to regard itself as an early champion of political and religious dissent, Australia framed a different myth. It was that of a continent to be explored and colonized by a nation of hardworking white people, with the help of a small contingent of carefully selected white foreigners, living in the hopes that the yellow hordes of Asia, growing at a terrifying pace not far from their shores, would not cast their eyes covetously in their direction. And when events did conspire to threaten this myth, Australia, the land where all but the Aboriginals are indeed immigrants, chose to introduce one of the most exclusionary immigration policies of any democracy, against a small number of people, some of them children.

. . .

WHEN SISTER CLAUDETTE of the Sisters of Mercy first visited Port Augusta in the 1970s, it was in answer to a call for help from Aboriginal people living in a reserve not far from what was then one of the largest ports in South Australia, transporting iron ore, lead, and silver from the Flinders Ranges. Like the Native Americans in the United States, many Aborigines were by now gathered on reserves. Reaching the camp, Sister Claudette found that the call had come from Aboriginal grandmothers, who had been taken from their parents as children all but illiterate and sent to work as domestic servants, some of them members of the "stolen generation," the generally half-Aboriginal, half-white Australian children removed from their mothers between 1910 and 1970 and sent to remote institutions with the purpose of destroying their Aboriginal roots. Now, growing old, the women wanted to learn to read and write so as to be able to help their grandchildren with their homework. It was, says Sister Claudette, who is an energetic and friendly woman in her sixties, shocking to discover these reserves full of people who had to ask permission to leave. "I knew about poverty," she says. "I had been working in the townships of South Africa. But here the Aborigines had been stripped of everything. They had no dignity left." She stayed with them for ten years, not unhappy, though in the summer the temperature rose to 114 degrees. She cannot forget that good Catholics in her congregation in Port Augusta did not choose to visit her reserve.

Two years ago, after an absence of fifteen years, Sister Claudette came back to Port Augusta. A detention center for asylum seekers was being built not far from the town, between the desert and the red streaky mountains, made out of "dongas," prefabricated huts designed for miners, shipped into nearby Port Pirie from West Australia and set down in rectangular blocks among the eucalyptus trees. The new camp was to take detainees from a troubled and much hated center called Woomera, about an hour's drive into the desert, which was to close down after a violent history of riots, suicide attempts, and arson.

Why the authorities decided to call the new camp Baxter, Sister Claudette is not entirely sure. The name might refer to Sir John Philip Baxter, chairman of Australia's Atomic Energy Commission from 1957 to 1972, for this was the area where the British and Australians jointly tested atomic rockets and missiles in the 1940s and 1950s. The explanation she believes likelier is that the camp is named after a man who once owned the land on which it stands, a settler remembered widely for the harshness with which he treated the Aborigines who inhabited it. Nor was Sister Claudette quite certain, the morning she took me with her to Baxter, to be tagged, searched, moved from one locked compartment into another, stamped with fluorescent identification marks, and then ushered through seven sets of security doors, how many detainees Baxter held. The numbers change from day to day and the authorities can be evasive about exact figures.

· · ·

IN MARCH 2004, almost forty years after my first and only previous visit, I went back to Australia, landing in Adelaide and going straight to Port Augusta, wanting to see what Australia's detention policy was actually like. Sister Claudette told me that in a month for which she had managed to get figures there had been 199 detainees, one of them a Kashmiri who had spent over seven years in detention; most were young men, from Afghanistan and Iraq, though there were also a small number of families with their children. Once I was inside the camp, she said, I would have no view of the outside world other than the sky above, the camp having been designed to let no one see either in or out. That, she said, as we emptied our pockets and stowed our possessions, was what she always remembered about Baxter, the enclosed dongas and the blue sky, along with the noise, the endless sound of whining and clanging metal, as the many gates and doors opened and closed, loud and harsh in the desert silence.

It was Salem who told me most about what it is to be a detainee in Baxter. Salem is half Iraqi, half Iranian, a geologist, a small, thin, worried man in his early fifties who looks considerably older, with thinning lifeless brown hair and very bad teeth. His wife, Emam, is thirty-eight and she, too, looks older, under her neat brown scarf and brown cotton gown. They come from southern Iran and they are Sabian Mandaeans, vegetarians and pacifists, followers of St. John the Baptist. Their Christian sect is neither recognized nor tolerated in Iran, and the difficulty is made worse in their case by Salem's mixed parentage. Salem was at Teheran University when the Shah was overthrown and the universities closed; only in 1980, lying about his religion, was he able to complete his degree in geology. Forbidden to apply for full citizenship in Iran during the long war with Iraq, and unable to find geological work as a foreigner, he met and married Emam and worked with his father as a goldsmith. The couple had three boys, Masoud, Majid, and Youhana, and Salem paid $800 every year in bribes to keep the family's papers in order. But the day came, early in 2000, when Salem was informed that he would no longer be entitled to a work permit or to a visa to stay in Iran. He was ordered to leave the country and to move to Iraq, though Iraq under Saddam Hussein was known not to welcome Mandaeans, and in any case would not accept either Emam or the boys. They were now a family without a country.

Salem knew people who had already been forced into exile. In the goldsmith's shop, he had heard stories of people-smugglers and of foreign countries prepared to give refuge to the persecuted. Most of all, he wanted a Christian, not a Muslim country. A friend who had fled sent him the telephone number of a smuggler in Indonesia, who was known to have transported other Mandaeans to new lives in Canada and the United States. Fearful of the journey and unwilling to leave relations behind, Salem delayed his departure despite the order to leave. Then, one morning at around ten o'clock, he received a call from his sons' school to say that Masoud had been gravely hurt in one eye after a fight with a group of Muslim boys, and when it took him until four that afternoon to find a doctor willing to treat an injured Mandaean half-Iraqi child, he knew he could delay no longer. He had been saving a little gold. He sold it all, together with his business, his car, and his furniture; he had no house to sell, being forbidden, as a half Iraqi, to own property. Following the instructions he received from Indonesia, he bought tickets on a plane from Teheran to Malaysia, for which no visas were needed. From there, after a month spent waiting anxiously in a hotel, the family was told to fly on to Bali. In Bali, where Salem handed over $7,000 in cash to the smuggler arranging their journey, they waited another month before being taken by boat to Indonesia, and then on again by car to a deserted beach. Their destination, they were now told, was Australia, a country good to refugees. They had three suitcases and two bags with them, their only possessions. They stared out across the sea and thought it looked very dangerous. "We feared," says Salem, "that we would die."

There were 126 people on board the frail wooden boat that came to collect them that night after dark fell. It was soon too rough to eat the rice, eggplants, and tomatoes that Emam had prepared, and in any case most of the passengers, who had never seen the sea and could not swim, were being sick. "Sometimes," says Salem, "we were sure that we would capsize. We prayed. Some of the young men on the boat fought over the drinking water, because there wasn't enough. We had brought with us some water of our own, and a little honey and biscuits, and this is what we fed to the boys." Among the 126 passengers were thirty young children, including Salem and Emam's boys.

The asylum seekers, most of them Iraqi, Iranian, or Afghan, had been told that the boat would take them to Ashmore Reef, a fair way from Australia's northern coast. Before they reached it, an Australian naval patrol spotted them and, judging their boat to be close to sinking, towed it into shore. Salem and his family were taken to a hostel, given rice and fish, then put onto a boat for Darwin, where they stayed for a week, waiting. At two o'clock one morning, they were woken and taken to a plane. They found themselves in Adelaide, where a coach waited to drive them to the recently opened camp at Woomera. And there, for many months, they remained, confused, uncertain about their fate, questioned from time to time by immigration officials, spending each day trying to keep the boys cheerful and healthy while around them there was constant violence between detainees and guards. They witnessed fires, self-mutilation, suicide attempts.

In October 2002, the family was moved to Baxter, shortly after it opened. They had by now learned that they had failed, after their first interviews and without a lawyer, in their first application for asylum. In December, detainees in one of the dongas lit a fire, causing $2 million worth of damage. There followed a rash of fires in Woomera and the camps at Port Hedland, Villawood, and on Christmas Island, causing the authorities to clamp down further on the freedom of the refugees. The boys were now aged six, twelve, and fourteen. They had been behind razor wire for almost a year. In keeping with a slight softening in attitude toward children in detention—and perhaps in response to the growing public opposition to the policy—Salem and Emam were asked whether they would prefer that the boys and their mother live in a guarded compound within Port Augusta, where they could eat home-cooked food and the children could attend the local school, though under guard. With misgivings, hating the separation that this would entail, they accepted. Emam and the children were moved to a house in the town, and Salem was told that he might make two visits to his family each week, also under guard. His sons are now eating again, Salem says, which they would not while in Baxter, and they do not cry, as they did in Woomera. But he worries about them growing up without a father. Alone in Baxter, he spends the days asleep; sometimes he reads the newspaper and sometimes he smokes a cigarette. "I am a geologist," he says. "What is there for me to do?"

Salem, Emam, and the three boys have now been turned down definitively by the Australian immigration authorities. The "discrimination" suffered by the Mandeans in Iran is not deemed to amount to persecution. They have been told that, as Salem is half Iraqi, and Iraq has now been liberated from Saddam Hussein, they may safely go to Iraq. The Refugee Review Tribunal, which hears appeals, has also turned them down. All that is now left is a last appeal to the High Court, and then to the Minister for Immigration and Multicultural and Indigenous Affairs, Amanda Vanstone, personally, under what is known as Section 417. If refused, the family has just two choices: to remain indefinitely in an Australian detention center, or to return either to Iran, which would accept Emam and the boys but not Salem, or to Iraq, where only Salem has the right to live. Neither Iran nor (even now) Iraq looks favorably on the Mandaeans. "They have held us in prison now for a very long time," says Salem, holding on to my arm tightly so that I will understand what he is saying to me. Emam, who has been allowed to come out to Baxter that day, speaks little English; she nods and smiles. "What have we done? Ordinary criminals do not live as we do, abandoned, not knowing whether we will ever be free. As Mandaeans, we need every year to be baptized. In three years, this has not once been allowed to happen. Sometimes I think that I will kill myself, but I cannot speak to my wife about this. I am an honest man. I should not be in prison."

When I left, back through the series of locked compartments and security checks, through the double rows of fencing and wire, and out into the yellow desert landscape, I could see Salem waving gently to me until I passed through the metal gate that cuts off all view in or out of the outside world. Driving back into Port Augusta with Sister Claudette, we passed a minibus driven by a guard from Baxter, with another guard on board. In the backseat sat Emam, being taken "home" to the guarded hostel and her sons.

Salem and his family are not without friends. Sister Augusta is only one of a group of local people, schoolteachers, pastors, librarians, farmers, who now take an interest in Baxter's unhappy inmates. In October 2003, Sister Claudette told me, there were 4,000 visits to Baxter. Some of the visitors were people like herself who went out to the camp several times, and others were strangers who drove many miles across the desert to register their protest at Australia's refugee policy and to offer their support to the interned people. They do not often have a language in common with the asylum seekers, but they bake cakes and cookies and bring nuts and olives, and they sit together companionably under the eucalyptus or, when temperatures make the desert unbearable, they retreat into a portacabin with air-conditioning and crowd around small gray plastic tables with plastic mugs and plates. There is nothing sharp in Baxter, no glass or metal or pottery: violence has caused too much damage in the past. When Sister Claudette asked Salem not long ago what he would do first if he was released, he thought for a long time and then said that he would like to eat a meal on a porcelain plate with metal knives and forks.

Two days after my visit to Baxter, I read in the newspaper that the camp had been closed briefly to strangers. A young detainee, showing signs of disturbance and suicidal behavior, threatened with solitary confinement, had climbed onto the roof of the compound. The other detainees, in sympathy, had taken over the compound and barricaded themselves in. Fifty guards, in full riot gear, had forced the gate.

· · ·

IT WAS UNDER Paul Keating's Labor government, in 1992, that Australia passed laws to lock up unauthorized arrivals in remote holding camps and keep them there as long as it took to process their applications for asylum, but the harsh full sweep of Australia's refugee policy crystallized only much later, in the wake of a series of specific events. Had these events happened at different moments, or at a different time in the political calendar, or even not so fast one upon the other, it is possible that Australia's ways of dealing with refugees might well have remained similar to those in place throughout the West, a little tougher perhaps, but just as piecemeal, contradictory, and unpredictable. As it was, the events were so dramatic, and so political, that within weeks Canberra had created a tight, clear, new, and radical asylum policy. And it is this model that is now being looked at enviously by Western governments, including the United Kingdom, for which the issue of refugees and asylum has become equally politically alarming.

It came about like this. Australia needs and welcomes immigrants. It needed them after World War II, to work in the mines and on the land. In the 1950s, there was a poster showing a kangaroo perched on a map of Australia, hauling toward it a boat with a beaming family on board. "Bring out a Briton," read the caption, "room for millions more." And Australia still needs migrants today, to feed its prosperous economy and to boost an aging Australian population now standing at around 20 million people. More than 6 million people have come to Australia as new settlers since World War II. Since the 1970s, multiculturalism has been a pivotal plank of Australia's self-image. Today, one-quarter of the population is born abroad. Australia has what it calls a nondiscriminatory immigration policy, which means in theory at least that anyone from any country can apply to enter, regardless of religion or race, providing they meet Australia's rules about good character and health. In the last ten years or so, government and opposition have tended to take a common line on immigration; in 2002, a new migration program was put in place, to last four years, allowing between 100,000 and 110,000 migrants per year, of whom 12,000 would be humanitarian or refugee entrants; another 99,000 people could enter on temporary visas for work or business. When it comes to official resettlement, Australia is generous: of the twenty-one countries that resettle through UNHCR, it takes the most people per capita— 620,000 refugees over the last half century—but it should also be noted that in absolute terms Australia is only thirty-eighth in number of refugees received. Australia has one of the world's most sophisticated electronic entry processing systems with a computer database of those it wishes to exclude.

The difficulties come with asylum seekers. There is nothing orderly about flight from persecution. Some arrive legally, on a tourist visa, and subsequently apply for asylum; others are overstayers, "unlawful non-citizens," who fail to depart after their visas expire.

There are some 60,000 of these in Australia at any one time, and 21,000 are caught each year. The real problems start with those the Liberal government calls illegals—wrongly, as it happens, because Australia has ratified the 1951 Refugee Convention, which specifically recognizes that refugees are not obliged to have documents. These are the asylum seekers who reach Australia without a visa (most often by boat operated by a smuggler, usually from Indonesia) and then ask for asylum. The use of the word "illegals" suggests criminals, people who have done wrong, terrorists, certainly not people entitled to anything. They are seen as "queue jumpers," stealing the places of the "good" refugees who have been patiently waiting their turn. On their way to Australia, it is said, the "queue jumpers" have passed through a number of "safe and secure" countries but rejected them in favor of greater affluence in Australia.

In 1992, when Keating introduced mandatory detention for these "illegals," only about 220 were actually arriving by boat each year. They were soon processed. All through the 1990s boats clandestinely brought mainly Chinese and Sino-Vietnamese. Those found to be true refugees under the Convention—a minority—were allowed to stay; the rest were sent home. However, in 1999, in response to political instability throughout much of the Middle East, the number of people arriving by boat and asking for asylum rose to 3,274. Most of them were Iraqis, fleeing Saddam Hussein, or Afghans, fleeing the Taliban, and almost all came with smugglers from Indonesia, following an already well-established route. These, unlike the Chinese and Vietnamese, were "genuine" refugees under the 1951 Convention, and as such had valid claims for asylum. It was the fact that they could not, in theory, be turned away or deported that posed the first problems, as well as the fact that while Canberra felt a certain sympathy for anti-Communist refugees from Hanoi, it did not feel quite the same about people escaping from the Middle East. What was Australia to do with all these people, and were there many more to come? It was in 1999 that the Liberal party introduced a "temporary protection visa," under which asylum seekers who had been recognized under the 1951 Convention received three-year visas, which they could turn into permanent visas only if they could persuade the immigration authorities that they were still in need of protection. Then, and only then, would they be able to apply to have their families join them, a measure that changed the nature of the boat arrivals, for whereas before men came alone and asked for their families to join them, now families, if they wished to stay together, had to travel together. Boats once full of men were now full of women in the gowns and veils of the Muslim world, and of small children and babies in arms. They were not deterred by a video put out by the Department of Immigration depicting Australia as inhabited by poisonous snakes, fearsome crocodiles, and man-eating sharks.

And people kept coming. In 2000, there were 2,937 new applicants. In the first six months of 2001, 1,640 people arrived. These numbers were, of course, trivial compared with the numbers of those who apply for asylum in Germany, the UK, Italy, or France, but the Australian detention camps were packed, frantic, and beset by violence, much of it involving self-mutilation and suicide attempts provoked by the uncertainty and delays. The immigration authorities let it be known that they did not want anyone to mistake the detention centers for "holiday camps." Meanwhile, given the changing nature of modern conflict and the outbreaks of armed conflict across large parts of Asia and the Middle East, the procedure for deciding who was or was not a genuine refugee was moving more and more slowly. Those in detention were now spending months and even years with no idea what would happen to them. And some, of course, were children.

Meanwhile, a wild political card had entered the game in the shape of a flamboyant, red-haired "old Anglo-Australian" called Pauline Hanson, whose parents had migrated from Britain before the First World War. Hanson ran a fish-and-chips shop in Queensland. In 1997, as an independent, she won a seat in Parliament on an unambiguously racist anti-Aborigine platform. Since everyone knew her feelings about the Aborigines—she was once quoted as saying that they were cannibals who sometimes ate members of their own families—she decided to give her maiden speech on the subject of immigration. "I believe," she declared, "that we are in danger of being swamped by Asians." Though Pauline Hanson had no discernible political skills—her grammar was patchy, her voice was grating, and she had trouble reading her own speeches—a large number of Australians loved her. She expressed what they most feared about the boatloads of desperate people clamoring to reach their shores. Hanson formed a party, One Nation, and won a fair number of votes. In response, five former prime ministers—Whitlam, Fraser, Hawke, Keating, and Gorton—issued a joint statement condemning her racist views.

As it happened, John Howard, about to run for a second term as Liberal prime minister in the forthcoming 2001 elections, was not among those condemning Hanson. And though she soon lost her seat and was eventually sentenced to jail for three years for electoral fraud (she was acquitted on appeal), and although the country soon got back to its usual concerns about health, crime, and unemployment, Hanson had reset the boundaries of what was acceptable in a public discussion of race. The Liberals, whose chances of winning the election were at this point dim, took note.

And then, on August 24, 2001, a sixty-foot gray wooden fishing boat called the *Palapa*, coming from Indonesia to Christmas Island, was spotted drifting helplessly at sea, its engine dead. Lying below Java in the Indian Ocean, Christmas Island belongs to Australia. On board were 438 people, most of them Afghans. Children were seen, and many women. When the news reached Canberra, alarm bells sounded. There was no room on Christmas Island to take anyone else, a boat on the sixteenth having brought 345 asylum seekers, and another on the twenty-second, 359. Australia's other detention centers were also full. The current minister for immigration was Phillip Ruddock, a man described by the Australian writer David Marr as having the "soul of a great bureaucrat" and an interesting political past, having on one occasion crossed the floor of Parliament to vote against his leader. Ruddock, as people would soon be saying, was a man of contradictions, a member of Amnesty International, yet very hard on refugees, whose importance in the Liberal party had been growing with the growth in importance of the refugee issue. Here was the very challenge he needed.

At first, Australia tried to lean on the Indonesians, on whom Ruddock had already tried to bring pressure to act more firmly against the people-smugglers. Indonesia, a vast, poor, corrupt country, refused to be drawn in. At midnight, a storm blew up. Waves dashed over the *Palapa*. A hole opened in the hull. The people on board cried and clung to one another. At dawn, a man was spotted holding up a scarf, on which he had written, in engine oil, "SOS" and "HELP." Conditions on the boat continued to deteriorate. After waiting eighteen hours, the Australians realized that they could delay no longer or the boat would sink. A call went out to all shipping in the area, soon answered by a 44,000-ton Norwegian tanker called the *Tampa*, three city blocks in length. The *Tampa*, on its way to China and Japan, had a crew of twenty-seven and carried a cargo of steel pipes, dried milk, other food, and timber. Its skipper was the highly experienced Arne Rinnan, and its owner, Wilhelm Wilhelmensen ASA, had done business with Australia for many years.

Captain Rinnan, obeying the laws of humanity and the sea, took the 438 people off the *Palapa*, which was now sinking. Among them were two pregnant women and a one-year-old baby. What Rinnan proposed to do was to drop them on Christmas Island, which was precisely what the Afghans wanted him to do, some on board having already tried once before to reach Australia and failed. What the Australians wanted was for him to take them back to Indonesia—or anywhere else, provided it wasn't Australia. Though the rules of the sea are clear on the paramount need to save lives, there is no rule to say that a nation may not close its borders to unwanted strangers. Responsibility, argued Ruddock, lay with Indonesia, because the rescue act had taken place in Indonesian waters; or possibly with Norway, whose flag the *Tampa* flew; or perhaps even with Singapore, because that had been the *Tampa*'s next port of call. But it did not, he insisted, lie with Australia, even though the Australian coast was nearest the rescue. Following early orders, the *Tampa* put back for Indonesia, then turned back to Christmas Island, Rinnan buffetted by the pleas and threats of the asylum seekers, the orders and counterorders of the Australian government, and the diplomatic maneuverings of the Norwegian government, the human rights lobby, and UNHCR. For the next eight days, through bouts of food poisoning and diarrhea, with near revolts and times of raging and despair, the asylum seekers from the *Palapa* remained on the *Tampa*'s decks, hot, miserable, terrified, and confused, treated with kindness by Rinnan and his men and corralled and marshaled by a unit of Australian SAS men, sent in to maintain order. Across the liberal world there was horror that traumatized people, many now severely dehydrated by the heat, and a few barely conscious, could be treated in this fashion. Behind the scenes, frenetic exchanges continued night and day between the *Tampa*, the Norwegian shipping company, and the Australian government and navy.

Until this moment, despite Pauline Hanson, immigration had not been dominating the coming elections. Overnight, it became the only topic that mattered. The *Tampa* had unleashed an apocalyptic vision of a future overrun by the yellow hordes Australians had always feared. One of Howard's first moves was to try to push through, in the heat of the moment, new legislation that would allow Australia to return to the high seas anyone who entered Australian territory without permission. And though Jim Beazley and the Labor opposition effectively defeated the bill, Labor's slightly hesitant protests and lack of leadership combined to dash its prospects of an easy election victory. Labor, it was said, looked like "a party trying to walk both sides of the street." Howard and Ruddock between them gave the impression of being not just in control but of being the leaders of a party able to secure Australia's threatened borders. They were thus able to draw toward them voters otherwise heading for Hanson's One Nation. "We will decide who comes to this country and the circumstances in which they come here," Howard announced, defining what was to be the essence of his refugee policy. His words touched some chord among Australians who feared that at any time Indonesia might collapse, sending thousands of economic migrants their way. The largest Muslim nation in the world was, after all, no more than a boat ride away.

It was about now that the infamous Pacific Solution was born, a strategy with a gentle name and terrible consequences. It was not new—the British had blockaded Palestine in the 1930s, refusing to let Jewish refugees land and pushing them to Cyprus—but in the context of modern refugee politics it was dramatic. No future boatload of "illegal" people would be allowed, Howard decided, to reach Australia. Refugee vessels would, if possible, be intercepted at sea and returned to Indonesia. If that was not possible, they would be transferred to "off-shore processing centers" and to a number of designated countries willing to hold them in detention while their futures were sorted out. At no time would they have access to Australia's legal processes, and there would be no right of appeal. Like the game of tag played along San Diego's fence, getting past the guards would become part of Australia's immigration process.

Nauru, in the Pacific Ocean, is a small, bankrupt republic, once famous for the richness of its guano deposits, sold off long ago for phosphates. In August 2001 it was said to owe $16.5 million on its desalination plant alone. In exchange for $26.5 million Australian, Nauru now agreed to take 150 of the *Tampa*'s asylum seekers and hold them in detention, as well as to take others from other boats; Papua New Guinea agreed to do the same, lending Manus Island for the experiment. In both places, the claims of the detainees would be assessed by UNHCR and the Australian government. At the same time, a number of islands regularly reached by smugglers from Indonesia and used as drop spots for their passengers—among them Christmas Island and Ashmore Reef—were "excised" from Australia for purposes of migration. Australia had effectively, by a stroke of its pen, shrunk its borders. What was so cunning about this move is that it put the *Tampa*'s asylum seekers, and those who chose to follow their example, beyond the reach of the Australian courts, where they might have had access to lawyers, appeals, and review hearings.

The Australian Migration Act is now one of the most powerful instruments in the country, able to sideline even the judiciary.

When, after ten days, the fracas had died down, the deals had been struck, and the requisite administrative orders put in place, the asylum seekers were transferred to an Australian naval vessel, HMAS *Manoora*. A very lucky 150 went to New Zealand, which took them as part of its normal humanitarian response to such situations. They were quickly processed; all but one proved to have valid claims under the Refugee Convention and were offered asylum. The queue jumpers were, after all, genuine. Others were taken to Nauru, to a hastily built camp rushed up by Australian military personnel on a sports field and the remains of a phosphate mine, in makeshift huts built of corrugated iron, plastic sheeting, and green cloth. Howard and Ruddock now set about tightening up the whole process of asylum. The measures they took were bold, bolder in fact in their entirety than had been attempted elsewhere. In "Operation Relex," a task force of naval vessels and aircraft was assigned to patrolling Australia's coast with orders to turn back asylum seekers approaching from Indonesia, and with new powers to search boats and to detain passengers and remove them, if necessary by force; and the government attempted with great success to restrict access to Nauru, which now proved virtually unreachable by journalists, human rights advocates, or lawyers, and discouraged the press from publishing "personalising or humanising" images, anywhere, of asylum seekers. Officials of the Department of Immigration and Multicultural and Indigenous Affairs entered into close relations with the border police of neighboring countries, to try to stem the flow of boats. And the temporary protection visas could now be renewed only as further temporary visas, with no chance, ever, of having families join the applicant. The Labor party, which could have opposed and defeated the amendments, endorsed them. The fact that it was illegal, under Nauru's constitution, to lock people up indefintely without charge or trial was soon solved by declaring the asylum seekers to be visitors, on special visas that confined them to the camp. That Australia had effectively bribed one of its poorest neighbors to break its own laws drew little comment.

The *Tampa* was not, however, the end of the story. For a while at least, before Australia's message of deterrence spread, boats kept on arriving, and the navy went on turning them away, without taking time to discover whether they contained genuine refugees. Between September and November 2001, thirteen Indonesian boats filled with asylum seekers tried and failed to reach Australia. Four were intercepted and sent back. One sank. Of the remaining eight, either unseaworthy or actually sinking, all were intercepted and their human cargo transported to Nauru or Manus Island. Those who tried to influence or restrain Howard—the United Nations; a number of lawyers, politicians, and commentators—achieved almost nothing. There was a moment's pause, when the Australian government ill-advisedly released photographs purporting to show parents throwing their children overboard from an Indonesian boat, in order, so it was claimed, to blackmail Australia into accepting them. The asylum seekers, it was suggested, were not human beings with the same values as ordinary Australians, since they were capable of treating their children this way. (Howard appeared on television saying that the kind of people who threw their children overboard were not the sort of people Australia wanted.) But the pictures were later shown to be misleading. The children had indeed been thrown in the water, but only because their boat was sinking. And there was a further, heart-rending pause when a boat code-named *SIEV-X* sank, drowning 353 asylum seekers; the forty-six survivors later described how their boat had broken up in high seas, how they had floundered in the water, swallowing the fuel that flowed from the boat, how they had watched those who could not swim struggle desperately before slipping underneath the waves. A young mother called Sundous lost her three daughters, Emaan, Zahra, and Fatima. Another, Ronkayya Satta, saw first her five-year-old daughter, Kawthar, stepped on in the frenzy to leave the sinking boat and drowned; her second daughter, Alya, who was two, slipped out of her arms. A woman who had just given birth was seen drifting away, one survivor later recalled to

David Marr and Marian Wilkinson for their excellent book *Dark Victory*, her baby attached by the umbilical cord. Wherever you looked, you saw "dead children like birds floating on the water."

It was hard to imagine that things could get worse, but they did. September 11 had now put terrorism at the front of all political agendas, and Peter Reith, Australia's defense minister, was able to point out that unauthorized boats could well become a "pipeline for terrorists." When election day came, Howard swept to victory. Tough border protection, Operation Relex, September 11, the destruction of the One Nation party, and the new Pacific Solution had among them proved a vote-winning formula, though the country had been polarized as never before. Neither the Australian judiciary, nor the refugee advocates, nor the human rights campaigners, nor the many ordinary Australians who had raised their voices against Canberra's overbearing directives, had been able to do much.* What Ruddock repeated, and what Amanda Vanstone, his successor, repeats, is that Australia's resettlement package is generous and that countries whose national policy is to accept fewer refugees are ill-placed to be so critical. The Liberal government said, and continues to say, with some reason, that steps must be taken to formulate coherent asylum policies that actually work, and that first among them is the need to end the vast and lucrative trade in smuggled people, which can only be done if smugglers are shown not to be able to deliver what they promise.

Australia's new policies had not, of course, come cheap. Between August 2001 and the middle of 2003, Australia was said to have spent $500 million on its Pacific Solution. But it had, in a very practical way, worked. Punishment and deterrence had born fruit. Only three boats arrived in the next three years. The question, people were left asking, was at what moral cost this success had been achieved. What had it all done to Australia itself? And how does one justify locking up people who have broken no laws?

---

* The disdain of some of the international community for Australia's stand was expressed by the award of the Nansen Medal to the captain of the *Tampa*, for outstanding service on behalf of refugees.

· · ·

ONE OTHER EVENT, which made little stir at the time, grew later
to challenge the whole spirit of mandatory detention as nothing had
before. It is the story of an Iranian boy called Shayan. I met Shayan,
who is now nine, in a park in Parramatta, a suburb just outside Sydney. He is tall for his age, very thin, with mouse-brown hair cut
short. He would look much like any other nine-year-old, fit and
brown from the Australian sun, except for the extreme wariness of
his expression, which makes him look rather like a startled young
animal, and the way he sits, or stands, extremely close to his parents,
stirring when they stir, watching their faces. Saeed and Zahra,
Shayan's father and stepmother, drove me to the edge of a small lake
in the middle of Parramatta's green and tropical park, and there in
the sunshine, looking out across the water, while Shayan was persuaded to sit in the car very close by and listen to music, they told
me his story.

Saeed is a computer technician, a Kurd who belongs to an Islamic sect, Al Hagh, regarded in Shiite Iran as heretical. He married
young, and unhappily, and his wife soon left him, yielding him custody of their only child, Shayan. Saeed remarried a Shia Arab,
Zahra, who converted to the Al Hagh faith. In 1999, Saeed became
involved in student protests at his university, and though he was not
among the many to be arrested, he was already marked down by the
police for his religion, and for the fact that he had converted a Muslim, a serious offense under Sharia law. The family fled, arriving in
Australia on an Indonesian fishing boat in March 2000. Shayan was
almost five and, according to his father, liked watching the flying
fish; he was bright, intensely curious, and regarded Zahra as his
mother, having scarcely known his own. Zahra was pregnant.

In keeping with the immigration policy then current, the family
was taken into detention and sent to Woomera until its application
for asylum could be processed. There were at this time about five
hundred refugee children in detention in Australia. The family had
been in the camp less than a week when a riot broke out among a
group of detainees who had been allowed no contact with the out-

side world for over three months. A fence was torn down. Guards in riot gear used tear gas and batons to restore order. Shayan watched. Later, he asked his father to explain what had happened. "I had no answer," says Saeed. "I didn't know what to say." Soon afterward, a detainee driven beyond endurance broke a bottle and held it to his heart, threatening to kill himself unless he received some kind of response from the Australian authorities. Shayan watched this, too. "Gradually," says Zahra, "we were becoming scared about him. He didn't seem to want to play with the other children, and he seemed easily frightened." It was at about this time, she says, that Shayan started having nightmares and wetting his bed.

Woomera, by all accounts, was a desperate place; it was hot and crowded, and when it rained the dust and sand turned to mud. By the spring of 2000, violence had become common. The atmosphere was tense and wretched. One day, a young Iranian climbed to the top of a tree and said that he would jump to his death. There were endless fights between guards and inmates. Fires were lit. Guards often wore riot gear. Shayan watched.

The center was divided into various compounds. Sierra, a little to one side, was the punishment block, in which unruly people were placed in solitary confinement. When a batch of new arrivals was due, Shayan and his family were moved into Sierra to make room for them. This seemed to frighten Shayan out of all proportion: he believed that only "bad" people were sent to Sierra. Apart from his new baby sister, Shubnam, he was the only child in the punishment compound. He refused to eat, saying to his father: "You eat my food. It will make you strong to fight off the guards when they attack us."

After eleven months, it was clear to everyone that Shayan had become extremely disturbed. Doctors diagnosed him with post-traumatic stress disorder, and in his report to the authorities, Wayne Lynch, a counselor who had taken an interest in the family, listed "bed-wetting, nightmares, anorexia, insomnia, fearfulness" among his symptoms. Shayan was now six. On March 3, 2001, the family was transferred to Villawood on the edge of Sydney, a detention center generally regarded as calmer and better for children. By now they knew not only that they had been turned down as refugees by the immigration authorities on their first interview, but that their appeal to the Refugee Review Tribunal had failed as well. They were running out of options: only the High Court and a direct ministerial appeal remained.

Villawood proved no easier for Shayan. In fact, he quickly grew worse. He witnessed more violence, more self-mutilation, other suicide attempts. He was taken for observation to Westmead Hospital, where a consultant psychologist, Dr. Timothy Hannan, warned of the consequences of returning Shayan behind bars. His disorder was becoming chronic, he told the Australian authorities, and each return to detention would trigger again all his symptoms. Shayan was sent back to Villawood. On April 30, he watched a detainee cut his wrists and bleed heavily. He stopped eating and drinking; soon he refused to speak. He was taken back to Westmead.

Under Section 417 of the Migration Act, Ruddock had the power to release the family on humanitarian grounds. An application, by lawyers and doctors, was presented: Ruddock turned it down. Shayan went back to Villawood. "For the next forty-five days, he would not eat or drink or talk," explains Zahra. She speaks excellent English and is a gentle and quiet young woman. Saeed, whose English is less fluent, leaves the talking to her; he is a slight, short man, with receding hair and a small mustache. Like his wife, he is soft-spoken. "Every four days, they took him back to Westmead and put tubes down his throat and his nose. Then twenty-four hours later, they sent him back." Shayan lost more weight and there were fears that his kidneys might be damaged. When in Villawood, he preferred to spend his days in bed. One day, as the guards were returning him from the hospital to the detention center, he managed to slip away. They chased him, and as he ran, he shouted: "I don't want to go back. I don't want to go back."

Shayan's case was now beginning to attract attention in the medical and legal worlds. Psychiatrists were writing reports and letters to the immigration authorities. Shayan, they warned, was "acutely traumatized." In August, a video camera was smuggled into Villawood and on the thirteenth—less than two weeks before the *Tampa* rescue—a national news show put out a film showing Shayan lying in Saeed's arms, limp and apparently lifeless. Again, Ruddock could have acted. Instead, he let it be understood, speaking on a news program, that there was more to the family's story than met the eye, and that the fact that Zahra was Shayan's stepmother was in some way significant. On four separate occasions, he called Shayan "it." Challenged as to why he was not prepared to show more compassion, Ruddock said that he could not make exceptions to government policy. Were he to let Shayan and his family in, would other families claiming mental illness in their children not demand the same? The Melbourne *Herald Sun* and the Sydney *Daily Telegraph* both carried stories hostile to Saeed, accusing him of having kidnapped Shayan and of deliberately starving him.

The family, nearly all legal avenues having failed, were told that they would almost certainly have to return to Iran. Meanwhile, Shayan could be fostered in the community. Saeed and Zahra hesitated. Doctors insisted that a child in so desperate a state needed above all to be with his parents, but they worried that keeping him in detention any longer might prove too dangerous: Shayan had by now witnessed three serious riots, four suicide attempts, many acts of self-mutilation, arson, fights, and the repeated humiliation of his parents. One day, while his parents, doctors, and authorities discussed what would be best for him, Saeed was led into another room in the hospital. Zahra remained with Shayan and Shubnam. She describes the scene: "Shayan was clinging on to me. A guard came up and said that they were going to take him. He began to pull him away from me. Shayan screamed: 'Mum, help me.' What could I do? They pulled him away and locked us in a room and took him away."

For the next few months, Shayan lived with a Muslim family in the community. His parents and Shubnam were taken to visit him two to three times a week, for an hour, always with guards who stayed with them even when Zahra went to change the baby's diaper. Their uniforms seemed to terrify Shayan. He was eating and drinking again, but his foster parents noted that he clung to them all the time, that he could not sleep unless one of them sat with him, and that he was still wetting his bed. At night, he often screamed. After four months, Ruddock granted Zahra, Shayan, and Shubnam bridging visas, which meant that they could live in the community; but since bridging visas do not include financial support, they were forced to live on the charity of friends. Saeed stayed in Villawood for the next eight months.

In August 2002, the Federal Court having referred the case back to the Refugee Review Tribunal, Saeed and Zahra were found to be refugees after all, on the grounds that they would face persecution on account of Zahra's conversion if they returned to Iran. Looking back over the long nightmare, Saeed asks: "If we are refugees now, why were we not refugees then?" He and Zahra took their case to the Human Rights and Equal Oppurtunity Commission, which found that their rights had indeed been seriously violated.

But Shayan sleeps little, has severe nightmares, and wets his bed. When he draws, he draws pictures of people behind bars. He has few friends his own age, saying that they do not know what it is like to have lived inside a prison, but he plays affectionately with Shubnam, who is now three. He will not watch children's television but prefers to see the news, though when he sees people in uniform, he cries. For a while, Saeed and Zahra hoped that he would get better on his own, in the flat that they have been given on a Parramatta housing estate. But since he seemed to remain so depressed and so fearful, and his screaming fits continued, they agreed to put him on medication. Every week, he sees a psychiatrist, who has told them that Shayan may take a very long time to get over what he experienced and witnessed; and that, possibly, he never will. As for his parents, their difficulties are not over, either. They have been granted temporary protection visas, like all "unauthorized arrivals" who are recognized as genuine refugees. At some point in 2005, they will have to apply to have their visa renewed for a further three years, and it is not impossible that they will be turned down. If they judge it too dangerous to go back to Iran, too likely that one or the other would be imprisoned or killed, then Shayam may once again find himself behind the razor wire.

. . .

SHAYAN'S STORY HAD pitted the Australian medical profession sharply against the government. Doctors realized that whatever treatment they might offer their patients was meaningless unless they were removed from the environment causing the trauma. At no time in the past, not even over the "lost generation," the children stolen from the Aborigines, had the suffering of children been so starkly juxtaposed against political indifference. A Professional Alliance for the Health of Asylum Seekers and Their Children was set up, bringing together 50,000 doctors and health workers from across the country—the largest alliance ever formed on a single social issue in Australia's history. Drawing on earlier studies from the concentration camps of the Boer War and the Nazi years, and on comparable detention center reports from the United States and various parts of Europe, they began to submit evidence, draft appeals, and draw up statements. Shayan was not the only child to stop eating and become mute. Elsewhere in other parts of Australia, it now emerged that other children in detention had become anxious, anorexic, and agitated; they were wetting their beds and walking in their sleep. One small girl was described as wetting herself every time she saw a guard. Mothers reported aggressive and violent behavior in otherwise placid children. One, anxious about the failure of her newborn baby to thrive as it should, was reported as saying: "I am afraid that she takes in my unhappiness from my milk." A young boy, deciding that he wished to die, was found digging his own grave. Another, asked why he had burned his hand with a lighted cigarette, replied: "Because I can't feel anything."

I could only talk to Shayan's parents and not to Shayan himself; he was too wary and too young to speak to strangers. It was from Morteza, another young Iranian already in Woomera when Shayan first arrived, that I heard at first hand what it is like to be a child in the Australian camps. Morteza spent three years and eleven months as a detainee, from early 2000 to his release—as a recognized refugee—on November 20, 2003. He was sixteen when he first saw Woomera. He was flying in low over the desert, after a terrifying and stormy journey by boat with smugglers, and he thought: "Where are we going? There is nothing there." He was right. Woomera had not yet been completed, and the first detainees lived in huts as the razor wire went up around them. There were soon 150 children in the camp, the youngest a newborn baby.

Morteza had been there about five months when the 1,500 detainees, who had had no contact with the outside world for a long time, asked for a mobile phone to be brought in so that they could call their families. What started as a peaceful demonstration turned rapidly into agitated confrontations with the guards; tear gas was used; the detainees fought back; the ringleaders were taken to the punishment block. It was Morteza's first experience of violence, and he joined the ranks of the protestors. His younger sister, Mena, was by now so depressed that she became incontinent and barely spoke; his younger brother, Hussein, was growing thinner all the time. The months passed and the family seemed to have been forgotten. The riots multiplied. There was a breakout and Morteza was among those who got as far as the town of Woomera itself, after which concessions were made concerning phones and the pace of the processing interviews. There were even some releases, but not of Morteza and his family. At some point during this period, Morteza tried to hang himself; later, he joined others on hunger strike; later again, he slashed his wrists with a razor blade. In the right-wing press, those who tried to kill themselves were labeled crazed, selfish, and manipulative.

In January 2001, the family, the two younger children very troubled, was moved to Port Hedland. By now Mena was writing in her diary: "If suicide were not a sin in my religion, I would have done it already." One day, Morteza and Hussein watched as a Turkish detainee took out a razor blade and began to cut from his neck downward, across his chest, his hand and arms and stomach. It was his third suicide attempt. Hussein, says Morteza, had a peculiar smile on his face. That night the little boy began to cry and couldn't stop. He started to wet himself and to stutter. "Please God," wrote Mena in her diary, "if you want to finish my life, finish it quickly." In Woomera there had been two girls her own age; in Port Hedland, she had no friend. Morteza spent his time with older boys. One night, trying to prevent his father being taken away by the guards to another compound, he was knocked to the ground and beaten with batons. There were more riots; some of the huts were burned down.

On May 21, 2001, the family, having had its application for asylum turned down at every stage, was sent to Villawood. In a friend's room one day, the young men discussed what new tactic they could try; someone suggested sewing up their lips. The three boys did it to one another, carefully pulling the thread through; it caused surprisingly little pain, Morteza remembers, though it hurt a lot when the blood had dried. His mother fainted when she saw him. He agreed to take the stitches out when the family was promised bridging visas in the community. The visas did not come through, and Morteza spent the next nine months under observation, a guard checking on him every two minutes for the first three months. Even so, when it became clear that the promises about the visa had been false, he tried to kill himself by swallowing an entire bottle of shampoo while in the shower.

In May 2002, his parents decided that they could take no more. They had spent $32,000 trying to make a new life in Australia, and had failed. Morteza's mother seemed to be aging very quickly, and neither his younger brother or sister was thriving. They agreed to return to Iran. For Morteza, the decision was more complicated. As with Shayan, a smuggled videotape had been put out on television, showing him being beaten by guards, and his case had received much publicity. His father did not think it safe for him to go home. What was more, he had converted to Christianity. And so his parents flew home to Teheran, and Morteza spent another eleven months in detention, ticking off the days one by one on a calendar on his door, before he, like Shayan, was perceived to be a genuine refugee after all, in a way that he had not been three years and eleven months before. He is now living in Sydney, on a three-year temporary protection visa, a friendly, almost jaunty young man of twenty, his long black hair pulled back in a ponytail. If he is extremely lucky, his visa will be renewed. But there is no way, as things stand, of seeing his parents, for if he leaves Australia, he will not be able to return. "I look at guys my age and think: I have lost my family. I lost four years of my life. No education, no training. It is like a movie: the action freezes, then starts again. I think: what a terrible waste."

Zachary Steel is a psychologist, working for the school of psychiatry at the University of New South Wales. Soon after mandatory detention for asylum seekers was introduced in 1992, he began to explore the possibility of investigating the mental health of the new detainees. Wherever he turned, he was blocked by the authorities. It was not until almost ten years later, in the wake of the *Tampa* and its repercussions, that he was able to start drawing together separate strands of research, joining forces with Derrick Silove, a psychiatrist from South Africa, whose interest had been kindled as a medical student doing autopsies on political prisoners who bore the marks of torture, and with Aamer Sultan, a physician who had fled persecution in Iraq and was a detainee himself in Villawood. Over eighteen months, Dr. Sultan, who had become a confidant and counselor to his fellow inmates, had watched their mental health deteriorate. It was with his help that the camera had been smuggled into Villawood to picture the listless Shayan lying in his father's arms.

Gathering information where they could, these doctors, psychologists, counselors, and therapists throughout Australia put together an alarming but altogether convincing picture. The asylum seekers, they observed, were arriving with backgrounds of torture, violence, grief, and extreme fear, and were thus at great risk for psychological trauma. They believed that the Australians would treat them kindly and with sympathy. Instead, they entered a world of horror and indifference, in which they were confined, seemingly indefinitely, behind rows of razor wire, with multiple daily musters and head counts, sometimes in the middle of the night; they were subjected to a constant barrage of orders over the loudspeaker system that they could not understand; they were handled harshly and moved suddenly, without warning, from one camp to another, in handcuffs. Referred to by the guards by number rather than by name, they were subjected to room searches and solitary confinement. They witnessed violence and self-mutilation; their guards wore riot gear, and there were periods when they were locked up for a long time in their rooms, denied access to the phone, to mail, or to visitors. As it became clear to them that their futures depended on the credibility of their claims, and on how well they handled their interviews, they became highly anxious about what to say, particularly as, like asylum seekers all over the world faced by immigration interviews, they felt confused and uncertain about their memories. Many, believing that they would be judged by how they were behaving in detention, were unsure of their every move.

In this new world, so different from the one they had expected to find, the asylum seekers, as Dr. Steel and his colleagues noted, behaved in a number of characteristic ways. Their initial shock and dismay were replaced, when they received news that the immigration authorities had turned down their first applications, or simply when months had passed with no news of a result, by guilt about the people they had left behind, by depression, and sometimes by aggressive and confrontational behavior. Many had arrived in Australia already suffering from post-traumatic stress disorder, and the symptoms most commonly associated with this illness began to emerge: extreme anxiety, sleeplessness, fear of others. Some never left their rooms; others slept by day and paced by night. Rejection by the Refugee Review Tribunal usually comes between six and eighteen months after arrival. At this point, acute depression was common, with feelings of doom and self-obsession, paranoia, hallucinations, sometimes even repetitive rocking and aimless wandering. The rate of suicide among detainees was ten times that of the normal population.

Papers and reports of these findings began to appear. One study, described in a keynote speech delivered by Dr. Steel and his colleagues before the Congress of the Royal Australian and New Zealand College of Psychiatrists in May 2003, concerned ten families, consisting of fourteen adults and twenty-two children between the ages of three and nineteen, with an average stay in detention of two years and four months. Using a wide battery of internationally accepted tests and criteria, the doctors found that a third of the adults had resorted to some form of self-harm; that every adult could be diagnosed as suffering from a depressive disorder; that all the children showed signs of at least one psychiatric disorder, and 86 percent of them had multiple disorders. More than half the children spoke of killing themselves. Five had slashed their wrists or banged their head violently against a wall.

Another study, carried out by Dr. Sultan in Villawood, looked at thirty-three detainees, twenty-eight of them men, the other five women. All had been inside at least nine months. Nineteen, Dr. Sultan discovered, had arrived in Australia having been tortured, and nine had seen relations murdered or disappeared. In Villawood, all but one reported sleep disturbances, nightmares, loss of libido. Nineteen were on anti-depressants. Thirteen suffered from paranoid delusions; thirteen had begun to stutter; twenty-three admitted to suicidal thoughts. All spoke of feeling helpless and despairing and of being unable to concentrate or to remember simple things. It was clear to Dr. Sultan that there was a strong degree of correlation between length of time spent in detention—waiting to hear, not knowing what would happen—and the level of distress and disturbance. It should be noted that it is not unusual, under Australia's current policy, to wait two years for news; some people have been in detention for over five years.

When I met Zachary Steel, his verdict on the system was clear. "I simply no longer believe," he said, "that it is possible for anyone to be kept in this kind of environment of coercive control, threat, uncertainty and fear without developing severe psychiatric consequences. Detention of this kind is a situation that cannot be rendered meaningful by anything. Even political prisoners, kept in similar circumstances, know why they are there. The asylum seekers know that they are innocent people, and no aspect of the current structure has any care or compassion. On the contrary they feel that they are hated, and that the authorities will do everything in their power to return them back to where they fled from."

It has long ceased to be a source of surprise to Dr. Steel when he hears that teenagers in one center have sewn up their lips, or that young men in another have gone on hunger strike. Morteza's repeated attempts to hurt and kill himself are familiar symptoms. The culture of self-harm has become so prevalent in the detention centers that it is impossible to prevent people from mutilating themselves.

When the first studies appeared, Dr. Steel assumed that action would follow. Instead, the Department of Immigration announced that it was not aware of any "independent" scientific or rigorous research to "support claims that mental illness is endemic among detainees held in immigration detention." Psychiatrists and other doctors redoubled their efforts to produce more research, in the process putting Australia at the forefront of current medical knowledge of the effects of detention on asylum seekers. The Department of Immigration labeled the work flawed and full of preconceptions, and Ruddock declared that it was far from certain, in his view, that you could in fact "regard depression as a mental illness." And so it has continued, says Dr. Steel: more research and more rebuttals, at times accompanied by personal attacks on the researchers. It makes him feel that he was once very naive. It is true, as he acknowledges, that efforts have been made to get children out of the centers and into the community, and that under Amanda Vanstone the numbers remaining behind the razor wire have dropped substantially.* His protests, and those of his colleagues, achieved at least this. But, as he sees it, the adult detainees who remain are getting sicker and sicker. It is a tenet of psychiatry that past traumas, dealt with in safety, can be mitigated and eased. In detention centers, they are only exacerbated. The environment, far from curing the pathology, is both cre-

---

* In the spring of 2004, fifteen children remained in detention, but there were many more living in the community under guard.

ating and perpetuating it. "The trauma," Dr. Steel has written, "is not past, but present, and extends indefinitely into the future." His words have a forlorn air: "Our ethics require us to prevent what harm we can and to document what we cannot prevent."

. . .

SHAYAN'S AND MORTEZA'S stories had stirred the medical profession to anger. And though the government remained obdurate, even choosing not to publicize its few concessions, something else had in fact happened. Of all the responses to the refugee predicament in the world, this is one of the most remarkable and certainly the most heartening. Ordinary Australians, people who had tacitly accepted the fact that asylum seekers—the "illegals" and "queue jumpers"—could be locked up indefinitely in detention camps in the desert, could not quite stomach the idea of children losing the will to live. It shook their image of Australia as an essentially humane place, challenged the cherished notion of "fair go," decency, which is deeply rooted in the national psyche. The publicity surrounding Shayan and Morteza, brief and contested though it was, made clear something that had not been perceived before: that Australia's camps were not the model centers described by Howard and Ruddock, but grim and terrifying places in which people were going mad.

The backlash started slowly. It has not grown to any overwhelming size, but it is evidence, to use Michael Ignatieff's phrase, of the "expanding moral imagination" of our times. It started among writers, lawyers, actors, academics, and in small pockets of the churches, with nuns and lay sisters and Jesuit priests, inspired by the reports put out by Dr. Zachary Steel and his colleagues and by the growing body of critical evidence emerging from research carried out by the UN, by UNHCR, by Human Rights Watch and Amnesty International, and by the Australian Human Rights and Equal Opportunity Commission. It spread through cities, into towns and villages, into the outback, a surge of moral indignation carried by telephone and e-mail. It drew in veterans of the old Aborigine rights campaigns, and prominent barristers including Julian Burnside, a Melbourne QC, who began to question the legality of each and every process, and younger advocates, such as Deslie Billich, who helps run a public interest law firm in Adelaide for the refugees. It prompted the birth of a now prominent human rights group, Chilout, campaigning on behalf of the imprisoned children. It took in novelists and poets, including Thomas Kenneally, Linda Jaivin, Arnold Zable, Eva Sallis, and Peter Carey, who produced fiction and plays, and journalists and commentators, such as David Marr and Robert Manne, who wrote essays and books; it became fringe and street theater; it provoked articles and poems and films. The Howard government called these activists the "elites," or the "Chardonnay liberals."

In Port Augusta, a Catholic churchwoman called Penny Kelly was in church on October 18, 2002, when the children in the congregation prayed for the families of asylum seekers being transferred from Woomera to Baxter. She was disheartened to note the hostile reaction of the townspeople, who either wanted the refugees sent back as quickly as possible, or pretended that nothing was happening. That Thursday, she went out to the new camp, taking with her a cake and some cookies that she had baked. She had never really been able to understand how ordinary Germans, living around concentration camps during the Third Reich, maintained that they knew nothing about them, but now she began to understand. Her neighbors concentrated on other things. Friends, however, eventually listened to her stories and took to accompanying her on her weekly visits to Baxter, and when she told her husband, who works for the Port Augusta prison, that the detainees had too few men visitors, he started going too, driving out to the camp in the desert, taking with him nuts and cookies, but really going in order to talk. Among these very different people, the visitors and the visited, country Australians and lawyers, doctors, teachers, goldsmiths, students, housewives from Iran and Iraq, Turkey and Afghanistan, real friendships began to grow. In the visitors' room, there is much laughter and affection. People celebrate one another's birthdays and remember, with amusement, the day someone brought in an enormous fish, so big that it would not fit on the X-ray machine through which everything must be checked, so that eventually it came in as a visitor instead. Like Sister Claudette, Penny Kelly feels her life to have been changed by her weekly involvement with an issue that for her raises huge moral questions. But she is also saddened. "I grew up proud of being Australian. Though I was aware of how badly we had behaved towards the Aborigines, I still felt we were basically a good country. I am no longer proud. I feel there is a hole inside me, like an ulcer. I think of the horrible things we are doing to these people. Australia will look back on this as a black day."

Around the time Penny Kelly was beginning to hear about Woomera, in the mountains not far from Sydney three women friends were watching television footage of the *Tampa*. Two of them, Susan Varga and Ann Coombs, were writers. "We felt depressed. This was something different, something that seemed to have gone too far," says Susan Varga. They called a public meeting in their town of Bowral and worked the streets with petitions and posters. Five hundred people turned up. Television covered the meeting. The next day, e-mails started arriving, many from Australians who had never protested against anything before. What was happening to the asylum seekers, they wrote, was not "fair." It was counter to everything that Australia was about.

For a while, Susan and Ann kept on with their writing. More e-mails poured in. They put their work to one side, gave up their lives to founding what they have called Rural Australians for Refugees, drawing up a ten-point plan calling on the Australian government to overturn its current policies, undo the Pacific Solution, and return to a more moral past. "It grew," says Susan, "like Topsy." By the spring of 2004, there were seventy-one groups across the country, doing whatever seemed most useful locally: writing letters, collecting money, drawing up petitions. A pharmacist called Elaine Smith has turned all her free time over to keeping in touch with the detainees on Nauru, updating her Web site with every legal move. It was Elaine Smith who broadcast information about a hunger strike on Nauru in December 2003, when four detainees, goaded beyond endurance by their endless indefinite sentence, sewed up their lips. In the years of its existence, no outsider has been allowed to visit the Nauru facility. What is known about it comes from relations in Australia, who talk from time to time to the detainees, some of them wives and children who followed their husbands to Indonesia only to find themselves ensnared by the Pacific Solution, or from the occasional illicit reporter, like Kate Durham, an artist in Melbourne who is married to Julian Burnside and went in without permission. Others, nearer the "front line" of the detention centers, visit prisoners. Others again invite those released into the community to stay with them. All over Australia, farmers have offered jobs to those on temporary protection visas. The mayor of Young has championed a group of Afghans to work in the town's slaughterhouses.

Like all other ventures concerning the asylum seekers, the Rural Australians for Refugees has built upon its own success. This is the second most noticeable aspect of Australia's moral crusade: it was not the television images of Iranian children being maltreated that alone caught the country's imagination. It was the fact th   ary Australians began to meet the asylum seekers face-to-   lore than 9,000 refugees are now out in the community. They all have stories to tell. As the Australians, who knew about them only from their demonized images, have discovered, they are neither scroungers nor exploitative, but anxious, troubled men, women, and children who have fled torture, persecution, and possible death, endured horrific journeys, lost everything they once possessed, only to spend months and even years in an Australian camp. As they have made friends and told their stories, so the absurdity and cruelty of their treatment have come to inspire and impress Australians, particularly as their visas are so punishing—the temporary visas do not allow for a permanent solution, nor for being reunited with families, so even those who have been released live in endless uncertainty—and even as so many prove hardworking and capable. What possible threat are such people to Australia's security? Why keep punishing them?

Some of those on TPVs are now approaching the moment when they will have to apply for a second visa for another three years. Few of their new friends and supporters are likely to take kindly to their possible redetention or deportation.

Australia has no Bill of Rights. Even if, at the time of the drafting of the Universal Declaration of Human Rights in 1948, it recoiled at the idea of letting people enter another country without invitation, it did sign the 1951 Convention. What bothers Father Brennan, a Jesuit priest, lawyer, and author of a book on refugees, *Tampering with Asylum*, is not merely that Australia is in breach of several conventions that it has signed and ratified—the treatment of the asylum seekers violates several articles of the Universal Declaration of Human Rights, the Convention for the Rights of the Child, the Statute of Rome, and the International Covenant on Political and Civil Rights—but that it is becoming so hard to justify a policy that is so discriminatory and inhumane. Were every Western democracy to follow Australia's model and introduce indefinite mandatory detention—indefinitely locking up asylum seekers who have committed no crimes as recognized under international law—the very meaning of the Refugee Convention would be forgotten.

What is more, Australia, unlike Europe, is not trying to deal with the arrival of tens of thousands of economic migrants, who need, if the Refugee Convention is to be upheld, to be sorted out from the true asylum seekers. On the contrary, those who took to the boats in Indonesia did so out of genuine need. Up to 90 percent of unauthorized arrivals, like Morteza and Shayan, have, after years in detention, been found to be true refugees after all. Nor has a single terrorist ever been known to enter the country on a leaky boat. As Robert Manne puts it, the country is being mobilized by a specter. With no new arrivals, it has become a policy about no one. It is an immense sledgehammer, to crack a very small nut.

Since the frenetic days of the *Tampa*, the mood of the immigration authorities has remained defiant, with much talk of teaching smugglers that Australia is not a soft touch. Fewer children remain in detention. Of Nauru's detained, who at the peak numbered 1,546, all but 284 have left. Most of those remaining are Afghans, and Australia has signed a $22.5 million deal to extend detention on Nauru at least until June 2005. Across the whole of Australia, 1,097 boat people are still in detention, either awaiting final decisions, or because their countries refuse to take them back, or because they have been turned down but know that if they went home they would face persecution, and so decide to wait and hope something may change. Just one man, a twenty-five-year-old Palestinian called Aladdin Sisalem, remains on Manus Island, costing Australia a reported $23,000 a day. How, asks Father Brennan—veteran of earlier campaigns to secure rights for Aboriginals—can Australia maintain a policy that demonizes a small number of innocent people, and treats them with such brutality, if not in the spirit of punishment and deterrence that it so vehemently denies? A system that risks the sanity of children, he argues, makes a nonsense of the family values that Australia so prizes. What alarms him, as it alarms Steel and others, is that Australia, having proved that it can get away with anything when it comes to asylum seekers, may well prove a model for countries now trying and failing to come to terms with these problems, and that far from publicizing what it does well—the resettlement of refugees—as an inspiration to others, it is instead exporting all that is most shameful. Australia has seen four waves of boat arrivals over the years; there are, argues Father Brennan, bound to be others, as new Talibans or Saddam Husseins drive more refugees into exile by their atrocities: now is the time to put in place policies that, while securing Australia's borders, are also humane and decent.

For what the Pacific Solution has done to Australia itself, he adds, is to divide the country more savagely even than the battles for indigenous recognition and rights, making the Liberal party more conservative, the Labor party more fractured, and battering those Australians who have long supported human rights and multiculturalism. "Howard sang a song until the people believed him," says Robert Manne. "It was a horrible song, and it allowed hateful things to happen in a democracy in a way that no one would ever have believed Australia would allow." Far from expanding the world's moral imagination, as Father Brennan sees it, Australia, under Howard and the Liberals, has shrunk it.

. . .

BEFORE LEAVING AUSTRALIA, I went to visit Villawood, Sydney's detention center, about which Thomas Kenneally wrote so bitterly in *The Tyrant's Novel*. Many of Villawood's detainees are overstayers, and it is here that they wait while their futures are determined. But it was also the camp where Shayan spent the last wretched months of his incarceration, and where Morteza sewed up his lips and later drank a bottle of shampoo.

The camp is in a suburb, a green, quiet area of calm streets and pleasant gardens; like most of the detention centers, it is somehow hidden away, cleverly concealed behind trees and virtually unmarked. By the beginning of visiting hours, people were making their way in ones and twos up a dirt road through the first set of gates, to join a queue inside the first wall of razor wire, to be searched, screened, and stamped with an ink that shows up under ultraviolet light. Inside the compound is a grassy area, perhaps an acre in size, with plastic chairs and tables and a jungle gym for children.

It was Behnam's birthday, the third he has spent in detention. He was eighteen. His family is Mandaean and their story is similar to those of most boat people. They found a smuggler in Indonesia, endured a harsh sea trip, were subjected to a slow process of interview and rejection, only then to be moved from camp to camp. Behnam's life is made tolerable by the fact that both he and his younger brother and sister attend school outside the camp, where all three are doing well. His mother is a purposeful, strong, outgoing woman. It is clear that she has played an enormous part in keeping the family together. On his eighteenth birthday, Behnam looked well.

But it was the scene around Behnam and his family that was memorable. They have made many friends during their time in Villawood, men and women who regularly make the long trip from the city to talk to the detainees and to show support. To one side of the grassy compound, under a large eucalyptus tree, several plastic tables had been pulled together and a tea party was in progress, celebrating Behnam's birthday. There was an elderly woman in an enormous red floppy hat. There were several middle-aged men, some wearing baseball caps. There were two or three lawyers, some nuns, a journalist or two, a few writers. There were two girl students, new visitors to Villawood. The atmosphere was festive. There was a fine cake with candles, and plates of Iranian food brought in by other Mandaeans already settled in Sydney. Rather late, a woman arrived out of breath, carrying in her arms a great many brightly colored balloons, which rose high among the branches in the breeze. Among them all, charming and collected, wandered Behnam, receiving his birthday greetings.

If you half shut your eyes, fixed them carefully on the cheerful tea party, avoided seeing the tall banks of razor wire rising steeply on all sides, the guards patrolling, the barracklike blocks separated by more wire fences, then you might just have believed yourself to be in an ordinary place.

NEWCASTLE AND THE POLITICS OF DISPERSAL

It may often be easier to live in exile with a fantasy of paradise than to suffer the inevitable ambiguities and compromise of cultivating actual, earthly places.

— EVA HOFFMAN, *THE NEW NOMADS*

It was on New Year's Day 2002, a still, cold morning, so gray that at nine o'clock it was barely light, that Suleiman Dialo, a thirty-year-old asylum seeker from Guinea, decided that the moment had come to end his life. Though the coroner, Terence Carney, would later record an open verdict for his death, saying that he had no way of knowing what was in Dialo's mind when he jumped from Newcastle's Redheugh Bridge to fall a hundred feet onto the towpath below, narrowly missing the waters of the river Tyne, Dialo's friend Bertrand has no doubts.

Like Monica Bishop, area manager for the North of England Refugee Service in Newcastle, like Katherine Henderson, Dialo's lawyer, like the city's fast-growing population of African asylum seekers, Bertrand knows precisely why Dialo chose to die. Dialo had reached the end of a legal line he had been crawling along for the past eighteen months, and he had finally come to believe that he had nowhere left to go. Sometime in the middle of November he had been informed that his appeal for asylum in the United Kingdom had been refused; and with it his accommodation, his English lessons at Gateshead College, his health care, his money, the £38 given to him each week by the government (calculated nicely at 70 percent of what is deemed the minimum necessary for a decent life, and therefore not a sum to be envied). He knew that any morning now, probably around dawn because that is a good time to catch people in bed, there would be a knock on his door and police would escort him to a detention center and from there to a plane bound for Conakry. Several times, during the year of their friendship, Dialo had told Bertrand that, were he to be finally rejected by the Home Office and the courts, he would choose to die. He could imagine no existence for himself back in Guinea, however hard he tried; and sometime in those next few weeks the Tyne must have come to seem to him better than the torture and death he told Bertrand awaited him at home.

This is not a plaintive tale about a cruel bureaucracy condemning a vulnerable young man to death; rather, it is a story about the loneliness and fear common to asylum seekers everywhere, made worse perhaps in Dialo's case by the fact that his native language was Fula, which is spoken across parts of West Africa, while there were no other known Fula speakers in the whole of northeast England; that his French was very poor and that he spoke scarcely a sentence of English; and that, in all his childhood in Guinea, he had never learned to read or write. Signposts, letters, instructions, telephone calls, the television and radio, ordinary daily conversation—none of this was available to him in England; his sense of aloneness was both overwhelming and shocking to him. He had not expected it. "He didn't ever really understand what was happening to him," says Katherine Henderson, the efficient and involved lawyer who had not long before taken up his case and was still hoping to redeem some of the earlier errors and misunderstandings, and so win Dialo, if not permanent leave to remain in Britain, at least some measure of breathing space. "The world about him had shrunk to almost nothing."

Even Bertrand, perhaps his closest friend among the Africans in the northeast, was never able to get very close to him: "He didn't speak much. It was as if he couldn't bear to talk about himself if he couldn't explain properly, if he couldn't put into words what had happened to him and why he so feared to go home. He seemed frightened in case he said a wrong word, and there was no one to know or check."

I first heard about Dialo in the early summer of 2003 from Gaby Kitoko, a medical student who fled eastern Congo in 2000, leaving behind him a wife and two children, after he was accused of spying for the United Nations. Gaby was one of the first asylum seekers to be sent to the northeast to await news of whether he would be accepted as a refugee, back in the days when Newcastle had no asylum seekers living on its housing estates, and before the Home Office in London started scattering young men and women from some ninety countries around Britain. Gaby walks with a limp, from what the Congolese soldiers did to him before letting him go. Three years later, he is still waiting to hear whether he may be granted leave to remain in Britain, and with it permission to apply to be joined by his family; but in the meantime, frightened on behalf of himself and other asylum seekers of the sense of isolation and incomprehension that afflicts all who wait, he has started a small local center for Africans in Byker, one of Newcastle's housing developments.

Patrolled, back in the nineteenth century when it was still a country district, by one of Newcastle's only two mounted police-men, Byker was once home to Newcastle's thriving community of dock workers. Now it is all battered redbrick housing and desolate streets, with shabby terracing and occasional shops, protected by thick sheets of metal and iron bars. On top of the few taller build-ings, where police have put closed-circuit cameras to catch signs of disorder and crime, razor wire has been fastened to safeguard the cameras from theft and breakage. There is an air of poverty and abandonment. To open his community center, with the help of local funders, Gaby took over three derelict shops and knocked them into a single cheerful room, in which each day he listens to the ills and worries of the Congolese, Zimbabweans, Angolans, and Rwandans who come to consult him. Gaby barely knew Dialo, he said to me, while behind us, on a vast television donated by a local well-wisher, a portly and energetic gospel preacher in pinstripe suit and waistcoat exhorted his studio congregation to heed God. Gaby greeted Dialo when he saw him, but as a fellow African, not a friend. It was only after his death that Gaby was asked, as a leader of Newcastle's African community, to say something to journalists; his words were toned down by a local refugee officer, anxious that his valediction should not sound too accusatory. Dialo died, said Gaby, because of despair; it was threat of deportation that pushed him, literally, from the bridge. These were not words that people want to hear.

Dialo didn't have many close friends, since he couldn't talk to them as he wished to. Photographs show a thin, wiry, good-looking young man, with dreadlocks and a quizzical smile; in one, he is leaning against a door, his elbow outstretched, one foot, wearing a fashionable sneaker, crossed rather jauntily over the other, his head dipped to one side, the dreadlocks falling along his cheek, a half smile on his face. Monica Bishop, the goodhearted and motherly woman at the Newcastle refugee service, told me that hugging clients was not something that she normally ever did, but that with Dialo, she had broken her own rules. "He used to come into the office frequently, and we had no time to look after him. He didn't say very much. He just sat and smiled. And I would say: 'Suleiman, you'll be all right. You really will be all right.' And then I would give him a cuddle." He was, Monica repeated several times, a greatly liked young man, a "lovely lad."

When Dialo ceased to be all right no one really knows. He reached Britain in July 2000, at twenty-seven somewhat older than many of the other African asylum seekers, from a small Guinean village far from the capital. He told Bertrand, whom he met that November at Gateshead College where he had gone to study English, that he had been forced to flee because his parents and brothers and sisters had been murdered. He said that he had left behind him a shop and a good life as a trader. Monica told me that Dialo had scars all over his back, from being beaten by the people who killed his parents. I asked Bertrand if he knew whether Dialo had been tortured. He looked puzzled: "Of course." I had made the same mistake before: forgetting that torture is now endemic across many parts of Africa, and how many asylum seekers come to Britain bearing scars from cigarettes, bayonets, rifle butts, boiling water, or whips. "There was also something wrong with his feet, because when I started a football team for Africans, he would come but only watch." Falaka, the beating on the soles of the feet practiced by torturers all over the modern world, can leave injuries that are slow to heal.

Bertrand and Dialo met only in the evenings, because Bertrand was a regular business student at Newcastle University, with a French passport to ensure him smooth passage in and out of England, while Dialo was an uncertain asylum seeker, who seemed to find learning to speak English extremely difficult. But in the evenings, when the Africans met and played music and talked, Dialo would sit and listen. Bertrand didn't ask him questions about his past. In any case, in those days, Bertrand wasn't much concerned with refugee matters. It wasn't until Dialo's death that he really began to wonder about the fairness of it all. All he thought about before that was how hard it must be for Dialo, with no friend who spoke Fula, and no more than perhaps a dozen people in the whole area who could understand some of his broken West African French, with its words of dialect and distinctive intonation, difficult to unravel even for those who speak French well. He worried when Dialo told him that his first legal representative in London had insisted on interviewing him only with a French and not a Fula interpreter, and that Dialo knew that he had not been able to get across either to him or to the Home Office the many terrible things that had befallen him at home.

All through the summer and autumn of 2001, in her office in the middle of Newcastle, not far from the statue of the eighteenth-century Whig reformer Earl Grey, under which the refugees of Newcastle like to meet, Monica Bishop worried about Dialo. She repeatedly wrote to the Home Office, in order to have his hearing adjourned while she desperately combed the northeast not just for a decent solicitor to take his case but for a Fula interpreter who could understand and translate what he had to say. Even now, she cannot bear to consign his file to the archives, but keeps it buried in a drawer of her desk. She found it and gave it to me to read. "He is extremely distressed," says one of her letters to a reputable firm of solicitors, written in May, "and I hope that you will be able to represent him." This particular firm was unable to, already having more cases on their books than they could deal with. Other solicitors declined as well. I went through the file. There were other letters: to sort out problems over accommodation, to ask for travel warrants to attend hearings, to request further postponements. There is a brief note describing the fact that Dialo had been imprisoned several times in Guinea, where some of his teeth had been extracted as part of torture, and that his feet were damaged. By the time Dialo was accepted by Katherine Henderson, who has specialized as a solicitor in asylum cases for several years now, his appeal had just been turned down.

The last time Bertrand saw Dialo alive was at the beginning of December, not long after he had received a letter from the Home Office telling him that they did not consider him a "Convention refugee," a person recognized under the 1951 Convention as having a justified fear of returning to his own country. He seemed confused, and he complained that he couldn't understand how it was that some of the asylum seekers he had met had made up stories, fabricated events and dates and even torture, and yet been granted asylum, while he had told everyone the truth and been turned down. It was at this last meeting that he told Bertrand that he would never go back to Guinea. It had taken too much to get to Britain, too much emotion and courage and too much money, and he had nothing and no one to go back to. He felt, he said, like an *échec*, a failure. He had left Guinea in order to save his own life: why go back now to die? And it had all become too difficult: the language, the fact that he was not allowed to work, the way he couldn't understand anything. He wanted a private life of his own, not to be treated like a child, and he could no longer bear to depend on others for everything. And he was afraid; inside himself, he was afraid about what he would find waiting for him.

Bertrand was shocked by Dialo's death; he had not anticipated it. But when it happened, it made sense to him. Dialo was not enjoying life. He wasn't the kind of person who would ever have been able to slip into Britain's underground economy and live along the margins, and he had nowhere else to go. He was, as Bertrand sees it, a strong individual, with a strong instinct for survival, or he would never have managed to overcome the torture, his parents' murders, and his own escape to Europe. But his strength had all been used up in the waiting, the uncertainty, the humiliations, and the sense of rejection. What haunts Bertrand now is that he did not see all this sooner.

On New Year's Eve 2001, Dialo went to visit a group of Africans in Gateshead. Some time after midnight, he disappeared. No one knows how he spent the rest of the night. It was the driver of a car, crossing the deserted Redheugh Bridge from the Gateshead side at nine o'clock the following morning, who saw him jump. There was no one about. The city center was empty, the shops and offices closed for the holiday. It was very quiet.

Dialo's funeral took place on January 11 at 1:30 P.M., in the Central Mosque in Elswick Road. It was, says Monica, icy, with a terrible biting cold. Gaby was there, too, and Bertrand, recently returned from a holiday in France, and a teacher from Gateshead College, who had grown fond of her silent pupil; Katherine Henderson came, too, reproaching herself for not having tried harder to make sure that Dialo had understood that all was not yet lost, that despite his failed appeal she might still be able to win him a reprieve from deportation by having his case reopened, on the basis of an accurate translation and a medical report testifying to his torture. In Monica's file are noted the arrangements for the ceremony: the cloth, towels, and soap for the preparation and wrapping of Dialo's body to be provided by the Gateshead Muslim Society, the grave to be filled by members of the African community, the women mourners to "attend at a little distance from the grave"; later, the coffin to be laid in Gateshead's Saltwell cemetery, at the farthest end, where other Muslims lie, their feet pointing toward Mecca. An imam came from London to officiate. The sum of £1,236.20 was raised locally to cover the costs.

Why, I asked Bertrand on one of our meetings under Grey's statue, did Dialo chose to jump over a bridge? "He wanted to make certain he would die. He was not silly." Dialo's death has sent Bertrand's own life in a new direction. He has become more aware of his own blackness in a white country, more conscious that to be black in northeast England is most often to be an asylum seeker, and that to be an asylum seeker is hardly to be a person at all. He wishes that he had known then what he knows now, that there are a number of Fula speakers in London, and that some way might have been found to bring them together with Dialo. In the weeks following Dialo's death, he began thinking about the isolation and apprehension that had weighed so heavily on his friend, and he started an organization with his friends to bring together Newcastle's African refugees to help them with some of their immediate difficulties. He has called it Baobab, after the West African tree under which villagers traditionally sit to discuss their problems; Baobab has its own soccer team and Bertrand talks of opening a club where the Africans can dance.

· · ·

SUICIDES ARE NOT unusual among asylum seekers in Britain. Not all are committed by men and women who have reached the end of the legal line and are facing imminent deportation, for the life of an asylum seeker is precarious, confusing, beset by contradictions and reversals, subject to sudden uprooting and dispersal, and most of it is conducted in a foreign language. For some, the waiting and the uncertainty are already too much. For others, the loneliness is more than can be borne. When, early in July 2003, a young Iranian used a knife to try to hack himself to death in Bigg Market, just in front of Monica Bishop's offices, he left a note: "You have to kill yourself in this country," he had written, in large scrawled letters, "to prove that you would be killed in your own country."

Katherine Henderson, in the summer of 2003, had two clients she feared would not survive the wait: one was a South African woman, gang-raped by soldiers in front of her family, whom she was then obliged to watch being murdered; the other, an Iranian, who learned that he had been refused asylum even without an interview, and who had already attempted suicide once when the Home Office mistakenly stopped answering his letters and cut off his benefits. She believes that some 50 to 60 percent of her clients, frantic and highly confused, traumatized by fear and grief for those they have left behind, are in need of some form of mental help. Monica Bishop has a handful of others she is keeping a close eye on. People working with asylum seekers have become attuned to this particular despair.

In 2002, according to official figures, 110,700 people asked for political asylum in the United Kingdom on the grounds of persecution and justifiable fear of return, under the 1951 Refugee Convention to which Britain is party. This was the largest number that had ever applied. (In 1993, for example, there had been 22,370.) It was also the highest number of applications in the developed world; the United States came in second, with 81,000, Germany third, with 71,100, and France fourth, with 50,800. But the numbers have been dropping. Only 2 percent of the world's asylum seekers, however, are currently in the UK, and as a country, Britain is not generous with its contributions to UNHCR, to which it gives half what the Netherlands gives. (Nor is it generous with resettlement, recently announcing that it would be offering places to five hundred people, but then allowing the plan to stall.) Just why Britain is such a magnet for asylum seekers is not easily explained, but it is generally attributed to a mixture of things: a cumbersome appeals procedure (which gives asylum seekers the hope that they may enjoy longer periods in the UK, while their case is being considered, than in other countries); smugglers' awareness that border controls are weak; the draw of already established communities; the fact that Britain retains its reputation as a place of welcome to persecuted people and that English is a language many people speak; and the realization that when it comes to deportations, the Home Office is relatively lax.

Since 1997, the rules and regulations governing the asylum process have been changed three times, on each occasion becoming tougher and more restrictive, and adding to the impression, as the Refugee Council observed not long ago, that the system is not working. Asylum seekers today (as has always been true under the Convention) may enter the country illegally—there is no other way—and claim asylum either at the port of entry (airport or seaport) or directly at the Home Office, but they must do so "as soon as is reasonably practical." Failure to do so means forfeiting all financial support, the assumption being that only a bogus asylum seeker would not apply on landing, but this rule, which is known as Section 55, is now being challenged in the courts as being in breach of the Human Rights Act article on "inhuman and degrading treatment." Having completed a statement of evidence—a history of what has happened to cause flight—then been interviewed and submitted any further evidence, the asylum seeker may be given refugee status, and eventually allowed to apply for citizenship. (Initial decisions are widely agreed to be made in an ill-informed way, and to rely on confusing and out-of-date country information.) Alternatively, he may be offered humanitarian protection for varying amounts of time, which means that though he has failed to qualify as a refugee under the 1951 Convention, valid concerns about danger and security prevent him from being sent home. If refused on both counts, the asylum seeker can launch the first of four possible appeals to various authorities and tribunals. A proposed "ouster" clause, which would have removed the right to judicial review or appeal to a higher court, was recently rejected by the courts. After appeals of various kinds, some half of all those who ask for asylum are refused leave to remain, and are then meant to leave the country. Not all do so. Many slip into the underground economy, or simply wait and hope to escape deportation.

It is not easy for people who have fled violence and persecution, or even poverty and despair, to stick to the strict truth. When their story is their only real passport, when they have thrown away their documents and tried to reinvent themselves, it is hard not to embellish the hardships of the past. Refugee life is rife with rumor. Among those waiting to be interviewed, word circulates about how some nationalities are more likely to get asylum than others, about how some stories are more powerful than others, more likely to touch the hearts of the interviewers. The buying and selling of "good" stories, stories to win asylum, has become common practice in refugee circles, among people terrified that their own real story is not powerful enough. How easy then, how natural, to shape the past in such a way that it provides more hope for a better future. Traffickers and smugglers, transporting clients to the West, are known to recommend identities, to advise assumption of an origin in one of the countries to which people asking asylum cannot be returned without breaching the Refugee Convention clause about nonrefoulement.

In recent years, as the numbers of people arriving in the West and claiming asylum began to grow steeply, and pressure mounted on immigration officers to turn away as many applicants as they reasonably could, the idea of what is truth and what is a lie has acquired a very particular potency in refugee matters. Credibility has become a benchmark on which everything depends. Asylum seekers found not to be telling the truth are automatically rejected, however genuine their need may be. "Lack of credibility"—that is to say, the supposition that the person asking for asylum is lying—has become, in most of the West, the main reason for refusal. For asylum lawyers, convincing their clients that they must tell only the truth has become of major importance. And spotting a lie, however trivial, has become a challenge for immigration officers, who admit that a falsehood, even one concerning method of travel or date of departure, enables them to throw out a case. The tragedy comes when the real story, the true story, is stronger than the made-up one, and would guarantee refugee status while the false one does not; this is particularly poignant in the case of those who receive poor legal advice or whose experience of torture makes telling their stories painful. The situation is not easy for the asylum seekers, certainly; but not easy for the interviewers either, to be forced to be so vigilant for lies in the stories of desperate people, knowing that there are among them people, using the asylum route, whose pasts contain no persecution, and others again, whose stories are indistinguishable in terms of pain and anguish from those of true refugees, but who fall outside the narrow definition of the Convention.

• • •

THERE MAY BE as many as 25,000 asylum seekers in Britain who, like Dialo, have reached the end of their legal road. They have been turned down on their first interviews and lost their appeals; some have tried and failed to win a reprieve under the Human Rights Act or before a tribunal; and some have been able to take their cases before the High Court. In every case, the immigration officers, judges, and adjudicators involved have decided either that their stories lack credibility, or that the applicant has in fact nothing to fear from return to his own country, or that his reason for coming to Britain is only a desire for a better life. Many will have suffered from lazy and exploitative solicitors; Katherine Henderson says that more than half the clients who have been sent to the northeast and come to her for help bring their entire life stories, including accounts of torture and prolonged family persecution, reduced by their first solicitor to three quarters of a sheet of A4 paper. Others, like Dialo, will have been offered poor or inappropriate translation, and been victims of clerical errors and misfilings. All, at the end of a process that will have lasted somewhere between four months and four years, will have been notified that their case has been rejected and that they are to leave the UK; in June 2003, the Home Office's list of "safe countries" (nations to which asylum seekers can "safely" be sent back) stood at twenty-four. Deportation—ticket to home country paid for—may follow immediately, or may follow a period in detention, in case the failed applicant absconds. The number of people for whom there was room in detention centers stood at around 2,000 in 2003 and 2004, but the government announced not long ago that they were increasing the number to 4,000.

Rejection also means the end of all financial help. Those with special needs can apply for continued support as hardship cases, but must sign a form to say that they are willing to be voluntarily repatriated at any time. Only the Iraqis, in the summer of 2003, were not obliged to sign this form, Iraq alone being deemed, for the time being at least, to be a country to which return was not a possibility. For each one collected at dawn, taken to a deportation center, and put on a flight, dozens more are said to vanish into Britain's black economy, sleeping on the floors of friends' houses, working illegally for appallingly low wages in factories, farms, and garages. Their particular limbo, refused asylum, always fearing deportation, the limbo that Dialo could not bear to contemplate, is not describable in figures. "They do not sleep," explained an acquaintance of Dialo, when asked by reporters about his friends who had been rejected for asylum. "They do not sleep because they know their futures."

In April 2000, "Interim Dispersal Measures," created under the 1999 Immigration Act, were put into place to alleviate the pressure on London to accommodate asylum seekers waiting for the answer to their application. In theory, the Home Office, through the National Asylum Support Agency (NASS), disperses people in "clusters," sending like with like, Iraqis with Iraqis, Angolans with Angolans, to cities around the UK where housing is available, either in council estates or with private contractors. In practice, people are dispersed as they arrive, with no time to match them up with others from their countries, which was why Dialo found himself with no other Fula speaker in Newcastle. When, in March 2003, NASS sent a first batch of asylum seekers to Stockton-on-Tees, they sent 675 Somalis, Algerians, Kuwaitis, Pakistanis, Ethiopians, Eritreans, Macedonians, Guineans, Zimbabweans, Turks, and Sierra Leoneans; all but a handful were young men, born in the 1970s and early 1980s. One result of this inchoate system is that they are now to be found everywhere, in ones and twos, these people who no longer exist, whose legal process has run out and who do not know what to do next; in the absence of some radical and farsighted solution, their numbers are set to grow all the time.

Both Katherine Henderson and Monica Bishop talk of the future with apprehension, as a time of inevitably rising suicides. "It's a bomb waiting to explode," Mohamed told me, when I went to see him in his office in Sunderland. Mohamed, the general manager of a local refugee office, is a Sudanese chemist who applied for and was given refugee status and asylum in Britain fifteen years ago, but has never been able to find a job to match his qualifications. Until 2000, Sunderland had a small Bangladeshi community, but few strangers, and certainly no strangers from Asia or Africa, had ever settled in the town. In the spring of 2000, Sunderland was earmarked as a good dispersal town. Asylum seekers from sixty countries have since arrived. Month by month, rejections are increasing; in ones and twos, like Dialo, they are losing their homes and money. "The implications for putting so many lonely, desperate, and confused people on the streets are terrifying," Mohamed said to me. "It will totally destroy the good work of all the refugee organizations in breaking the negative image of asylum. And what does it do to them? These people were active in their own countries. Even if they had been tortured and persecuted, they were people who had work and professions and positions in society. Here they are condemned to doing nothing. They were somebody at home. They are leftovers here."

In the summer of 2003, of the 50,000 official asylum seekers scattered by NASS in sixty-four cities, towns, and villages across the UK, about 5,000 were believed to be in the northeast. None, under legislation passed in 2002, are allowed to work, however great and necessary their skills—as doctors, for example, or chemists, or biologists—and however protracted their wait. Lack of work was, according to Bertrand, the single most painful thing for Suleiman Dialo to bear, since he had left behind him a good and profitable job as a trader; it is also mentioned most often, by those applying for asylum, as the single worst aspect of the waiting. Extrapolation from national statistics, however imprecise, suggests that at least 2,500 of these people in and around Newcastle will ultimately be refused asylum. For a long time, while Byker absorbed, first, some of the hundreds of Romanians who arrived suddenly from Timișoara on Christmas Eve, 2001, then Zimbabweans fleeing Mugabe's political

madness, then Iraqi and Turkish Kurds escaping systematic persecution by their governments, then Afghans in flight from the Taliban, the housing estate experienced mainly arrivals; now, it witnesses
many departures as well.

It is said that in the UK in 2004 there may be several thousand
Iraqis, most but not all of them Kurds, who have reached the end of
their legal line and moved into the limbo that Dialo so feared. Because of the war in Iraq, their particular position, rejected yet not liable to immediate deportation, is more anomalous than most;
though they may stay, they may not work. Cut off from the support
that kept them going, they now work as ill-paid laborers or in factories, or they exist on the charity of those still supported by NASS.
No longer asylum seekers, yet neither refugees nor deportable, they
do not exist, except as names of people who should not be in the UK.

Ali arrived in Dover on October 5, 2000, in a truck full of boxes.
He does not know what was in the boxes, having been ordered by
the smuggler not to look. He is a Kurd, from Sulamaniya, a short,
wiry young man in his late twenties, with fashionably cut hair and a
pleasant grin. He speaks no English, having had neither the desire
nor the aptitude to learn while not knowing his future, and therefore
never having profited from the variety of English programs offered
by local council and voluntary organizations up and down the country. A prospering shoe shop owner, with a large family of brothers
and sisters, Ali was driven from Iraq after he refused to work for a
local *akha*, a powerful gang. Arrested on their orders by the police,
detained in solitary confinement in a cellar, beaten up and badly
scared, Ali emerged from captivity and fled to Istanbul; from there
he found a trafficker to bring him to Britain. His first application for
asylum was turned down; the immigration authorities pointed out
that his troubles were not with the state but with local hoodlums,
which made him ineligible for refugee status. He appealed. On June
5, 2002, Ali learned that his appeal, too, had been rejected.

Within a few days, the money that he had been receiving each
week was stopped. He left the room rented for him by the NASS
while he was an asylum seeker and moved in with friends. And there,

fourteen months later, he remains. When I met him, under Grey's column, he had a friend with him to interpret. He hoped I could get his money reinstated, as he was having trouble finding even casual low-paid work now that he had no papers of any kind. I asked him whether he thought of going home. He looked surprised. "Never," he said, through his friend. "It will never be safe for me." Like other Kurds in Newcastle, he is haunted by the story of another Iraqi Kurd who, hearing that he had been refused, hanged himself two years ago in the park, on a spring day in 2002, holding a daffodil in his hand. Hassan Omar Saloh was an older man of forty-seven, Ali explained, and he left a wife and eight children in Iraq.

I asked Ali about his life in Newcastle. What sort of work could he find? He looked anxious, evasive. Did he have friends? Yes, he replied, he had many friends, nearly all of them Iraqi men like himself, waiting; they met when they could, they sat and talked, they watched television. Did he have a girlfriend? "How can I? There are no Iraqi women in Newcastle, at least, no single ones." At night, when the Iraqis meet, they talk about work and loss and depression, and about Halabja, the city in Iraq where Saddam Hussein ordered 5,000 Kurds to be gassed; they remind one another of the fathers tortured to death in special centers, and the children whose corpses were still warm when their parents, in answer to a call from the police station, arrived to collect them. They discuss the Americans and the war, and whether Iraq will ever be a viable country again. They have spent their money, and their future is not so much empty as impenetrable. They stare at a vast blank wall. The legitimacy of their claim for asylum, in this world of nuances and degrees of persecution, has become almost irrelevant, and is certainly irrelevant to them. In escaping Iraq, in the long and frightening journey to freedom, in the imagination it took to conceive a new life and carry out the moves required to obtain it, they crossed some invisible barrier in their own minds. They are refugees, living in an alien land, but that land is immutably now theirs. They have no other. It is as if Iraq has become a chimera, a place of make-believe; the war, whatever its implications for the rest of the world, has no relevance to their lives.

Going back to what was once home is not an option any longer. They have traveled too far.

. . .

THE FIRST REACTION of most asylum seekers sent to the Byker area of Newcastle is one of astonishment. They have come from all over Africa, from the Balkans, Southeast Asia, and South America, expecting a sense of order, predictability, tranquillity, a tangible feeling that there is someone in charge and that that person is benevolent. This was what they had grown up imagining, a Britain in which things happened in an orderly and safe way; and because what little news trickles home from people who have preceded them into exile is always cheerful—those who have sacrificed so much, endured so much to go abroad, tend not to report poverty and failure—nothing has shaken their faith in all things British. Theirs is a curiously old-fashioned view, surprisingly little shaken by the realities of modern migration. What they find, in Byker, in derelict housing estates up and down the country, is very different from anything they expected. It is frightening, shabby, and unpredictable.

When Gaby arrived in the northeast in May 2000, he was among the first Africans ever seen in Byker, apart from the few who, over the years, had jumped ship in Newcastle or been smuggled into local ports in containers. In the streets, people asked him why he was there, and how long he was planning to stay. He felt ashamed. He wanted to explain that he had lost his honor as a human being, and that being a refugee had never been among his plans. He wanted to point out that he was thirty-two, alone, separated from his wife and children, and that he was aching to work, to give something to the country that seemed willing to look after him. "I wanted to ask them," he says now: "'When am I going to start my life?'" No one, back in 2000, when the Interim Dispersal Measures took effect, had thought to prepare the local community for the sudden arrival of Zimbabweans, Sri Lankans, North Koreans, and Iraqis, with their longing for different food and their languages and accents no one could understand; the far-right British National party was quick to make gains among residents perplexed about what this influx might spell. The northeast has some of Britain's most disadvantaged communities; unemployment, already high through loss of jobs in mining and the docks, created further strains. There were clashes, broken windows, thrown rocks. In Byker, Gaby was called a monkey and told to go back to the trees. Some asylum-seeker children were given urine to drink by boys in the street.

Though much has certainly improved in the three years since Gaby began his long wait in Newcastle, not least in the form of a consortium of organizations that tries extremely hard to broker good relations and better understanding for asylum seekers, everyday life for those who wait remains extremely tough. And it is growing worse. There have been discussions about sending asylum seekers to camps in western Europe as part of a "no nonsense" regime to prevent "bogus" refugees from flooding into Britain, while, in the wake of September 11, the shadow home secretary, Oliver Letwin, has been demanding that Britain derogate from the European Convention on human rights, to underline the right of Britain to deport failed asylum seekers if they represent a "threat to national security."

Not long ago, a report from the European Monitoring Centre on Racism and Xenophobia found Britain to have some of the most hostile attitudes in Europe toward asylum seekers. Racial harassment is increasing, and with it the number of actual physical assaults, much promoted by the scaremongering that has become the habit of the day. The Web site of MigrationWatch UK, a one-man research group run by a former British ambassador to Saudi Arabia, Sir Andrew Green, has warned that "we can expect at least 200,000 and perhaps 250,000 non European Union immigrants a year," figures that have little grounding but that have been much quoted. The Richmond (Yorkshire) MP William Hague, campaigning for the Conservatives not long ago, spoke of sorting out "criminals and asylum seekers."

None of this process has been helped by an explosion of ill temper in the tabloid newspapers, viewed throughout the rest of Europe with wary disbelief as responsible for a climate of xenophobia toward refugees nowhere justified either by numbers or events and not matched by the media in other countries. Because the tabloids, which portray asylum seekers as parasites, scroungers, criminals, and terrorists, do so in English, they are followed with interest by the rest of the world. (And some are copied: in Switzerland not long ago, the Swiss People's party won 26.6 percent of the popular vote in a general election, partly, so it was said, on the strength of its poster campaign, which showed a black face with the slogan "The Swiss are becoming Negroes.")

It was at the turn of the millennium that the *Sun*, the *Daily Mail*, and the *Express* sharpened their campaign against immigrants. (A survey not long ago revealed that every time one of the tabloids put asylum on its front pages, with warnings of Britain in the throes of losing control of its borders, circulation rose by some 10,000 readers.) Headlines have included "Swan Bake—Asylum Seekers Steal Queen's Birds for Barbecues" (the *Sun*), "Official: Asylum Tearing UK Apart" (the *Sun*), and "Widow, 88, Told by GP: Make Way for Asylum Seekers" (the *Mail on Sunday*). As the feeling grew that reporting in the British media gives undue prominence to scaremongering claims from fringe groups, portraying asylum seekers as threatening young men with contacts in the criminal underworld, so in the spring of 2003 the anticensorship organization Article 19 carried out a research project on media reporting of refugee matters. They found that fifty-one words of a disparaging nature were regularly used to describe asylum seekers, words like *bogus, fake, cheat*, and *failed*. They also concluded that statistics were "frequently unsourced, exaggerated or inadequately explained," that the tabloid press failed to distinguish between economic migrants and asylum seekers, and that the hostility of media coverage was provoking a sense of alienation and shame among refugees, who are rapidly being perceived as "untermenschen," the unwanted underclass, nonpeople, victims at best. UNHCR and the National Union of Journalists joined forces to produce a memorandum on good reporting, and in October 2003, the Press Complaints Commission issued guidelines to counter inaccurate and inflammatory stories.

Even so, hostile and bigoted reporting continues, with continued casual disregard for any distinction between asylum seeker, refugee, failed asylum seeker, or economic migrant, and totally neglecting a very simple but important fact: that in 1999–2000 alone, according to Home Office research, migrants, including asylum seekers and refugees, made a net fiscal contribution to Britain of approximately £2.5 billion.

In the *Daily Mail*, Ross Benson has been running a series of stories about the Roma, warning of an invasion of Gypsies as the European Union is enlarged. The Roma are one of the most despised of all European ethnic minorities. In January 2004, the *Sunday Times* took up the theme, suggesting that up to 100,000 Roma were on their way. The next day, the *Sun* added that after three months in the UK, these Roma would be "entitled to health, education, pension and welfare benefits." The *Daily Express* then inflated the figure to 1.6 million: GYPSIES PREPARE TO INVADE BRITAIN. Though two days later the *Express* amended this figure to 40,000, it predicted an "economic disaster" just the same. Even the *Economist* spoke of the "coming hordes." On January 22, 2004, the *Mail*'s front page covered a report by the Organization for Economic Co-operation and Development, saying that Britain, which was taking one in five of the Western World's asylum seekers, had "failed to turn the asylum tide." The article, it later turned out, ignored the fact that the UK is currently eighth among western European nations in the number of refugees as a percentage of its population, well behind Austria, Norway, Sweden, Switzerland, and Ireland. By contrast, there are very few articles describing what asylum seekers are fleeing from, the violence and terror and loss that they have left behind.

It was at least in part because the mood of the country encouraged such intolerance that Jack Straw, when foreign secretary, suggested that Britain might decide not to reaffirm its commitment to the 1951 Convention. Britain thereby became the first government in the world to threaten to pull out. Other countries, unsure whether the threat was real or tactical, watched what became known as the "nuclear option" with interest. Though, eventually, Britain did uphold its commitment, Straw followed up his hesitations when he was made home secretary, proposing that, instead of processing asylum seekers and their applications on British soil, they be sent to "offshore" centers, either on the fringes of the extended European Union, or in the regions from which they had come, where the whole procedure could be done in a consistent and orderly way. An exception might be made for some special groups, such as children. Coming so soon after Australia announced its Pacific Solution, Straw's proposals provoked strong and angry reactions in the refugee world, and were eventually rejected by other EU countries, though not before Denmark, Ireland, and Austria had expressed interest. Soon, the UK government came up with another idea: to pay Tanzania £4 million in aid in return for taking all the UK's failed Somali asylum seekers and putting them into a zone of protection; this of course would shift still more responsibility to the poor countries that are already housing most of the world's refugees. Though striking bargains over refugees is far from unknown, Tanzania declined. The enormous inherent problems that would be posed by Straw's "offshore" centers and "Zones of Protection"—Will people in flight from persecution be able to proceed in an orderly manner to a designated center? Who would run the show? How would compliance with international standards be guaranteed?—were all too obvious. What frightened the human rights world was that these proposals had been made at all.

In Byker, in his community center, Gaby warns new arrivals not to expect too much, to take great care not to antagonize their British neighbors, to make no fuss, to provoke no one. "It's very hard," he says, "for us Africans to accept abuse and say nothing. We knew it wouldn't be like home here, but we didn't expect to be made to feel so useless."

Gaby has reserved a small, airless room at the back of the community center, a windowless area that was once a storeroom, as his office. Among the crammed desks and computers, he listens, day after day, like a doctor with his patients, to the fears and bafflement of those scheduled for deportation. Whether, like Dialo, they came from violence and persecution, or are refugees from lives so impoverished and hopeless as to make the dividing line between economic necessity and physical safety lose all meaning, their response to forthcoming departure is fear. They come in search of the impossible, a postponement of the evil day.

On a Monday morning in the middle of August 2003, Gaby had two visitors. Claudette was from Rwanda, a round, nervous woman with three young boys. She is a Hutu, from a prominent Hutu family, and before the birth of her sons she worked for the Ministry of Commerce in Kigali. Toward the end of the war in 1994, after the massacres of the Tutsis by the Hutus were largely over and when the Tutsi soldiers were closing in on the capital, Hutus suspected of supporting the genocide were rounded up. Claudette's sister-in-law and a niece, both Hutus, were killed in a local skirmish. Soon afterward, her parents were killed, and with them one of her brothers and a sister. After threats were made against her Hutu husband, who was accused of having led a group of Interanhamwe killers to their victims in the genocide, what was left of the family fled to the Congo, where they spent two years in the relative safety of a refugee camp. But then rebel fighters overran the camp; Claudette, her husband, and the children found themselves forcibly repatriated to Kigali, where she and the boys were led one way, and her husband another, into prison.

In the months that followed, Claudette was repeatedly visited by soldiers from military intelligence, eager to get evidence against her husband. She was raped, beaten in the small of her back with rifle butts, kicked in the stomach, and forced to kneel on gravel while soldiers whipped her, tortures designed to extract from her a confession that she was indeed an "enemy of the state" and that her husband had been a leader in the genocide. In October 2002, Claudette was detained for a fortnight and told that unless she testified against her husband, she would be held in prison indefinitely.

She agreed, and was released pending her husband's trial; but she knew that the deal was meaningless, as she had no evidence to give, and other women who had agreed to testify had sent their husbands to their deaths and remained prisoners themselves. From earlier travels in the area, she knew the surrounding countryside well. Disguising herself as a peasant woman and taking her three small children, she walked several days through the bush toward Uganda, where a friend of her husband's helped them to escape, first to Kenya and then to Britain. Claudette and her sons reached London on a cold winter's morning. They knew no one, but were treated kindly and with respect. The three boys were now at school and doing well. Claudette recalled with appreciation how her neighbors in Byker took pity on the family and brought them, in the first days of confusion, food to eat.

On July 4, 2003, Claudette learned that her appeal had been turned down. Refusing her case, the Home Office allowed that her account of persecution up to her return from the Congo in 2001 was probably true; but went on to say that her assertion that the family had been targeted because they were Hutu intellectuals was not credible. Taking this together with her account of her escape—which he found improbable—and the reasons she gave for her husband's detention—that he had written a hostile thesis on Rwandan prison conditions—the Home Office interviewer concluded: "I cannot find her honest as to the core of her case." Hard as her life would surely be in Rwanda, he said that he believed that the country was indeed returning to normality, and that she and her children were unlikely to be mistreated again. Furthermore, given her past employment, Claudette was obviously a clever and resourceful woman, and she would manage. "How can we go back?" asked Claudette. "What chance would the children have with a father in prison in connection with the genocide?" While waiting and dreading the knock on the door that will spell deportation, Claudette has dreamed of finding ways of leaving her children in England, where they could at least survive.

Gaby could do little for Claudette. He was trying to find her a new solicitor, willing to take her case to the High Court, but knew that this was unlikely. Nor could he do much for Nsamba, who talked in careful, measured sentences, with the precise enunciation of those educated in the French system, and whose right leg was so badly injured during torture that the muscle had withered away and he now walked with a limp. Nsamba was a professor of economics at the University of Kinshasa in the Congo, a man too interested in opposition politics to remain safe for long, and whose account of his five-day trek to freedom in Zambia had been disbelieved by the Home Office on the grounds that no one with his injuries could have walked so far, and that, as an educated man, he would have described his journey more articulately had it been genuine. Nsamba, who had spent his months in Britain building an effective political opposition to the government at home in the Congo, learned at the end of June that his case had been rejected. As he saw it, choosing his words with care, Britain was once a country where respect for human rights was absolute. He came, admiring what he thought he would find. Now, having lived among the refugees for many months, he was not so sure.

. . .

BRITAIN'S ASYLUM WORLD is a busy, anxious place, full of currents and hopes, misunderstandings and deferments. Nothing is as it seems to be, and nothing stays the same. Rules change, in response to surges of hostility in public feeling, then change again, as they prove unworkable, or simply too harsh to implement. In the confusion and uncertainty, those whose daily work brings them into contact with refugees—the doctors, lawyers, refugee organizations, churches, human rights campaigners—are buffeted by a discourse that becomes more unpleasant day by day, as politicians make mileage out of scandals, as faraway countries drive political opponents into exile, as droughts and famines destroy communities, as travelers and television programs continue to peddle the image of a safe and welcoming West.

Before leaving Newcastle, I heard about Angel Heights, a former nurses' hostel opposite the main hospital. An imposing manorlike building, it was once the pride of 1930s town development and is now a home for "dispersed" asylum seekers. Angel Heights is all that is wrong and all that is right in British policy; it is both decent and dreadful, both humane and cruel. For a while, it was home to 140 single Afghan men, but not long ago, in response to new waves of arrivals and departures, the building was turned over to single African women sent up from London and the south to await the results of their applications for asylum. There are relatively few such hostels for single women, reflecting the fact that few young women have the courage and money to make the journeys in search of safety, that they often have children or elderly parents to care for, and that their movements are far more restricted. As a place to visit, it is impressive: brightly painted corridors and large meeting rooms hung with prints of fruit and plants; comfortable single rooms, each with a television and a kettle and a small fridge; a large inner courtyard with plants and benches. But Angel Heights is also a waiting room, a building in which nothing happens. Few of its inhabitants speak English, and few can speak to each other. Because it provides full board and lodging, the women receive just £10 each week. Forbidden to work, they have, literally, nothing to do; nothing, that is, except to worry: about those they were forced to leave behind, of whom they seldom have news; about the torture and rape most have endured; about their cases and their lawyers; about themselves. They sit, alone, in large rooms, full of cobalt-blue chairs in rows; they stand in the corridors; they queue by the single pay phone. Angel Heights is quiet; when the women speak, they speak in whispers. Outside the window is a forlorn garden with an abandoned greenhouse and an unkempt volleyball court, reminders of the days when nurses strolled on the grass and organized matches against each other.

Looking for someone to talk to about life inside Angel Heights, I found Madina, one of the two non-African women in the hostel at present; the other is an older Belorussian woman in her fifties, confined to her room with severe diabetes. Madina is a geologist from

Azerbaijan with a master's degree, a dark, thin, bony woman in her early thirties, her hair lank and very black, her clothes black. She has a thin, awkward smile and speaks some English. Her story told me everything I wanted to know about Angel Heights.

Madina last saw her eleven-year-old son, Kolya, on January 12, 2003. He was then in a hospital in St. Petersburg with severe frost-bite to his face and hands, having been thrown from a police car into the snow and found by a passerby. Kolya is half black. He was in shock and unwilling or unable to say much about what had happened to him, beyond the fact that the police had picked him up as he was walking to a school party and that in the scuffle he had lost the present he had been carrying. Madina was told by the doctors that he would be fine, and that she could return to collect him on the fourteenth. When she returned, his bed was empty. Kolya had been moved, she was informed, to a children's ward in a psychiatric hospital, with severe mental problems. She hastened to the hospital and was refused entry. Kolya was far too ill to see her.

Though terrified and baffled about what to do next, Madina had long expected trouble—but not this kind of trouble. For almost a year, she had been involved with a group of campaigners protesting against the war in Chechnya and what the Russians were doing to Chechen refugees. She already had to flee her home town in Azerbaijan because of death threats against her second husband, Salimov, a Chechen, and because of her own work with Armenian refugees, and she was no stranger to violence. Her first husband, Kolya's father, who was Congolese, had been killed in a bomb attack when he returned to Brazzaville after completing his studies in Azerbaijan, and Kolya had endured many racist attacks as a small boy. Since arriving in St. Petersburg, the city chosen carefully by her as the most liberal in Russia, Madina had been harassed by the police; her office had been ransacked and her computer and files confiscated, and she had been hospitalized with concussion and severe bruising after being arrested. "I'm not the kind of person who can sit back and do nothing," she said to me, sitting in the empty dining room in Angel Heights, reminding me again how often I feel surprised by the instinctive and apparently unhesitating courage of political activists. "I feel suffering like it's mine." A second attack by the police had left her with two broken ribs and a dislocated shoulder. And on September 19, almost four months before Kolya's abduction, Madina was again hospitalized, this time with severe depression. Soon after she was released, Salimov was arrested and charged with spying.

By this stage, not surprisingly, Madina had lost what little faith she had ever had in Russian human rights. Even liberal St. Petersburg was turning out to be dangerous for dissidents. But the abduction of her son was more than she could bear. Having been refused permission to see him on January 14, she went home in despair. The telephone rang as she entered the apartment. Her caller did not give his name. "We have taken your husband and your son," the voice said, "and now it is your turn." Madina fled to her nineteen-year-old sister's apartment. Later, they went out because the sister was going to the dentist. As they left, there was a shot: Madina's sister fell into the snow, dead. Madina saw a policeman run away. "Next time," said the telephone caller that night, "we will not miss." Again Madina fled. Friends helped find an agent who provided her with a ticket for London and a visa for Italy, where the plane was landing. She reasoned that she must stay alive for Kolya's sake. At Heathrow, she asked for asylum. She was put into a small hotel near the airport and, three months later, sent to Newcastle.

These, then, are Madina's reasons for being in Angel Heights, waiting to hear whether the Home Office will decide to send her to Italy, for which she still has a visa, and let the Italian government decide on the legitimacy of her claim, or whether they will grant her leave to remain in Britain. The familiar and sad story of violence, fear, and torture explains Madina's haunted look, her fragile thinness, her anxious pacing. She has no idea how or when or where she will ever see Kolya again.

Meanwhile, she waits, and thinks. She sleeps little, thinking obsessively of her son, who she knows from friends is still in the psychiatric hospital in St. Petersburg. She also knows that there is still no news of Salimov, who, she now suspects, has been "disappeared." She spends her weekly £10 on phone calls to Russia. From dawn until late each night she wanders around Angel Heights' long bright yellow corridors, occasionally leaving the building to walk down the hill into central Newcastle and to the main library, where she can receive and send e-mail. She found a book on geology in Angel Heights' small library and uses it to work on her English. Every morning, she forces herself to translate something from a newspaper, as practice. Had she tried any of the novels on the shelf? "They are," she said mournfully, "not serious." Most days, she spends a few hours with one of the African women, recently granted leave to remain in the United Kingdom. The African woman is too frightened to walk in Newcastle's streets on her own since some boys threw eggs at her; asked by the Home Office whether there was a close family member she would like to apply to have join her in Britain, she replied that no, she had no one, soldiers had killed them all. At six o'clock, Madina eats dinner in the refectory, alone; afterward, she sits in her small, perfectly comfortable, totally silent bedroom, with its bright purple walls, and thinks. So the days pass, each one like the last, in an outer appearance of calm, and an inner feeling of desperation and terror. I didn't feel there was much more I wanted to know about Angel Heights: a benign prison, lived in by solitary women, waiting.

. . .

AS GEORGINA FLEXNER, who works for the Consortium for Asylum Support Services, sees it, the real messages spread by government go all one way. For all the pious words about integration, about preparing local communities for the arrival of asylum seekers, about the enormous advantages to both sides of having refugees in the community, "regionalization"—the currently popular word—is effectively all about policing and little about care. Asylum seekers are not meant to feel welcome; if their reception is too good, then they might want to stay. Since Flexner started work in the north

three years ago, she has decided that the dispersal program, with all
its contradictions and confusions, its ever changing regulations and
its arbitrariness, is designed chiefly as a deterrent to others who
would follow. It is rife not simply with contradictions, but with ab-
surdities, which serve mainly to give ammunition to the anti-
immigration lobby. Monica Bishop told me that not long ago, four
young women asylum seekers needed to be transported from a hostel in one part of Newcastle to a YMCA in another. The journey was
about two miles. But because the contract for transport by bus orig-
inates in Kent, a bus was sent from Ashford to Newcastle to take the
four passengers, a distance of over three hundred miles. The total
cost, she estimates, was around £1,000; a local taxi would have
charged £5.

Georgina Flexner is not, however, altogether discouraged.
What no one reckoned with, she says, are ordinary human feelings
of sympathy. The northeast, impoverished by unemployment since
the collapse of mining and the dockyards, its housing estates van-
dalized and shabby, has grown fond of the strangers drifting into
their city centers since 2000. Many of its inhabitants have found
themselves, against their expectations, enjoying the fact that members of ninety new nationalities have settled in their empty houses,
bringing with them new music, new customs, and even new food in
the markets. When, not long ago, the Beamish Museum decided to
draw asylum seekers closer into the community by offering two
busloads of them a free day's visit, there was outrage from the
British National party and some of the newspapers, but an equally
loud backlash from local people, who liked the idea of all these
Zimbabweans, Iraqis, and Sri Lankans inspecting Stevenson's
Rocket and early railway stock. Refugee families, expelled suddenly
as the result of a negative decision by the Home Office from
neighborhoods in which their children had grown up, faced with
deportation long after they had settled and put down roots, have
found vociferous champions for their cause among neighbors and
community groups. Georgina Flexner talks warmly of the enthusi-

asm of northern plans for integrating refugees. Willing to turn their hands to all forms of employment, bringing with them skills that might transform dying housing estates, these are the very people, as she sees it, who may contribute most to a new prosperity. Studies done in recent months have shown that 80 percent of asylum seekers in the northeast would chose to stay there, should they win the right to remain in Britain, providing they can find work and housing; they find the north friendlier, less intimidating than London. As she moves between local communities and the ever growing refugee population, Flexner observes how neatly balanced are the ancestral fears of losing England to a tide of foreigners, against the newer fear of seeing the northeast become a mere transit area.

. . .

EARLY IN 2004, the Home Office announced that the number of applicants for asylum in the UK was down by 40 percent, to 61,050. The government's delight was not shared by those who work with refugees: they view the growing restrictions with unease, and worry about all those people who, fearing rejection, are now not even bothering to try to make the journey to safety. Asylum specialists would like to see many changes, including the setting up of an independent documentation center, to provide reliable country information. They worry that the Home Office is paying far more attention to securing its borders and building up Fortress Europe than to making the system on the ground workable for those who manage it or supportable for those who live it, and that the government does little to counter the hostility fomented by the tabloids.

Lies, inaccuracies, exaggerations, untruths: this is the climate in which the current British asylum world lives, in which policy is made not so much on evidence as in response to media and public perception, and in which those seeking asylum, buffeted by the chaotic, contradictory, and discriminatory asylum procedures now in operation across the Western World, scramble for a toehold using any method they can. Not long ago, UN Secretary General Kofi Annan told the European Parliament that European anti-immigration rhetoric was "dehumanizing people." "This silent human rights crisis," he went on, "shames our world."

LITTLE BETTER THAN COCKROACHES

Guinea's Long-term Camps

Contemporary history has created a new kind of human
being—the kind that are put in concentration camps by
their foes and internment camps by their friends.

— HANNAH ARENDT

It was in 1958 that Sékou Touré, Guinea's first president, won independence from France and embarked on twenty-six years of socialist
dictatorship. Touré's isolationist views, and anger at them on the
part of De Gaulle and other Western leaders, effectively ensured
that all through the sixties, seventies, and eighties, Guinea remained
one of the most isolated of Africa's postcolonial countries, a distant,
shuttered land, with a small stretch of Atlantic coast and thousands
of square miles of semitropical forest, little touched by the material
and economic development that came to other parts of the continent. Even today, despite the forest region's many natural resources,
Guinea vies with Sierra Leone and Liberia—the three Mano River
Union countries of West Africa—for the title of the world's poorest
and least settled country. Her 7.5 million people are said to live on
less than a dollar a day.

The capital, Conakry, is an old-fashioned place, with its fringe of palm trees along the shore and a wind that blows constantly from the ocean. It is very hot and very humid and the city is growing fast, but outward, simply, poorly, in shantytowns that vanish into the distance, with few of the plate-glass-and-steel skyscrapers that mark other developing capitals.

Guinea's leaders since Touré have proved little more accepting of dissent: even today, twenty years after Touré's death, opposition politicans prefer to lie low during election time, and few of them are said to sleep in their own homes while polling takes place. A courageous Guinean professor of law, Dr. Thierno Maadjou Sow, has since 1995 been running the Organization Guinéenne des Droits de l'Homme, one of the country's handful of campaigning bodies. His dealings with the government are wary. *"Tout le monde ici,"* he told me when I first arrived in Conakry, *"a quelque chose à coeur.* We are all victims of terrible things." He was talking about his many colleagues and friends who have spent months and years in prison and who expect to spend many more there.

In the year 2000, thirty-three of the world's forty-one most indebted countries lay in Africa. Forty percent of the world's refugees, and 70 percent of its AIDS victims, were also African. In the early and mid-1990s, when civil war inside Liberia and Sierra Leone had turned some 7 million people into refugees, either displaced within their own countries or driven abroad into nearby ones, Guinea, a long fat country wrapped around its neighbors, had willingly absorbed one of the largest per capita refugee influxes in the world. Seven hundred thousand people—a tenth of Guinea's own population—had found shelter there, either within camps run and financed by the international community, or scattered around the country. As Guinea belongs to the West African Economic Community, Sierra Leoneans and Liberians, who also belong, are allowed to reside and work there. By the spring of 2003, according to official UNHCR figures, 185,000 refugees were being protected and cared for by Guinea, though the true figure, including new arrivals and those who for one reason or another had not been registered, was certainly far higher. Of all those now crossing over from Liberia and

Sierra Leone, 70 percent, over two thirds, I was told, were under the age of eighteen.

As Cairo's Liberian boys had left their roots along this rainy belt, having fled Charles Taylor and the rebel commanders either alone or with their families and crossed the nearest border to safety, Guinea seemed to be the place to go in search of them. A visit would give me, I thought, not just a clearer picture of what had driven them into exile in the first place, but a sense of what they had left behind. Some, like nearsighted Mamadu, working off his smuggler's fee in Tel Aviv, had spent many years here, in one of the long-term refugee camps at Guékédou, and I wanted to see for myself these camps, so established and so problematic. Izako, the customs officer forced to abandon his wife and small son and daughter in Monrovia, had told me that he believed that his family might have made their way into Guinea; by going there, I half hoped that I might find them.

In Guinea's *région forestière*, so I was told, I would see the gamut of African refugee life, the cycle in all its stages, from new arrivals to the residents of settled camps, indistinguishable, after long years, from the villages that surround them. In UNHCR's headquarters in Conakry hangs an immense map, marking with arrows and bands of color the flows of people around West Africa, making me think once again, as in San Diego, of the migratory paths of birds around the world. Along the southern borders of the area, where the forest runs for almost a thousand miles, there is a swath of red. This is refugee territory, refugees coming and going, crossing and recrossing borders, settling and dying, making lives and being moved on; it was there that I wished to go, to see for myself what Africa offered its moving populations.

. . .

THE CAMP OF Kuankan lies 700 miles from Conakry, in a clearing cut out of the semitropical forest that seems to stretch forever along this part of West Africa. It can be reached by flying to Nzerekore, the nearest town, either hitching a ride on the twice-weekly UN and aid agency plane on the rare occasion when one of the thirty seats is not taken by an aid worker, or taking one of the infrequent flights by a very ancient commercial plane. Then there is a long drive, at first along a new tarmac road laid by foreign funders to make the delivery of aid easier, then along a dark red-earth track between the tall teak and palm trees, the feathery acacias and deep green baobabs. The track is full of craters, deep crevices that become rivers when the rains come.

For a passenger lulled by the green, the denseness of the forest shade, the sudden clarity and light of the camp's great open space is startling. Here, in over two square miles of mud huts with thatched roofs, and in tarpaulin tents, live 33,000 refugees, all but a very few of them Liberians escaping Charles Taylor's long and murderous civil war. None of the Cairo Liberians had been to Kuankan, but all knew of friends here, and it was just possible that Izako's family might be among them. My visit was in March. With the start of the eight-month rainy season in February, water begins to soak through the thatch and the torn and patched tarpaulin above the refugees' heads, and in the bright sunshine and great heat of the morning of my first day in the camp, people were laying out their possessions to dry. The air was humid and absolutely still. It seemed an isolated, hermetic place.

In the autumn of 2002, Human Rights Watch sent a mission to these borders with Ivory Coast, Liberia, and Sierra Leone, where Guinea dips down into a narrow prong they call the Parrot's Beak. Researchers visited Kuankan. The report they came back with was alarming: it spoke of incursions by Liberian rebels and government forces over the border and as far as the camp, of complicity by Guinean soldiers and police, of forced recruitment of young refugees as boy soldiers and porters, of rape and looting. A third of the food eaten by the rebels in Liberia is said to have been stolen from camps like Kuankan. The picture painted by Human Rights Watch was disquieting, but it was not unexpected. Other reports written by similar organizations in recent years have dwelt on the violence and confusion now endemic along one of Africa's most permeable borders, where Sierra Leoneans, Liberians, and Ivorians cross regularly from country to country in response to the ebb and flow of war. In Kuankan, at any one time, there are Liberians who have gone back and forth into Guinea in response to the fighting; Sierra Leoneans who fled first into Liberia when the rebels began amputating the arms and legs of villagers to terrorize the country-side, and then fled again, into Guinea, as conflict pursued them; Ivo-rians who have spent much of their lives circling around the camps of West Africa. That many come from the same ethnic groups, for the most part Mandingo, Krahn, and Gio—the groups that I had heard so much about from the Liberians in Cairo—and speak the same language would make the fact of the border itself almost irrel-evant, were it not that soldiers from all sides use it to intimidate and plunder those who wish to cross. Simply crossing the frontier, with soldiers behind and predatory guards ahead, is a terrifying ordeal.

Reading the reports before I arrived, I had been struck mainly by the violence of these forest camps, the sense of constant vigilance, the almost casual brutality of a state of war that never seems to end. Listening to the young Liberians talking in Cairo, their long litany of loss and fear, I had expected unease, tension, a sense of anticipa-tion. What I actually saw, when I got there, was poverty.

Ordinary Guineans, for all the vast natural resources of their country, their diamonds and gold and bauxite, are poor in material things; Guinea has limited electricity, few roads, no train service or postal system, inadequate schools and health care. But the refugees are even poorer. Whether inside the camps or outside, they are so poor that in a literal way, they have nothing. Most of them do not even have a bucket, and they think about one and talk about one with longing. Some of the Liberians have been in Kuankan for over ten years, an entire lifetime in the case of the many small children who make up about a third of the camp's population. Poverty is very hard to describe. It is an absence, a nothingness. But the poverty of camp refugees is about more than just not having things; it is about having no way to get them, no means of altering or controlling one's own life. Their poverty curbs and crushes all hope and expectation. Kuankan's refugees are destitute of possibilities.

Kuankan has twelve sections, which are known as zones, as if a word so official could lend definition to a place of such sprawling sameness. Each zone reflects a wave of new arrivals, refugees from a fresh outbreak of fighting within a radius of perhaps a couple of hundred miles. The most recent consists of white tarpaulin tents on wooden frames, donated by Médecins Sans Frontières (MSF), each one the same, and each one divided into compartments for different families. The tents are set up in regular lines, at a certain distance one from the next. Zone 12 stands a little apart from the others, near the edge of the forest. Its first site, closer to the main body of the camp, was abandoned after last year's rains, when the red earth between the tents turned to deep mud and everything the refugees possessed became damp and encrusted. In the camp, there is fresh water, provided by one of the international agencies, but there was not enough to keep the children of Zone 12 free from the mud; by the end of each day they were streaked with red, slippery and wet.

At the time of my visit, Fatima was a recent arrival in Zone 12. She is a thin, tall woman in her early thirties, and she has five living children, two others having died in Liberia before she was forced to flee to Guinea last July. When I was taken to see her, by a refugee employed by the camp to guide the few visitors who make the journey into the forest, she was wearing a bright yellow sarong, her black hair pulled tightly back in the plaits many of the Liberians wear; her face is gaunt and bony, but she was brisk, without self-pity. One night, while the family slept in their house, the rebels attacked their village in Lofa county. Pulling three of her children behind her, carrying the two youngest on her back, the smallest still a baby, Fatima managed to get them all to the safety of the nearby forest. In the dark and the confusion, terrified by the sound of shots, she lost sight of her husband. She and her children stayed hidden for some days in the bush. I asked her what they ate. "Bananas," she said. "And some leaves and roots." From others who came to join them in the forest, she learned that her older brother had been killed and that her closest friend had been shot in the leg.

It took her ten days to reach the border, where she found people from UNHCR waiting to ferry the refugees in lorries to Kuankan. Médecins Sans Frontières has given her, along with her portion of a tent, which measures about ten square feet, a wooden frame bed, four mats, four blankets, two pots, and two bars of soap. Her entire home was too small for us to stand inside together. She pointed to a small pile of straw, neatly raked into one corner. Here, she said, two of the children, who can't fit in the bed, sleep. Not one of them has shoes. The middle girl, who is eight, has one set of clothes. It consists of an adult's T-shirt, and it is so full of holes that it hangs half off her body. She wears it as a dress. She has no pants. Both the baby, who is now two, and her older brother, who is four, are breastfeeding. Fatima's breasts are thin and withered, like those of a very old woman.

Like all the registered refugees in Kuankan, Fatima collects food rations each month from the UN's World Food Programme. Stored in sacks at the end of her wooden bed are bulgur, cornmeal, a little salt, some dried beans. There is an old tin with a few inches of peanut oil. In the most generous days of the early 1990s, the food package included rice, sugar, and tinned fish, but what Fatima showed me was the family's entire ration for a month. In the open spaces between the tents, some of the refugees have planted sweet potatoes. The growing cycle is too long to wait for the actual tubers to grow, but the leaves, which grow quickly, can be used to make a sauce for the bulgur. Neither Fatima nor her children like bulgur, which they had never eaten before they arrived in Kuankan, the staple grain of this part of West Africa being rice, but the refugees say that the World Food Programme has great stocks of bulgur, so bulgur is what they distribute. Later, I watched it being boiled up, in huge vats of glutinous porridge. Fatima has no other food, and no means of getting any, but she accepts without apparent envy those refugees in neighboring tents who somehow manage to buy pepper and dried fish from a market in a nearby village, or even some of the onions and tomatoes, most no larger than marbles, that are for sale near the entrance to the camp. No one has money for sugar, or milk, or tea, and she had not fed her children meat or fish or eggs since she left home nine months earlier. The five children, accustomed to the oranges and vegetables that grew in their garden in Liberia, to the chickens the family kept and to their eggs, are not doing well on their new diet. They miss the sugar and the fresh fruit.

Fatima has learned that her surviving brothers and sisters managed to escape and are now in another camp in Guinea, about seventy miles away, near the border with Ivory Coast, and that her parents are with them. She talks of the fact that they are alive with surprise and pleasure: she had not expected so much. Of her husband, who used to hunt small deer and wild pig in the forests around their village, she has had no news since the rebel attack in July.

Fatima's closest neighbor in the camp is Peter, an anxious and agitated former civil servant who comes from Liberia's Lofa County, which was home to almost half the young men who came as refugees to Cairo. The enforced inactivity of the camp has begun to weigh heavily on him. Escaping his burning village in the faint light of dawn in July 2002, carrying his youngest daughter in his arms, while his wife took the baby, he was unable to help his elderly parents. The last time he saw them was when he looked back over his shoulder as he ran into the forest: they were standing by their hut, watching helplessly. Peter is now haunted by the thought of what has become of them. In Kuankan, you seldom see anyone above the age of fifty; many of the older refugees who did set out on foot are said to have given up or died along the way.

At first, Peter believed that he would find some means of contacting his parents and arranging to have them brought out to safety with friends. He questioned new arrivals, sought out the aid officials in charge of the camp, pestered the refugee organizations. But as the months passed with no news, and people coming from Lofa reported no sign of the couple, he began to accept that they are probably now dead. He sits, day after day, in front of his small, hot tarpaulin tent, thinking about the past, in an agony of boredom and despair, looking out at the thick green forest where the refugees are not encouraged to roam, for, under the terms set by Guinea's president, they may not use the land to plant crops, nor hunt the wild pig and porcupine and deer said to be plentiful in the surrounding countryside.

"I wish, at least, we were learning," said the young interpreter, lent to me by the Liberians who manage some of the camp's basic functions. "It is the fact that we sit here declining that is so hard." This young woman, wife of an engineer with a mining company, fled for the second time from Liberia into Guinea in 2002, having spent the early 1990s in a refugee camp along the border. Her dress is Western and smart, and on her feet she wears flimsy sandals, as if to convince herself that she does not belong here. She picks her way through the rough muddy paths with difficulty. Once a cabaret singer in Monrovia's nightclubs, she has found occasional work as an interpreter in the camp with one of the aid agencies. Her husband, the mining engineer, helps the camp's carpenters. Her manner, though friendly, is distant and a little skeptical; a muddy refugee camp in the middle of a forest clearing is not where she planned to spend the middle years of her life, and not the place she now means to stay. With the passing of so much time, and with so little to do, expectations take on an urgent and uncomfortable dimension.

Fatima, with her five children and small tent, is perhaps luckier than some, for unlike many of Kuankun's inhabitants she has not spent her adult years as a refugee, going back and forth across West Africa's borders in search of safety. She and her family survived the first nine years of Liberia's civil war without being driven from home. Unlike most of her neighbors in Zone 12, this is her first experience of a camp. She takes this reduction in her life calmly, preferring to focus on a few very specific thoughts: she worries that her children may not be growing as they should, on the bulgur that they find so hard to eat and on a diet deprived of everything that has a taste they know or like; and she fears that she will not be able to send the older children to the school run by an international agency in the camp, because they have no clothes and no shoes in which to go. She wonders how she can acquire the things she most needs: a bucket, a lamp and some kerosene, a mattress, and one more blanket. And, just occasionally, she dreams of getting hold of a bouillon cube, to give the bulgur some flavor.

In the daytime, and for much of the night, the tarpaulin tent is stiflingly hot; the children sweat and turn in their sleep in the long hours of darkness, when the camp is lit only by cooking fires and the occasional kerosene lamps of the more fortunate refugees. I could only imagine the scene. Night falls in Guinea at about seven, and it does not grow light until twelve hours later. There is no electricity in Kuankan, and no generator, and, with the fighting so close, and the regular incursions of rebels and soldiers from across the border, no foreigners are allowed to remain in the camp after nightfall. It is then, say the refugees, when it grows dark, that the presence of rebel fighters, come to visit their families in the camp, or in search of food for themselves and their companions, becomes apparent. I tried to picture Fatima and her children in the dark, with the forest thick and black not far from their tent, and the quiet footsteps of people coming softly from behind the trees. I thought how frightening it must be for the parents of young boys, waiting for armed men come to prey on their sons, wondering if they would ever feel safe again.

I wondered too, if the fighters ever came into the camp as they are said to dress for battle, in women's frocks and long wigs, their faces painted white or hidden by masks. These grotesque outfits gave Liberia's seven-year civil war its macabre reputation and made commentators speculate that, together with Somalia and Rwanda, Liberia was evidence that Africa had turned its back on progress and was sinking into barbarity and superstition. Faced with apparitions like these, with men of war said to eat the hearts of their vanquished enemies in order to draw strength from them, for whom the invisible world of the spirits is a far more potent force than that of humankind, Fatima might well keep her children very close to her after the hours of darkness.

* * *

THOUGH THE PRECISE origins of Liberia's savagery lie in a complicated web of politics and plunder, the events that ultimately drove Fatima and her neighbors in Kuankan into exile, and the band of young men I knew to Cairo, began with the death of Samuel Doe, Liberia's twenty-first president, on September 10, 1989, at the hands of a psychopathic warlord called Prince Johnson, a good-looking man with a charming smile. Liberia was the first emergency in Africa after the end of the Cold War, coming soon after the dismantling of the Berlin Wall and Saddam Hussein's invasion of Kuwait. To understand something of the nature of Kuankan, something of the camp's past and its continuing existence, the way it has become a place of refuge for people buffeted by a civil war that never seems to end, and how it has for many of them taken the place of everything that went before, I had to learn about Liberia. Where refugees come from and what conditions turned them into exiles is often something that people do not want to know. In Cairo, talking to the Liberian boys, I had learned about massacres and heard the names of rebel leaders; I had also begun to understand about the value of the past as a passport that cannot be taken away. Looking around Kuankan it was impossible not to ask: for this to be acceptable, what had happened at home?

Samuel Doe had been a master sergeant in the Liberian army. A small, burly man who sported an American military beret, he was, for a while at least, a protégé of the United States; he came to power in a coup in 1980, after which he executed thirteen leading members of the former government on the beach at Monrovia. Of Liberia's sixteen official tribes, Doe favored the Mandingo, descendants of the ruling dynasty of medieval Mali and now inhabitants of Guinea's forest region; he took up against the Gio and the Mano and slaughtered them. Despite his appalling human rights record and the widespread knowledge that he was embezzling millions of dollars from Liberia's rich diamond and gold resources, Doe continued to be supported by the United States, for whom Liberia had been a steady provider of rubber—to counter Britain's monopoly—since the 1920s.

Liberia, land of the free, was invented by the United States in 1847 as a place to send freed slaves, mainly from Ghana. For over a century, power lay with an oligarchy, American-descended, Christian, literate in English, and enjoying American-style institutions and American bank loans. In the late 1980s, nearby Burkina Faso became a rallying point for exiled Liberians, who, funded by Qaddafi's plans to train revolutionaries for his pan-African dreams, plotted to overthrow Doe with the help of neighboring Sierra Leone and Ivory Coast. Among these plotters was another psychopath, Charles Taylor, who numbered among his disaffected followers adults as well as many young children, pressed into "small boy units." At one point, 20,000 out of the country's 75,000 fighters were children. Though it was the warlord Johnson who closed in on Monrovia and cut off Doe's ears before parading him in his underpants in a wheelbarrow through the streets, it was Charles Taylor who, in control of much of the country, was able to make the deals and secure the dollars with which to buy arms and followers. Between 1990 and 1994, $75 million a year was said to have made its way into Taylor's war coffers through taxes levied on diamond exports, timber, rubber, gold, and iron ore, as well as the marijuana that he supplied to his child soldiers. Taylor might never, of course, have been so successful, had it not been for the fortuitous timing of the first Gulf War, which drew American attention away from Liberia and let in a corrupt Nigerian-led international force called ECOMOG, who themselves plundered at will, providing arms to those warlords most open to their deals.

During the worst years of the civil war, between 1990 and 1997, Charles Taylor's irregular forces, in weird and fantastic outfits and fueled by greed, revenge, ethnic rivalry, and drugs, went on frenzies of looting, Rambo style. They had developed a taste for Western possessions and they used drugged children to man checkpoints that became infamous for casual murder and theft. All Liberians in exile have a particular fear and horror of checkpoints; it was at a checkpoint, for instance, that Mohamed saw his godmother's head hacked off and used as a football by the rebels. Headless corpses appeared in the streets of Monrovia. Not surprising, then, that Liberia's people fled. In a single year, 700,000 left the country, for the most part taking little or nothing with them. All through the 1990s, Liberians crossed into Ivory Coast and Sierra Leone, and into Guinea, where first hundreds, then thousands, then tens of thousands settled in Kuankan and similar camps along the forest, where they were poor but at least safe. And the longer the war went on, the more the splits and factions multiplied—to be manipulated and engineered by ECOMOG, which dealt in looted resources and teak and other valuable hardwood—and the more refugees fled.

The trouble was not, of course, just in Liberia. Though the *région forestière* of Guinea shelters mainly Liberians, there are many other Africans there, too. The 1990s were barely more peaceful in Sierra Leone, a largely Muslim former British colony that emerged from three decades of one-party rule only to descend into a ten-year civil war, triggered by an invasion of disaffected Sierra Leoneans from Liberia. Sierra Leone's own war would see executions, abductions, rapes, and at least 100,000 people mutilated by having limbs amputated; whole neighborhoods of Freetown were set alight, often with their residents inside.

By 1997, when Charles Taylor brought his own kind of peace to Liberia, there were said to be 7 to 8 million firearms in West Africa, transferred from one area to another as conflicts developed. UN investigators have discovered a network of arms brokers and transport companies leading back to Slovakia, Moldova, Ukraine, and Kyrgyzstan. The heady mixture of greed, ethnic tensions, ruthless warlords, and the conviction that power has its roots in the invisible world and that man's destiny can be revealed through marabouts, soothsayers, priests, and "heartsmen" (providers of human hearts) had effectively created a generation of refugees, driven to choose between starvation, life in a camp, or death at the hands of marauding soldiers dressed as women. "I identified with those crazy people," a former government official and later employee of a foreign food agency told a journalist. "We all wear masks. Behind those masks is a mad, horrified people."

When, on July 19, 1997, an exhausted people voted Charles Taylor, the most successful warlord of them all, into the presidency, the flow of Liberian refugees into neighboring countries briefly stopped, and UNHCR and the international aid agencies turned their attention to the consequences of the fighting within Sierra Leone, where rebel forces against the government were now cutting off the arms and legs of their own citizens and driving abroad those who survived. These horrors fueled further speculation that what was now being seen was a taste of the future: desperate, deracinated youths driven into frenzied wars by environmental degradation, vast movements of the population from countryside to city, and high birthrates. Not everyone agreed; the critics of the "new barbarism" idea argued that, on the contrary, war was always war, whether fought with machetes or smart bombs, and that these West African wars were not different but only cheaper. For a while, in Liberia, it seemed as if peace might even be made to work. Taylor's victory in the presidential elections, closely observed by international experts, was accepted as generally legitimate. But not for long. By the spring of 2002, Liberia's fragile five-year peace was coming to an end and rebel forces were once again challenging Taylor's rule; new men of war "with no contrite hearts" and no compassion were again looting, raping, and murdering. The insecurity was worsened still further by violent xenophobia in Côte d'Ivoire, where leading government officials were inciting ethnic and religious hatred, and security forces were targeting victims, mainly in the Muslim north. Liberian refugees from the looting, the abductions, and the burning of villages were again on the move, Fatima and her five children among them. As people fled north into Guinea, Liberian government soldiers and rebels were moving west into Sierra Leone, to abduct fighters and recruit mercenaries for the next stage in their war.

These, then, are the causes of Fatima's flight, and the flight of Peter her neighbor, and that of the Liberians in Cairo: violence, loss, grief in comparison with which the uncertain waiting of the camp takes on a different aspect.

· · ·

BENEDICT IS FIFTEEN, a lively, slender boy, watchful and old for his years. He is one of Kuankan's large population of single, unaccompanied children, the term by which the aid world designates children who have lost their families. When Benedict was thirteen, fighting broke out in Liberia's Lofa County, which borders Guinea, and whose contours I had grown to know from the stories of the Liberians in Cairo. As soon as his family heard that both the rebels and the government forces were looking for boys to take as soldiers, they sent him into the bush to hide. All the other villagers, watchful of the approaching trouble, sent their young sons, too. In the bush, the boys quickly learned to survive. They found yams and plantains, and cooked them over a small open fire, cautiously so as not to attract attention with the smoke, and they added these to the food brought out from the village from time to time by their parents. Weeks passed, and still the rebels were known to be in the area. One of the boys fell ill from something he had eaten; after a few days he died. Messengers from the village came to tell them that it was still not safe to go home.

Then, very early one morning, Benedict woke to see smoke rising on the horizon, from the direction of his village. It was too far away to see more than wisps of white against the blue of the sky, and too far to hear any sounds, but later that day villagers appeared and told of a rebel attack. The smoke on the horizon grew thicker and new arrivals described their huts being set alight; many of the occupants, they reported, had been herded inside and burned to death. Next morning, a neighbor of Benedict's arrived in the boys' camp. He told Benedict that his parents, his younger brother, and his elder sister had all been burned to death inside their house.

It took Benedict and some of the other boys orphaned in the rebel attack four days to reach the border with Guinea; fortunately, they had no difficulty surviving on foraged roots and fruit. Like Fatima, Benedict was welcomed by UNHCR and eventually taken to Kuankan by truck. Offered the chance to live as a foster child with another refugee family, he asked to be allowed to live on his own, preferring the independence he had learned in the bush. Once a month, together with the others, he collects his dried rations from WFP, which he cooks for himself, together with a few onions, sweet potatoes, and peppers that he has planted next to his hut. What he has left over, he sells, and buys dried fish and sugar. However much he saves, he is never able to afford a second set of clothes or a pair of shoes. When he arrived in Kuankan a year ago, the Guinean Red Cross gave him a T-shirt and a pair of shorts. Since he owns nothing else, he cannot wash them and is now embarrassed when he goes to school in such ragged and dirty clothes, though nothing will keep him from class. He wants, he says, to become a scientist. Because of the school, if for no other reason, he believes that the camp life is better than the one he was leading in the bush, though he says that he is hungry at the end of every month, just before the rations arrive. He does not like to talk about his parents or the past.

It is not easy to care for all these lost and orphaned children, those who saw their parents hacked to death or watched their homes burn down, those who were separated from their families during flight and cannot find them again, or were abducted and forced to do things as child soldiers that they are now too ashamed to confront. In the spring of 2003, there were just over 1,500 of these separated children in Kuankan. Some of them are babies and children so small that they do not know their own names, so they cannot say where they came from. Other refugees found them abandoned along the route toward the border, picked them up and carried them, and later gave them to UNHCR to care for. Photographs of these children are posted throughout the camps of West Africa, in the hopes that someone will recognize and claim them. I wondered whether Izako's son and daughter might be among them, and whether, not having seen them for so long, he would recognize them now. They made me think of the posters of small, nameless children separated from their parents in the European exoduses that followed World War II; their photos hung in post offices and stations throughout liberated Europe in 1946, as 40 million displaced Europeans wandered in search of what had been or could again be home.

Throughout Guinea, the task of caring for the separated children falls to one of the most impressive of the international aid organizations, the International Rescue Committee, which, as implementing partner for UNHCR, runs the entire educational program of the camps. Christian, who is in charge of the separated children, has eighteen local offices and a staff of 127, who act as tracers and social workers; when parents are found, the children are driven or even flown to join them. These reunions can be terrifying for the children, particularly for those long separated from their families and shocked by all that they have experienced and seen. Boy soldiers, in particular, face the prospect of rejection, if not by their parents then by people from their villages, against whom they have sometimes been forced to perform acts of great cruelty. Not long ago, Christian, whose office is in Conakry, arranged for a young boy called Sekou to be repatriated together with some of the Sierra Leoneans going home. He knew that the boy's parents were alive, and despite Sekou's evident reluctance, persuaded him to try to live with his family again. A few weeks later, Sekou was back, having walked through the bush for ten days to return to Conakry and the safety of the children's center. When he was eleven, Sekou had been kidnapped by the rebels. As a boy soldier he had been ordered to lock some people from his own village into their hut and set fire to it. The survivors of his community would not accept him back, and for his parents the shame of what he had done was too great for them to take him in.

The size of the task facing Christian, and the delicate complexity of its demands, became clear to him not long ago when he heard about two refugee children living in a village just inside the border. He set off to find them, driving one of the white Toyota Land Cruisers that have become the hallmark of international aid the world over. On making inquiries, he discovered that there were another 205 separated children in the same village, having stopped there as they fled the war in Liberia, and now stuck as a kind of indentured labor force for the Guinean villagers, who see nothing wrong in using these young children to work in their fields and houses in return for food and lodging. If there were 207 lost children in a single border village, Christian reasoned, then how many more must there be in other villages, where their escapes had been brought to a halt by hunger? Few of the children had ever heard about the refugee camps, and none knew what they were for or how to find them.

Finding ways of tracing these lost children's families, ensuring that in the meantime they are safe and not exploited, persuading the families who have taken them in and are benefitting from the work they do that the children would be better off in the camps is a time-consuming and complicated process. In eighteen months, Christian and his staff have found 7,500 separated children along the border and in Conakry. These children were all traveling absolutely alone. The true number of the separated may be three or even four times as high, for it is widely accepted that somewhere between 5 and 7 percent of children who become refugees from war are separated from their families in flight. How many die on the way, too tired or hungry or frightened to go on, no one can say.

In Conakry, in a shabby building with a large inner courtyard shaded by mango trees, Christian runs a transit center for children who are on their way to be reunited with their families, or whose problems are so acute as to make camp life too hard. He keeps it intentionally shabby, and the dormitories have bare foam mattresses on the floor and ragged sheets: he does not want the children to see the place as anything but the most temporary pause, between a past that they are putting behind them, and a return to their families and a new life. It must not, he insists, become home. There are no toys and few books. The boys fashion cars out of old tins, ingenious contraptions of wire and cotton reels and flattened bits of metal, which clatter around the concrete at the end of strings.

In spite of the center's transitory nature, Abu and his three brothers have been there for over a year, waiting for papers that will allow them to join an uncle in the United States. The boys are the sons of a prosperous and influential businessman and politician, a man much envied and much disliked, according to Abu, in their small town in Port Loco in Sierra Leone. When the rebels reached the town in 1997, his father was one of the first to be surrendered and killed. Their mother, eight months pregnant at the time, was shot and killed while struggling to squeeze out of a back window of their house with the younger children. The nine children, three of them by the politician's second wife, who had died in childbirth some months before, were caught and tied up. Abu's eldest brother was asked where their father kept his money. He did not know. So the rebels cut off first one of his hands, and then, when he still said nothing, the other. Abu's father had confided in him alone out of all the children; when his turn came, he led the soldiers to a hiding place in another house. While the men were clearing out the money, he managed to untie the other children and run off into the bush. He lost sight of his two sisters and two of his brothers, including the one whose hands had been amputated. When it was clear that they would not be able to go home, he set out through the bush with the four younger boys, carrying the smallest, then only two, on his back.

Once across the border, encountering no UNHCR officials, Abu stopped at the nearest village and asked for help. A farmer agreed to take in the boys and feed them in return for work. Every day, Abu, then aged twelve, worked in the house and in the market, before going out into the cassava fields. One day, many months later, he heard about the camps; he set off again with his little brothers, eventually reaching Guékédou, the large camp for Liberians run by UNHCR. They had not been there very long when the camp itself was attacked by rebels coming across the border, and in a skirmish one of his brothers was killed. Abu took the surviving boys and set out again, only to be rounded up by the Guinean military, who accused them of being boy soldiers with the rebels. Eventually released, they made their way to Conakry, where they were found by Christian.

Only Abu can now remember their parents, though his twelve-year-old brother has a vague memory of their village and life before the war. The four boys sleep together on two mattresses pushed together, waiting for the moment when they may be sent to America. Two other brothers who share their room are also waiting to know their future. After many inquiries, Christian discovered that these two small boys' father was alive and living in Chicago, having escaped Liberia early in the war and gone on to make a life as a lawyer in the States. Their mother had died in the fighting. But their father has taken a new wife, a woman considerably younger than himself, and by whom he has two new children. Christian has written repeatedly but the letters that come back are vague; and to his last one there has been no answer at all. Some of the children who arrive at the transit center do not speak. They listen, and will do what they are told to do, but they will not talk. It can take several months, says Christian, for them to say a single word.

Before I left Conakry, I asked Christian to look out for Izako's children, and I gave him a little money for the center. He seemed pleased. We drove slowly back into the center of town, in a traffic jam of overflowing communal taxis and decrepit trucks; the extreme humidity of the day was giving way to cooler evening. The money, Christian told me, would go toward food for an evening of remembrance for Muna who had died two weeks before. Muna was twelve years old; Christian thought that she had died of AIDS. He had found her living in the house of an elderly Guinean shopkeeper. Neighbors had told him that Muna had only been fed when she agreed to sleep with the man, and that once, after she had tried to run away, she had been kept locked in a cupboard for two days. At the transit center, the other children had asked to have a party at which to remember her.

. . .

KUANKAN IS JUST one camp, along a border crowded with settlements that have shifted, opened, closed, opened again as fighting has ebbed and flowed up and down the *région forestière*. On December 6, 2000, as it was growing light, the small market town of Guékédou, a few hours' drive from the camp of Kuankan, was attacked by rebel soldiers coming across the border from Sierra Leone and Liberia and up into the Parrot's Beak. It wasn't the first attack in the area—rebels and government soldiers from both countries had been making forays into Guinea all through the autumn—and it would not be the last. In the months that followed, many Guineans and refugees were killed in sudden incursions of fighters. In Guékédou, in December, the inhabitants fought back, anxious to defend their town, and soon the Guinean army arrived with reinforcements. When the locals seemed to be making little progress against the attackers, when they had been forced to allow the rebels to occupy a village nearby for several weeks, the army sent in helicopters, which machine-gunned the central market square in Guékédou, having been informed that among the crowds were many Liberian and Sierra Leonean soldiers. The townspeople scattered and took to the bush. By evening the town was practically empty.

Guékédou happened at the time to be a base for UNHCR's eastern operations in Guinea, and several large houses and offices had been built to accommodate a substantial number of expatriate and local staff. There were also new offices and houses for the people working for the many international organizations that make up the aid constellation. It was a bustling, purposeful place. On the first day of fighting, UNHCR's office was destroyed. Then one of their staff was killed in Macenta, not far away, shot by rebels as they retreated along the road on which he lived. Another UNHCR employee was abducted, though later he was released alive. Seeing no signs of a quick end to the fighting, UNHCR ordered its staff to pull out of the area and retreat, in their Land Cruisers and trucks, to Kissidougou, a town farther from the border.

Until that autumn, Guinea had appeared to be a place of safety for West Africa's refugees. The Guinean government had been allowing the Liberian rebels to use the refugee camps as bases; now, the armed incursions looked like Liberian government reprisals for that support. Guinea's president, Lansana Conté, made a speech in which he called on his people to defend their country against all invaders. Widely reported in the papers and broadcast over the radio, his words were seen as signs of a tough new stand against the refugees. The Liberians and Sierra Leoneans in the camps, declared President Conté, were supporting the fighters with food and arms. They should either go home or be confined to the camps, and in any case they should be controlled. Refugees were, he added, little better than cockroaches.

In the days that followed, Guineans formed vigilante groups to harass the refugees. Previously harmonious relations between Guineans and their country's vast foreign population were soured by attacks and accusations. There were large numbers of casualties. When the fighting died down, UNHCR and the international agencies took stock. One request made by President Conté was that the camps should be pulled back from the border areas, to make their use as rebel bases harder. Since the aid agencies no longer felt it to be safe to leave staff in such troubled places, they closed up operations around Macenta and Guékédou—at the time, UNHCR's largest branch office in Africa—and opened up new camps about 200 miles farther north, around Albadaria.

Early in 2003, I drove through Guékédou, to see what remained of the camps that had been home to 400,000 Liberian refugees for almost six years. Mamadu, the boy who as an eleven-year-old had been dragged away by rebels from his parents and four younger brothers and sisters, had spent six years in a camp in Guékédou. He had, he said, been happy here. There is now almost no trace of it left. The sea of tarpaulin that once stretched across the plain as far as the eye could see has gone, as if it had never been there. The tents and huts have long since been pulled down, and the surrounding land has reverted to savannah and forest; only a few of the more solid international offices still stand, but they are empty and abandoned, with the look of mildew and imminent collapse that comes quickly to these rainy areas. Guékédou itself is now poor and run-down, the fine houses lived in by the expatriate staff shuttered and derelict. Not long ago, an aid worker from Kissidougou visited Guékédou to discuss the possibility of setting up a small education project in the town. The mayor greeted her with great caution. He would not wish the proposal to go ahead, he told her, unless the foreign investors were prepared to appoint a number of foreign resident staff and open a proper office. Guékédou simply could not risk a second economic collapse. It was a mark of what prosperity the refugees, however poor, bring.

Kissidougou, meanwhile, is booming. It is here that the aid organizations have settled, and built themselves offices and air-conditioned houses around central courtyards, behind tall gates. They have brought generators, provided Internet access and e-mail, and improved the roads. At night, after dark, they gather in the Hotel Savannah to eat, drink beer, and talk over their day, parking their identical white Land Cruisers in rows outside the door. The food is good, with distant memories of the French who once occupied this part of West Africa, and there is plenty of beer. The night I ate there, there was *steak au poivre* on the menu, and *poulet chasseur.* In Kissidougou there are doctors from Médecins Sans Frontières, logisticians and protection officers from UNHCR, sanitation experts, community workers, teachers and water engineers, men and women from several dozen different countries for whom the sense of purpose and adventure that comes with aid work offsets the punishing humidity and constant attacks of malaria and diarrhea. At dinner, I was introduced to a woman from the Southern Illinois Trauma Center. She is in Kissidougou, she told me, to train refugees to counsel and otherwise help those among them who have been tortured. "Just do it," reads the logo on the Nike sports cap worn by many of the foreign workers. I had known from Izako that his wife and children were not in Kuankan, but I had hoped to find some trace of them in Kissidougou. No one knew of them, and their names were not on UNHCR's lists.

• • •

UNHCR IS AT its most impressive when conducting the emergency operations for which it is best known. Long-term situations—camps that endure year after year—are not its strong suit, and much of their administration is sensibly left to implementing partners. These include the IRC, which besides providing for separated children organizes much of the education in the camps, and Médecins Sans Frontières. All are aware of the envy that local people understandably feel over the relatively generous help given to the refugees; in keeping with current thinking, efforts are made to integrate and widen services wherever possible. The challenge is made easier in Guinea, where refugees and the surrounding people speak the same language and poverty is universal. Among the experts I passed along the tracks through the forest, hastening between camps and villages, were community and welfare officers, development experts and environmental consultants, come to improve conditions throughout the entire forest region. Refugees as "agents of development" has been a catchphrase since the early 1970s, when it was first noted that relief and emergency assistance, leading to dependency, were an increasing burden to the countries that took refugees in, but not much progress has been made. UNHCR is not a development agency, and other organizations have been reluctant to undertake expensive projects promoting self-sufficiency, particularly since refugee aid and development have none of the urgency and drama of emergencies, and funds are hard to come by.

Just as it is not easy to care for separated children, whose lonely migration has left them troubled and uncertain, so it is not easy to attract foreigners to work for very long in Guinea. The constant humidity and endemic diseases, the sense of insecurity and lawlessness, and the widespread disinclination to stir up trouble, lest worse be unleashed, leaves permanent posts unfilled or quickly abandoned. Short-term missions are greatly preferred. The idealism that drew many into the work has long since given way to despondency, thanks to the endless cutting of corners as funds eat into already meager supplies and the logistics of caring for so many people with so few resources become more intractable day by day. The very nature of the daily issues—the arrival of insufficient quantities of tarpaulin, the axing of nonfood items from the basket of provisions for each registered refugee, the quarreling and rivalries of people reduced to so little—induces inertia and exhaustion. Guinea, one aid worker told me, has the reputation of being the worst country in the world in which to work.

Conakry itself has little to offer either foreigners or refugees, of whom between five and six thousand are said to live in the capital's poorer quarters, harrassed by their Guinean neighbors and prey to demands for bribes. For these refugees who do not wish to live in the camps, there is very little that UNHCR can do, beyond offering them a measure of protection against detention or *refoulement*. Danger, insecurity, is something everyone refers to, but they use the words "fluid" and "vulnerability," as if the risks were made more manageable by softer language. David Kapya, who in 2003 was running the UNHCR office in Conakry, compares refugee flows to a bush fire that may spread at any time and that has to be contained and dealt with. Kapya's language is about the movement of populations, the raising of grants, the delicate administration of 200,000 desperate and confused people. He has little time for global policies.

Not long ago, in keeping with the world's declining budget for UNHCR and more pressing needs elsewhere, there were calls for cuts in spending in Guinea. Already pressed to the edges of necessity, UNHCR had no choice but to pare away at inessentials: an end to the occasional tins of sardine or bars of soap distributed in the camps, a cutback in adult education and prevention programs for gender-based violence. But with the borders officially closed—though unofficially passable—who knows what new crisis may be bottled up beyond the confines of the camps, deep inside the forest areas that no one visits? The head of UNHCR's Nzerekore office is a Peruvian, Cesar Ortega, who has run refugee programs in many parts of the world. Contemplating the bridges and crossing points along the many miles of frontier, he waits and worries. "Sometimes," he says, "I am lost. I think of all the people out there, who may be waiting to come in."

In 2001, a scandal erupted in the enclosed world of Guinea's camps. Refugees, who live so close to the surface of life, constantly alert to the possible fulfillment of wishes and needs, are particularly vulnerable to exploitation, so the news that a team of researchers doing a report on the protection of refugee children had discovered that women and young girls were being sexually exploited by other refugees and aid workers alike came as no great surprise to the foreign community. But the scale of the activity and the implications were shocking. It became clear that prostitution, in the sense of bargaining the bare necessities of life in return for sex, had become endemic in places where small items—a few fish, a pair of shoes, a pretty scarf—can transform a meager daily life into something with light and color. Where people have nothing, even a bouillon cube acquires a powerful lure. In the soul-searching and recriminations that followed, seven teachers were dismissed from Kuankan's schools. When challenged, they reacted with surprise. "This is Africa," they said. "This is our way." Like the Guinean families providing the separated Liberian children with a refuge in return for work, they appeared genuinely astonished at the fuss. What the inquiry also brought out, more worryingly, was the extent of the sexual coercion and outright rape visited on refugee women all along the forest region and on their long journeys to find safety—including rape by aid workers.

UNHCR, and in particular the High Commissioner, Ruud Lubbers, were not thought to have handled the situation well, initially dismissing it a little lightly. But later, realizing the extent to which any scandal of this kind is damaging to the entire aid world, Lubbers set up a department in the Geneva headquarters to investigate all allegations of misconduct within UNHCR. In 2002, 125 separate complaints were explored, from corruption to harassment. More important perhaps, the scandal raised disquieting questions about the harm that humanitarian intervention can unthinkingly bring in its wake.

Not all Kuankan's refugees find it easy to accept the invisible line that keeps them in the camp, free and yet not free, dependent always on the whim and charity of others, enclosed in poverty few can see any way to escape, beholden at every step to foreigners who have apparently boundless power yet are often curiously pedantic and ungenerous. Something of the anger simmering among people condemned to permanent inactivity and supplication found expression not long ago in a teachers' strike. Mary, the head of education for the International Rescue Committee, is a brisk and purposeful American in her fifties from Seattle, who, having climbed in Tibet, felt the moment had come in her life to pay something back for the pleasures she had enjoyed. What an administrator and former Peace

Corps worker had to offer was schooling. IRC gave Mary a job.

Mary has 1,200 teachers and their assistants under her, having won a battle to include a woman assistant in every classroom as a way of protecting and encouraging girl pupils. Classes have seventy to eighty students, and it is often a struggle to keep them functioning. The few schoolbooks go missing and have to be coaxed back with threats and the help of sorcerers; new pupils pop up unexpectedly in class, having been sent over the border from nearby Liberian villages now that education has collapsed in Liberia with the renewed fighting, and many students are far behind their ages and abilities. Mary is acutely conscious that she is running programs that she herself has never been present to see work, like all the evening education classes. These begin after dark, long after she, as a foreigner, is obliged to leave the camps. She is also extremely aware that the children under her care would do far better in small classes in which they could overcome their fears. She was in her office in Nzerekore when she was informed that the teachers had gone on strike in Kuankan. "Though it seemed to be about pay," she says, "it was really about anger. That was all I heard when I went to talk to them. 'We have no dignity' was what they said. 'Why can't we have a plot on which to grow some food? Why will no one give us seeds?' Some of these people have been in Kuankan for ten years. They feel abandoned. They don't feel like real people anymore. Our intentions are good, but we do nothing for their self-esteem. It doesn't make me feel good to belong to a system that so diminishes people. So I talked to them about hope and the future and, even if I am a teacher, I began to think of ways to find them seed and hoes. These people are farmers. If you devaluate and demotivate them, what will happen to their children?" What struck the aid workers trying to resolve the strike was that some of the teachers had gone above their heads, written directly to the headquarters of UNHCR in Geneva, taken the law, as it were, into their own hands. It seemed to some of the aid workers bold, even a little impertinent. To Mary, it was an excellent sign. It suggested that the teachers were taking control over their own lives. But the ambivalence of the relationship between helper and helped is never far below the surface.

No one really believes in camps, not in the sixty or so camps in Guinea, not in the camps dotted all over the world, wherever refugees are on the move. Neither those who care for refugees, nor the people who live in them, regard them as more than temporary constructs, meant to be holding facilities until something better is worked out. The skills at which UNHCR excels, the creating and designing of these tented cities, lose their edge as months turn into years, and something of the early bustle and energy is lost in the apathy and unhappiness of unresolved situations. Once the humane and efficient answer to crises, now forgotten by funders and resented by their hosts, these camps have become places where people wait, and where they do not want to be. Jason Scarpone, the new country director of IRC, shares Mary's longing to see more integration and development, more boosting of local economies, and less pursuit of unending crises. Like most of the new players in the international refugee world, he talks, with passion, about refugees as agents of development and the importance of widespread income generation.

Yet more than 3 million people in Africa today live in what have come to be called protracted refugee situations, long-lasting and intractable limbos in which dispossessed people are sequestered, concentrated, and kept out of danger as most closely suits host governments, the international community, and often the refugees themselves, who feel safe in the company of others in the same position in a strange land. Camps are places dealt with by other people. However, camps are also profoundly destructive places. More fundamentally even than prisons, they deny all freedoms, even the freedom to make the most basic choice. Those who service them do so humanely and with certain standards in mind, but in practice these standards are extremely low. In practice, too, as an evaluation report produced by UNHCR in 2003 concluded, the "circumstances and conditions" of these refugees are deteriorating all the time, as conflict becomes endemic and asylum ever more unpopular, and as the refugees themselves turn into pawns in larger political games.

In Africa "protracted refugee situations" are to be found where the land is poorest, the climate harshest, the conditions least hospitable. Though agreements in Burundi, the Congo, Sudan, and elsewhere may bring a measure of peace, violence has become a way of life for a generation of young Africans. And Kuankan, like the other camps up and down the forest, is full of children, single women, and adolescents. As world attention shifts away from them, toward new, more imperative crises, so do money and rights—rights to move about, to have a proper legal status, to freedom of choice, to an education. The camp dwellers feel truly forgotten. It was this world, of camps without seeming futures, so poor that even a bucket spelled riches, that Suleiman and Mamadu, Mohamed and Musa had all turned their backs on when forced to flee the war in Liberia. However terrifying the journey, however unpredictable the future, staying in a camp was not an option any of them considered bearable. Although I had not found Izako's family, I had seen the conditions under which, somewhere along the *région forestière*, they were probably living; and I had come to understand better the desperation of the Liberians in Cairo, their ferocious need for education, for another life, in a better place.

The tragedy for Fatima and Peter and their neighbors goes well beyond the refugees to Guinea itself, its present and its long unfinished business with the past. Guinea, as a country, is neither poor nor without possibilities. It is a fertile and rich land, in which four of Africa's major rivers rise. Its economy stagnant, its borders under constant assault, its population swollen by huge numbers of refugees it has neither the resources nor the desire to care for, it is not flourishing.

．　．　．

IN KUANKAN, I asked about depression, whether people so long frightened and displaced showed signs of deep sadness and apathetic despair. At the far end of the camp, in a single-story brick building, is a mental health clinic, opened in 2002 by a Norwegian agency. It is run by a Liberian former nurse, Sophie. In 2003, the UN carried out a survey of the health of the refugees in the forest regions and concluded that 12 percent suffered from some degree of clinical depression. Sophie rejects the figure as grossly low.

In Kuankan, Sophie explains, depression is described by a curious phrase, brought by the Liberians from home. Any profound lowering of the spirits goes by the name of "open mole," meaning the fontanelle, on the crown of the head, where the skull does not fuse shut for some weeks after a baby's birth. In later life, as Sophie's patients tell her, this hole can open once again and let in depression.

Sophie's treatment is simple. She asks an herbalist attached to the clinic to cut the patient's hair, clean the head, and rub in herbal potions; she herself provides paracetamol and counseling. But what she really does is listen. Behind every open mole, as she is very aware, lies a terrible tale of rape, loss, violence. As the story unfolds, the mole is felt to close. The day comes when the patient appears proudly in the clinic to announce that the gap has gone.

· · ·

THE REFUGEES KEEP coming. In the far east of Guinea, there are twenty crossing points from the Ivory Coast, and nearly as many from Liberia; but there is often little, in this hilly, densely forested countryside, to mark a frontier. At Thio, a path winds away through a clearing down toward a patch of forest, with the river beyond. It is hard to write about the richness and thickness of this tall forest, or the variety of the leaves that spread out like giant hands or whispery feathers over the bush below. This is the boundary with the Ivory Coast. Up the path, when I visited it in the early spring of 2003, were walking small groups of people, thirty to forty a day, weighed down by bundles and small children. Thirty, across a single border point, is worrying for those who work with UNHCR, for it suggests a pattern of oppression that might easily produce panic. It is when the numbers reach the hundreds, a hastening, jostling, anxious crowd, pushing its way across, over bridges and through rivers, that a state of permanent half emergency becomes a crisis. At Thio there is a small military post, with a policeman and several members of the Guinean Red Cross, waiting to process the day's arrivals from the Ivory Coast, the first step in this particular odyssey to safety, one that will involve, in the days and weeks that follow, medical checks, registration, the allocating of a tent or hut, a few clothes, a ration book, the promise of a school.

At Lola, farther into Guinea along this particular route, there is a transit center. It used to be a reception center for children, but necessity has turned the immense hangar into a staging post for new arrivals. I stopped to look. A young Guinean working with the Red Cross was standing by the door with a clipboard. He told me that there were 1,002 people inside, 444 of whom were children. Reading off his clipboard, he gave me the figures: 925 Liberians, 1 Ghanaian, 13 Nigerians, 28 Ivorians, 20 Nigerois, 11 Malians, and 4 Guineans, themselves former refugees in the Ivory Coast, now driven back by fighting in the country they had made their home. The hangar was busy, noisy; it made me think of Ellis Island, except that it was dark, with shafts of bright light, like searchlights in the surrounding dimness, the motes of dust clear in the air. On the floor, the refugees have built themselves a mosaic of small patches of territory, their mats, boxes, containers, jerry cans, baskets, and bundles, the luggage of West Africa's refugees, each denoting a small, private area. Within these spaces lay small children. It was a strangely peaceful scene.

Fallah was born in a small village in northern Liberia, not far from the border with Guinea. She is a restless, assertive woman, eager to talk and full of gestures, and she is uneasy in the hangar, eager to get on and sort her life out. She said that she was not married, but that she has two sons. In 1996, when the older of the two was ten, rebels came to her village in search of boy recruits. She heard stories about women on their own being abducted and raped. Fallah took her children and fled over the border, not into nearby Guinea but toward Ivory Coast, where she sensed that they would be safer. She is strong and energetic, so the three-day walk, carrying clothes and mats on her head, pulling along the five-year-old, was not a problem. She settled in Danane, a town well inside the border, and found work on a cassava farm. The two boys went to school. With her wages, she bought cocoa, which she was able to sell in the market at a profit. She found a friend, a younger woman, Maja, who like her had fled the fighting in Liberia. Maja, too, had children but no husband. After the elections in Monrovia in 1997, and Charles Taylor's doubtful victory, she thought of going home to enjoy the promised peace, but by now the two women and their children felt settled in the Ivory Coast.

Late in 2002, political unrest in previously safe Ivory Coast, sparked off by politicians fanning ethnic differences, began to spread to the countryside. Fallah and Maja watched and waited. But then the day came when Ivorian rebels began to close in on Danane, and word came that they, too, were looking for recruits and porters. Fallah's sons were now aged ten and fifteen. The two women packed up what they could carry, Maja put her eighteen-month-old daughter on her back, and they set out for the border with Liberia, planning to travel on to Guinea, just as I imagined that Izako's wife must have done, carrying one small child and pulling along the other. They walked for three days, stopping at night to sleep under the bushes, aware that the rebels were not far behind them, occasionally hearing shots in the distance.

On January 28, 2003, they reached the Cavally River, which separates Ivory Coast from Liberia. The bridge across, which acts as frontier between the two countries, was closed. By now they could hear persistent shooting in the forest behind them. The river was not very deep, though the current was strong. Between them, the two women managed to get their four children and baggage across. They laughed, telling me their story, two women friends who have endured much together. But then they stopped laughing. They said that it had been all right for them, because they are strong and fit, but that sitting alone on the banks of the river were small children, terrified by the fighting in the forest behind, but unable to swim and too frightened to cross. Then Fallah described watching a little girl hesitate, then slip into the water, where for a second she seemed to hold steady against the current; but almost immediately, she lost her footing and was pulled under and swept away, her yellow T-shirt bobbing brightly in the water as it was carried along until it vanished from sight in the sunshine.

THE CORRIDORS OF MEMORY
The Naqba and the Palestinians of Lebanon

We find stories tossed in the streets of our memory.

—ELIAS KHOURY

When Mahmut went to collect the few belongings, the mattresses, quilts, and cooking pots that his family had salvaged from their house, he brought them piled high on a camel that had been borrowed for the journey over the mountains. His daughter Zainab remembers the animal well. She had not been expecting anything as exotic, and she can recall it with the sharpness of a photograph, just as she remembers with perfect clarity the earlier flight from Balad al Sheik, stumbling without shoes across the rocky hillside as dawn was breaking and the first slit of sun touched the horizon, crouching down in the gullies, dragging her younger brothers and sisters by their hands, while behind them she could hear the crack of the rifles and see the flames as the soldiers set fire to their house. It was cold and very still.

That was New Year's Eve, 1947. She was twelve. The Haganah, the Jewish underground armed organization, was beginning its assault on the mountain villages above Haifa, flushing out the Arab fighters, of whom her father was one, driving them farther back up into the mountains, toward the isolated stone shack that her grandfather had built for the hot summer months, when he lent his village house to guests.

The attack on Balad al Sheik, one of the first acts of reprisal in the war between Arabs and Zionists, had been prompted by the killing of forty-one Jewish oil refinery workers the night before, itself a gesture of revenge for the deaths of six Palestinians at the gates of the refinery. Mahmut, unlike many of the other villagers, owned a gun; he was a man of standing and land, some of which he had sold to buy the gun and the ammunition to go with it, for the Arab resistance was very short of weapons. He was a farmer, she explained to me when I visited her in the autumn of 2002, who grew carrots and cabbages, as well as corn, wheat, and barley; he grew olive trees and grapevines, pressing oil from the olives and fermenting a little vinegar from the grapes; her mother supervised the making of jam, and there was a small shop in which the produce was sold. There were cows, large black and white Dutch cows that gave milk three times a day, and some sheep. Their house had many rooms because her father was a well-known man, and many people came to call on him and drink the coffee that was always kept ready for visitors.

Zainab can also remember, and can recite, step by step, the stages of their journey into exile, the weeks in Majed al Koroum, while her father crept back to their village under cover of dark to see whether it was safe to go home; the drive on by hired truck in search of greater safety when he returned to tell them that there was little left standing of the fine house, with its two stories and many rooms, and that many people in the village had been slaughtered, whole families lined up against the village wall and shot in reprisal for Haganah deaths. An account written later recorded that orders had been given by Haganah to "encircle the village, harm the largest possible number of men, damage property, and refrain from attacking women and children." After they left Majed al Koroum, they heard that twelve of those who elected to stay had been executed in the village square by the Israel Defense Forces. Zainab can describe the months spent in a rented house over the border in Lebanon, waiting, trying to understand the nature of the war, while Mahmut crossed and recrossed the border, visiting his family only by night, and the women prepared food and provisions for the fighters up in the hills; and the arrival, many months later, at Shatila, the refugee camp opened not long before on Beirut's western slopes.

Fifty-four years later, she remembers these things very clearly, and particularly the family house and their lands and the way the fruit trees grew and the many celebrations of village life, and the occasional trips into Haifa, by Bus Number 1 from the village square, to see her aunts, or to buy clothes and shoes and the fruit that could not be found in the hills, because she rehearses these memories every day, savoring the image of lost and stolen happiness. Balad al Sheik had, she says, two coffee shops, and a school dating back to Ottoman times. And when Marwan, her eldest son, who has never been to what are now the Palestinian territories, takes his mother out on Fridays in his car and up into the hills around Shatila, she points up at the bald ocher mountains that surround Beirut, their lower slopes spotted by trees and scrub, and says: "That is what our mountain was like. That house, over there, on that hillside, was what our house was like. Those fields, below, those could be our fields." Memory is, and has been for half a century, the defining element of her life.

Zainab is sixty-seven, a mild, silent woman with a soft, round face and sad eyes. On her face can be seen what Edward Said once called the "marks of disaster uncomprehended," the reflection of "a past interrupted, a society obliterated, an existence radically impoverished." In her expression there is a look of profound resignation and a complete absence of all expectation, as if her life has been a series of improvisations and suspended hopes. For the past fifty-four years Zainab has been a refugee, a displaced person living in the Palestinian refugee camp of Shatila, which, in 1982, became a byword for Israeli violence and aggression. Among its inhabitants there are not very many today who remember the Naqba, the "disaster," the name Palestinians all over the world give to the uprooting from their homeland in 1948, when the British pulled out of their former mandate territory and the new state of Israel was carved out of land the Palestinians believed to be theirs. There are few still alive who experienced the flight into exile, either in Shatila or in Lebanon's eleven other official Palestinian refugee camps, or in the diaspora that has taken Palestinians to camps in Jordan, Syria, and Kuwait, and scattered them from one end of the world to the other. Refugee life is hard on the elderly, and diabetes, high blood pressure, respiratory problems, and heart disease have all taken their toll on those who fled as children in 1948. Zainab, like all the older refugees, looks much more than her sixty-seven years. She is severely diabetic and has had one heart attack. She walks slowly, with a slight stoop. The "notables," the men and women who were already adult and leaders in their communities when they fled, are regarded as people apart, both for what they have been through and for what they remember. They are custodians not simply of the Palestinian collective history, but of the affirmation that the Palestinians exist, and have always existed, despite all the attempts to make them disappear from the mind and conscience of much of the world.

Over half of those now living in Shatila are children, the grandchildren of the Naqba. Neither they nor their parents—born when the camp was a rocky field of tents, tethered precariously in the hard ground—have ever been to the territories, but they hold on to the dream of going home with an intensity that, like Zainab's, defies questioning. Ask a passing child in the camps where he comes from; he will reply with the name of the village from which his grandparents came over half a century ago. Ask him to draw a flag, and he will draw the flag of Palestine. The "right of return," in Palestinian Arabic "awdah," the much debated, much disputed Resolution 194,* which no one except the Palestinians really any longer believes could possibly be enacted, is more than a tenet of their faith; it is an immutable fact, a necessity. "I want to go home," says Zainab. "I

---

* Under the 1948 UN General Assembly Resolution 194, all Palestinian refugees wishing to return home were to be permitted to do so "at the earliest practicable date." But fifty-six years later, except in special cases, the refugees have not been allowed back.

want to go home and grow old there and be buried in our cemetery." That the village of Balad al Sheik has long since been bulldozed; that the square in which the men once sat and talked is now a
concrete playground played on by Israeli children; that the marble
slabs have long since been stolen from the tomb of Shaykh Izz al-
Din al-Qassam, the great fighter against British rule; that a Jewish
settlement stands on what were once her father's olive groves; that
apples grow in place of corn; and that her identity card, categorizing
her as a Palestinian without a state, forbids her from going anywhere—these facts are neither interesting nor important to her.
Balad al Sheik does not even exist as a name any more: it is now Tel
Chanan, part of the larger town of Nesher. But what concerns
Zainab is very simple: it is her right to go home, and the right of her
children and grandchildren to inherit the land of her father and her
husband. That dream, the certainty that return will happen, has sus-
tained her for over half a century; it has held her together during the
years of poverty and deprivation, through the shelling and the civil
war, the fear and the uncertainty. It has made possible an entire life
lived in a corridor of the mind. Like all dreams, it has become an al-
ibi, a shadow; and like all such shadows, it does not bear disturbing.

Jabra Ibrahim Jabra, writing about his boyhood in Bethlehem,
described his childhood as a "blend of memory and dream, of exis-
tential intensity and poetic trance, a blend in which the rational and
the irrational interpenetrate and intertwine." Jabra, who spent his
life in exile in Iraq, said that these memories formed a well full of
water gathered "from the rains of the heaven and the flow of experiences—to go back to when we are seized by thirst and when drought
afflicts our land." But childhood memories, as he noted, are susceptible to alteration, and when a person draws on that particular well,
he can never be sure that the water will rise cool and clear or turbid
and muddy, while the memories of the lost Palestine are frozen in
time, immutable and forever happy.

Return to Palestine is not, of course, all that Zainab wants. She
wants, so much that it makes her cry to talk about it, to see her third
son, Tariq, again. Tariq was forced to flee Beirut after the Israeli in-

vasion of 1982 when he was a young fighter for the Palestine Liberation Organization, and he now works in Oxford. In the last ten years, she has seen Tariq just once, when he was living in Cyprus and was smuggled into Shatila for a three-day visit when she was ill, but he had to leave early when it became known that the Lebanese army was still looking for him. "Tell him," she said, when I explained that I would soon be meeting Tariq in Oxford, "tell him that I am well and healthy. Tell him that you found me…" She paused, looking for the right word, her expression of anxiety and defeat barely visible in the dim room. "Tell him that you found me fresh."

. . .

SHATILA, IN THE pale twilight of an early winter evening, is a wretched place. Long before you reach the camp itself—walking past the bombed Gaza hospital, once the pride of the Palestinian doctors and now home to some 900 "displaced" refugees; walking through the street market that divides the former camp of Sabra from Shatila—you begin to notice the smell. It is sweet, heavy, sickly, and it catches in your throat. It comes from the meat, newly butchered and piled on barrows; from the chickens, penned in wicker cages and piled one on top of another; from the vegetables rotting on the ground; and from the sewage, which seeps up steadily from the gutters, so that the dirt road is wet and sticky. It is a smell of too many people, living too closely together, in too great poverty.

There are said to be a few more than 12,300 people in the camp of Shatila, occupying an area of six hundred yards by six hundred yards where Palestinians mix with Syrians, poor Lebanese from the south, Kurds, and Africans seeking asylum. It has one of the densest populations outside Gaza in the world. Walking deeper into the camp—because there is no perimeter fence, no army checkpoint, the residents of Lebanon's other camps dismiss Shatila with scorn as not a true camp—among people shuffling their way past stalls and donkeys and carts and barely moving cars, the road narrows first into alleys, and then into passages and corridors, some no wider than a man's shoulders. Below, where water pipes coil along the uneven ground, and rubbish and rubble choke the gutters, lies a patina of dirt and water. Recent plans by the UN Relief and Works Agency and the European Union to install sewage, drainage, and water systems have stalled; there is never enough water, and what there is arrives by main pipes laid alongside sewage drains, with latrines that flow into open drains and along the pathways. The descendants of the original families have built rooms one above another, precarious cinder-block boxes that seem to teeter as they rise. The buildings almost touch. Forbidden to build outward—the Lebanese are reluctant to confer any sense of permanence on the refugees whose arrival they were forced to accept—the Palestinians have built upward, accommodating children and grandchildren on the same site where the first arrivals pitched their tents in the 1940s and 1950s. When there was no space left between the buildings, the owners filled the air above.

Today much of the inner camp is almost completely dark, the daylight reduced to a pale glimmer by the overarching buildings and the canopy of wires that dangle not far above the head. Windows open onto walls. The air smells damp. Within the houses, the flickering of uncertain electricity—supplied for eight hours a day—and the twenty-watt bulbs are hardly enough by which to distinguish expressions on people's faces. Talking to Zainab, wanting to learn what being a refugee means to the Palestinians of her generation, I couldn't see what she was thinking. I peer at my notes, unable to make out what I was writing.

Zainab has three ground-floor rooms, which she occupies with her two unmarried daughters and her husband, who, like her, fled the Naqba as a child from Balad al Sheik, and to whom she had been betrothed long before the families came to Shatila. There is almost nothing in the main room to suggest a past: no early photographs, no pictures, no ornaments. There was no time, she says, to bring them. To one side, at the end of a damp, almost entirely dark passage, lives one son, Eyad, with his family; on the floor above, Marwan, her eldest son, now fifty, with his wife, Naifa, and their three sons. A third son, Ghassam, was knocked down by a car when he was ten; he spent many weeks in a coma and his speech has never fully come back. A daughter, Aziza, who is married to a pathologist, is close by. Zainab has fifteen grandchildren, two of them, Tariq's daughters, in Oxford. Her father was one of the first refugees to settle in Shatila. The site of his tent, chosen by another leader in the community, near to his own tent and to the mosque, was a good spot in the early days. Now it lies in the dark inner heart of the camp.

Zainab remembers Shatila as she first saw it, in the winter of 1949, a hostile, unwelcoming place, where the winter winds blew the sand and grit into the food and the tents, loosening the tent poles and making the canvas flap. In those days, the hundred or so tents, of many shapes and sizes, were scattered among the cactus; and in the daytime, when the men went off to look for casual labor on Beirut's building sites, the women would take the children and sit in the shade of the pine trees at the edge of the camp to escape the glare of the sun. At night, there was no room for the boys under the canvas, so they slept outside, on the sand; when they woke they found themselves covered in dew. There was very little water; what there was came by truck, brought by UNRWA and rationed, distributed by the Palestinian men too old or frail to go looking for building work. Some of the water vats had been used to transport oil, so the water came out dirty, undrinkable. With the water came food rations: flour, sugar, rice, a little oil. The newcomers were destitute, wholly dependent on charity. The life was harder on the city Palestinians, educated and professional people from Haifa and Jaffa and Acre, not readily absorbed into the idle and impoverished existence of a camp where they were closely controlled by a foreign power and denied citizenship, working permits, or travel documents.

Zainab did not go to the first school, opened in a tent not far from the newly built mosque and the separate latrines for men and women, though her younger brothers did. She stayed with her mother to look after the youngest children. She has never learned to write, but Marwan says that when he was a boy, it was his mother who knew when he had failed to finish some part of his homework and sent him back to study until it was done. Two of Zainab's sons today have master's degrees; one of her four daughters is a teacher.

The first years in the camp, for all the hardship, were the best years. Then, the Lebanese people in the villages around were welcoming and sympathetic; they had been told, and they believed, that the Palestinians were temporary visitors, soon to go home. They saw them suffering and gave them fruit and vegetables. As the tents grew old and worn, they were reinforced, first by low walls, to keep water out, then by tin walls and roofs, the tin taken from the drums used to supply oil and flattened with a hammer. However carefully they prized open the drums, there were always holes, which let in the rain at night, and the tin was covered with the logos and names of charities and suppliers, so that the camp looked like a mass of billboards. It was a long time before there was anything on the ground except for bare earth and the sand, which seemed always too hot, so that the children were given wooden clogs to wear. Water pipes, of a kind, were laid. Electricity appeared, after two enterprising refugees negotiated with a man who owned property near the camp to tap into his source. It was rationed, like everything else, but it was enough to power a radio and provide dim lighting after dark. As the years passed, it became clear that there were more and more people in the camps, more children, more arrivals fleeing fresh fighting in the villages of Israel; as the camps grew and as economic conditions in the Middle East worsened, so the neighborly Lebanese became suspicious, resentful. When those of the Naqba talked at night about all that they had left behind, their longing was greater. They were not just poor now; they had been betrayed—by the British, by the Israelis, by the Arabs. No one, it seemed, was willing to see in the Palestinians a people dispossessed of their land and in need of political and economic support; truly they had become objects of charity, without voice and without rights. It gave the past a sharper edge.

. . .

THERE IS NO one single culprit for the Naqba, no one cause to explain how or why, in a little less than a year, between 700,000 and

800,000 Palestinians—almost two thirds of the population—fled their houses and lands, taking with them little more than the clothes they were wearing. It was not only the British who were responsible, though the Balfour Declaration of 1917, which promised a home-land for the Jews and respect for the rights of the Palestinians, is spoken of today as if it had appeared last week, and with the full force of blame. Nor was the flight caused only by the Arab coun-tries' irresolution in supporting the Palestinians, or by the fact that the Palestinian leaders were divided and poorly organized, while the fighters with their few thousand rifles, of varying ages and efficiency, were equipped neither physically nor psychologically to fight side by side with others. Nor was the cause just the particular brutality of the Haganah and other Zionist groups, though they were indeed better led, better equipped, and more than willing to make the most of all weakness they encountered. By the early autumn of 1947, the Yishuv, the Zionist party, was said to hold over 10,000 rifles, 702 machine guns, and many submachine guns and mortars; and, unlike the Arabs, they had factories in which to produce more weapons. The Naqba began and grew out of war.

On November 29, 1947, the UN General Assembly voted to support the partition of Palestine into two states, one Jewish and one Arab. There were attacks by Jews on Arabs, whose leaders com-pletely rejected partition—which would have given the Jews much of the coastal plain and Galilee—and attacks by Arabs against Jews. The skirmishes grew sharper. The exodus of the Palestinians began in late December 1947, starting with middle-class families from West Jerusalem, Haifa, and Jaffa, towns already earmarked as lying within the borders of the new Israeli state. Their flight proved infec-tious. As household after household packed what they could into cars, taxis, and rented trucks, and onto the backs of mules and horses, so neighbors lost their nerve and began packing too, mindful of the spreading brigandage, the stories of attack and revenge, the outbreaks of fighting, and the ominous shadow of future Israeli rule. Palestinian businesses closed, then in their wake clinics, offices, schools. Already by January 1948, before the British left, the clashes between Arab irregular forces and the well-trained Haganah were growing more murderous; there were snipers, bomb attacks, kidnappings. A sense of imminent catastrophe clouded people's thoughts.

When, in the late spring, the Haganah launched a number of carefully targeted attacks, it was against a people already fragmented and disoriented by departures and defeats. With every Haganah victory, the resolve of those who had determined to stay and fight weakened. Tiberias, Haifa, Jaffa, Safad fell, one after the other. Their populations joined the exodus. By the beginning of May all but 3,000 to 4,000 of Haifa's 70,000 Arabs had left. The inhabitants of the villages and the countryside, who had always looked to the city dwellers for leadership, followed them, though they, like the city people, assumed that they would soon be back. No one bothered to take much with them. Right up to April 1948, it had not been part of the official Zionist strategy to precipitate Palestinian evacuations, though the assumption had always been that the fewer the Arabs who remained within Israel the better the prospects for the new state. The Haganah expulsions, which started as isolated decisions to clear areas of particular strategic concern, soon turned into conscious efforts to encourage people to leave.

Events were now moving very fast, with Israelis taking over Palestinian lands, and Palestinians continuing to leave, their departure hastened by killings. As villages were deserted, so they were destroyed, to make way for new Israeli settlements. Walid Khalidi, author of a study of the destroyed villages, *All That Remains*, calculated that 416 villages were occupied and razed. There were massacres like the one at Deir Yassin, a village near Jerusalem, where at least 107 people were killed by the Stern Gang, a Zionist group calling for the occupation of all Jewish territories in the Bible, in April 1948. The Arabs had abandoned their cities, David Ben-Gurion said, speaking to the People's Council, the Provisional Government of the Jewish State, "with great ease, after the first defeat, even though no danger of destruction or massacre confronted them.... Indeed, it was revealed with overwhelming clarity which people is bound with strong bonds to this land." The rest of the world found it convenient to believe him.

By the summer of 1948, it was apparent that almost a million people had crossed the borders into Lebanon, Jordan, and Syria. Count Folke Bernadotte, the UN mediator for Palestine, appalled by the enforced exodus, began pressing Israel to accept repatriation as part of a comprehensive settlement for the area. In December, the "right of return" for all Palestinians was endorsed by the UN General Assembly. But by now the Zionists had perceived that an almost completely Jewish state was a real possibility, and that to let the Palestinians back would be to accept a fifth column in their midst. Where, in any case, would the repatriated Palestinians go? Their villages had already been bulldozed and their lands occupied by Jewish refugees newly arrived from Europe. In the spring of 1949, while Zainab and her family lingered in the house near the Lebanese border, trying to gauge the possibility of return, the United States tried to force Israel to take back 250,000 people, a third of all those who had left. Tel Aviv's offer to take 65,000 to 70,000 was judged too derisory to discuss, and the United States proved unwilling to press further.

In any case, it was too late. Palestine's exiles had become refugees, to be used in the decades to come by Israelis and Arabs alike as pawns for propagandists and politicians. And they were not simply refugees: like Zainab's family, most had left nearly everything behind—photographs, deeds of ownership, family records, mementos, clothes, books, furniture, the fabric of each and every history. Only a very few have ever been able to reclaim a single item. The Palestinian refugees had become a people without a past, and their minds, as the Lebanese novelist Elias Khoury would write, "a black cave full of obliterated memories."

* * *

IT IS ZAINAB'S son, Tariq, working today as a manager in a printing firm in Oxford, who talks most easily about the violence that came to Shatila in the late 1970s. Tariq is forty-eight. With his three brothers and four sisters, he grew up listening to his grandfather talk of Balad al Sheik; and not just to his grandfather, but to members of all the other families who came to Shatila from the villages above Haifa, united under a renowned fighter called Fakhri el Hassan. In exile the Palestinians have chosen to keep to the configurations of their villages, neighbors often living close together within the camps. The different quarters take the names of villages. One day, when Tariq was already a grown man, he saw a photograph on a calendar of a view overlooking Haifa; "And I knew," he said, when I met him in Oxford, in a small trim house with a garden out along the Cowley Road, "that it was Balad al Sheik, just by seeing the photograph. All my childhood my parents had talked about it. I came to be able to almost feel it." He has never been there.

Tariq was born in the tent into which Zainab moved when she married. By then she was sixteen; Tariq was her third child. He remembers his first years of tent life as perfectly normal, though even as a small child he was conscious that it was considered a temporary arrangement, which would end any day, when the family returned to Balad al Sheik. He was a naughty but loving child, a tyrant to his mother, whose favorite he knew himself to be. When she walked to collect water in a pitcher, and carried it back balanced on her head, he demanded that she carry him as well.

Tariq's father, who had spent the first years in the camp as a casual laborer on Beirut's building sites, had gone to work in the Red Crescent hospital, in the sterilizing unit. The family collected the tin drums from their UNRWA rations, beating them into flat sheets to use as walls and anchoring them to wooden posts; Tariq remembers the tent gradually being transformed into a shack, with a corrugated iron roof and a mud-and-straw floor. There was always trouble with the door, the tin proving too flexible to keep upright; his father, says Tariq, became very skilled at mending and repairing. By 1973, when Zainab was twenty-five, there were eight living children, but Tariq believes that there had also been some stillbirths. Shatila had only one midwife, and many newborn babies died. Those who survived started life in clothes made out of UN flour sacks and Tariq remembers how the women artfully used the logo of two hands meeting over the flags of the UN and the United States to adorn the children's underclothes. In the summer, Shatila was full of small children running around with the flags and logos on their pants and undershirts.

They were the first family in Shatila to have a refrigerator, and a gramophone, inside a wooden box, on which they listened to recordings of famous Arab singers. His father, says Tariq, insisted on the boys wearing clean shoes to school and later to work. "He was proud of us. He made us proud. He spent all his time looking after us, working." Their house, then as now, was "rubbish," as Tariq puts it, "and we all knew it. But my father made the best out of every square centimeter." His own father, Tariq's grandfather, treated the Halimi family's tent site exactly as he treated his land in Balad al Sheik: if he discovered anything out of place, he was furious. "He was a very small man," says Tariq, "very short. He sat guard on a chair and watched."

Tariq grew up angry. He hated hearing about what had happened in Balad al Sheik, and hated the position he saw his family reduced to. "It was the most important thing in my life," he says, "being a rebel." He hated the way that the sitting room was also the bedroom and the room in which they ate, and he was ashamed that they ate on the floor. He wanted to become someone, someone who could fight back. His chance came in 1968, when the Palestinian Liberation Organization took root in Lebanon. It started with a soccer club. His grandfather, still a respected figure in the community, had a friend who had rented rooms bordering on the back of the camp, and the rent included a small backyard. Tariq persuaded him to let him use this yard. He got hold of some bricks and some sheets of corrugated iron and built a shack; along the front he painted the words "Cubs of Palestine" and invited his friends to join, Lebanese boys as well as Palestinians. He managed to find uniforms and booked his team to play in tournaments. He was fourteen.

Fatah, Arafat's political group within the Palestinian resistance movement, was already active in Shatila, though the organization proper remained secret and underground. They were looking for energetic young boys with initiative. Tariq, who sometimes walked around the open walls at the top of the half-built cinder-block houses four and five stories up—he had no fear of heights—was just the kind of boy they wanted. His father was already a member of Fatah. One day, he asked Tariq to come and sit with him in the main room. They sat on the floor together, on mattresses. His father showed him a gun he kept hidden in a wardrobe. This, he said to Tariq, "is for Palestine." The occasion stuck in the boy's mind, and though the gun was later destroyed when the camp was shelled and part of a wall fell on the wardrobe, Tariq always remembered the solemnity with which his father had spoken. Before he was sixteen he had had several brushes with Lebanese policemen, when they came flaunting their authority over the refugees around the perimeters of the camp.

In 1973 the eighteen-year-old Tariq graduated from school with high marks and was among the handful of boys chosen to take the entrance exam for the American University in Beirut. To his great pleasure, he passed. He began to attend classes in the handsome colonial building in West Beirut, passing between the medieval dark alleys of Shatila and the airy lightness of the Lebanese capital each day. But the work was hard and unfamiliar, and by this time Tariq was far more drawn to the political discourse of Fatah and the PLO anyway. It was a good moment for the new generation of Palestinians, who were better educated than their parents and beginning to challenge the authority of the traditional elders. There was money in the camps, and work, and the freedom to meet and talk in the evenings at classes and in clubs.

Soon, Tariq was skipping classes in favor of full-time politics, attracted, like his friends, to the increasingly influential resistance movements, each with its slightly different ideology. Fatah, which held that the struggle was nationalist and something apart from the overthrow of conservative Arab countries, remained a secret organization, with cells, wings, and branches. Tariq liked its brand of nationalism, its aim to free Palestinians from the arbitrariness of

Lebanese control, to give an impetus to nation building. For a while, he was made a probationary member, but by 1974 he had been selected to work in the schools that surrounded Shatila because he was popular with the young Palestinians. By that summer, he had recruited and was training more than two hundred students, and by the time the civil war broke out in 1975 he was leading his own unit of a hundred teenaged boys and girls. Fatah opened a war operations room and Tariq led a section of the militia, young fighters with guns but no military experience.

There had been tensions between Palestinians and Lebanese for years, ever since Nasser of Egypt had persuaded the Lebanese to allow the Palestinians to govern their own camps. From the mid-1960s, when it became clear that conventional warfare was never going to be anything but ineffectual against Israel, because the Arab forces were worse equipped, worse trained, and disunited, the importance of Palestinian guerrillas began to grow more apparent. And when the Palestinians lost Jordan as their power base and moved their forces into Lebanon, the tensions with the Lebanese led to confrontations, the participants egged on by Christians and Falangists who found it convenient to blame the Palestinians for Lebanon's ills. The Israelis decided to expand their security zone and, in March 1978, invaded South Lebanon. A thousand civilians died, and eleven villages around Tyre were destroyed. The Palestinian fighters adopted guerrilla tactics, withdrawing before the attacking forces, and the Lebanese grew increasingly angry at the Palestinians for causing Israeli aggression.

While the civil war between the alliance of the Christian Falangists and the Israelis on one side (Israel had been training and arming the Falangists since 1976) and the Muslims and the Palestinians on the other was becoming more bitter, Tariq was rising through Fatah's ranks, coordinating missions of fighters against the Falangists. Wounded one day by a sniper, he came around from a series of operations to find that his injuries had relegated him to office work. Fretting at the inactivity, he agreed to go to Moscow to learn Russian, most of it now, he says, forgotten. The plan had been

for him to stay seven years and take a degree. He liked life in the Soviet Union, and he was intrigued by Palestinians from other parts of
the diaspora whom he met in the university halls, but he felt too dis-
tanced from the things he really cared about. Before the first year
was over, he was making his way back through Egypt and into
Beirut. When he got there he found that seventeen of his own recruits were dead, killed in the fighting. He blamed himself for having recruited them and began to drink heavily, uncertain about his
own future. The Syrians were now bombing Beirut; Tariq and the
rest of his family, who had connections in Ein el-Helweh refugee
camp in Sidon, moved to greater safety along the coast.

Then, on June 6, 1982, the Israelis again invaded, in response to
a series of Palestinian guerrilla attacks launched from Lebanon.
Bombing and shelling, they made their way along the coast, reaching Beirut, their tanks bowling along the Corniche. The highest casualties were in Beirut itself, but many also died in Sidon and the
Palestinian refugee camp of Ein el-Helweh, and hundreds more in
the villages of southern Lebanon. It was a while before people realized that the Israelis were using cluster bombs, having bought them
from the Americans on the express understanding that they would
never be used against civilians.

Tariq was in Shatila in late August when the PLO agreed to
evacuate the camp under a UN-sponsored cease-fire agreement,
taking its fighters into exile in return for guaranteed safety for the
civilians and families left behind. He was not among the 12,000 or
so who left, but instead avoided the dragnet and hid himself and
some weapons, fearing some dark event of retribution, but not
knowing how and where it would come from. He was in the camp
the night of September 14 when Bashir Gemayel, the newly appointed Falangist prime minister, was assassinated and the Palestinians were blamed for his murder, and he was at home, in the family
house, the night the Israelis began advancing on Sabra and Shatila.
He began to try to organize some kind of resistance, seeking out
those few Palestinians who still had weapons, bringing together one
with a rocket launcher, another with a Kalashnikov. Most of the

night of September 16, the Israelis and the Lebanese forces shelled the camp; inside, the rubble from the falling houses, their cinder-block walls and powdery foundations pitifully inadequate as protection, blocked the path for those trying to reach the wounded. Tariq decided that his job was to rescue the injured. His friend Jamal, shot in the head, died as he was carrying him in his arms. Talking of the killings now, Tariq weeps.

His family had scattered in the shelling. Some of his relations were taking shelter in Sabra, where the massacre would continue next day. Others were hiding in a basement under the offices of Fatah, or behind the main water tank supplying the camp. For the next three days, the killings and arrests and disappearances continued, but Tariq and his father and uncles succeeded in getting the family together and to safety. Israeli soldiers with loudspeakers were rounding up all Palestinian men and Tariq fled to Lebanese friends at the other end of Beirut, only to be turned away. He felt bitter, but not surprised. Returning, he was arrested with his father and two brothers. A Lebanese friend, working with the soldiers, intervened to have them released. Many Palestinian men were led away to the sports stadium whose tall stands still loom over the camp; few were ever seen again.

No one has ever established precisely how many people died in the attacks, though it was later said that the Israeli offensive, and particularly the shelling of Beirut, killed 18,000 people and wounded 30,000. When reporters were at last able to approach Shatila they noted, first of all, the smell, and then the flies. As they advanced, they found bodies everywhere—small children, women, elderly people—lying in the alleys, inside the houses, by the roadside, on the rubbish dumps, knifed or machine-gunned to death. When they reached a hundred corpses, they stopped counting. There were pools of blood on the ground, still wet.

Tariq escaped and was hidden by American friends in the city. Three weeks later, he took up an invitation from a printing school in the UK to study abroad. "My mother told me to go. She was terrified that I would be killed if I stayed." He was slipped out of

Lebanon and eventually found himself in London, in the gray solitariness of a foreign autumn day. He had become not just a refugee, but doubly an exile, without possibility of return. Behind him, he left attacks and resistance against the Israelis fueled by Amal, an increasingly vocal Shiite Muslim militia. He was in Oxford, not in Shatila, where he felt he should be, when in 1985 the Israelis withdrew, the Syrians returned, and Amal launched an attack on Shatila, which was still largely in ruins. The "war of the camps," pitting Amal against the Palestinians, would last until the end of 1987. Sabra, and Gaza Hospital, which stood along its edge, were destroyed; patients and staff from the hospital were led away by Amal militia, many never to reappear. Those who had survived the massacre in Shatila now lived through a series of sieges that took them to the very edges of endurance. Intensive shelling drove them as far underground as they could burrow, in garages and basements. Medical services for the wounded and dying became minimal, as the one trained doctor remaining used coins and Band-Aids to stop air escaping from perforated lungs and made splints out of wooden doors. Under assault, Shatila's inhabitants grew close together. Communal kitchens produced food, contributed by those who still had supplies. Zainab and the other women left their dark houses, with a freedom they had never had before, and carried food to the fighters. The rationed water and cigarettes were shared until they ran out altogether. At one point, 6,000 shells a day were falling on the 245 acres of the camp.

Unable to carry the dead for burial to the cemetery on the edge of the camp, the people buried them in the mosque, in the concrete floor. Today it is a shrine to 350 men who lost their lives in the fighting. A flat platform of gray marble covers the place where they were laid, swaddled roughly in sheets, alongside and on top of one another. It is one of Shatila's stopping points for visitors, with its grille looking into the makeshift tomb, decorated by Palestinian flags, the names of the dead engraved down one marble wall. After the invasion and the wars, a floor was built above, where today the men gather to pray.

Between the three sieges, which saw 2,500 Palestinians dead and three of every four of their houses destroyed, it was, says Marwan, Tariq's elder brother, like 1948 all over again, with the women queuing for powdered milk and building materials. Only now the camp was poorer and dirtier, the women queued in filthy water that reached above their ankles, and the camp looked like a war zone. Rosemary Sayigh, a British writer and academic working on a study of Palestinian women at the time, listened as they compared massacres, the old and the new. There was a story in the camp about how someone had found the bodies of three small children blocking the drains. Children slept fitfully, wet their beds, woke screaming from nightmares. It was not like 1948, the women said, it was worse. They were now hated by the Lebanese, who blamed them for the savagery of the invaders. When peace finally came, Shatila was little more than rubble surrounded by a wasteland, and the road to Jerusalem, so it was said, no longer led through Beirut but through Washington.

A wasteland, in many respects, Shatila remains: a wasteland of garbage and ruined buildings, the jagged fragments of former houses left standing empty, or camped in by the poorest of the refugees; a scene of devastation both utterly violent and utterly ordinary. To this day it is illegal for the PLO to have a presence in Shatila, or for the Palestinians to have their own militias. The memories of those days are violent, and when the inhabitants of Shatila talk about the massacre and the sieges, they talk about the snipers who waited in the surrounding houses to pick them off as they ventured out for food, or the day that someone found a head, impaled on a pole.

In twenty years, Tariq has seen his sisters only once, the time that he was smuggled back into Beirut. "Tell him how long my hair is," Souha, the younger of his two unmarried sisters, said to me as I was leaving, shaking her thick black hair loose so that it fell right down her back. "Explain to him how much it has grown." When they last met, she said, it had been cut very short. "That is how long we have not met: almost two feet of hair."

Zainab visited Tariq in Oxford once, sixteen years ago, when his first daughter, Hanan, was born; she has never seen his second, Rasmiyya, who is now thirteen. His father has also traveled to England once; he stayed for six weeks, then said to Tariq that though he found it peaceful and the countryside green, and though he liked the fruit and vegetables, he could not bear to stay any longer. One uncle went to Libya for eight years to earn money to rebuild his house in Shatila: it had been destroyed three times by shelling. Another uncle has worked in Abu Dhabi. A nephew is in Norway, where he has asked for asylum. Tariq used to keep a record of where the members of his family live, the uncles and cousins and nephews and nieces. Three years ago, he reached thirty-six living scattered among Abu Dhabi, Britain, Sweden, Jordan, Denmark, and Germany, and then he stopped counting.

For Tariq, too, displacement is mostly about loss, though it is also about memory. When he speaks to his mother on the telephone, he asks her what she is wearing, and what she is cooking for dinner that night. "When I think of her," he says, "I think of a little girl who never left her home in Balad al Sheik. Everything that happened to her afterwards is a nightmare, with happy moments. For my mother, her children became the personal possessions she had lost. It is cruelest for her. What she wants more than anything in the world is to have her four sons together in one room. She will never have this."

Hanan is embarrassed by the insistence with which her father talks about the past. She does not like to see tears come into his eyes when he speaks of his own father, and the way that he cleaned his sons' shoes and was so proud of them. "My daughters," Tariq says, "have become English. They understand Arabic but speak very little. My wife and I speak Arabic together, but now we speak to the girls in English. They are growing up, and the most important thing is that we communicate properly. I try to avoid confusion. The worst, for us all, is a clash of cultures—one world with their friends and another with us. But I have to live knowing that if I told my mother these things, if I told her that I can accept that they may marry English boys, she would be devastated." Hanan herself, a neat, pretty girl who seems sensible and reflective, is clear: "I do not feel like a refugee," she says. "I feel Palestinian. But England is my home."

Tariq, like Zainab, dreams of a return to what was once Palestine, where he has never been but which he feels he knows better than the orderly English terraced houses and green fields that surround him. But for him, return is only a notion. The quality of his life, the possibilities for his daughters, have come to interest him more; less angry now, more accepting, he wants a settlement, the right to *something*, if return is denied. "Something" might only be, perhaps, the world's recognition that the Palestinians exist as a distinct group and that though they may have left the lands on which they lived, they cannot be simply absorbed without trace into surrounding Arab countries. "I always talk about myself as a refugee," he says. "I will never be anything but a refugee. Even if some day I manage to go back to finish my life in Balad al Sheik, I will call myself a refugee who returned. I was born a refugee, I grew up a refugee, it is how I think." Tariq has indefinite leave to remain in Britain and has applied for citizenship. Under his current status, he needs a visa to travel to an Arab country, and may not go to either Israel and the Occupied Territories or to Lebanon. Laughing, a little embarrassed, he says that he has an obsession with boxes and cases, and that he keeps every container that comes into the house. "Always I feel I might need it to pack things in. In my heart, I know that I will be moved on. I own this house, but I forget." "Record!" wrote Mahmoud Darwish, in "Bitaqit Hawia," a poem that has become famous throughout the Arab world, "I am an Arab / Without a name—without title / Patient in a country / with people enraged." Where collective existence assumes the shape of a philosophical paradox, where a civilization is regarded as essentially disposable and its people transported, dislocated, and dispossessed, then *awdah*, the right of return, becomes a matter of identity, too.

For some years after the Naqba, the Palestinians were silent. The "black cave of obliterated memories" was so shocking that no one cared to write about what had happened. It was not until 1953 that the first literary work by a Palestinian appeared in Arabic, a collection of poems by George Naguib Khalil called *Roses and Thorns*. Novels, as a literary genre, are not part of Palestinian cultural tradition. It was only when the Egyptian Naguib Mahfouz began writing his novels in the 1950s and 1960s that a fictional voice emerged among the Palestinians; even so, it was not until the 1970s that Palestinian women began to write and publish. The voice that has developed since is distinctive, but more, Edward Said has argued, for its form than its content. The themes are those of dispossession and exile, of houses and lands wrecked, abandoned, destroyed, rebuilt, and destroyed again, of collaborators—"tails," slanderers, dangerous scorpions—and of Israeli domination in the figures of soldiers, security men, officials, employers. In Ghassan Kanafani's *Men in the Sun*, three Palestinian refugees choose to suffocate inside a tanker transporting them illegally over the border into Kuwait, rather than make the fuss that would alert the driver to their existence. These writings employ little narrative in the recognized sense of one scene following sequentially upon another, but rather a series of broken, fragmentary compositions. It is through this form that the vulnerability of Palestinian life comes across, with sentences expressing instability and fluctuation, and self-conscious set pieces and testimonials, in which the present is always subject to echoes from the past.

To talk to Palestinian refugees today is to understand what dispersal and loss really mean. A higher proportion of Palestinians than of any other people in the modern world live away from the place they identify as home, and they can neither return to the places of their youth nor travel freely, nor do they feel safe in countries that were once open to them.* They also live, to a great extent, away from each other. A people singularly attached to and depend-

---

* According to official UNRWA figures, there were approximately 4 million Palestinians in exile in the Near East in 2003, and a further 428,000 outside UNRWA's area of operations.

ent on family, for whom, until recently, to have fewer than seven or eight children was seen as a misfortune, they live separated not just by distance but by papers. Palestinians have identity cards, not passports. They are moved around at the whim of others' governments. To succeed, to be educated, to find jobs and send money home, they are obliged to travel, but not necessarily to places they wish to go. The "stability of geography and the continuity of land," wrote Said, do not exist for them. Many are required to live with the certainty that they will never see a child, a parent, a cousin again. Listening to a Palestinian describe his family is a long and complicated undertaking.

Not long ago, Mourid Barghouti wrote: "At one thirty in the morning Mounir [his brother] informed me from Qatar of the death of my father in Amman. I was in Budapest. At two fifteen in the afternoon, seven years later, my brother 'Alaa informed me from Qatar of the death of Mounir in Paris. I was in Cairo." This is how Palestinians live.

. . .

THERE ARE TWELVE official Palestinian refugee camps in Lebanon, of varying sizes and degrees of segregation from the Lebanese, and more than 380,000 Palestinians, around half of whom are registered with UNRWA and live in the camps. No one knows the exact figure, for more Palestinians live in seventeen "informal" camps, in conditions of great hardship. According to recent research, camp "dwellings" average two rooms for every six people, and less than two thirds of these dwellings are connected to any form of sewage system. Among the larger families, those with seven children or more, 96 percent are said to live below the poverty line.

The camps in the south, near the border with Israel, are those the Lebanese patrol most assiduously. The largest, the one people talk of as the most Palestinian, in which the life of Palestine is least diluted, is Ein el-Helweh, the camp on the edge of Sidon to which Tariq and his family fled in 1979. The name means "Sweet Spring." Here, in a dip between the sea and the mountains, surrounded by hilltops capped by Lebanese gun posts, encircled by wire and walls, entered only via checkpoints run by casually contemptuous young Lebanese soldiers, live 45,000 Palestinians; or so says UNRWA, for the Palestinians themselves, for whom there is no census, put the figure at closer to 60,000. Unlike Shatila, with its cocktail of displaced people, Ein el-Helweh is regarded as a "pure" camp, for it has no outsiders. The only exceptions are a handful of wanted people, hiding out in the alleys and turned over to the Lebanese when the military search for them becomes too insistent. Ein el-Helweh is poor and cramped but has none of the claustrophobic intensity of Shatila, though the former villages of Palestine are reproduced in the same way and families live in the same kind of compounds, new rooms sprouting above and alongside the old ones on the sites of the first tents. Yet the place has a more robust, lively air. Ein el-Helweh, say its inhabitants, is truly Palestine, a Palestinian town that might just as easily be on the West Bank; unlike Shatila, it is also highly political, with eleven political parties, and a Fatah headquarters, which is itself a source of employment.

To the north of the camp, on a slight elevation and some way back from the camp's main street, where the market takes place each morning, lies the proxy village of Sousouf. It covers some hundred square yards of ground and contains about forty families, all descendants of men and women who fled the real Sousouf near the Lebanese border in the spring and summer of 1948. In Roman times, Sousouf was Safsofa, a village with many goats and beehives. In September 1948, Ghazi was a boy of seventeen. His family was the last to leave the village. They would have left sooner, but on the ninth his father, pressing oil from their olive crop, harvested early in response to the conflict coming their way from the valley below, was kicked by their horse, fell, struck his head, and was killed, leaving a widow and seven children. On Saturday, September 18, not long after night fell, planes began to bomb the village. The bombing lasted all night, says Ghazi, and soon there was also shelling. At dawn, Israeli soldiers entered the village. Some of the men were lined up, in batches, in front of a wall, and shot; others were dropped into the village well. A fourteen-year-old girl was raped. One old man was shot in his bed. In all, says Ghazi, forty-five died; he would have fought, but he had no weapon, the only gun owned by the family being with his uncle, who was away fighting in the hills. Ghazi on this point is absolutely clear: the British are to be blamed for the Naqba, for arming the Jews and repressing the Palestinians and for spreading propaganda that Palestine was a free and empty land; for the rest, he blames the Arabs, for promising but then failing to support the Palestinians with arms and men. The Naqba was indeed a catastrophe, not for any one person alone, but for a whole people. The Palestinians, he says, calmly but also firmly, have lived in uncertainty for fifty-four years. This uncertainty has marked his life and ruined it. It has ruined all their lives. For him to talk to me, to tell me what the last fifty-four years have been for him, was "like pulling off a plaster, opening a wound. I want to do it, but then I cannot stop talking."

Like Zainab, like many of the 2,000 or so people still alive today who remember the flight from Palestine, Ghazi recalls life before the Naqba as a time of happiness and ease. His father had three wives and seven children; his mother was the middle one, and he her middle child. They were farmers, growing wheat, corn, tobacco, watermelons, chickpeas, and figs; they had an olive grove and vines. They kept the chickpeas, beans, and small crops of vegetables for their own consumption, and sold the figs, olive oil, and grapes. When his mother judged the moment had come when they had no choice but to flee, they crept out from where they had been hiding and ran toward the mountains during a lull in the shooting. They took nothing with them. The border with Lebanon lay just over an hour's walk away; they crossed over to a village called Yarcun, then on to Bint Jubeil. From there, after a month wondering whether they might be able to go home, they moved on to a camp outside Tyre, Bourj el Shemali, from which UN officials were already distributing the Palestinians to camps farther away in Lebanon as well as to Jordan and Syria. In May 1949 all those who had survived the killings in Sousouf were moved to the new camp of Ein el-Helweh.

They were given tents close together. In 1950 Ghazi married a girl from another Sousouf family.

It was, says Ghazi—at seventy-one a strong, upright man, with thick wiry gray hair cropped short—better than chaos, though it was not perfect. The two families built a fireplace near their tents, and made piles of firewood they collected from the hills around the camp. UNRWA handed out flour, sugar, and rice, and, for the first year or so, occasional tins of fish. Water was delivered in barrels to the different village quarters: theirs was known as the fountain of Sousouf and it ran out every evening, around seven. Relations with UNRWA were good: most of its employees were refugee Palestinians like themselves. The camp was surrounded by wheat fields and citrus orchards, later cut down by the Israelis when they invaded Lebanon in 1982. Ghazi got occasional jobs as a building laborer in Sidon. "I used to roam and wander the fields looking for work," he says. "But it was very hard." He was the eldest son, and he and his younger brother were responsible for his mother and sisters. Electricity reached Ein el-Helweh only in 1970. Until then, the younger children studying for their exams carried their books out of the camp in the evenings and sat along the highway, under the streetlights, in order to be able to read.

It was about three years, he says, before he began to realize that they were not just about to go home; then he started to talk about the need for independence, the importance of not relying on the people around them. He began to make plans; he planted a tree and found work with local farmers. But he went on thinking about Sousouf, and at night he would dream that he was still there; in the daytime, when he was working in the farmer's fields, he would look up at the mountains around, very like his own mountains, and pretend that he was working his own fields. "I lived in the past," he says, "remembering, all the time. At night, we sat and talked about what it had been like." Ghazi was then nineteen. He has not stopped remembering since. "Every moment," he says, "something reminds me. This is how I live. I remember how we used to take our olives to the press and how I used to stand around with the others and we used to laugh and joke. I remember the weddings and parties in the village and how in the summer we used to dance. I remember the way the men sat together and talked and how as I grew up I used to sit with them, listening. I remember the way the richest man in Sousouf always had coffee ready for visitors and how the women used to visit each other in their houses while the men sat in the rich man's house and talked. Yes, we live here with our neighbors from Sousouf and, yes, we meet and talk. But you cannot transport the life. There, our houses were surrounded by our lands. Here, it is like a prison. The land we look out at is owned by others. There, the weddings and celebrations and burials were all part of our lives, and we all shared in them. Here, unemployment and stress have driven all that away. We have become too busy thinking how to pay the rent and feed our families. We still do those things, but not with our hearts; we do them out of duty. We bring up our children to keep to our ways. But we are frightened that they will become thinned with exile."

It is only in the last ten years that historians and researchers have started committing to film and archive the store of oral memory that almost alone conserves the history of the Palestinian people. This is the only way to preserve the meaning of what it is to be a Palestinian, and prevent the Palestinians from scattering into twenty different peoples. "Basically," the Palestinian historian May Seikaly wrote in July 2002, "people turn to memory when they are afraid they have lost it."

By the Israeli invasion of 1982, Ghazi and his family had been living in Ein el-Helweh for over thirty years. Early in August, the camp was surrounded and Israelis and Falangists shelled it from the hills, before posting snipers to pick off Palestinians who were driven out into the streets below in search of food or water. When the Palestinians decided to fight back, they lost a hundred men trying to take the hill directly above the camp, where a lighthouse with an ungainly stone Madonna perched high above its beacon looms. After houses around the perimeter had been knocked down, bulldozers were sent in to flatten what remained.

Over loudspeakers, orders were given for all men between the ages of fifteen and seventy to leave the camp, carrying white flags to indicate that they intended to do so peacefully. The men fetched white sheets and bedcovers and came out; they were led down toward the beach in a long line. It was, says Ghazi, repeating what Marwan had said to me in Shatila, like 1948, all over again. With the others, he was taken to Ansar, a prison camp run by the Lebanese military. In 1982, I had just started writing about human rights for *The Times* of London, and I remember hearing about the camp at Ansar in southern Lebanon, about the way 9,000 Palestinian men of various ages had been rounded up and how there were stories of disappearances and deaths under torture. Palestinians throughout the country were now subjected to threats, kidnappings, and attacks, and with most of the fighters and weapons gone they had little protection from the assaults coming at them from all sides. The Palestinians, it was said, would rather be arrested by the Lebanese army, from whose camps they usually returned alive, than by the Lebanese security forces, where torture and summary executions were common. *Khang*, strangulation, is the word used by people in the camps today to described what happened to them after 1982.

Even so, they were not quite crushed. The PLO, who had been generous employers, were gone, the Lebanese economy was in ruins, and the war had seen their homes and livelihoods destroyed. The day nurseries, nursery schools, clinics, and workshops had all closed down. But the younger women, in particular, had been galvanized and strengthened by their role in the resistance, and a spirit of retrenchment settled over the camps. Families long used to hardship pulled in their belts and returned to the strong roots of their traditions. The Palestinian flag and photographs of the martyrs, those who had died in the five years of conflict, were potent symbols of resistance. Bit by bit, new projects flowered in the ruins. The Internet and e-mail have brought the outside world to the camps, particularly to the young, who have been helped by international organizations to make contact with other teenagers in the Occupied Territories, meeting online. They call these meetings the electronic intifada, and the players global nomads.

Ghazi is one of the very few Palestinians to have visited the village in which he spent his childhood. In 1982, at the time of the invasion, one of his daughters became very ill. The road between Sidon and Beirut was blocked, and the nearest hospital with the treatment she needed was in Haifa, across the border in Israel. He asked and received permission to take her there. On the last day of his ten-day visa, he took a bus to Sousouf, now renamed Bar Yochay. Two of the original houses, standing on the main road, were intact, but the rest of the village had been bulldozed. Piles of stones, buried by rough grass, were all that remained of the houses he remembered so vividly. His father's fields, once covered in wheat, tobacco, and corn, were now planted with apple and peach trees. The olives had gone. The land around was thickly forested. It all looked absolutely different. He found the visit extremely painful. He does not want to go back, at least not as a visitor, not before the return he believes is rightfully due him.

But when he returned to Ein el-Helweh, he felt more like a stranger than ever. "I had regained my sense of belonging, and now it had gone again. We are not Lebanese. We are strangers here. I cannot change."

. . .

THERE IS DEPRESSION in the camps, though no suicide: in Ein el-Helweh, Ghazi can recall just one case, thirty years ago. And there is little or no crime, for no one has anything to steal. But there is much anxiety, and when problems arise people are quick to quarrel and come to blows. The mood is wary and conversations are full of ambiguity. Children fight and argue as they never used to in the 1970s and 1980s, say the teachers who work in the camps, and the noise is far louder than it ever used to be. The failure rate at school is high, and since space is so tight children seldom get a second chance. Many of the classes have fifty pupils or more. One woman in three is said to be illiterate. Fatima, who runs one of the rare successful projects in Shatila, a vocational training center for women, where they encourage one another while learning how to type and read and write, says that thirty years ago, when she was a thirteen-year-old in the camp, there were open spaces where the children could play. Now, in the damp, sunless winter days they sneeze and wheeze and their noses run. Television flickers in the murky light of the camp, where it is as hard to see along the pinched alleyways as inside the houses, and parents try to monitor programs for the violence and consumerism that they fear can only feed their children's keen sense of discontent. To these children, Fatima says, everything seems expendable, impermanent, unstable, especially where there has been so much destruction. "Why," asks her small daughter, seeing the Barbie dolls and tricycles on television, "can't I have a doll with its house and its wardrobe? Why can't I go on holiday to the seaside?" Fatima's regret is that she does not know what to say to her daughter; she does not really know the answer herself.

Nor does she know what to say to her own mother, who came as a girl to Shatila in 1949 and who sang ballads about Palestine all through Fatima's childhood, and who now tells her that her one wish is that someday, someone will take her home. Fatima's mother has very high blood pressure; in the camp, she lives in one small room. Last summer, a former neighbor from their village in Palestine, who now lives in Sweden, was able to return to see what had become of their lands. He visited Shatila on his way back to Sweden and showed her parents a video of what remained of their childhood homes. Fatima's mother, who had not talked much about the past for some time, began remembering and describing her home all over again. At night, she again began to dream of when she was a girl. "Where is home?" asks Fatima. "We have no home. I feel conscious only of being a refugee." Fatima has two brothers and five sisters. Her eldest brother is in Utah, where he buys and sells cars; the younger is in Germany, where he fled after the war of the camps and now has asylum. One of her sisters is in Denmark and another in Canada, having moved there after working in the Gulf. The three married sisters are all in Shatila, and the last, who is single, lives in Ein el-Helweh.

Refugee populations have long attracted the attention of statisticians. UNHCR, for many years barred from work with Palestinian refugees through its mandate and the existence of UNRWA,* is now carrying out a project to identify the unmet needs of the Palestinian diaspora. Lebanon is one of the countries it plans to look at. It is said, for instance, that well over half the Palestinian men in Lebanon are unemployed, and that what little work is to be found is only of a laboring kind; that the Lebanese camps have a particularly high number of "hardship" cases—widows, single mothers with children, the handicapped; that only a handful of Palestinian children manage to go on to higher education; that the number of hospital beds available to Palestinians has dropped by half in recent years. Exiled Palestinians are the subject of countless statistics, percentages, graphs, made more poignant by the fact that so much of their documentary history, their family papers and photographs, their maps and civil records, were lost with the Naqba, and the 45 million documents said to survive lie scattered, like the Palestinians themselves, through the Occupied Territories, in Jordan, Syria, and Lebanon, in the American Friends Service Committee headquarters in Philadelphia and the International Committee of the Red Cross archives in Geneva. History, the oral history that is now the subject of much attention in the camps, is coming to be seen as a potent form of resistance against the suppression and distortion of Palestinian culture and history by Israel. "In the end," Edward Said once remarked, "the past owns us."

The events of the last decade have not been kind to the Palestinians in Lebanon, and across the Arab world it is now accepted that they are the most unfortunate of all the Palestinian refugees, for the once friendly Lebanese government has in recent years closed many

---

* At the insistence of Arab states, Palestinians registered with UNRWA were excluded from the competence of UNHCR, both in its statute and in the 1951 Convention. UNRWA provided stability in a strategically important region by materially helping refugees and preserving the internal security of the Arab states as a bulwark against Communist subversion. See Gil Loescher, *The UNHCR and World Politics*, Oxford University Press, 2001.

doors against them. After the Gulf War, the rich Arab states where so many had found work and from where they sent money home began to expel the Palestinians, whose labor they no longer needed. Professional people and laborers alike found their contracts abruptly terminated, the salaries that had supported large extended families in Shatila and Ein el-Helweh and Burj al Barajinah stopped. I remember writing a story for the London *Times* about a Palestinian who was put on a plane from Kuwait because his visa had been withdrawn, and who was then not allowed back into Lebanon. Instead, he was shuttled around the world, as country after country closed its doors to him, and he spent his nights sleeping on the benches of airports, before being put on another plane to another country and another airport. Then, the story attracted attention; now, the odyssey of refugee life is not remarkable.

UNRWA's funds in Lebanon, once ample for sustaining the 70,000 or so Palestinians of the Naqba, have been diminishing steadily and make little headway against the needs of the well over 380,000 their numbers have now reached, including the children and grandchildren of those who fled. It is a very long time since tins of tuna and sardines made their way into camps along with the rice, oil, and sugar. Like the rations of the Liberians and Sierra Leoneans in Guinea's long-term camps, the Palestinians' rations have been cut again and again. Today about 3,500 people live in buildings destroyed during the fighting in the 1970s, heaps of rubble patched up by cardboard or strips of corrugated iron, which they are forbidden by law to rebuild. Without sanitation, electricity, or heat, without papers or identity cards, unregistered by UNWRA because not living inside the camps, these are the most dispossessed of all refugees. Like the rejects in Cairo, the "File Closed" asylum seekers, they are not subpeople but nonpeople, human beings without official existence.

Within Lebanon today, Palestinians may not work as doctors, dentists, lawyers, architects, taxi drivers, bankers, or teachers—in all, seventy-three occupations are forbidden them—and recently the Lebanese government passed a new law prohibiting them from owning property or, if they already owned it, from passing it down to their children. There are stories about the Lebanese guards who man the checkpoints around the camps forcing the young Palestinians to remove their sunglasses as they pass in and out, and about the way that they have been known, as idle persecution, to order car drivers to remove all the wheels of their cars. As I was traveling into Ein el-Helweh with Mahmoud, Ghazi's nephew, recently returned from collecting his master's degree at the University of Malta, we were stopped by a stout young Lebanese recruit in battle fatigues, his Kalashnikov slung over one shoulder. He demanded to see what was in the trunk. It was full of books. After a thorough rummage, as thoughtless as it was arrogant, he waved us dismissively on. Mahmoud told me that not long before, a friend of his had been ordered to dismantle and remove all his car seats, and had to send for his wife inside the camp to bring him a screwdriver. When, some hours later, the car seats had been removed, the soldiers told him that they had no further interest in the car.

Mahmoud was twelve when the Falangists and Israelis shelled Ein el-Helweh; his uncle's house was hit and two rooms collapsed. A grandchild asleep in one of them was saved because a heavy wooden wardrobe fell across his cot, making a protective cover. Too young to be rounded up with the men and taken to the beach, Mahmoud watched from the edge of the camp and listened to the loudspeakers ordering them out. Today he has one brother in Sudan, another in Saudi Arabia.

Those who manage to travel abroad on scholarships are forced home when their visas run out, to a life with only the barest possibility of professional work with UNRWA or a foreign nongovernmental organization, while those offered the chance to visit the Palestinian Authority hesitate, fearful that the Israelis may stamp their passports so that the Lebanese later refuse to let them come home. They prefer to take buses to the border, where they stand behind the wire, looking across to the hills of Galilee, contemplating with bitter sentimentality what was once theirs. Some, driven by poverty and enforced idleness to seek the services of human-smugglers, find themselves trafficked to Europe to battle their way past asylum restrictions and onto work quotas. In the seventies their destination was Germany, crossing from the East into the West, in search of jobs not even the Turks would take. Today, they aim for Scandinavia, Holland, and Britain.

Until recently, Palestinians were able to attend university inside Lebanon because fees were low. In the 1960s and 1970s, Palestinians were said to be the best-educated people in the Middle East, for, like all dispossessed people, forced to live by their abilities alone, they felt passionately about education; now fees have risen sharply and Palestinians have been reminded that they are "non-Lebanese" and told that they must pay the fees charged to foreigners, some three times those paid by the Lebanese students. With UNRWA's funds falling, a decision has been made to pay for no major health care for people beyond the age of sixty—thereby cutting off older people with cancer, heart conditions, or strokes. One serious illness can cripple an entire family. Into this hermetic world, encircled by prohibitions and restrictions, it is not surprising to find that Islamic fundamentalists have made inroads, and that young Palestinians are once again joining political groups, where they receive a little money and a sympathetic hearing. In Lebanon, Hamas is said to be second only to Fatah in numbers of members, though no one speaks openly of its activities. In the camps, the language of politics is about power, not ideology; survival, not democracy.

"The Palestinians are resigned to suffering," explained Bassam Jamil Hubaishi, a Palestinian in his fifties working for a human rights organization. "But for how long will they be willing to watch their well-educated children working as manual laborers? We need to find a solution to this soon. No one is living as a human being should. No one meets even the minimum requirements." It was Bassam who pointed out to me that while those born in the camps and now in their forties and fifties are more interested in a decent life than in return to Palestine, the young by contrast are once again growing up more militant. "If they are given no chance to improve their lives, who can blame them for talking of a homeland? They feel precarious, unwanted. They don't belong anywhere. When they look around them at the hovels and alleys in which they grew up, they think: at least that isn't home, home is somewhere better, home is where I can live in dignity and where I will be wanted."

Not long ago, a researcher asked Palestinians what they felt about the right of return. A little over three quarters of those interviewed did not hesitate: it was their entitlement, they said, and not something they would be prepared to negotiate about. Their words were both sad and chilling. It is many years since the right of return to the lands they left over half a century ago has been anything but a bargaining tool, useful in talks conducted by people who themselves live far from the camps. This gives the Palestinian refugees—the more than 5 million people spread out today through Jordan, Syria, Lebanon, and the whole Arab world from the Gulf States to Iraq—a true feeling of abandonment, an almost biblical sense of betrayal and forsakenness. The notion of redemption by return is an absurdity, a game played by politicians. There can be no homecoming for those of the Naqba. (Not long ago the Palestinian political scientist Khalil Shikaki, questioning 4,000 Palestinians about where they would choose to live, found that the overwhelming majority wanted to live, not back in what is now the state of Israel, but in a Palestinian state, a finding that has been used and interpreted in different ways in the Arab world.) Ghazi, who had farmed his father's fields of olives and vines in Galilee as a boy, and imagined that one day they would be his, tried to work as a farmer in the fields around Ein el-Helweh, and for a while was even able to rent some small fields and farm them. But they were not his fields. Before I left the camp, having spent nearly a whole day listening to him describe his life with more anger than self-pity, he took me up to the top of his house. In old kerosene and gasoline cans on the roof, he grows onions, marjoram, and mint. He picked some herbs and gave them to me, saying that he would willingly have given me an onion, except that since I was traveling, I would probably have no use for one.

"All those who have been destined to exile share the same features," wrote Mourid Barghouti, not long ago. "For an exile, the habitual place and status of a person is lost. The fortunate ones are looked upon with suspicion, and envy becomes the profession of those who have no profession except watching others.... The calm of the place of exile and its wished-for safety is never completely realized. The homeland does not leave the body until the last moment, the moment of death."

THE ILLNESS OF EXILE

Exile was not so much a geographical dislocation as a
state of mind, something that consumed and branded and
left one maimed for life.
— MANDLA LANGA, "THE NAKED SONG"

When Lamine was seven, his mother's only child, and living in a
suburb of Algiers with two younger half brothers, his father was assassinated. The killing had been carried out in error, and the military men who ruled the new Algeria did what they thought was best
for the eldest son of a martyr: they put him in a uniform and sent
him off to military cadet school over 500 miles away, across the
desert and near the border with Morocco. There Lamine stayed,
year after year, bewildered, frightened, and lonely. The descendant
of an Armenian Orthodox Christian, he was the only boy in the
school who was not Muslim; though he agreed to read the Koran, he
would not convert, and this added powerfully to his sense of apart-
ness. The freedom fighters who came to train the little future officers were hard men from the Atlas Mountains, more used to
guerrilla warfare against the French than to the ways of small boys.
When Lamine went home to see his mother in Algiers—he had two
ten-day holidays each year, several days of which were eaten up in

transit—he found her always in tears, lamenting her loss of his childhood. He did not cry himself, having quickly learned that, to survive among soldiers, one must suppress one's emotions. "I had lost my loving," he says. "You can't hold on to love when no one treats you gently." But when his twelve-year penance was coming to an end, and he had been made an officer, he began to dream of another kind of life, one not circumscribed by bullying, orders, and desolation. Behind the outer shell of impassivity, he nurtured a longing for a gentler life.

Today, Lamine is no longer so innocent; he is a watchful, taut figure, precise and knowing. But in those years there must have been something innocent about the slim, boyish officer who stares boldly out of graduation photographs, because when he was just eighteen, about to embark on the next step in a military career of which every twist and turn had long been ordained, he questioned his superiors about his future. Was it absolutely necessary, he asked, for him to remain in the army? Might he not now return to civilian life?

It was 1983. Algeria had not yet begun its long descent into civil conflict, but the military rulers who held the country in their grip were not in a mood for vacillating young officers, with who knew what dark plots and secrets in their minds, particularly as Lamine was not alone in his discontent, but one of a group of similarly troubled young cadets, boys who had been together since the age of seven and shared a profound revulsion for the military life. Lamine was accused of wanting to overthrow the government, of being a ringleader with contacts abroad. He was sent to spend the next three years in secret military detention, sharing a cell with twelve other prisoners, men also deemed to present a threat to the stability of Algerian military rule. From time to time, in order to extract the names of fellow conspirators, guards put electrodes on his genitals, kicked him with their heavy military boots, and sprayed him with freezing jets of water. They told him that he was a rebel and that he deserved such punishment. They said that he was an animal and should not exist on this earth. One day, they kicked him so hard that they broke his leg and knee; most days, he was carried unconscious from the torture room and zipped back into the overalls they had stripped from him before they began their work, blood pouring from his nose and mouth and ears. He survived, Lamine says now, for one very simple reason: he was accustomed to ill-treatment.

One morning, as his torturers prepared their electrodes, Lamine laughed out loud. He had, he says, realized a profound truth: either they would kill him, or they would stop torturing him. Either way, he had ceased to care; he was free. After this, they tortured him all the more: the pain became so great that he deliberately moved to another room in his mind, and tried to imagine himself another person. Since they had teams of torturers, working around the clock, they came for him at random moments of the day and night. "They wanted us to die," he says.

But the time came when the military was forced to recognize that there was in fact no plot afoot, that they were dealing simply with a group of disaffected boys. All but a handful were released. Lamine was among the seven supposed ringleaders to be sent for court-martial for plotting against the security of the state, since all these years of punishment could not be allowed to appear a mistake. He received a six-year prison sentence, with hard labor. He was greatly relieved: he had heard from a cadet friend that the seven "ringleaders" would be shot as an example to others, and believes now that he was spared because of a campaign mounted on their behalf by Amnesty International, which had long regarded them as conscientious objectors and had convinced the Algerians that their deaths would bring worldwide criticism. In his prison life, Lamine had seen many others lined up and shot against the wall of the courtyard where they exercised. Sent to a civilian prison—but obliged to keep wearing his military uniform—he offered to teach and write letters for illiterate detainees, in exchange for extra rations of coffee and cigarettes. He learned a lot about death, he says now, for many of those he helped were due to die, and often in the mornings, when he went on his rounds, he found their cells empty.

After six years, Lamine and his surviving friends were set free. One had died while in detention; another had gone mad, and a third would shortly die from the effects of the treatment he had received. A fourth had agreed to work for the regime. Lamine had lost almost ten years of his life (he tends to look back on his twelve years in cadet school as lost years, too); but now, at last, he was allowed to become a civilian. He applied to the Ministry of Health to train as a paramedic, and though they kept a close eye on him lest he show any signs of political activity, they taught him about epidemiology and tropical diseases and sent him off to work for the World Health Organization in Africa. He was constantly in pain, all down his spine and around his neck, as well as from his broken knee. In the years that followed, while he kept his eye on the military rulers in Algeria, hoping and waiting for the day when his country might become a safe and free place for him to live, Lamine roamed on behalf of WHO: the Congo, Zaire, Guinea, Ivory Coast, Mali, and the southern deserts of Algeria. For a while, he was based in Djanet, an outpost deep in the Sahara, where early nomadic hunters had painted antelopes on the walls of their caves, and where he would go in search of the missionary fathers of Père Charles de Foucault, to whom he was drawn because of their spiritual certainties, even though he sensed that they did not have quite enough to offer him. Until 1994, when the political tensions and pressures of the civil war caused those in power to begin to fear even shadows from the past, Lamine came and went between Algeria and the rest of Africa, restless, always alone, but free. But his record stalked him. "They wanted," he explains now, "to do away with the silent opposition. They saw me as hostile." When he felt the threat growing closer, when he saw others arrested and imprisoned for milder pasts, he slipped over the border one day and crossed to Spain. With his known file, his story, and Amnesty International's testimonial, he was granted asylum.

Lamine had become a refugee. And it was now that his real problems began.

People have forgotten a very simple truth: no one wants to be a refugee. Exile is a terrifying, lonely, confusing experience. "Imagine," said a psychiatrist I went to talk to one day, "being a baby in a loving, happy family. Your mother loves you, feeds you, smiles at you, hugs you. You wake up one morning to find that she no longer appears to know who you are. She doesn't smile. She doesn't even look at you. You cry, you laugh, you make noises. She remains withdrawn and silent. All that was familiar and safe has gone. That is my image of what it feels like to be a refugee. A world without known contours, its geography hostile and alien." No surprise, then, that exile can become a form of mourning, as memory invades the present, as traumatic events—torture, flight, the death and loss of those you love—flare up, like sudden fires, into despair.

For Lamine, the descent into grief was slow. In Spain, he started teaching French, Arabic, and Russian, which he had studied at military school; when he ran out of money, he washed plates in a restaurant. In his spare time, he interpreted for other refugees, helping them to prepare their applications for asylum; he reminded himself how fortunate he was to have papers no one could challenge. He felt neither happiness nor misery, though, looking back on those years today, he knows that day by day, he was growing sicker. When he worried, it was about the constant pain in his knee, spine, and shoulders, which no doctor seemed able to cure. He did not feel part of his new life, but he had friends and work, and when he woke in the middle of the night, with tears on his face, from dreams about cadet school and prison, he pushed the dreams firmly to one side. He dismisses the word "integration," saying that it is actually the bane of every refugee's life and that it means nothing in the vocabulary of displacement, but has been invented by those who like to pretend that the past is a country easily left behind. He was helped by his nature, he says, which is to struggle and look for solutions, though he wonders now how far his refusal to confront his sense of alienation paved the way for what was to come.

Lamine might have lived out the rest of his life as a refugee in Spain, speaking his many languages, helping other refugees, keeping his demons at bay with willpower, writing occasional articles for a Catholic magazine about the poor and the dispossessed of the modern world. But late one night, going back to his room, he was stopped by a group of men. They were Algerians—agents of the Algerian government, he assumed—and they had come to find him. They had knives. He was stabbed, but survived.

When he recovered, friends urged him to move on, to leave Spain, but to avoid France, with its large Algerian community. The UK agreed to take him, and a transfer of his refugee status was swiftly arranged; he was not even interviewed by the Home Office. Late in December 1996, Lamine arrived in London. "It was cold, so bitterly cold that I thought I would die," he said to me, soon after we met. "Believe me, I didn't see how I would ever be warm again." Though fluent in five languages, he spoke not a word of English. He found a small room in a cheap hotel at King's Cross and lay down on his bed, his bones aching from the prison torture, and the wounds from the recent stabbing raw and painful. Days passed. When he could, he slept. The rest of the time he lay still, staring at the wall, thinking. He was assailed by flashbacks—of being bullied as a small boy, of having his leg broken, of the electrodes—and now he could not keep the thoughts away. His life had been fractured, the word he uses again and again, and this time, he feared, he would not have the courage to start over. He was forty-two. "I had reached a black hole. I was lost. I had friends, a life, work in Spain. In England I had nothing. There I had been wanted, useful. Here, I did not exist. I could see no point in going on."

•   •   •

THE LITERATURE OF exile is full of pain. "We, the exiled survivors," Virgil has Aeneas lament, as he flees the burning city of Troy, carrying his father, Anchises, on his back, "were forced by divine command to search the world for a home in some uninhabited land." In these journeys into loss and the unknown, the past, as Nabokov wrote in a long essay about memory, overshadows the present and dims the future "into something thicker than its usual pea soup." Like the false prophets of Dante's Inferno, Nabokov saw the exile's head "forever turned backward, and his tears or saliva . . . running down his shoulder blades." Edward Said is not the only writer to have remarked on the ambiguities of the condition: exile, he wrote, "is strangely compelling to think about but terrible to experience."

Whether Greek or Roman, European or Arab, whether contemporary or ancient, all those who write of exile describe a world in which the past is safer territory than the present, even when the past was full of horror, for at least the past has already been experienced. One of the most frequent themes of exiles is that of recapturing and reliving their lost past, earlier images providing a solid counter to the fluidity and rootlessness of the present. The native shore, observed Milan Kundera, the Czech émigré writer, is after all the only known shore, but the exile, to survive, has no choice but to step off onto a precarious, rickety bridge, from the land where all is familiar and where he speaks a language known to him from childhood—from, that is, his real world—and grope his way across toward a new country, a world hitherto only of the imagination, in which nothing is understood or familiar. In the process, by some sleight of hand and hope, he must reverse these two worlds, the real and the imaginary, so that all that was once familiar becomes imaginary, and the imaginary becomes real. Both to remember too much and to forget too quickly is perilous; a "fetish of exile," as Said described it, distances the refugee from "all connections and commitments." Willing himself to forget his cultural background, he finds that he has nothing to put in its place. The bridge is fragile and terrifying. Yet this profound dislocation of the spirit has to be borne, because it cannot be avoided. When Eva Hoffman used the haunting phrase "lost in translation," she was describing what it means to live not only linguistically but spiritually in a new language. "The words I hear now," she wrote, "don't stand for things in the same unquestioned way they did in my native tongue." For all of us, the word "exile" resonates as an ultimate image of loneliness and need, touching an atavistic fear of losing all we most cherish, and all that we feel has shaped our identities and continues to define our tenuous image of ourselves. For Mandla Langa, one of the African writers who have put on paper the experience of exile that has dislocated their conti-

nent for the last half century, exiles are branded and maimed crea-
tures, condemned like animals who have left limbs in a snare to wander through life "crippled, their minds locked on that fateful
moment of rupture."

It was not until after World War II that systematic attempts were
made to link the experience of exile with that of the traumatic events
that so often led to it. As the stories of those who had survived the
Holocaust became known, so a literature of trauma began to take
shape, and with it a realization among doctors that terrifying and
destructive events have the power to cripple and maim, even if they
left their survivor apparently unscathed, and to reappear later as illness. None of this was new, of course: Freud had written extensively
on childhood trauma, and John Bowlby about the lasting effects of
loss and bereavement, but something about the intensity and simi-
larity of the symptoms reported by many different patients began to
attract attention beyond psychoanalytic circles. Exile, it became
clear, particularly when accompanied by brutal experiences, overwhelming loss, and torture, was a potent and disabling event. When
Primo Levi and Bruno Bettelheim, who had survived Auschwitz and
Dachau, killed themselves at the end of long and productive lives,
people were quick to say that the past had finally caught up with
them. When the survivors of the concentration camps began to
reach retirement, when the huge efforts to keep the past at bay
through work and activity began to lessen, their minds were invaded
by all that they had lost and endured. It became clear, too, that the
aftereffects of the camps were being handed down to a second generation, the heirs of the Holocaust, who seemed to share an an-
guished collective memory in their dreams and fantasies, waking up
at night with terrifying images of gas chambers, firing squads, and
extermination camps. They live, as a psychiatrist put it to me, in the
reality of their parents' past, identifying with parental behavior and
patterns of thought, caused by a history they feel they share but did
not themselves experience.

Like the children of Holocaust survivors, the children of refugees
grow up in a world circumscribed by fear, unrealistic expectations,

and overprotectiveness, with parents whose profound sense of powerlessness in the face of annihilation and loss expresses itself often as self-blame and guilt. Because they are in limbo, and because all their concentration and energy have to go into surviving and helping their children survive, they feel they have no permission to mourn and grieve. Seen this way, exile and the memory of trauma and loss produce an experience of bereavement many times over: loss of country, status, activity, social networks, reference points, and family, all compounded by a sense of lost time, the lost hopes and ambitions of youth and young adulthood. Yet delay in mourning, psychiatrists have long agreed, is known to increase the difficulties of adjustment. "That which cannot be spoken cannot be treated," wrote Bruno Bettelheim not long before his suicide in 1990. "If they are not treated, these wounds will continue to ulcerate from generation to generation."

Toward the end of the 1970s, there came a move to encapsulate this experience of breakdown, to give the condition a name and a label. As more and more clinicians saw patients who had suffered traumatic events, either recently or far in the past, whether of sudden unexpected horror or consciously self-inflicted harm, they began to document a number of specific emotions. Their patients told them of feeling depressed, fearful, sleepless, irritable, unable to concentrate; they said that they felt estranged from other people and that they kept forgetting the most obvious and important things. They reported flashbacks of great intensity, and terrifying dreams that woke them night after night. They returned, again and again, to their feelings of guilt about the people they had left behind, and those they had failed to save. A new diagnosis, post-traumatic stress disorder, was invented to cover all these symptoms, which seemed to occur, disappear, and then reoccur, sometimes with no apparent reason, sometimes triggered by a smell, a few notes of music, an unexpected encounter. Most people reported a feeling of profound worthlessness. Some spoke of suicide. Others came to their doctors complaining of headaches and constant pains in their arms, legs, necks. Others again described seeing shadows or hearing screams. They spoke of "frozen memories," obsessive and intrusive thoughts that came back, unchanged, again and again. Many had panic attacks. A few became hostile, and paranoid, and turned to alcohol or drugs. Some wanted to talk, and then could not stop talking. Some said little, preferring to retreat into silence, where the past was buried deep. "Some stories," wrote Anne Michaels in her book, *Fugitive Pieces*, "are so heavy only silence helps you to carry them." When physiological studies were made, changes were found to have taken place in neurotransmitters, hormones, and the immune system. And these various symptoms, twice as common in women as in men, and particularly present in women who had been raped, seemed to occur in people from every different ethnic and cultural background. Rape has its own particular horror, especially among people whose culture views it as extreme dishonor: to overcome the feelings of shame, to survive in a new world where there is no shame attached to rape, may mean rejecting the culture and faith of the past, and with them much that once lent comfort and support.

By the 1980s, post-traumatic stress disorder was attracting the attention of many researchers, drawn not least to the apparent existence of a disorder that seemed, uniquely among mental illnesses (though not, of course, unique to refugees), to be triggered by a trauma from a single specific event. Patients appeared to alternate between reexperiencing their traumatic memories and avoiding them. They were using different defense mechanisms to keep away what felt so acutely painful, to lock into the unconscious what they could not bear to experience. But then the moment would come when the conflicting need to integrate this information into their existing cognitive world became too powerful, and memory broke through these defenses and into the conscious again. These two tendencies, argued the psychiatrist M. J. Horowitz in the early 1980s—the tendency to complete what was missing and the tendency to repress—led traumatized people to oscillate. When they proved incapable of processing the traumatic material, so that it remained permanently in active memory, chronic post-traumatic reactions followed. Criticized for failing to explain how it is that some people seem to survive traumatic events relatively unscarred, while others react to the same situations by becoming disturbed, Horowitz's theory found interested supporters in a world in which terrifying and destructive events seemed to be such a feature of the times.

Nowhere, perhaps, is the term "post-traumatic stress disorder" more used than among those who work with refugees. They argue that the asylum seekers of modern days undergo some of the most extreme events that life can deliver: torture, killings, violence, loss. Lamine's story is not unusual in its horror or despair, and this fact explains the difficulty people experience in believing the stories of asylum seekers, preferring to find them exaggerated or untruthful simply because they are too painful to absorb or comprehend. Exile, once the fate of individuals, is today the fate of millions—some 40 million people, perhaps, between those driven abroad and those displaced within their own countries.

In a field known to be short on reliable statistics, a few figures nonetheless stand out: depression has been observed in up to 90 percent of people who have been displaced, and post-traumatic stress disorder in about 50 percent; many people who have been tortured have also suffered injury to the brain from beatings to the head, suffocation, near drowning, and starvation. There is, it appears, something singularly traumatic about the combination of forced exile and extreme violence. At no moment is that combination of experiences more disabling than at the moment of arrival in a safe place, when the asylum seeker, frozen in a state of insecurity, not knowing whether he will be allowed to stay or be deported, denied access to work or study, assailed by memories of loss and brutality, oscillates on his bridge, unable to go back or to proceed. And it continues to be disabling, during the long limbo of the asylum process, when those who wait, condemned to passivity and uncertainty, experience feelings of being disliked and despised, which in turn feed existing feelings of failure and valuelessness.

. . .

TORTURE IS NOW documented to take place in 124 countries. Two thirds of those are recognized by the United Nations, whose Convention Against Torture most have signed and ratified. Torture alone—physical pain and degradation inflicted as gratuitous punishment, in order to achieve social control through terror and coercion, to obtain information, or as an expression of loathing—is enough to produce consequences; but the severity of these consequences will be influenced by the duration and severity of the ill-treatment, by the age of the person being tortured, by his biological vulnerabilities and his personality, by his expectations and perception of torture, and by the models of the world that he brings to the experience. Victims of torture are individuals, but they are not alone. As with the survivors of the Holocaust, the effects of their torture will be felt on wives and husbands, parents, children, neighbors. As with the Holocaust, torture involves societies that appear on the surface to be civilized, societies in which people who could be expected to treat their fellows as human beings instead turn on them, brutally stripping them of all dignity, safety, and humanity while continuing to behave apparently normally in other ways. This duality and the way that seemingly mindless persecution destroys the deepest-rooted expectations about human behavior are understood to be among the cruelest aspects of torture. Helplessness and pointlessness, the inability to protect either oneself or others—these are what refugees who have been tortured talk about.

In May 1984, two doctors from the Chilean Medical Association traveled from Santiago to Washington to appear before the House of Representatives Committee on Foreign Affairs. They had come to testify about the activities of some of their colleagues who were collaborating with the military dictatorship in the practice of torture. As the torturers beat their captives into unconsciousness, the two doctors explained, suspending them by the arms and shoulders from poles and hooks, clamping electrodes to their testicles, and stubbing out cigarettes on their bare arms, so these medical colleagues stood by to make certain that the prisoners did not die, but instead lived on to be tortured another day. Disgusted by what they had heard, the committee issued a report. It called for a worldwide campaign to make these facts known, so that torturers everywhere would be shamed into abandoning the practice; and it urged doctors to study the long-term mental and physical effects of torture itself, and to set up centers where those effects could be documented and treated.

As it happened, the committee's words, though important politically, had already been heeded. Eleven years earlier, in 1973, Amnesty International had organized a conference on torture. It was held in Paris; to it came interested doctors, lawyers, and researchers from many parts of Europe and North America. Among them was a Danish doctor called Inge Kemp Genefke, who set up the world's first medical center for the study of torture, in Denmark; others soon followed, in Canada, America, and France. Bit by bit, torture's insidious legacy was unfolded: by leaving physical scars, deformities, and pain that prolong it far into the future, torture also destroys the mind. Some physical injuries were discovered to be susceptible to treatment, but others were not. Few victims, it was found, had been tortured in only one way; most had known many variations. Listening, recording, analyzing, doctors began to discover how clever torturers had become, tailoring their methods so as to cause most pain and distress while leaving the fewest traces. They learned that while the Turks preferred falaka, beatings on the soles of the feet, the Chileans liked to administer electric shocks. Soon, they came to certain conclusions. Three quarters of people who have been tortured suffer from severe mental consequences, and often these take the form of and are accompanied by extreme physical pain. They discovered, also, that treatment to mitigate the effects of torture is virtually always difficult.

In London lived a medical secretary who had gone into Belsen with the Allies in 1945 as a nineteen-year-old volunteer, and stayed on for two years to work with the survivors, then spent the next seven helping children who had been through Auschwitz. She had long been interested in the aftereffects of horror and grief. Her name was Helen Bamber; she was rather short, with a pretty, innocent face and a light, soft voice. Volunteering in her spare time for Amnesty International in the 1980s, she set up a medical group to document the stories of refugees arriving in England from countries like Argentina and Greece. Amnesty was a campaigning organization; it could lobby and collect material, but it could not treat. So, in 1985, Helen found the backers and the money to open the Medical Foundation for the Care of Victims of Torture, and when I first met her, she was working in two rooms in the National Temperance Hospital not far from Euston and King's Cross stations.

Because she believed so passionately in what she was doing, because she is a persuasive and remarkable woman, she was soon a magnet for a whole range of doctors, psychiatrists, and therapists, who came to her after their days in hospitals and clinics to treat, for free, people with dislocated shoulders and disfiguring burns, with agonizing pain in the soles of their feet, and with terrors and flashbacks that stalked them day and night. "The majority of those tortured do not survive," Helen would tell people who came to hear about the work of the foundation. The testimonies of those who do survive "cast a shadow on us all." Arthur Koestler, waiting in a prison to be executed during the Spanish Civil War, described himself as so restricted in time and space, so deprived of hope by the imminence of death, that he lacked even the substance to cast a shadow. Helen borrowed his image. The shadows of those who had been tortured, ethereal miasmas of agony and loss, pain so real that it had destroyed the will to live, needed addressing. In her quiet, soft, reasonable voice, Helen would explain how it was our duty, as people who had not suffered this way, to bear witness, to reclaim time and space for those who had lost both, and in the process to counter what she calls the "climate of disbelief" that colors the attitude of the West toward those who seek asylum. The people who came to work with her would document the experiences of those who had been tortured and would help them to live again. The question for Helen, though torture itself is full of nuances and ambiguities, has always been fundamentally simple: how do you coax back to a bearable existence people whose bodies have been attacked, whose brains and memories have been weakened by blows to the head, whose privacy and pride have been invaded by rape and sexual assault, who have seen their families destroyed and have lost everything that once mattered to them, though they have done nothing wrong? Torture, she would say, is about isolation and chaos, about the disintegration of the psyche. Tortured people have to be helped to reclaim their lives; they have to be freed, not cured, for the concept of cure is seldom appropriate; they have to learn to cope again.

Those she could not immediately see how to heal, those for whom the scars of memory were so deeply embedded that they obscured all possibility of brighter realities, these she would "accompany." Accompanying, traveling alongside, in Helen's view, is a crucial part of the process.

When I went to see her, early in 2003, Helen talked about a middle-aged Rwandan woman who had been referred to her not long before. For several weeks, Mrs. M. did not speak. She cried, she rocked, but she said nothing. Helen sat and held her. Week after week, she appeared in Helen's room, at the appointed time and on the correct day, and cried and rocked. Then one day she began to talk. She said that she was a Hutu, the wife of a Hutu businessman who sold spare parts for cars, and that she had three children, a girl of thirteen and two boys of ten and six. In 1994, some years before the birth of her youngest child, civil war came to her village. One day Tutsi soldiers arrived. They assumed that her family had been responsible for the deaths of Tutsis. They killed her father and her two brothers, with knives and machetes. Then they attacked her, using machetes and bayonets, and slashed her from side to side, almost amputating her right foot, and leaving her stomach and groin with open gashes. They raped her, vaginally and anally. Leaving many villagers dead or mutilated, they dragged her husband away with them. Later, she heard that they were holding him in a prison, and later still he suddenly appeared at home, having escaped. For a while, the family lived quietly, without trouble. But one day the soldiers came back and, finding her husband there, beat him very badly and took him away with them. Mrs. M. was again raped, by four men. When she fought off a fifth, she was again slashed and beaten. Her husband did not come back; a neighbor told her that he had been killed. One day, a villager came to tell her that the soldiers were on their way to get her. Mrs. M. fled. She hid in the bush, and then with friends, until money was raised to send her abroad. She left her children with her mother.

As Mrs. M. related her story, she told Helen that every day, as she lay on her bed in her lonely hostel room in London, she saw her children sitting near her. They were always there. Talking about the three children of whom she had no news, and had not seen for many months, Mrs. M. cried and rocked. One day, Helen asked her what she said to her children. Did she tell them that she was always with them in her thoughts? Did she tell them what disgusting food she was forced to eat in her hostel? Mrs. M. laughed. It was the first time she had laughed or smiled, in all the weeks she had been coming. And after this, things changed. The two women talked. It was the beginning, a breakthrough. Now Helen hopes that the day will come when Mrs. M. can accept that her children are not with her— and may never be. "But her reality is still that they are sitting on her bed. I cannot destroy that. I can't delve into her inner world. She wants not to live, but does not know how to die. I can only accompany her."

Over the years, the Medical Foundation, growing steadily in response to the victims of torturers in Colombia, Sri Lanka, Kosovo, Iraq, Turkey, Zimbabwe, and Liberia, has developed into a loose federation of skills and therapeutic methods, presided over, until her retirement as director in 2003, by Helen Bamber's accepting and benevolent eye.* Drawn to the work by their feelings of sympathy and recognition, bringing with them disciplines that range from Freudian analysis to cognitive therapy, clinicians have discovered at the Medical Foundation the freedom to listen and treat as they see

---

* Between 1986 and 2004, the Medical Foundation saw 37,000 clients from eighty countries.

best, feeling their way into methods that owe as much to instinct and common sense as to orthodox medicine. The Foundation is, say its admirers, one of the last bastions of eclectic medicine, in a field that grows more specialized and narrow all the time. While most clinicians accept post-traumatic stress disorder as a useful label with which to arm their clients in their requests for asylum with the Home Office, few regard it as more than a very broad diagnosis. As a recognizable set of symptoms, shared by many people who have been badly tortured, post-traumatic stress disorder provides a therapeutic base from which to start work. But recognizing the symptoms is just a beginning. The damage done by torture, its particular perversion of human relationships and intimate violations, leaves echoes not easily comprehended or dispelled. Listening always for the nuances of the possible, assessing the degree to which confrontation and direction are wise or premature, becomes part of an everyday process in which to the skills of doctor, psychiatrist, and therapist need to be added those of social worker, housing officer, and lawyer, for the needs of refugees are without bounds. For clinicians trained in precise disciplines, the very flexibility and imaginativeness of their work with clients are extremely attractive.

Though not, of course, to everyone. Some years ago, the senior clinician at the Foundation was a psychiatrist called Derek Summerfield. The longer he worked with clients, the more Dr. Summerfield came to feel that his skills as a doctor were less important in dealing with asylum seekers and refugees than his ability to find them homes and work. Torture, he accepted, is a devastating event, and can and does leave dreadful effects. But most people who came to the Foundation seemed to him to process and handle the experience themselves, with extraordinary resilience. What they needed was not medical help, which perpetuated their sense of being victims, but practical assistance in putting their lives on a tolerable footing. To call them ill was to detract from their many social problems. As his impatience with what he saw as the "medicalization" of the problem grew, Dr. Summerfield decided to leave and forge his own path. Though the Medical Foundation felt bruised by months of debate and discussion, the feeling did not last long. Soon, in the warren of offices and consulting rooms that spread across three buildings in North London, lawyers were taking down initial testimonies and working on submissions to government, physiotherapists were easing the pain of fractured bones, psychiatrists evaluating the effectiveness of different interventions, and therapists guiding clients through the minefields in their minds. To explain about the work of the Foundation, Helen tells this story: A young man from a central American country was sent to her one day, several months after his arrival in England. They started sessions together. He had been profoundly tortured, and been forced to watch others tortured. No one in England, he explained, had been able to imagine the degree of his anguish. Instead, he had found a forest, and there, among the beeches, he would run about and shout and cry. The forest, he said, became his doctor. After some months working with Helen, he told her that the Medical Foundation was now his forest.

In other clinics and counseling rooms, and in some parts of the National Health Service, other doctors, many of whom have done their stints at the Medical Foundation, are attempting to come to grips with the hideous legacies of torture and the long unhappiness of exile. Yet the fact that the Foundation is forced to rely on translators—albeit a team of translators, built up over the years, whose knowledge of the many variations of tortures is enormous—has long troubled some of the specialists, who feel the need for more direct contact. A new center to tackle precisely this question was started in London not long ago, by two women with personal experience of oppression and exile. Josephine Klein is the only daughter of a Polish Jew who fled to Holland at the age of seventeen to escape persecution at home, and who herself became a refugee at the age of thirteen, when the Germans invaded Holland. The family— Josephine, her parents, and her disturbed older brother—fled to England. They had hoped to make their way on to America, but when several convoys lost ships on the crossing, they accepted refuge in a village in the Midlands. England treated Josephine well. All she knew about the country came from *The Scarlet Pimpernel*, and she was not disappointed. The local authority found her a place in a good school and paid for her uniform; soon, she moved to the top of her class. There followed a successful academic career in psychoanalytic psychotherapy. It was a world in which chaos had been contained and regulated, and she was grateful. Josephine is now in her seventies, a smiling, understanding woman.

In 1993, after she had given a paper at a memorial conference for John Bowlby, the psychologist famous for his work on attachment, a young woman came up to her. Aida Alayarian was an Armenian refugee from Iran, studying for a master's degree; she needed a supervisor for her dissertation on torture. It was, Josephine says now, as the two women, interrupting each other frequently and affectionately, tell me their story, her day for good deeds. She promised Aida that when she had a vacancy she would accept her as a student, and she kept her word. It took her just three sessions to realize that Aida, who had trained in Iran in clinical psychology and child therapy, needed not a supervisor but a collaborator. As Aida wrote her dissertation about torture, the two women talked about their own lives, about Josephine's extended family, almost all of whom disappeared into the extermination camps, and about Aida's escape from Teheran's notorious Evin prison, and they told each other how they would like to start a treatment center for traumatized refugees, and how they would recruit and train therapists who could work with clients in their own languages, without need of interpreters. Interpreters, however sensitive and good, it seemed to them, inevitably blunted a process almost too fragile for words, and they were appalled when, in the work they were already doing, they noticed that people would bring and use as interpreters their own children, who had learned English quicker than they had been able to, rather than tell their stories through strangers.

Aida knew all about torture. As an Armenian from a vocal and politically active family in Teheran, she had seen her father imprisoned and lose his sight, and her brother and several cousins executed. Iran in the late 1970s and the 1980s was a brutal and terrifying place, with revolutionary courts and committees presiding over a regime of torture and summary executions, many of them carried out in Evin prison. When I was writing about human rights for *The Times* of London, I spoke one day to an Iranian physicist who had escaped to London. We met in secret; he was too frightened of the long arm of the Iranian secret services to tell me his name. Talking about the months he had spent in Evin prison, he described being taken one day by a guard along a corridor toward the torture rooms. On the way they passed an open door. I have always been haunted by what he said next: "I looked into the room. It seemed to be a hall, stretching for many meters in all directions, with a high ceiling. All I could see were legs and feet, hanging from hooks in the ceiling, rows and rows of them. Men's legs, with trousers; women's bare legs; children's legs and tiny bare feet. Bodies, hanging, dead, dozens of them. I realized that this was where the torture ended."

When her daughter was four and she was heavily pregnant with her second child, Aida was arrested and taken to Evin. She was tortured. Her guards wanted the names of Armenian activists. When the time came for the baby to be born, nothing happened. She laughs now, sitting in north London, as she recounts her story. "A month passed, and then a second. Still no baby. This is medically extremely rare in human beings, but it happens in bears. When there is danger, they simply hang on to their unborn cubs. When I reached the end of the eleventh month, one of Evin's doctors took pity on me. He was a young man, and he was terrified of the system himself. They were still torturing me, and I begged him to help me die. Instead, when at last it was clear that my son was going to be born, he diagnosed me with puerperal fever and transferred me to a hospital outside the prison. A guard accompanied me, but he was not allowed inside the women's ward. The young doctor [from the prison] told me to pretend that I was Turkish, from a village far from Teheran, and that I was a simple peasant girl. When the [hospital] doctors discharged me, I telephoned my sister from the hospital telephone and she came to collect me and the baby from the back. The guard never knew that I had gone."

After this, heavily veiled and living in hiding with her two children, her mother having forfeited her house on account of Aida's disappearance, Aida returned to her underground work with refugees and dissidents, until it was finally just too dangerous for her to stay in Teheran. With the help of friends, she and her children escaped to Turkey—she had parted by now from her husband—but as an Armenian in Istanbul she was again suspected of having dissident connections, and again arrested and again tortured. A United Nations commissioner heard about her and secured her release. The family now moved on to Holland, and then, in 1991, to England, where they were given refugee status and where Aida started work with HIV patients and asylum seekers.

By 2001, Aida and Josephine had gathered enough funders and enough volunteers to open the Refugee Therapy Center. They found therapists able to work in seventeen different languages. Both are practical, realistic women and they share a similar vision of the effects of torture. Terrible experiences, they agree, can and do lead to trauma; but trauma is cloudy, not solid like measles, and how it will be experienced owes much to how an individual perceives himself and how resilient his past has made him. Good parenting, they say, that leaves children feeling loved, with a strength that lies beyond words, will make a vital difference to the way a person is able to process torture. For Aida, the help she seeks to provide is all about trust, the breaking of isolation, and allowing people to feel safe. "We provide," she says, "a space in which people can be while they learn to trust again." As she sees it, not all people who have been tortured need to or can or want to relive the experience; rather, they need to be helped to build up structures that contain and imprison it. Then they need to learn to live. "Until recently," she argues, "the accepted view was that in order to get better, people have to talk about what has happened to them. But for some people, the best thing is to build a wall around that particular moment in their past, and then move on." Aida, too, like Helen, "accompanies" her clients. And they know, she says, when the time has come for them to end their therapy. They get bored and they simply stop coming.

The image of victim and survivor is always present in this field. Doctors who work over long periods of time with people who have been tortured marvel at the spirit and dignity of their clients, and at their enormous powers of self-regeneration. Much, they note, depends also on the expectations of torture victims. "When people come from societies where repression is severe and where torture is routine," says Dr. Michael Peel at the Medical Foundation, "where they have witnessed others disappear and heard stories of torture, these people tolerate it better. It is not a catastrophe, striking from nowhere. It is part of their map. They assimilate it because it does not shatter their feelings of what is predictable." Cultural differences have become important to him, as has the need to gauge, person by person, what works best. For many, it is a question of reducing the traumatic past into "bite-sized chunks," which can be absorbed and, one by one, assimilated.

And people find their own strategies to survive. Helen told me about a man in a Middle Eastern country who had been arrested and severely tortured. One day, he was made to watch a friend being tortured. Afterward, he tried to comfort the friend. "Old man," he said, "we cannot strike them back now. But while we are here in prison I shall teach you to read and write, and that will be our victory over them."

* * *

THE FIRST TIME Michael Korsinski saw Lamine, he was lying on the floor of Korsinski's office at the Medical Foundation, scrunched up like a fetus, racked with pain. He could neither sit in a chair nor walk normally around the room. That day, the two men, Lamine an Algerian former military cadet and refugee in his mid-forties, Michael an American therapist some ten years younger, embarked on what would become a very long and very arduous program of work, the therapist, a tall, thin, gangling man who uses his hands a lot, lounging in his chair, his client crouched over and cramped, or shuffling around the room, looking at his feet, unable to meet the therapist's eye. In prison, as Lamine would tell me, there is no horizon, and to look into people's eyes is to invite trouble. Michael is an ideal example of the Foundation's eclecticism: he is a dancer, who learned about physical pain through a bad accident; a practitioner of the Alexander technique who came to Jungian analysis through his need to bridge what he saw as an uncomfortable gap between his own mind and body; a somatic psychotherapist who came to the work not through the theories of earlier doctors and analysts treating functional disorders as Reich and Charcot did, but through his own interest in the body. At the Medical Foundation, among people stunned into chronic pain and despair by torture, Michael discovered the setting he needed in which to do his work. In the early 1990s, recruited by Helen, he began to listen to people's bodies.

In many ways, Lamine was also Michael's ideal client. He was a clever, articulate, reflective man who had reached a moment of such profound desperation that the vast edifices of his defenses were weakened just enough to allow them to be breached. Safe, at last, from threat and danger, he could permit himself to collapse. He was caught, as Michael saw it, in that quasi-world familiar to all who work with tortured refugees, in a state of pain that is neither all physical nor all mental but some complicated amalgam of both, trying to dissociate himself from his body so that he might survive as a psychic entity; the two, the mental and the physical, needed to be brought together again. While Lamine rocked and groaned, Michael got down on the floor next to him and did exactly what his instincts told him to do: he took hold of Lamine's head and supported it. "I could feel this huge tension," Michael says. "I had to do something to release this unbearable physical pain." For Lamine, the moment was both shocking and intensely moving. He felt humiliated; but he also felt comforted. Never, he says now, had he lain on the floor in this abject fashion, not even during the worst of the torture. However, lying on his bed in his bleak hotel room in King's Cross, he had decided against suicide and he knew that he needed help: medical help, for his old injuries, and above all mental help, though he could not imagine that he would ever meet anyone he could trust. Particularly not in this alien country, where he could not speak to anyone and where he felt permanently cold. Through Michael's hands, in a room full of the brightly colored rubber balls and odd objects that are among the tools of his trade, with a translator looking on, Lamine wondered whether he had found his man.

Nothing happened quickly. It had been luck that had taken Lamine to the Medical Foundation, luck in the form of a perceptive nurse at his local doctor's office in King's Cross: she remarked on his wounds and suggested that he try the place up the road, which she believed looked after people who had been tortured. It took great courage to go there. Helen's flash of humor helped release Mrs. M.'s story: now it would be Michael's willingness to stick by him until he got better that would open Lamine's first door. "He promised me something. And he kept his word." Lamine did not expect people to keep their word. He had been betrayed since early childhood. That sudden feeling of trust became his key.

Although the doors opened only very gradually—and not all are yet open—Lamine returned week after week to see Michael, longing for the day when he would not need a translator; and, slowly, the pain began to ease. "There were two aspects to talking," he says. "One was talking or not talking. The other was really talking." It was his whole, painful life of lovelessness and violence that Lamine was forcing himself to face, of which torture was just a part. Michael knows that doors cannot be forced open, just as he knows that torture may do many different things to people, but that one thing it always does is alter them. Lamine was looking for the person that he had been, Michael for ways to help him metabolize his experiences, to face up to and question his own carefully constructed defense mechanisms and find the strength to let them go, and then move on. As he saw it, his job was to decide when Lamine was ready to confront the past, when he was sufficiently strong to start rebuilding. He was listening for the signal. "You need a very broad palette to work in this field," he says.

When I went to see him, Michael, like Helen, told me a story. "There was an Asian man who was blind. One day, he found himself by an elephant, but did not know what it was. 'This,' he said to himself, stroking the trunk, 'must be a snake.' Then he felt the elephant's body. 'And this is a breathing mountain.' After this, he ran his hand along a leg. 'And this is a tree.'" No one, Michael says, "knows the whole picture. All we have are the pieces of a complex puzzle which says that people don't react well when they are badly treated."

. . .

ON FRIDAY AFTERNOONS, over several years, I have listened to refugees at the Medical Foundation talk about what torture has done to them, and about their sense of exile. I have heard about rape, about burns and electric shocks and what it is like to watch children and parents die; often, describing what has happened to them, people cry; sometimes, they barely speak. I have come to learn that rape, of both men and women, and betrayal, both real and perceived, cause a particular kind of pain and grief neither easily conveyed nor ever eradicated. In Muslim societies especially, the shame of rape is so profound that many women so victimized have never told their families, or mentioned the rape to the immigration authorities when asking for asylum. Easier, by far, to describe survival, the steps to safety, than to confess.

There is Mary, a neat, contained Ugandan girl, who speaks good English from her days in missionary school in Kampala. Mary is twenty-two. Her mother died of AIDS when she was a child. During her first holidays from university, Mary volunteered to take some food and clothes to northern Uganda, to distribute in a camp for displaced people. One night, asleep alone in a tent, she was attacked by fighters from the Lord's Army. They raped her, took her away with them to their camp, and held her prisoner. Every night she was raped, often by several different fighters. She was also beaten. Three months later, the camp was attacked by government forces. Mary was freed, but then taken back to a military barracks. Here she was kept for two months. She was again raped. One night, she managed to escape and make her way back to Kampala. She found that her widowed father had died. An uncle bought her a ticket and put her on a plane to London. She arrived in England six months pregnant, too late to have an abortion, and when she came to the Medical Foundation she showed me her swollen stomach, disfigured by the blotchy scar of a huge burn: the Lord's Army fighters had poured boiling water and porridge over her. Mary, too, cried, when she first came to see me on a Friday afternoon at the Medical Foundation; she cried because she was alone, with no friends, and because she could not get in touch with her sisters and brother in Uganda, and because she had just been refused asylum in Britain and didn't know what would become of her, and she cried because she did not know whether to keep her baby after the birth.

There is Luis, who arrived in London in 1976, on another cold gray December day, from Chile; a rare survivor of Pinochet's death squads and torture centers, he had been a young political supporter of Allende. Luis's friends and pregnant wife had been murdered in secret detention. For many years, he had pressed on with his life, held the memories at bay, laughed when strangers told him he needed psychiatric help. He couldn't sleep and he ached and coughed, but he studied for a sociology degree at Middlesex Polytechnic and earned his living washing up, cleaning, repairing refrigerators and washing machines, and selling shoes in Camden Market. At night, he became a cleaner in a department of the civil service, where he fantasized that refugees were only permitted to clean during the night so that the staff would not be forced to meet their eyes, and when in people's offices he saw combs and boxes of Kleenex, cigarette packets, hats, or pairs of shoes, he would try to imagine their lives, and their families, picture them in the pub or at home after work, cooking dinner with their children. When the agency that employed him sent him to clean people's homes he would feel their beds and their half-empty cups of tea to see if they were still warm. In the little time that he wasn't cleaning, or mending people's stoves and refrigerators, or writing essays for his classes, Luis busied himself helping other Chilean refugees. Like Lamine, he has thought a great deal about exile. In this period, he says, he was running very fast to keep thought at bay; but inside, he was falling apart, "atomized, shattering."

Luis met Helen Bamber on a bus. They traveled the same route in the mornings and they began to talk. In her immediate, forthright way, she told him that he looked terrible; he told her that his left side ached unbearably, where the muscles had been torn by the torturers, and that his nights were filled with dreams of the people he had left behind, his dead wife and comrades, tortured and now dead, whose faces he saw in the darkness, smiling, alive, sad, asking him questions about why he had lived while they had died. In Chile, he had often beseeched his torturers to kill him; now, during the few empty spaces in his crowded life, he thought often of suicide. Panic attacks engulfed him, black holes in which he lost all sense of what was real and what was not. For several years he stayed at home; he gave up the studying and he cleaned people's houses only when sheer financial necessity drove him. He brought up a daughter he had fathered by another Chilean refugee, and her daughter by an earlier relationship, and he enjoyed the safety and happiness of being at home with the small children, pushing away thoughts about himself. That is, until the day when, like Lamine, he could push them away no longer.

With Helen's help, he found a therapist to work with; and, very slowly, he opened the past and began to reshape the present. His girlfriend had begged him to talk, saying that she was afraid at night of what was happening in the part of his mind that he kept shut. Now he could not stop talking, week after week, to a therapist in Brighton, though it was many months before he stopped imagining the moment when he would jump from the cliffs of Dover, stopped remembering continuously the heavy shadow of the dead, those who had been alone when tortured and "alone, their bodies mutilated, abused and broken, defeated when they died."

In a passage of a memoir that Luis wrote, when he decided that he should record his experiences for others, he used Helen's words: "I know their last words and their last sounds, because I was there too, because I accompanied them to the threshold." He thought that he would never survive the day one of his daughters was taken back to Chile; he had fought to win custody but was told that as an ex-convict he had no hope of keeping her. In time, he stopped denying the past and knew what it felt like to be angry. In time, too, he became a therapist working with refugees himself, and was able to return to Chile to give evidence at a trial of his torturers, confronting them at last, terrified that he would fail, shaking, sleepless, but elated. When he came back to London, he felt himself a stranger once more, with nightmares and memories he could not control, and which only more therapy helped put behind him. In his memoir, Luis wrote about the torture, the beatings, and the threats to the three-year-old first daughter he had by his wife in Chile, the mock executions and the solitary confinement, and the day when, like Lamine, he found a gate somewhere within his mind that the torturers could not enter. "'Here,' I said, pointing to my head, 'you will not enter. The rest of my body has been all yours and you have violated it, abused it, humiliated it and tortured it. But this is mine, only mine, and when I am gone, after you kill me, it will go with me, with all the secrets and my secrets and all the secrets before me.'" And then, much in the same way as Lamine had laughed aloud at his torturers, Luis had told his tormentors: "You can leave the room."

Almost a quarter of a century later, as we talked in a café in Victoria Station, where he is about to catch his train home to his new wife and their two young sons, with the sound of the trains and the clatter and din of a large station drowning some of his soft words, what Luis wants to talk about is loss. "The loss of all the people I loved. I want to be with them, the people I met in the camps, the ones who disappeared, the two who were machine-gunned in front of me in their car, those I heard screaming day after day in the torture center of Villa Grimaldi. I don't feel guilty. I wasn't a perpetrator and I begged them to kill me and they wouldn't. But I remember, and I think always of the loss. I keep company with the dead."

• • •

TESFAY IS ERITREAN, a tall, very thin figure with graying hair cut short and glasses that give him a distinguished, professorial look.

He is neat and trim. Tesfay never imagined, in all the years of his childhood and adolescence, that he would live outside Eritrea. On the contrary, he knew that what he liked best about his life was the sense of community that came from his large family, many relations, and small village. He would tell friends, when they talked about the world outside Africa, that perhaps, when he was old, he might visit Europe.

In the winter of 1995, as a twenty-six-year-old teacher and occasional political activist, Tesfay realized that unless he acted quickly he would be arrested and possibly executed. He had already been taken into custody on several occasions, sometimes along with his father. He had lost two brothers, and seen a sister wounded, in the long war with Ethiopia. Now, on this bright, sunny winter day, Tesfay decided to flee. He told only his father of his plans. He said good-bye to no one. Late one night, on foot, taking nothing with him, he followed a smuggler through the hills and across the desert. They walked for six days. In Sudan, he was put on a plane, still in the company of the smuggler. He thought he might be gone two years. By the time I met Tesfay, in a café near his small council flat in Hammersmith, he had been an exile for eight years, and there was little prospect of his being able to go home. As he told me his story, he kept stopping, to breathe deeply and steady himself. "You see," he said when he could breathe again, "whenever I talk about it, my chest becomes too tight to speak."

Like Lamine, Tesfay knew no one in London. It was January and, like Lamine, Tesfay remembers best the gray and the debilitating cold, after the light and sun of the high plateaus of Eritrea. The smuggler, who accompanied him all the way into the city, left him on a street corner in Finsbury Park, toward the north of the city, telling him that this was an area frequented by Eritreans. Tesfay walked around the streets, stunned by the feeling of unfamiliarity, terrified by the chaos in his mind. But many of the stories that refugees tell about themselves are lit by sudden episodes of luck and generosity: so something unexpected and good happened to Tesfay. Looking into a shop window, he saw an elderly woman who seemed to him unmistakably Eritrean in appearance. He went in and spoke to her. It turned out that her family came originally from his father's village in the mountains. She took him home with her, to the flat in Finsbury Park where she had lived since becoming a refugee herself in the 1970s, and she let him sleep on her sofa while he found a solicitor and applied for political asylum.

Because his flight had been so precipitate, Tesfay had not had time to prepare himself for London, to visualize what it might all look and sound like. He wandered the streets, fighting off panic, trying to understand what people were saying. He felt very cold and very lost; sometimes, overwhelmed by memory and desolation, he fell over, and lay under a car or along the pavement. Passersby assumed he was drunk. Although his Eritrean friend did her best to make his life tolerable, although the Home Office eventually granted him asylum and gave him a hotel room in which to live, his sense of loss and isolation grew stronger. His first hotel was inhabited by prostitutes and drug dealers, whom he found terrifying and strange. The shared kitchen was very dirty. He stayed in his room. One day, he bought a kettle and sometimes, when he felt weak from lack of food, he boiled pasta in it, switching the kettle on and off until the pasta was cooked. On several occasions, he came back from walks to find his room ransacked, his few possessions gone. He moved back to spend the night on his friend's sofa, but spent the days in his hotel room, in his pajamas, remembering the past, going over what he had lost and the life he would have been living, had he stayed at home. "I felt everything as a shock, a pain, a loss," Tesfay says now. "At home I had always felt safe. I was respected, popular, I had friends, I had money in my pocket. Here, I knew no one. Days went by when I did not speak to anyone. The more time I spent alone, the more I needed to be alone. I dreaded having to tell my story again and again, to lawyers, to the doctor, to the Home Office. The only place I could find to live was the past." He grew thinner. Constant agonizing stomach pains and feelings of nausea sent him to see doctors. Some, he says, treated him well; others were impatient and callous, and he left them feeling that he was not good enough to receive their care. From time to time, a new doctor would wonder whether some of his pains might not be psychological in origin. "I thought they were telling me that I was mad. I became defensive and insisted that they simply try to address my symptoms." In time, he says, his hotel room came to look like a little pharmacy.

It took almost two years for Tesfay's life to improve. Slowly, he learned English and began to make friends. The Eritrean woman went back to Asmara for a visit; she took letters to his family, and brought back replies. Now he knew that they were alive and well, and they knew that he was alive. I asked Tesfay if he had ever been able to speak to them. He said that his village had no telephone. He moved, first to a better hotel, then to the room in Hammersmith he now has, where the kitchen is clean. And the day came when he was referred to the Medical Foundation, and though he kept telling everyone that he wanted to forget, not to talk, he did begin to talk about himself, very slowly, often having to leave his sessions to vomit. "The therapist would say to me: 'How do you feel?' And I would say: 'I feel terrible, I have a headache and a stomachache and I feel sick.' And then I would quickly begin to generalize. 'Like everyone else, I...' And the therapist would say: 'I don't want to know about everyone else. I want to know about you.' Then he would ask me why I thought this or that, and I found this terrifying. I felt silly."

As Tesfay began to talk, he began to remember his dreams. He dreamed about police and soldiers coming to get him, and about the president of Eritrea arriving in his village by helicopter; he dreamed about his family. He felt bad all the time, and whenever anything upset him, he vomited. He gave up drinking coffee or tea or eating anything but the blandest food. He still cannot tolerate cigarette smoke. But, bit by bit, session by session, he began to grow more aware, to anticipate what gave him pain and made him sick. He learned to control it. And, after some time, he trained to become a counselor himself. Working with others, whose sense of shock and alienation he felt to be part of himself, "changed my frame of reference," he says.

But Tesfay, like Lamine, is alone. When I asked whether he had a wife or a girlfriend, he pulled a bowl of sugar lumps that was sitting on the table between us toward him, picked up a single lump, and threw it, almost violently, to one side. This, he said, was what his life was like: apart, not in a group, not close to anyone. "At home, you meet someone like you. To have a relationship, you need a network or a group, and there you find someone who shares your values and understands you. I want someone who can communicate with my mother. Here, I never know the extent to which people understand me. I have friends, but I have to work hard to communicate with them. I have to think, very carefully, about concepts. It is very, very hard work."

For Tesfay, for Lamine, for Luis who accompanies the dead, for Mary, who is shocked by her sense of aloneness, home has become an elusive idea, haunting and dangerous. Home was what defined them, and what they were forced to abandon. The image of home is always an image of abandonment—their abandonment of others, others' abandonment of them. And home, in a place of exile, rarely exists. It is a thought most find too frightening to dwell on. But Tesfay thinks about it often. "If I were to play with words," he says, "I would say that I was homeless. Even if I go back to Eritrea now, I will not belong there. I will be strange to people, and they will be strange to me. Eritrea does not now have everything to satisfy me: I have acquired new habits and manners. But here, I lack what I need to feel at home. Wherever I am, for the rest of my life, I will never be entirely at home again."

· PART FOUR ·

AFTERWARD

GOING HOME

Afghanistan

As a political unity, it is nothing but a chewed bone left
over on the plate between Imperial Russia and British
India.

— PETER LEVI, *THE LIGHT GARDEN
OF THE ANGEL KING*

In July 2002, with the Taliban not long gone, and the Americans
still pursuing Al Qaeda in the high southern valleys, I went to Kabul
to talk to refugees returning to their country after many years of exile. I decided I needed to see for myself what return meant to people
who had been gone so long that they remembered little of their
country, who were going back to a country petrified in time a quarter of a century earlier, and what it was like for a country so new and
so fragile to welcome and absorb so many expectant people who
were bringing with them so many new skills and foreign ways, and
so much hopeful memory. I wanted to learn what it felt like to travel
backward, in great number, all at once, and about what people who
had spent their lives—in many cases all their lives—in refugee
camps expected and hoped for.

Dubai, in the summer of 2002, was still the gateway to

Afghanistan from the West. Ariana, the Afghan state airway, owned a single elderly jet, which had been coaxed into service by foreign engineers, but it had as yet no booking system. Getting on a flight was a matter of turning up and waiting. At midnight, Dubai's modest second-string airport was humid, quiet, and very hot. Along one wall, with its single row of plastic seats, gathered the passengers hopeful for Ariana's dawn flight: a German television crew, with furry booms and metal boxes; foreign women aid workers, incongruous in Afghan dress and neat Western haircuts, leaning on their suitcases, reading fat paperbacks; a group of bearded Afghan men, standing apart, talking to one another. And there was Nasir.

Nasir stood out from the others. He was dark and clean-shaven, and he wore pale gray trousers of lightweight wool, brown loafers, and a checked poplin button-down shirt, newly ironed; his hair was cut short and very neat. Nasir had glasses, unmistakably Western, which gave him a mild, scholarly air; there was a mobile telephone in his shiny leather briefcase, and his new belt was probably, like his loafers, made in Italy. His manner was tentative; like his faint foreign overtones, it had something unsure about it, almost wary.

As the night wore on, as a second and then a third television crew joined the queue, and then some more aid workers, Nasir and I began to talk. He was, he told me in his uneven American accent, an Afghan who had been forced to flee Kabul in 1979, when, as the son of a prominent family, he had been suspected of political interests inimical to the incoming regime. One by one, all of his large family had been driven abroad, for fear that they would not escape the repressions of the Communist regime. No one expected to be gone for long. Nasir, his wife, and their two sons went to America. He did well as a businessman in electronics, and his wife gave birth to a third son. All the children were soon fluent in English as well as in their native Pashtu and Dari, and all later went on to earn master's degrees. Though Nasir's marriage did not survive the long exile, he built himself a large house in the suburbs of Washington and described to me with pride the fine tall trees in his garden. His business thrived. Year by year, he watched from afar the mujahedeen's struggle for power, observed the Taliban's rise, and later celebrated their defeat. He was intrigued by the new Afghanistan and what it might have to offer. He wondered what he had to offer his country himself, since he had money and a good house and an American passport, and his sons were grown men. He had come to look. Afghanistan needed trained and professional Afghans, he said to me, as the night wore slowly on; it needed people who spoke the languages, who remembered the past, and who wanted to shape the future. With his easy, Americanized ways, Nasir believed he might be the kind of person who was wanted. And he had cousins he had not seen for over two decades who had endured the Communist and mujahedeen and Taliban years in quiet, unobtrusive jobs at the university or in the civil service, making no enemies. Nasir had houses in Afghanistan, too, one of them a large compound in the center of old Kabul, where his grandparents had lived and his father had grown up. He had plans to open a factory and possibly broker a series of deals between foreign organizations and the new administration to provide water for the city. He was excited by what was waiting.

Kabul lies a little over two hours from Dubai by plane, over an unbroken landscape of ocher and beige mountains. There are almost no trees, though occasionally, far below, you can trace the course of a river cut into the rock, edged with a long green strip of wheat fields and orchards. The airport, six months after the allied invasion, was pitted with deep holes where shells had landed; just off the runways lay the burned-out planes of Afghanistan's small air force; beyond, by the ruins of hangars, were tanks destroyed in the last weeks of fighting. The air was clean and clear; the tawny mountains, tipped by snow that descended in rivulets of white along the cusp, stretched away forever in patterns of color that seemed to grow darker with distance; the sky was very blue. The airport hall was cramped, noisy, frenetic; there were soldiers and UN posters about land mines and security precautions. "Do not travel," said one, "to places that other people are not going to." Arriving passengers were given forms to fill in, with questions about identity and address. Not knowing what to write, I looked for Nasir, and found him leaning silently against a pillar in the chaos. He was biting his lips, his pencil poised in the air above his form, hesitating.

There was only one blank left on his form. "What," asked this last question, "is the reason for your visit?" As I watched, Nasir's pencil descended. In English, in a firm, large, rounded hand, he wrote: "Coming home."

• • •

THE AFGHANS KNOW about exile. Until recently, theirs was the country with the largest number of its people dispersed—refugees in neighboring Iran and Pakistan, or, farther afield, in America, Germany, Britain, and the Gulf States. During the 1980s and 1990s, when Afghanistan was almost totally cut off from the world, first by the Soviet invasion, then by the mujahedeen conducting their own civil war, and later by the Taliban, I used to read about the refugees, and wonder what it was like to come from a country from which almost one in every four of its inhabitants had fled. From 1979, when Nur Mohamed Taraki declared Afghanistan a democratic republic, and Moscow moved to shore up the insurgency with military equipment and advisers, Afghans had left in waves, via precipitate flights on foot, by car, truck, donkey, and camel, leaving behind houses and lands and possessions and, sometimes, elderly grandparents too frail to make the arduous journey over the mountains to safety. During the confused years of warlords and mujahedeen, during the reign of the austere and punitive young Taliban, bent on imposing their brand of implacable Islam, I used to hear about derelict and abandoned villages, empty except for a handful of elderly people, sometimes sharing a single room for warmth and safety. The young, for the most part single men in their twenties and thirties, but families, too, the women silent and watchful, came to the West with stories of torture and executions.

By the time the allies attacked, on October 6, 2001, those who stayed behind had endured twenty-three years of lawlessness, rape, killings, looting, expulsions, and displacement as, one after another, groups of fighters, often aided by foreign powers, had destroyed their fabled irrigation system, mined their orchards and fields, leveled their cities, closed their schools and hospitals, plundered their possessions, and driven many of their brightest and strongest abroad. One in four Afghan children could expect to be dead before the age of five. Kabul was virtually destroyed, and sewage ran along open gutters. The handful of tarmac roads that once linked the larger cities—Afghanistan is the size of Texas—had become all but impassable after years of neglect, erosion, and war. The water supply had once been the pride of Afghanistan: through underground canals, the people had irrigated wheat fields, orchards, and vineyards. That system had collapsed under mines and shelling. There was no postal system, no telephone, no national newspaper; all the law books were said to have been burned by the Taliban. There never had been a railway. And there were said to be as many as 10 million unexploded land mines—down wells, in fields, among the ruined houses. A country once self-sufficient had been reduced by war and drought to penury.

After the allies began their bombing, and the warlords, assisted by the Americans, began their advance on Kabul, UN agencies, long in waiting over the Pakistan border in Islamabad and Peshawar, started to prepare for what they assumed would be a new wave of refugees. For a while, there was confusion: Pakistan and then Iran closed their borders, and one heard of terrified and destitute families, clinging together in the rocky, barren no-man's-land, unable to move either forward or backward. But the predicted exodus never happened. When the borders opened, there were not many people wanting to leave Afghanistan. Most Afghans preferred to sit this conflict out.

On November 13, 2001, Kabul fell. The remnants of the Taliban took to the mountains to the east, along the North-West Frontier province of Pakistan, and to the south, where the valleys and high passes were full of tunnels and secret caves. An Interim Authority was sworn in, to prepare for a *loya jirga*, a grand council of elders, and for eventual democratic elections; in Bonn, the international community pledged $4.5 billion in aid to rebuild. Afghanistan was in the grip of a four-year drought, and 70 percent of the buildings in Kabul had been reduced to rubble.

In November, when the first humanitarian experts flew cautiously in to scout out the lay of the land, they found Kabul silent, empty, and eerie. The university lay in ruins; in the library, ancient religious tomes had been punctured by bullet holes. Nothing moved on the streets. Around the airport at Bagram, not a single house was standing. By February 2002, the UN agencies and the nongovernmental organizations that had been looking after the Afghan refugees for over two decades in Pakistan were frantically shifting their operations from Peshawar to Kabul, in anticipation of the waves that would now come home. In keeping with a report drafted by Lakhdar Brahimi, the UN special representative, Afghanistan was to be regarded as a model for a more coordinated and sensitive approach to UN assistance. "Consultation," "involvement," a "light footprint" became the catchphrases of foreign involvement. Kabul, overnight, became hectic, its residents boasting wanly of traffic jams, though apart from ancient yellow taxis, bicycles, and the jeeps carrying heavily armed militia and the ISAF peacekeeping forces, the traffic was all white Toyota Land Cruisers, the logos of aid agencies and NGOs painted on their sides. Kabul had become a place of expectations.

The refugees did start to come home. They came because President Hamid Karzai asked them to, promising that in the new Afghanistan they would prosper and be safe. They came because the UNHCR told them that it would pay for their journeys and give them food and money with which to rebuild their lives. They came because Iran and Pakistan were growing weary of their long-term guests and had started to make Afghans' lives uneasy with threats and random attacks and demands for bribes. And they came because they wanted to come home, because after years in a foreign land they wished to grow up, or die, in the place their families remembered as their own, where they belonged, and where they were beholden to no one. They were tired of being unwelcome.

By March 2002, though Al Qaeda still controlled some of the mountain areas, though land mines littered their fields, and though their houses had been reduced to rubble, they were on their way back. March is traditionally the first month of migration in this part of the world, when the snows have melted sufficiently to make the high roads passable and when enough months of light and sun remain to plant and build before the bitter cold winter weather descends. By June, they were coming in thousands, by July in tens of thousands, arriving at the outskirts of Kabul, where UNHCR had set up a reception center. They came in buses and trucks, streaming up over the high plateau in clouds of dust at first light, piled high with quilts and bales and buckets, their metalwork brilliantly decorated with peacocks and lovebirds, camels, palm trees, leopards, and lions stalking in jungles. By July, it was clear to everyone that this was likely to be the largest mass return in modern history.

· · ·

WHEN THE ENGLISH writer and historian Robert Byron visited Kabul in the 1930s, he found strongly scented yellow and white roses in the British minister's garden, along with sweet williams, peonies, canterbury bells, and columbines. He noted that the town was small, shady, and set in the middle of a great green plain, the houses surrounded by well-irrigated and neatly tended gardens, with long avenues of trees, mostly poplars. Three quarters of a century later, the city is a ruin, a shell of houses open to the wind and dust, with flies hanging in clouds over the deep gutters that act as open sewers along the roads. There are very few roses anywhere.

I note that the city is crowded with jeeps in which ride soldiers with their rifles at the ready, and that the boys in the streets are selling long green cucumbers that hang like fat worms from their barrows, and flat sheets of bread that look like loofahs, pinned up by pegs, much as the Chinese hang up ducks in the windows of restaurants. Half the women are wearing sky-blue burqas, with their small mesh panels for their eyes, while the rest wind scarves around their heads. After dark, when a curfew confines foreigners to their hotels and guest houses, the talk is of warlords, weapons, opium, and the assassination of the vice president, shot, it is said, on the orders of another warlord. The electricity supply is still erratic, there is not much water, and the telephones do not work, because the UN has installed one system for itself and the government, and aid agencies have installed another, for everyone else: the two are not compatible. This creating a new country is heady work for those who sweated out the Taliban years, for those who went into exile and spent the time dreaming of a better future, for the aid world, which perceives a virgin land on which to try its new theories, for lawyers who plan to draft a constitution full of the human rights so long denied the Afghans, for women, escaping the terrible isolation imposed on them by the misogynist Taliban, and for the UN, for whom Afghanistan may provide redemption after the debacles of Rwanda and Somalia. Playing at new countries is fun.

Not many districts of Kabul were as badly shelled as the west, traditionally home to the Hazaras, among the most persecuted of Afghanistan's main ethnic groups. The Hazaras are descendants of the Mongols and Turks who fought with Genghis Khan and lost their lands and lives in successive brushes with Tajik and Pashtun warlords, who killed or enslaved over half their number in the late nineteenth century. Wanting to learn what the returning refugees are up against, I went to West Kabul, which, in July 2002, still looked like photographs of Berlin in 1945. Mounds of earth and dirt marked where houses once stood, though the jagged remains of more solid buildings lined the main roads; the rafters for the roofs have long since gone, taken by the Taliban for firewood.

But West Kabul is already also a place of purpose. The Hazaras, accustomed to conflict and defeat, had planned their exodus two decades earlier with foresight. Fleeing the civil war and the Taliban, they had journeyed for the most part together, over the mountains to the east, to the cities and refugee camps of Pakistan. There, they had regrouped and waited. Twenty or more years later, they were still there, still together and waiting, and when news came that Kabul was again safe, they hired trucks with the money promised by

UNHCR and traveled back together to reclaim their part of the city. In Pakistan, the Hazaras had become renowned weavers of carpets, and now whole factories decided to make the journey home together, the owners and middlemen as well as the weaver families whose young children provide the bulk of the work force. They brought with them their vats, dyes, and wool. And because the workday for the children includes several hours of schooling, the Hazaras brought their schools with them, the teachers accompanying their pupils in the peacock-and-leopard-painted buses and trucks.

Since there was no building standing for the school to occupy, the first lessons took place in the shell of a compound, teachers and children crouching in the remains of former rooms that had been swept clean and divided by curtains of bright cloth. Within three days of their return, looms had been erected in houses that were hastily being rebuilt around them, and children as young as six and seven were sitting in their rows on long benches, plucking threads through the taut string. I found twelve-year-old Abdul Hakim, a thin, energetic boy with the quick movements of a small animal, eager to practice the English he had acquired in Peshawar. He led me from the school along dusty tracks between the ruins to where his five brothers and sisters were at work, chattering and weaving like a row of brightly colored little birds. It was their turn to go to school later in the day. The family has been lucky. They came home to find their house, though partially ruined, at least unoccupied. Their neighbors had found theirs intact, but inhabited by a family able to produce deeds proving ownership: the house had changed hands many times in twenty-three years, starting, after the original family's departure, with a new set of deeds, forged by a local warlord.

The teacher who walked with us was Jawad Wafa, a slender, gentle young man with soft brown hair. He is twenty-two. Jawad came from Bamiyan, in the high mountains of the Hindu Kush, and his family has spent the years of exile in Iran. Jawad himself had to stay in Pakistan. "My father," said Jawad in his soft, precise English, "was a farmer, with many fields of wheat, and a religious scholar. When fighting came to our village in 1988, he decided that we should leave and go abroad, though my two married sisters were to stay behind. We left one night on foot, with a donkey and a horse to carry our things to Qetta in Pakistan. But my eldest brother had heard that things were better for refugees in Iran, and he went ahead to see. He sent word that he had found well-paid work in a factory making loaves of sugar, and that there was work there for my other five brothers as well. I was only eight then. Even though the work was enough to support all of us, I hated Iran. In the street, people used to insult us and call us names. Our accents were different. At last, I was given a place in a religious school in Qom, but one day the religious police picked me up and held me in jail for a month and shaved my hair."

Jawad was never safe. He has the distinctive flat face and slightly slanting eyes of the Hazaras, and during the long years when Afghans were living in great numbers in Iran—2 million people at the peak—there were periods of mass expulsions back into Afghanistan, particularly of young men. They were picked up in the streets or late at night, held in camps near the border, then pushed across with orders not to return. The day came when this happened to fourteen-year-old Jawad, and he found himself in Herat, alone, with no money and no friends.

"The Taliban were just starting to be powerful. I saw them in the streets, with their great turbans and their scissors to cut the hair of men they thought wore it too long. They stopped me all the time to ask if I had said my prayers. After a few days I found a way to go back to Bamiyan, but it was six years since I had left and my married sisters did not recognize me. I got ill and didn't know what to do. I tried to get back into Iran, but I was stopped at the border and pushed back."

Jawal now had little choice but to find a home in Pakistan. He heard of a religious school in Peshawar, founded by an Iranian cleric, and for the next five years he lived and studied in the madrassa. He saw his parents only once: he got word that his father had had a stroke, so he slipped across the Iranian border by night to see him, returning the next day to the madrassa. Meanwhile, in Pakistan the mood was changing. Soon confrontations between the traditional religious teachers and their secular young pupils, who wanted to be taught to speak English and use computers, led to bitter fights and expulsions. Jawad was one of eighteen young men deemed to be troublemakers and expelled. He was trying his hand as an apprentice tailor when he met Aziz, an energetic and somewhat older Hazara, who was then in the process of setting up a school for Hazara weaving children in Peshawar. Aziz offered him a deal: he personally would coach the younger man in English and political science, if Jawad would join his school and teach the children to read and write.

Jawad was one of the teachers whom Aziz sent on ahead, as the Taliban were pulling out of Kabul, to prepare for the transfer of the school back to Afghanistan. He found an abandoned and derelict building, bought some whitewash, acquired tables and chairs. In May 2002, the school traveled across the mountains in a truck, with its textbooks. The children missed just three days of schooling. "I am very anxious," Jawad said to me. "I am anxious but also hopeful. I need a proper university education if I am to help my country. But I have too little time to study and no one to help me. I plan to become a lawyer. If we don't have social justice, we will never become men for ourselves: our destiny will be that of people who carry wheels on their shoulders for others."

• • •

IN 1836, LIEUTENANT Colonel Sir Alexander Burnes, visiting Kabul with a British military expedition, set out west from the city on a journey into the mountains. From Kareez-i-Meer, where he and his party halted for the first night, he noted in his journal that he could see, "in the hazy distance, a vast vista of gardens extending for some thirty or forty miles... No written description can do justice to this lovely and delightful country. Throughout the whole of our journey we had been lingering amidst beautiful orchards, the banks of which were clustered over with wild flowers and plants in profuse abundance." Among the "wide spreading plane-trees" and the grapes, "which imparted a purple tinge to the hills," Burnes spotted porcupines, hedgehogs, and marmots, though he observed, with his sportsman's eye, that "everything that yields a fur" was hunted by the Afghans. What Burnes had seen was the fabled Shomali plain, the former orchards of Kabul, a rich plateau irrigated by deep wells and the snowmelt, which flowed along the *qanats* or channels buried far underground to water vineyards and fruit trees. Babur, the Moghul emperor Zahiruddin Mohammed, descendant of Genghis Khan and Tamburlaine, who spotted sixteen varieties of wild tulip growing in the hills around Kabul, one of which bore the scent of red roses, loved the Shomali plain and came, in the sixteenth century, while on his way to India, to picnic beneath its mulberry trees. There he remarked on the excellence of the quinces and plums, and observed that the valley was home to parrots, mynah birds, peacocks, and monkeys, and that the local people laid snares for migrating herons and cranes, in order to decorate their turbans with the feathers.

But the Shomali plain was also where, during the 1980s and 1990s, the mujahedeen fought one another and the Soviets for the approaches to Kabul, and where the Taliban decreed a scorched-earth policy to level the ground for self-protection. Over a period of several years, acting alone or ordering others to do their work, the Taliban shelled the leafy Shomali villages into ruins, set fire to the vineyards to starve the economy, destroyed the avenues of planes and poplars to prevent the rebuilding of roofs, chopped down the mulberry trees that gave shade and fruit to passing strangers, dropped mines down the wells and *qanats* and laid them in the fields of wheat. The Shomali plain came to be a symbol of Taliban savagery. By the summer of 2002, when I saw it, it was a derelict, deserted, silent wilderness, broken only by the red printed warnings about unexploded mines, and by the clusters of green flags waving on the end of poles, each marking the grave of a martyr, a man who has died a violent death. It was a barren, desolate place.

But not, as it turned out, entirely empty.

Searching for signs of Babur's earthly paradise, I saw two men, with white beards and flat felt Afghan hats, at work in a half-burned vineyard close to the main road north toward Mazar-e-Sharif. Behind them were the ruins of a once large village and the great stumps of what must have been a magnificent row of mulberry trees. The men were gently picking up unexploded shells and putting them on a pile, ready for collection by a demining agency working in the plain. It was hot and still and very dusty. The men were cousins.

In the early 1980s, explained the older man, Haji Kamal, the village of Logar, named for the province of his great-grandfather, who had planted these lands, had been home to forty families, most of them related to one another. With its avenues of trees, its orchards of apricot, apple, plum, and pear, Logar had been a tranquil and shady place. Haji Kamal and his three brothers had owned, between them, 12,000 vines, from which they produced 600 sacks of raisins and many table grapes, sold in the bazaar in Kabul together with wheat, melons, maize, apricots, walnuts, and several kinds of cherries, as well as an abundance of the sugary white mulberries that the Afghans eat dried during the winter months. The Kandari red grapes were the sweetest, Haji Kamal told me, but not the most valuable; those were the white ones, which he dried slowly inside the house. He had grown eleven varieties of grape, drying most of them in the sun during the month of October, on the roof of his house or spread out on the ground. In the late 1970s, Chinese farming technicians had visited Logar and introduced pomegranates to the valley, and these, too, had made him a fine crop. Haji Kamal's family, with his children and his brothers and their families, had grown to eighty people by the time the mujahedeen came, and they shared between them eight milking cows and a donkey, as well as a small tractor. When the Soviets invaded in 1979, he had just opened shops in Kandahar and Kabul, and made a deal to sell fifty tons of raisins each year to China.

After the Soviet shelling began, and he began to fear for his family's lives, Haji Kamal sent his wife and children to Pakistan. They left by truck at dawn, taking with them the cows. It was a morning so cold that there was heavy snow in the passes and one of his pregnant daughters lost her baby. He stayed on fighting with the mujahedeen, then joined his family in a rented house in Peshawar, where he sent his young sons, but not his daughters, to school, and from time to time he made the journey home across the mountains to check on his abandoned fields and crumbling house. Until the Taliban were defeated, he had not judged it safe to come back, but here he was now, with his cousin Amir Jan, also one of several brothers, planning, with the help of UNHCR and various foreign aid organizations, which were providing rafters and windows, to rebuild the compound in which they had once lived. In the years of exile his family had grown from eighty to two hundred people; but if the fields could be made fertile again, there would be enough food for them all.

The two elderly cousins, with their lean bearded faces and elegant pale gray turbans, led me to see their compounds, now mounds of dust and rubble around the stumps of the mulberry trees that had once provided such dense green shade. In one, a large white tent, donated by UNHCR, sheltered some of the women and children who had returned with them; there was a cow, tethered to a pomegranate bush. It was a bleak but not despairing scene. The water from his well alone, Haji Kamal said, gave him great pleasure: very cold and very pure, it reminded him that he had come home from his borrowed life in a rented room in Peshawar, where he had always felt hot and cramped. "Though I found everything ruined, I knelt down and kissed the ground. I don't expect a harvest for two years. But at least we can walk along the road, in safety, even at night. We feel safe."

•   •   •

BEFORE I LEFT Kabul, early one morning I went to watch the families arriving at the UNHCR reception center at Pulicharki, site of a notorious Taliban prison, under a fold of the tall ocher mountains. UNHCR has put up tents and hangars, where they hand out rations of wheat, buckets, bars of soap, and plastic sheets, and where doctors from Médecins Sans Frontières monitor the health of the new arrivals and vaccinate against measles and polio. UNHCR gives small sums of money to every returning refugee, though the aid agencies are conscious that they must not show too much favor to the refugees and thereby produce resentment among those who endured the Taliban years. The money men, who are all Afghan, supervised by UNHCR, sit cross-legged behind wire cages, counting out the dollars. One tent has been made into a simulated mine field, where families are walked past the weapons they might expect to find, unexploded, in their fields. Over the mountains to the east, in swirling bursts of dust, come the trucks, their painted sides catching the sun, swaying under their loads of mattresses and blankets, mats and sewing machines, bicycles and cooking pots, accumulated in exile. The families who climbed out talked about how hard life had been in Pakistan and about the perils of the journey during which they have been preyed on by police and guards in search of bribes. Farmers in the 1970s and 1980s, they have since become cobblers and builders, shopkeepers and mechanics. The young boys speak little, but the girls are bold: egging one another on, they talked of the education many have received and about their plans to become doctors and teachers in the new Afghanistan. A small, robust, outspoken girl of fourteen, who can remember almost nothing of their village and had spent ten years in a refugee camp, said that her plan was to attend Kabul University. On her head, she wore a plain scarf. "I am not in the habit of wearing a veil," she said. By midday, the process of arrival was over; it had been an orderly, cheerful procedure. The morning's 5,000 returnees, with their buckets and bars of soap, were on their way, by taxi or in the cars of relatives come to collect them, to discover what was left of home; or what they have come to call home, for it is said that more than half of all those "returning" to Afghanistan in 2002 were in fact born outside the country. The brightly decorated trucks and buses were climbing the mountain passes again, to collect more returning families.

Before I caught my plane back to Dubai, Nasir took me to see a friend in government, Nabi Farahi, deputy minister of finance, whom he had known a quarter of a century earlier, when both were students at the university. Farahi sat out the Taliban years as a professor of Pashtu, lying low when others provoked the Taliban. A charming, bespectacled, bearded man in his sixties, he offered melon to counteract the intense heat of his unair-conditioned office, apologizing for the lack of elevator, telephone, computer, carpet, or fan. To wipe up the melon juice, he sent his assistant to fetch unused forms from previous governments. Farahi is appalled at the speed with which the refugees are coming home. "We have nothing for them yet," he said. "No jobs, no houses. This country doesn't work. It is too soon." Like all Afghans in positions of some authority, he worries when he sees the few good jobs going to men who have come back from exile with skills those who stayed behind had no chance to learn, and at the way that the foreign aid organizations are casually poaching the best people with salaries that can run to fifty times those the bankrupt Afghan state can offer. "I would like to see some dignity in the way people are returning," he said, licking melon juice from his fingers. "It is only chaos." It was Farahi who first mentioned to me the resentment many Afghans feel about how so much money has been promised, and so little visibly delivered.

Within six months, well over a million people had heeded Karzai's calls and UNHCR's promises and come home; this was more than had been expected for the entire year. At this rate, there would be 2 million by the time the snows came, returned to a country without houses, roads, schools, hospitals, water, or electricity. "I see our job as software," said a man working for the UN. "We are trying to provide the rewiring of the system, but we will not be here to run it. The Afghans have to learn to do it for themselves." For their part, the Afghans fear that the West will not fulfill its promises. As they watch the Land Cruisers speeding along the dusty roads, they remind one another that the West had promised things before, when they wanted the Soviets out, but that once the Soviets had gone, the West did not seem quite as committed as before.

Out on the Shomali plain, Haji Kamal is very conscious of the

fragility of the transitional government and the power of the encir-
cling warlords, and of the coming winter, when snow, and winds no
longer broken by trees, will turn his valley into a harsh and forbid-
ding place. It was in the next few months, he said, that Afghanistan's
future would be decided.

. . .

ALMOST EXACTLY A year later, I went back to Afghanistan to see
how the refugees had survived their first winter. I wanted to find Abdul, the ebullient small boy who had led me through the dusty alleys
of West Kabul; to see whether Jawad had won his place at the university; and whether Haji Kamal and Amar Jan had rebuilt their
houses in the Shomali plain and were growing grapes for raisins
once again. I had heard that the Hazara weavers' school was flourishing. Nasir, to whom I spoke from time to time on the telephone,
told me that he had reoccupied his family home in the center of
Kabul, but that there was nothing but confusion over the awarding
of the lucrative contracts for roads, telephones, and electricity. He
was still hesitating, flying in and out of Kabul on Ariana's ancient jet,
trying to gauge the stability of the new Afghanistan. He could not
quite make up his mind how far to commit himself, he kept saying,
over the crackling line. Money was pouring into the city, houses
were being built and fetching enormous rents, but there was no certainty anywhere. No one felt safe. Only the foreign aid specialists,
he said, seemed in control, and even they would soon be leaving.

Flying in low over the bare mountains, I found the airport still
pitted with shell holes, the burned-out tanks still in their places
along the runways. Inside the terminal, the chaos was unchanged,
but pictures of General Masood, the Northern Alliance warlord assassinated in the closing days of Taliban power, have replaced the
earlier notices about land mines. On my plane were two middle-
aged Afghan brothers. They had fled the city twenty-four years before and were now bringing the body of their father home for burial
in a Kabul he had never been able to visit in his long years in exile.
They were uneasy, talkative. In their pockets were the deeds to the

family house, long since occupied by others, over which they anticipated one of the fierce property wrangles in which many returnees
have been ensnared.

We landed in Kabul soon after a flight from Frankfurt, bearing
additional prosperous returnees, businessmen and engineers and
academics who have made lives in the West and were now, like my
friend Nasir, coming back to see the lay of the land. An elegant
Afghan woman in her forties, with many trunks, dressed in a stylish
combination of Afghan and Western dress, struggled to find her
luggage. *"Entshuldige"* (Sorry), she was saying loudly, pushing her
way through the Afghan porters with their turbans and flat hats,
"Entshuldige, entshuldige." A young Afghan man with a strong American accent, crew cut, cocky, and bemused, was telling all who will
listen that this was his first visit to Kabul and that he had come to
meet a grandmother he had never seen. His real name is Mohamed,
but he likes to be called Mo. Born and bred in Manhattan, Mo was
incredulous and a little scornful of the chaos. "This is not really my
place, you know. I don't belong here."

Kabul, I wrote that night in my diary, has changed little in a year.
There is more razor wire on foreign and United Nations buildings;
there are more women wearing burqas, a sign of the diminished
faith most Afghans now have in an independent future in which
women would be free to be bold. The crowds are thicker and the
city is dirtier and dustier, Kabul's population having apparently doubled to 2.5 million people. And the Land Cruisers are now lost in a
permanent traffic jam of taxis, trucks, old cars, donkeys, and bicycles. The pollution is so bad that to live in Kabul, it is said by foreign
residents, is to smoke the equivalent of forty-five packs of cigarettes
a day. There are many more beggars, mostly women in burqas with
babies, and small boys are selling tattered copies of a U.S. Marine
training manual by the roadside. A hundred thousand returnees are
apparently squatting in the ruins of the city, destitute. Afghanistan is
still, in the language of the aid world, a SCCPI, a "situation of
chronic conflict and political instability," its people short of food
and vulnerable to disease, physical assault, and forced displacement.

But there are roses out along the avenues leading into the city, and over a garden wall I saw a pink lavatera in flower. The fruit sellers have watermelons and mangoes, and the policeman was still where I had left him, directing traffic from a purple plush sofa, perched on a raised dais in the middle of the road. In the UN compounds geraniums and zinnias are growing, watered by channels cut out of the earth, and in the bazaar are new photograph shops, showing the unveiled faces of young women. Masood's hawklike, brooding, unsmiling face is on every billboard.

Though the city is bustling and full of energy, in a state of constant rebuilding and activity, the refugees, it is said, have become cautious. When the snows had melted and the migrations began again, in March 2003, they did not flock home in anything like the same numbers as the previous year and as it had been feared they would. They have neither been pushed by increased intolerance in Pakistan and Iran, nor pulled by promises of work and houses. The tales of resettlement that have traveled back over the mountains have not been altogether happy ones, and the numbers arriving at Pulicharki daily in their brightly painted buses are said by the UN to be down to six hundred. Also, something has been done to curb those who traveled back and forth over the border, again and again, each time collecting money and rations, soap and plastic sheeting from the World Food Programme and UNHCR. A sophisticated machine that photographs the iris of each returnee and keeps a print on a database has been introduced.

The Hazaras have been hard at work rebuilding West Kabul. Along the road leading out to the weavers' school, timber and brick merchants are doing a brisk trade. If the city buildings are still shells, their jagged walls in ruins, the side streets are by contrast full of builders and carpenters. The reconstruction of the capital is said to be in the hands of wealthy returnees, or warlords and their commanders, eager to control the money and the patronage all these projects entail. Aziz, the energetic young Hazara who is much involved in his people's return, had come to the airport to meet me and the friend with whom I was traveling, Frances D'Souza. He said that some 300,000 Hazaras have already returned to West Kabul, where his school now has 870 pupils, studying in two shifts, and that it has moved to a new compound, a series of classrooms built of cinder block, an innovation brought back with returning refugee builders from Pakistan and judged greatly superior to the old Afghan mud and straw. More than half his pupils, Aziz said with pride, are girls, and in the evening, when the rooms are given over to classes in literacy, he could fill his center six times over with women queuing for the education denied them by the Taliban. Aziz notes these numbers with delight. "People have come home from Pakistan and Iran believing that education is their passport to a better life." He is teaching humanism and human rights and what he calls a benevolent interpretation of the Koran to his top class, tightly packed rows of serious young men and women.

In the alleys behind the school, in among the building sites and timber merchants, the carpet trade is booming. Aziz believes that there are at least six hundred factories, some employing as many as five hundred weavers, mostly working in their own homes, the patterns drawn out by young apprentice draftsmen on graph paper and quickly memorized by the children at the looms. The work is slow: five to six hours weaving every day except Friday, precise, meticulous work that needs small fingers and affects the eyes and lungs, but brings in enough money to support the entire family. The looms stand in the cool, under the pomegranate bushes and the vines. It takes four months for a family to weave a carpet three yards wide and four yards long. In Aziz's school, the children talk of their futures as doctors, teachers, and engineers.

Not all the foreign experts who have made Kabul their base— there are said to be over a thousand registered NGOs alone—are as sanguine as Aziz about the country's future. In February 2003, four months before my return, a Brazilian working for the International Committee of the Red Cross was stopped on a busy road outside Kandahar by a militia group. The commander, recognizing the Red Cross painted on the front of the Land Cruiser, pointed to his false leg and thanked the Brazilian for having saved his life during an earlier skirmish. A Red Cross team, he told him, had been on hand and had amputated his leg; otherwise he would surely have died. Then, taking from his pocket a mobile telephone, the commander called his warlord. He spoke, listened, came back, drew out his gun, and shot the Brazilian dead.

Incidents like this have made foreigners wary and no one, now, feels safe. Within the UN compounds, behind the razor wire and the concrete pillars, there is talk of how much can be achieved for Afghanistan and how quickly, before the money runs out and with it the political will to restore such an ailing country to a semblance of democratic rule. Only, they add, it is of course not so much a question of restoration as of imposition. Afghanistan never was a democracy; it was, and is, a loose federation of tribal fiefdoms, ruled over by powerful warlords, and thus it seems set to remain. Andrew Wilder is a British academic who has lived in Afghanistan off and on for many years. Early in 2002, he arrived in Kabul with a small monitoring unit, funded by the Swiss and the Swedes, and a remit to do something seldom done in UN circles: analyze data on the spot. Wilder is not happy with what he sees around him. Over fourteen months, he has watched the UN agencies bicker over priorities and chains of command, nongovernmental organizations proliferate and go their own ways, and more attention and money go to the easier and more visible problems than to the more difficult and crucial ones. Sitting in a prefabricated hut on the grounds of a former prime minister's residence, Wilder fears for the future. The theories behind development and the delivery of aid have become more complex and sophisticated all the time, he points out, but they are not matched by performance; disillusion and disappointment fester over how few expectations have been realized. Security, argues Wilder, was always known to be the major issue in Afghanistan: how to make the country safe from the warlords and free of weapons? "Everyone, from Karzai down, knew that security should be addressed first. So what did we do? We provided assistance first, with the assumption that security would follow. It hasn't."

On my first day back in Kabul, I found a driver and went out to the Shomali plain, to see how Haji Kamal and his family had survived the winter. The dog roses were out along the hedgerows and the fields around Logar were full of men working at the grapevines, now watered and pruned and sprouting once more. The UN tent had gone. In both Haji Kamal's compound and that of his cousin Amar Jan, there were signs of building. Seven rooms had been finished, long whitewashed rooms with windows and rafters donated by a foreign aid organization, now furnished with felt carpets and lined with pillows in reds and greens. From the cool of Haji Kamal's main room, which he has painted a bright blue wash, visitors can look out over pomegranate bushes and chickens pecking in the dirt. There is a new outside bread oven, and a second cow and four sheep have appeared. He told me that all his children and grandchildren who can walk half an hour there and back are at the village school, and he and Amar Jan have planted tomatoes, radishes, potatoes, eggplants, and onions. Along the avenues of mulberries destroyed by the Taliban, new shoots are growing from the stumps of the trees.

Of Logar's forty original families, all but six have come home. Haji Kamal, the former member of the mujahedeen, is a man of peace now: he talked of his new orchards, of the apples and plums and almonds from which he expects a first crop in three years' time, and of the lessons he gives his grandchildren about the unexploded mines, still plentiful across his land. But he is pleased, every day, to be home. Not long ago he turned down the offer of a job for his eldest son in Dubai, saying that he no longer wished to have his children live away from him. He fears only the weakness of the central government in Kabul, and the power of the warlords, grown strong and lazy from looting and extortion. "What do I miss from my years in Pakistan? Nothing. There is nothing to miss. I have no single good memory of exile."

. . .

ON MY FIRST visit, it had been too dangerous to move far outside Kabul; this time I planned to go to the Hindu Kush to see for myself how the people returning from exile to the high mountain villages had fared during the long snowy winter. I knew that the numbers coming home dropped during the cold season, but that the refugees were again arriving, by bus and truck, over the passes. They worry that unless they come soon, their homes and lands will be occupied by others.

Nancy Dupree wrote her guide to Afghanistan back in 1972, before the Russians arrived, when foreign visitors still came to sightsee and fish for trout in the high mountains. She traveled up into the Hindu Kush to visit the valley of Bamiyan, where a Buddhist sect in the fourth century cut two immense Buddhas out of the mountain face, and a third smaller one in a niche between them. For the journey, she described two roads, not paved but decent. Neither the one that crossed the 12,000-foot Hijigak pass, nor the one that skirted the lower Shibar mountain, the watershed between the Oxus and the Indus, would take longer than seven hours, and either would offer a delightful and memorable journey. The journey remains delightful in many ways, but twenty-six years of neglect and fighting have reduced the roads to little more than riverbeds, pitted with huge craters and strewn with rocks; the few cars and trucks that make the journey prefer to travel in convoy, for fear of breakdown or attack.

Eleven hours of painful bucketing over the stones takes the traveler through some of the most dramatic scenery in the world, the bald peaks of the Hindu Kush, tinged for most of the year with snow, stretching forever into the distance in shades of beige and ocher and purple, against a sky of deep, pure blue. There is a constant sound of water, from the snowmelt down the riverbed. The million or so Kuchi nomads, who once regarded the highlands of the Hindu Kush as their summer pasture, have not returned to their grazing lands, for they have lost their herds to fighting and drought; there were no animals to be seen. In any case the Hazaras, who occupy this part of Afghanistan, do not want the Kuchis back, for the Kuchis famously sided with the Taliban in their battles, and many Kuchi leaders became Taliban commanders whose savage ways are remembered all too well. The summer grazing, say the Hazaras going home, will be excellent for the herds they now intend to build up for themselves.

Long before the traveler starts the long climb toward the pass, having left Kabul along a brief but very smooth stretch of tarmac, a legacy of the Taliban years, you come across a first long, lush valley, with a racing river to irrigate orchards and plantations of poplars. In the fields grow potatoes and wheat; in neat rows between the crops and trees, in plots of their own, are the poppy fields, white and pink against the bright surrounding green of the grass, the rocky mountains, and blue sky above. From far away, the poppies look like wild flowers, growing in profusion in this green and fertile valley; from close to they look like rows of tulips, their petals large and firm. They have a festive air. The nearest laboratories capable of transforming the poppies into heroin lie far to the south, around Kandahar. In the Hindu Kush, poppies are smoked as opium, though all but a very small part of the crop is sold to traders in Kabul. Before the Taliban came, Afghanistan was the world's main producer of heroin. The Taliban, for a while, curbed production. When the UN arrived, in the winter of 2001, it offered grants to farmers willing to substitute their most profitable cash crop for any other. But today Afghanistan is again at the top of world heroin production, the farmers having understood that by growing poppies they cannot lose: they are paid equally well to dig them up or to sell them to warlords and their middlemen. Along with much else that the refugees are bringing back from their years in Iran and Pakistan is a taste for drugs, especially, so it is said, among young Hazara men.

I wanted to see Bamiyan, because I had heard that Wadad Jafa, the young Hazara teacher from Aziz's school in West Kabul, was now working with the UN in the Hindu Kush; and because Bamiyan, which once lay on the silk route between Samarkand and Kabul, is a place of return for the internally displaced, refugees who did not have the money to make the expensive journey across the border into Iran or Pakistan and so had remained in Afghanistan, exiles in their own land. These internally displaced Afghans, like IDPs the world over, are not eligible for the dollars and the bars of soap going to those coming back across the mountains. UNHCR is doing what it can for them, but in a country of such overwhelming want, the ambiguities of the IDP stories do not lend themselves to easy bureaucratic assistance. In Bamiyan, I hoped the predicament of the displaced would become clearer.

Had the Taliban ruled for very much longer, the Hazaras claim, their people would have been wiped out altogether. The Taliban considered them inferior and hostile. Finding them weakened by the Soviet and mujahedeen years, they persecuted them with particular ferocity, and nowhere more than in the province that is traditionally home to most Hazara. Finally the Taliban brought to Bamiyan and its valley the heavy artillery with which to destroy their Buddhas. The valley of Bamiyan itself, with its escarpment running down the middle, is faced along one side by a long and sheer sandstone cliff, perhaps three miles from end to end. The sky and the light, at this altitude, are startlingly bright and clear. The air is pure and sharp. I tried to imagine the Taliban fighters laying the mines, then lining up the tanks that now lie scattered, rusting and broken, around the escarpment, positioning their heavy artillery, then giving the order to fire shells that boomed out in the silence, until the two great Buddhas, standing well over a hundred feet tall in their sheltered niches, with the faded touches of their once red-and-blue-painted robes, modeled out of mud and straw, crumbled and fractured into the valley below.

In the caves and grottoes that surround the Buddhas, pitting the rock face like the holes inhabited by the swallows that flit through the valley, there once lived a community of yellow-robed monks, said to number over a thousand people at its peak in the seventh century. In the summer of 2003, the cliff caves sheltered those coming home to Bamiyan, who had sat out the Taliban savagery in the high secluded valleys of the Hindu Kush where the Taliban seldom ventured. Though not regarded as refugees, they were exiles nonetheless; when they returned in the spring and summer of 2003, it was to homes looted and burned by the departing Taliban, to fields long since gone wild. Like the poppies in the green valleys lower down the mountain, their bright clothes—vermilion, turquoise, and many shades of yellow and purple—stand out dramatically against the dull rock face, as they flit up and down the perilous tracks cut by the monks through their mountain monastery. From the caves, the view over Bamiyan is sad: the old bazaar lies far below, destroyed to rubble when old scores were paid off and the handsome buildings that once dotted the valley, surrounded by magnificent gardens, were razed.

By the time I reached the valley, early in July, 260 returning families were said to inhabit the caves, six or seven people sharing holes once occupied by a single monk. The caves are cool in the summer, but damp and cold when the snows come to Bamiyan in late October. Inside, the frescoes of flowers, griffins, ducks, and musicians that once covered the walls and ceilings have long since been blackened by cooking fires. All but a very few of the cave dwellers are Hazaras, farming families who once lived in some comfort and prosperity on their lands in the valley, growing wheat and potatoes and raising small flocks of sheep and goats. Many of them are single mothers, their husbands and fathers having been killed by the Taliban as they fled. As Amir, one of the older men, explained, as the cave dwellers gathered around to talk, the children solemn and staring, the women breaking in to add their own memories, the final flight for most of them took place in the winter of 1997. The snow was already deep and the winds bitter, and they had put off leaving too long, hoping that the Taliban's attention might turn elsewhere. "Then the day came when we knew that we could not wait any longer. We hid what we could, carried a few necessities with us, like quilts and cooking pots, but there were many small children to help. The old people came with us, but many did not survive the journey. We don't know quite how many died, simply giving up in the high mountains and dying quickly of the cold. We dug mass graves for them at the foot of the mountains. When we found safety in the distant valleys, where the Taliban never came, the farmers there helped us, by giving us flour and shelter. We survived, but that is all."

It was from the women in the caves that I first heard a story that would come to haunt me.

Mira is an energetic, handsome, wiry woman, tall and black-haired, in a purple dress with much embroidery. She has a son of six, a jaunty child with cuts and bruises from falls along the cliff face, and two older girls, silent, pretty, and watchful. Mira's husband, the father of the children, was taken away by the Taliban in 1997, as a hostage after a Hazara attack. She has had no news of him since that day. When her neighbors decided that flight could no longer be put off, she gathered up her four children, the youngest a girl of six months, and followed her friends across the fields. It was soon clear that she could not keep up with them while carrying on her back both a baby and a child too young to walk. "We got to a road, and I knew I couldn't go on." Mira told her story briskly, without emotion. I began to dread what I knew must follow. "It was snowing lightly and dark. I wrapped the baby up in all the clothes that we could spare, and I put her down by the edge of the road, propped up against a rock. Then I picked up my son and, pulling my daughters behind me, I went on with the others to look for shelter for the night in the mountains. Later, I left the children with my neighbors and went back down into the valley to look for the baby. I found her quickly, still propped against the rock. But she was dead."

Mira is not the only woman to have left a child by the wayside in her flight from the Taliban. Talking quickly, pointing to surviving small boys and girls, other women begin to talk of babies set down and never found again, or discovered dead from exposure when they went back to get them. They had no choice, they said. They always picked the youngest, the one who could not stray and whose cries would be the least loud. I became obsessed by this image of small, silent babies, freezing to death alone in the dark and the snow.

As it became clear that the Taliban had left Bamiyan, in the winter of 2001, and that many of their men had disappeared forever, executed in the closing weeks of fighting, the survivors made the journey back over the mountains, better prepared this time, leaving no children or old people behind. They returned, however, to destitution; some of the women have lost five and six sons to the Taliban and are now caring for their grandchildren; the husbands of others were mutilated in the fighting. Some of the other returnees are children on their own. There are many small orphans in the dank holes in the cliff.

By the time of my visit, the people in Bamiyan's caves were living in a curious vacuum, an existence that they have grown used to and that many believe will never end. They send the fitter young men to work in the new bazaar in the plain far below, visible from the caves, where they pick up a little money as porters, and the young girls to make the daily trek to bring water from the river almost a third of a mile distant. The younger children are dispatched to collect firewood in the mountains. Because of the sheer cliff face, each small child requires a constant minder, and it is usual to see babies and small children who are starting to walk harnessed and bound to the older girls.

All along Bamiyan's lush valley, where the first crops of wheat and potatoes are growing, there are other families reduced by the war and exile to the edges of hunger. Many of them are widows unable to reclaim their farms after so many years of neglect, either because their lands have been appropriated by others, or because as women alone they do not have the strength or knowledge to farm them again themselves.

For all this, Bamiyan is not a sad place. Twenty-two expatriate experts, representing every form of foreign aid from Médecins Sans Frontières to Save the Children Fund, Japanese and French, Germans and British, Swedes and Americans, living in air-conditioned guest houses along the escarpment, are busy bringing water, electricity, schooling, family planning, and women's cooperatives to the area. Bamiyan's dusty tracks are full of boys wobbling on their new bicycles, gifts of UNICEF to encourage children to make the journeys to school. Along the higher ridge, where the ground flattens out to provide a runway for the aid world's planes, the American military have put one of their outposts, a "Provincial Reconstruction Team," composed of a mixture of regular soldiers and reservists, sent to offer both security and a campaign for the hearts and minds of Bamiyan's people. Surrounded by the safety of open space, towered over by the great mountains that stretch away behind, the

American base looks like a stockade from the Wild West, with its watchtowers and flagpoles, its row of concrete fortifications and rolled razor wire. Just to see the Americans walking around, with their radios and walkie-talkies and their army boots, makes them feel safe, say the people of Bamiyan, the way they have not felt safe for years.

I found Jawad Wafa, as neat and courteous as ever, in the UN compound, where two foreign aid workers were playing Ping-Pong. His life had not worked out as he had hoped. With the growth of the school in West Kabul, Jawad had lost his sleeping quarters to a new classroom, and, on a salary of $15 a month, had found it hard to survive. Dreams of entering Kabul University had been lost in the ever-increasing demands on him as a teacher. With his family reluctant to return to Bamiyan from their now established and comfortable lives in Iran, Jawad had accepted a job with the UN, in the hopes of becoming one of the first undergraduates at Bamiyan University, which the Americans have promised to rebuild. His pay in Bamiyan is good—over $300 a month—but he is very wary about the future, and disillusioned with the materialistic ambitions of the Hazara leaders, whose motives in exile had once seemed to him so pure, so far removed from personal power. The politics of returnees, their greed and desire for personal gain, have saddened him. He feels rootless, separated from a family he cannot visit: as a former refugee, he has no passport and no ID card, and he fears arrest and ill-treatment by the Iranian border guards if he is caught crossing over into Iran. He has never seen the five nieces and nephews born since he was last at home, five years ago, though his mother wrote to tell him that she has hung a photograph of him on her wall. Jawad has been a refugee since he was eight; he feels himself to be one still.

I went to two more villages before the long journey down through the mountains to Kabul, hearing more stories about babies abandoned along the road to exile, and about men executed by the Taliban; their widows pointed out to me the green flags that mark their violent deaths, standing out bright and clear against the rocky mountains. Then I set off down the rocky track again, past the wrecks of trucks that had slid over the passes and fallen into the ravines far below, past the valley where a dragon was said to have devoured a daily tribute of maidens until a warrior turned him to stone, a mountain stream flowing for eternity with the tears he weeps of remorse. The road leads down along the stony riverbeds where wild rhubarb grows in profusion, and through the pink and white fields of poppies and the orchards of late-flowering Lebanese apple trees, which are said to produce the sweetest fruit.

. . .

IT SEEMED CLEAR that Kabul, in the summer of 2003, nineteen months after the arrival of the liberating forces, was still an aid city, the strings pulled by foreign forces and foreign money, protected by the 1,500 men of the peacekeeping forces, more wary after a suicide bomber killed six of them, and ruled over by a fragile government. A great deal was happening, in terms of income-generating and cash-for-work projects, wells dug and mines removed, lawyers and teachers trained, and a new currency floated, but the city has, as Nasir warned, an uncertain air, as if the players are constantly looking over their shoulders. Nasir had spelled out their fears: the departure of the 15,000 American soldiers from their headquarters at Bagram, the dismantling of the UN operation as donors were lured to newer emergencies and able officials were posted to more sensitive trouble spots, the moving away of the now bustling foreign organizations as money and the interest of backers go elsewhere. "No one reads the history books, and no one listens to those who do," said one weary and seasoned aid worker. "It's all about quick fixes, and we do those very well. But we don't stick around for the real work." Like others, he feared that donors, agencies, the aid organizations with their high salaries, are in danger of overwhelming the fragile Afghan administration, distorting the economy, and losing sight of their most important task, that of building up institutions owned by and accountable to Afghans, while money is being spent almost arbitrarily, more in keeping with funders' whims and desires for a high profile than in response to what is needed. Though most Afghans now

see themselves as Afghans first—hence the vast numbers coming
"home"—this remains a country of some twenty ethnic groups,
ruled over by warlords, who like to call themselves commanders and
who control their fiefdoms with absolute authority and fill the vacuum left where the state should be.

In the summer of 2003 there were still more than 2,000 UN
people in Kabul alone, but there was talk of how there will soon be
no more than a few hundred, plans to "downsize" being already far
advanced. The young men and women, experts in water and refugee
returns and gender studies and security, who are the missionaries of
the modern world, are veterans of these campaigns. They knew one
another in Kosovo and East Timor and will doubtless meet again in
Iraq, the Congo, or wherever the next emergency calls for them.
Bustling about Kabul like doctors and nurses, they provide an efficient, cheerful service. They are fit and full of enthusiasm, and they
work extremely hard, stopping only on Fridays to exercise in the
UN's new gym, its treadmills and rowing machines flown in not
long before from abroad; but they are growing restless. UNHCR's
budget for 2004 has already been set at a quarter less than that for
2003. No one doubts the need for a stable Afghanistan. But the politics are unlikely to allow it. Nor will there be enough money.
Somewhere between $14 and $18 billion is needed in the next ten
years to put Afghanistan on its feet: $4.5 billion had been promised,
rather less than $2 billion delivered. One official told me: "It is not a
question of whether we are going to pull out of Afghanistan. It is a
question of when. In some senses, you could say that we are pulling
out already." Lakhdar Brahimi, a man widely admired and respected, was already on his way to Baghdad. He leaves behind him,
say the skeptics, a tinderbox, with echoes of Vietnam.

Not surprising, then, that the professional Afghans, those who
spent their years of exile studying and training in the West, waiting
for the day when they would cease to be refugees and would return
home to rebuild the new Afghanistan, are hesitating. They feel they
have been deceived, explains Nasir, led to expect things that were
not there. It is the poor who are coming home. And those who are

being forced home, either expelled by the Iranians, or put onto planes by the British. The latter's assertion that Afghanistan is now a safe and fit place for return, intended to placate constituents at home, is sending alarming messages to Iran and Pakistan. Both countries have signed temporary agreements that they will force no more refugees home, despite the huge numbers who remain.

Still in search of the internally displaced, trying to find some line of definition in this persistently hazy field, I wanted before I left to visit the camps set up by UNHCR outside Kandahar for the Kuchis, the now herdless and unpopular nomads reported to make up the greatest part of the 300,000 or so IDPs. (That was the number of people estimated by a mission from the European Union early in 2003 to still be adrift within Afghanistan.) But the shooting of the Brazilian delegate in February had proven the roads around Kandahar unsafe; I was taken instead, by local aid workers, to meet a young Afghan social worker called Amira, who had trained in her years of exile in Pakistan and come home to offer her skills to the interim administration. Amira had agreed to take me to visit three women living with their young children in the old city, widows who are, in her book, the truly displaced, the real IDPs, of Afghanistan today. We drove to the old quarter, where once fine houses, with courtyards and porticoes, are now derelict and ruined. Down one alleyway, through what looked like a mine shaft propping up a crumbling roof, up the remnants of a steep flight of stairs, live Anja, Fatima, and Salima, perching in the ruins in squalor and destitution. The three women have known one another for a long time. They come from the same village in the highlands of the Hindu Kush, not far from Bamiyan. Anja is in her early sixties, and the two younger women barely in their thirties, but all three look considerably older. Fatima's face is thickly lined and Salima is thin and listless. They are widows, their husbands killed at different times in the fighting, when the Taliban came to their valley and laid waste to their homes and fields. Together with nine children under the age of fifteen, they occupy two dark rooms. The smell of feces and rubbish is overpowering.

On one wall in the room Anja and Fatima share with Fatima's

two young daughters, hung high up as is the style in Afghanistan, is a single photograph of a young, scholarly-looking man, in spectacles and city clothes. Though there is very little light, the picture stands out, for there is almost nothing else in the room, beyond a neat pile of mats and quilts in one corner, and two burqas hanging on a peg. "That is my son," said Anja. "He was called Husein. When the Taliban attacked the mujahedeen in our village, he was caught in the crossfire. There was a bullet in his neck and another in his kidneys. He had been in Iran as a refugee, but we were all here in Kabul, because we couldn't afford to get to Iran, and he had gone back to the village to see what the situation was. We hadn't seen him for many months." Fatima is Anja's daughter-in-law. Too poor to make the journey into exile during the civil war, they are now too poor to go home to their valley; in any case, as women alone with small children, they do not feel able to reclaim the lands that were once theirs. Their houses have been destroyed in the fighting, the rafters stolen for firewood, their fields long since claimed by others, and they are skeptical that they would receive any of the international help promised by foreign donors to people going home.

Salima's husband, Mustafa, was the first of the three women's husbands to die. Five years ago, when the Taliban attacked their village, the family was preparing to flee to safety with other villagers when a stray bullet caught him as he was carrying a first load of belongings out of their house. "There was no hospital to take him to," she said. "I simply held him in my arms and he died. We just sat there staring at him, because we couldn't believe it: one moment he was alive, and then he was dead." Because she stayed behind to bury him, Salima and her seven children were forced to make the journey to safety alone, the other villagers having already left. "We were the last to leave. The village was deserted. It took us a week to get to Kabul, sleeping out in the mountains, and I had to carry my youngest child on my back. We left behind us a good and happy life. We were all farmers, and we grew potatoes, barley, beans, wheat, cucumbers, onions, and tomatoes. We had apple and apricot trees. We managed well."

When Salima and her children got to Kabul, in 1998, she found work doing washing for the more prosperous families, and began spinning and sewing quilts, skills she had used for the family at home. She found a room in the same building as Anja and Fatima. "Kabul was very empty then, and there was no landlord. We simply moved in and cleaned it up a bit and lived here. But when the Americans came and the landlord came back, he told us that we would have to pay ten dollars a month for each room and now I wonder every month how to pay the rent." Salima's rent bought her a single room, some fifteen feet square, which she shares with her seven children. It has a cement floor and a wooden ceiling, a window with glass looking out over the derelict courtyard, the use of an open latrine, and a small extra area she uses as a kitchen. Her eldest son, who is fourteen, sells soap and shampoo in the bazaar, but in recent months demands by police for bribes have reduced his profit to nothing. Other than the little Salima makes from her sewing, the family has no income. I asked her what they eat. "For breakfast and lunch, we have bread, and sometimes a little tea. For dinner, I cook potatoes and sometimes the cheapest rice. Sometimes I have to buy the food already cooked because it is very hard to find fuel. The children search for pieces of paper or cardboard, or old shoes, to use as fuel." At night, a very small kerosene lamp gives them a few hours of light.

The children, said the three women, are healthy, and some of them at least are now going to school. The women do not look well. Rheumatism from the damp and cold, TB, scabies, gastritis, and kidney problems from the polluted water and poor diet have hit the returning refugees hard. Anja has constant toothaches in her few remaining teeth, and Fatima suffers from recurrent bouts of untreated malaria. Anja and Fatima cry when they talk about Husein, saying that he would have looked after them, and that they had pinned all their hopes on him. "If he had lived," they said, "we would have gone home. We would have been all right." While the Taliban were still in power, Fatima traveled back to the village to find Husein's grave. But there was still fighting in the neighborhood and she had to flee back to Kabul without seeing where he was buried. She has not been back since. Her misfortune now, she says, is that she had two daughters and no sons: with no male figure to look after them, what future would they have?

Afghanistan, said Amira as we left, has become a country of displacement, people drifting from one end of the land to the other, in search of safety or food. Half the population no longer lives in the place they once knew as home. The European Union plan, drawn up to monitor the returning refugees, spoke of a people coming home "in safety and dignity." The Belgian branch of Médecins Sans Frontières, which has opened a first clinic for mental health problems, has been overwhelmed by cases of anxiety and depression, men and women shocked and traumatized by events they were forced to witness, by loss and death, and by the utter desolation of the life they are enduring now.

I asked Amira whom she considered to be worse off in the new Afghanistan, the families who had had the resources to flee abroad during the years of fighting, or those who, like the three widows, could not find the money to reach the borders. She looked surprised. "Kabul is full of displaced people like these women. There are hundreds, perhaps thousands of women just like Anja and Fatima and Salima, in cities all over the country. Unlike the refugees, who are coming back with new skills and languages and education and even possessions, they have nothing to offer. They have lost everything—husbands, lands, homes. They are entitled to nothing and they have nothing. What little money they manage to earn all goes in food for the children. It is hard to see how they will survive." It is hard, too, in Afghanistan, to see where the internally displaced end and the urban poor begin; indeed, the distinction is increasingly allowed to blur among those who work with them, who say that the ever growing numbers of people displaced by extreme poverty and moving to the big cities are now indistinguishable from the beggars and squatters who have long filled the capital.

• • •

BEFORE LEAVING KABUL, I went to visit Babur's tomb, fabled like all his settings as a place of greenery and peace. The greatest and most civilized of all the humane Islamic travelers and geographers, having conquered Delhi and founded the Moghul dynasty, Babur asked to be buried in Kabul, saying he liked its gardens of shady trees and the cool of its summer months. Babur's last wife was an Afghan; after her husband's death, she brought his body home, and in 1640 his grandson Shah Jahan built him a tomb on the hillside above the city, looking out across the river, under mulberry and plane trees. Babur wanted his tomb left open to the winds, but sometime later a memorial pavilion was erected to protect the site, left open on three sides, carved in small delicate panels of pink, green, and black marble. The writer Peter Levi, who visited Babur's tomb in 1972, had expected to find the place in ruins. Instead all was tranquillity and elegance, the gardens stretching away in formal parterres, with fountains of bubbling water and the avenues of mulberries the philosopher warrior had so loved.

The civil war has not been kind to Babur. His garden today lies in chaos, the fountains dry, the pavilion chipped and pitted by bullets, and the plane trees blackened stumps. Babur's tomb is said to be a place where young returnees come after dark to take drugs. But by day two municipal pools nearby are full of children swimming, coming out of the water to eat hard-boiled eggs sold from baskets and dyed russet brown by the skin of onions, and the occasional visitor to Kabul still makes the long hot dusty walk up through the former gardens where now only marigolds grow, to where Babur and his obedient wife Bibi Mobaraka lie, Bibi in a smaller, more modest tomb not far from his feet. Only the inscription above his tomb has not been harmed. This tomb, it says, was constructed "for the prayer of saints and the epiphany of cherubs."

At the airport, where Red Cross and UN flights leave for Kandahar, Herat, or Mazar-e-Sharif, where Ariana brings back from Dubai returning refugees, professional people keen to observe their reclaimed homeland, and where there is a new sign saying that no one may traffic in precious saplings, threatening devices, or "Knife-Swords," I found Mo from Brooklyn. He was still chewing gum, but he was very jaunty. Kabul is a great place, he said, and he loved his mom's family. He planned to stay around and see what Kabul had to offer him, as soon as he got back from a quick visit to Dubai to meet a cousin.

DEAD DREAMS

The Dinkas of Oulu

An exile reads change the way he reads time, memory, self, love, fear, beauty: in the key of loss.
— ANDRÉ ACIMAN, *SHADOW CITIES*

What," asked Shinfig, who is nine, "is this?" He was pointing to a picture of snow, a mountain slope covered in thick white snow, down which people were skiing between the fir trees, somewhere in northern Finland. Shinfig is Sudanese, a Dinka from southern Sudan, the second son of Mary and Maum Awol, whom I had met in Cairo in the spring of 2001, soon after I started working with the refugees. Mary had been brought to see us by our Sudanese interpreter, David Deng, another Dinka, a huge, genial man whose fluent English made him a leader in the large Sudanese community of asylum seekers in Cairo.

Mary was well over six feet tall, with rather large front teeth, and hair neatly cornrowed across her rather small head. She had a limp, which made her gait slow and awkward. She spoke no English and was often solemn, but when she smiled it was with great warmth. Mary was a "closed file," David told us, an asylum seeker not just refused refugee status by UNHCR, but informed that any further appeal would be useless. Would we, he asked, consider interviewing her again and trying to put together a new case for UNHCR? Without it, she faced not deportation—Egypt had no money to send Mary and Maum and their four children back to Sudan—but a state of permanent limbo on the margins of Egyptian life, her children without education and often with little to eat. I still have the first lines of the testimony she brought to us. "My name is Mary Agum Masayo Kou," she had written. "I am from Southern Sudan and a member of the Dinka tribe. I was born in the Rumbek Lake States in 1963. My father, Mayo Kou, worked as a medical assistant in Rumbek hospital. My mother was a prison warder in Rumbek while my grandmother looked after me and my many brothers and sisters. When I was very small, I contracted a childhood disease, which left me lame in my left leg."

But there was more that she hadn't thought to explain to UNHCR, or she had said it badly or too fast. Mary and her family had been forced to flee Rumbek when it was captured by the Sudan People's Liberation Army, and her father had died of heart failure before they reached the safety of nearby Wau. Later, when she was a young married woman working as a dental nurse, fighting had broken out between the Dinka and the Fartit, and her husband and small daughter had been shot dead. She had fled to Khartoum, taking her remaining child, a boy, with her. There she had met a childhood friend called Maum, and married him and had four children, before being harassed and pursued by the security forces, anxious to use her services as a spy on other southerners. When she refused, they arrested both her and Maum in the middle of the night and took them to security headquarters. "I was kept for two days and given torture," Mary explained carefully through David. "Many times I was beaten with leather lashes all over my body. I was beaten on my feet. I was burned with lighted cigarettes. From all these punishments, I have scars. I was all the time insulted because I am a Dinka." Down the corridor, the security forces had also been torturing Maum. When Mary and her husband were allowed to go home, she saw that he had a tooth missing and that the front of his body was covered with welts from a whip. Six months later, having been constantly followed and watched, the family bought false passports and early one morning slipped out of Khartoum and made their way to Egypt. Mary was forced to leave behind her eldest son, who had been forcibly conscripted into the army.

Having heard her full story, we helped Mary to prepare a new statement for UNHCR, then persuaded them to reopen her case. And then she waited, for month after month, to hear what they would say, and each time I returned to Cairo I would go to see her and her children, Majok, the eldest boy, who was eleven; Shinfig, the boy who had marveled at the snow; a girl of seven, Anwen; and a little boy of three, Nuomshett. For several months, the six of them lived in two rooms in a shantytown on the edge of the city, sharing the small space with David and another young Sudanese man. Maum could not find work, but Mary found an occasional job as a cleaner, always badly paid since as an asylum seeker she was not officially allowed to work and was often exploited by her Egyptian employers. When she was away from home, the children stayed indoors, because Mary feared for their safety on the streets. Most months, she expected to be evicted for paying the rent late, and the children seldom had much to eat besides beans, rice, and onions. When I went to see her, I took with me clothes, oranges, milk, and a tray of the pastries that Egytians love to eat. Mary never complained about her life.

Once, she was evicted. By now she was also looking after her thirteen-year-old nephew, Joshua, who had fled southern Sudan to escape forcible conscription as a boy soldier. I heard from David that she was living in a new apartment, in another part of Cairo; it proved to be an empty shell of a flat, due shortly for demolition, with no electricity or running water, where the floors sloped and the ceilings sagged. The place was completely bare except for a few tattered velvet hangings and two enormous damask sofas without springs, remnants from a more splendid past, abandoned by their Egyptian owners as they moved on to better things. In this dark and cavernous space, Mary, Maum, their four children, Joshua, David, and the other young Sudanese man, all lived on the very little Mary earned as a cleaner and on the money David brought back from occasional jobs as interpreter. They slept on the floor. Mary's health was often poor, and weeks passed when she could not work. From time to time, Father Anastasi at the Coptic church gave her a little money and some secondhand clothes for the children. Mary was always cheerful when I saw her. "Ooooooooh," she would say, a long-drawn-out sound of pleasure that was the greeting she gave to visitors, and which I had grown used to over the phone on the few occasions I had managed to reach her from Europe. Her embrace was enormous.

Late in 2002, Mary heard that UNHCR, against all probability, had decided to grant her and her family refugee status. With it came the much-prized blue refugee card, which gave them a measure of protection against the Egyptian police, and a small monthly allowance of around £12, which helped buy food. This was also the year that Finland decided to open its quota of resettlement places for refugees to people from Sudan, and early in 2003 Mary learned from the Finnish embassy that they were being offered new lives in Finland. They visited the embassy for the orientation talks for refugees who were about to be resettled, about Finland's weather and education, work and living conditions; it was a brochure about the snowy Finnish countryside that Shinfig showed me when I went to see them. Snow is not easy to describe to a nine-year-old boy accustomed only to varying degrees of great heat. Only much later, when I went to Finland, did I hear an immigration officer describe how she tries to convey what snow and ice will feel like to refugees who have never even worn a coat: "I ask them whether they have ever seen a freezer. If they say yes, I tell them to imagine putting their hand inside and keeping it there for a few minutes. Then I tell them about the way that we deal with the cold, about the thermal underclothes and the padded jackets."

Describing his first encounter with snow, when he arrived to live with the Eskimos in Greenland, the Togolese writer Tété-Michel Kpomassie wrote: "So thick were the flakes, you'd have said that all the white birds in the world were shedding their feathers."

. . .

THOUGH THEY HAD taken in a few hundred Chilean asylum seekers fleeing Pinochet's persecution in the 1970s, it was not until 1989 that Finland adopted a formal resettlement program. The Vietnamese boat people became its first experiment. Resettlement was not an option then widely offered in Europe, which, throughout the 1980s, had remained a place of refuge principally for the "good refugees," those fleeing communism. Only Australia, Canada, New Zealand, and the United States had opened their doors to UNHCR's Convention refugees, people for whom there was no possibility of ever going home. In Finland, the Vietnamese, taken in, cared for, eventually granted citizenship, flourished. They seemed to adjust without too much pain to the freezing darkness of Scandinavia and soon began to open restaurants and small shops. Other Southeast Asians followed, and they too appeared to thrive and to meet with their hosts' approval. There was something pleasing in their temperament, something about their quiet reticence that ordinary Finns, quiet and reticent themselves, found soothing. Kielo Brewis, who works for the Ministry of Immigration in Helsinki, has become interested in what she calls the intercultural exchanges between the Finns and the resettled refugees, the way that the Finns and the Asians share patterns of noncommunication that are both subtle and remarkably similar. "We Finns take a long time to talk," she says. "We never talk very much and when we do, we really take our time. We are never too explicit. The Asians, too, take their time. It has worked very well here."

But Finland is not immune to the new crosscurrents of refugee politics. Its borders, with Russia to the east and Sweden to the west, make it vulnerable to the arrival of asylum seekers by train and sea, and all through the 1990s, when a direct train service linked Helsinki and St. Petersburg, refugees arrived in their hundreds in search of work and asylum. The numbers have dropped in recent years, now that the border with Russia is heavily guarded and thickly mined and the train has been stopped; people trying to enter Finland without papers are swiftly returned. However, Finland still has about 3,000 asylum seekers entering its territory every year, for the most part using the services of smugglers, to begin a process of interview, appeal, and acceptance, or rejection followed by deportation, that closely mirrors what happens in other parts of the European Union. But with at least one difference: Finland is both small—it has fewer than 6 million people—and orderly. It is not a country in which it is possible to disappear. Failed asylum seekers—some 60 percent of all who apply on arrival—are sent speedily home, often accompanied by police to see them returned to their original countries. "We are good at clarity here," said Leena-Kaisa Aberg, head of the Finnish Red Cross refugee team, when I went to see her in Helsinki. "There is no one in Finland who is just in limbo. We like to have things orderly."

I had come to Finland to study not asylum but resettlement, the acceptance of refugees given status by UNHCR under the 1951 Convention as eventual citizens with full rights. The main countries for resettlement remain the United States, with some 70,000 places each year, followed, at some distance, by Canada, Australia, and New Zealand. The Scandinavian countries have been generous, in proportion to their small populations: both Norway and Sweden take around 1,000 people every year. Finland, too, has always said that it intends to honor what it sees as its obligations under a Convention it was one of the first countries to sign and ratify. Unlike the United States and Canada, which are accused of skimming the "best" of the refugees, those most educated and most likely to contribute to their new country, the Finns offer homes to the most vulnerable and the most needy. Around 15 percent of the Finnish annual quota, which started at 500 people in 1989 and has since built up to 750 (there has been talk of raising it), goes to single mothers with many children, to the elderly, and to the sick. For some years, Finland steered away from Africans, particularly after a large influx of Somali asylum seekers, arriving without warning on a direct flight from Mogadishu to Moscow and on by boat via Estonia in the 1990s, caused tension and unease. The Somalis, unlike most of the Asian refugees, struck their hosts as neither reticent nor quiet. Then, in 2001, mindful of Africa's apparently unsolvable problems, the Finnish government took the decision to offer 500 places, over several years, to those escaping Sudan's long civil war. Mary and her family were among them.

Over the past fifteen years, the Finns have made an art of resettlement. Having realized their initial mistake—they sent three single Kurds to three separate towns in Finland, to avoid producing a ghetto of foreigners, and thereby left them miserably confused and lonely—they have come around to the idea of communities. They study the needs of their new guests carefully, and prepare their own inhabitants for all eventualities. Before the arrival of a number of Burmese not long ago, talks were arranged in the municipalities where the newcomers were to go. They were enthusiastically attended. Policemen, librarians, school cleaners, and mayors flocked to learn about Burmese politics, culture, dress, and food. Municipalities—twenty-five have now joined the resettlement program—have considerable autonomy in Finland. They are invited by the national government to make offers to resettle refugees, for which they will get generous national support, including interest-free loans for any new housing they will need to provide. For the refugees, the package is also generous: at least three years' guaranteed full support, and many years beyond that if necessary, on a par with that given to unemployed Finnish citizens, as well as help of every kind from the Red Cross, from municipal social workers, and from the ministries of education, health, and labor. "Sometimes," said Ann-Charlotte Siren-Borrego, who has worked in resettlement affairs since the program began, "we say that this is just like a laboratory. We can test things out. We are a microcosm of what resettlement can provide. And because we know each other, and talk and cooperate, we iron out problems before they arise." As Argentina, Chile, Brazil, Burkina Faso, Benin, and Ireland are all considering resettlement as a policy, Finland, whose experiment is small and neat, is being looked at as something of a model for other countries to follow.

It took me a while to find Mary and her family. Between UNHCR and the Finnish embassy in Cairo, which processed her papers, her family's names underwent a number of changes. But the Red Cross tracing methods are impressive; eventually I was informed that Mary, Maum, and their children had arrived in Oulu, in Finland's far north, not far from Lapland, where it is totally dark for several months each year, and where it is not unusual for the temperature to sink below minus 30 degrees Fahrenheit. Born in heat, color, and light, the family was to be resettled in ice and universal winter dark.

. . .

OULU WAS ONCE famous for its tar. It was here, among the lakes, ponds, bogs, marshes, rivers, and creeks of northern Finland, that in the seventeenth century enterprising loggers built ships to sail the world. A fire, impossible to control amid so much wood and tar, destroyed the fine old timber city in 1822, and what was left of the painted wooden houses were bombed by the Russians in World War II. Since then a new town has been laid out on a grid system, a town of square, flat-roofed, boxlike buildings, with cement and stucco facings and metal-frame windows. Oulu, windy, icy, perched on the edge of the Gulf of Bothnia facing Sweden, on a latitude with Siberia, Greenland, and Alaska, has little charm. Logging has long since given way to technology, and Nokia is Oulu's main employer, though there is still a paper mill, and as you drive in from the airport, along a wide, flat, empty highway between the fir trees and the silver birches, you can see the smoke from its chimneys curl slowly into the still clear sky of winter. In summer, tourists come to cycle along Oulu's paths and by the side of the water, and to sit drinking in the market square until late into a night that never grows dark. In winter, the town is quiet, empty, dark, and very cold. The sun never rises. Ice makes the pavements lethal. No one moves on the streets, and very few cars go by. Oulu has 123,000 inhabitants. Contemplating the scarcely imaginable contradictions, the move the resettled refugees have to make, the extraordinary journey through climate and culture, Heike Estolen, area manager for the Red Cross, tried to describe what it must be like adapting to surroundings in which nothing was like anything you had ever known. If Oulu had become a world apart for him, a world of silence and difference, after a two-year posting among the refugees in Bosnia, what, he asked, might it be for people who had traveled many thousands of miles, from color into gray?

Though most of the seventy-one Sudanese sent to live in Oulu are Christians and all but a very few are from the south, among the first to arrive was a Muslim called Malish. With eight other Sudanese families, Malish reached Oulu on October 15, 2001. It was snowing. He was on his own, having left his wife and unborn daughter in Cairo, and by the time he went to bed the first night, he had been allocated a small, warm, pleasant apartment with pale wooden floors. The town office that looks after refugees—the Sudanese had been preceded by some Iraqis, Bosnians, and Somalis—gave him a few pieces of basic furniture, and his first allowance was enough to buy warm clothes. Malish had been a teacher in Sudan, with a hankering after a degree in philosophy. He had studied for some years in an English-speaking seminary, and in Cairo, because his English is so good, and because he is ambitious and energetic, he had even managed to get a little work teaching. "I had no real idea of any kind about what I was coming to," he says. "In junior school, I had read about Finland but it didn't actually mean anything to me. In Cairo, the Finnish embassy told us about the weather, but how do you describe great cold? I was shocked by the dark; that is what I felt and that is what I still feel: shock. I couldn't understand why it was all so quiet, why no one spoke in the street."

Malish came to interpret for me with the Sudanese, who, alerted by Mary, gathered to talk in the community center. Like all the Sudanese he is finding Finnish, which they all study every day for six hours, extremely hard. It is a language with immensely long words, and no prepositions, in which pronunciation counts for everything.

Even the Swedish minority in Finland seldom speak Finnish without an accent. And as Malish described how the Sudanese in Oulu are living—the little apartments they have been allocated all around the town, the television channels they watch, the friendly distance shown them by their Finnish neighbors, the lack of spices and dried fish or okra on sale in the local shops—other Sudanese arrived to join us, slithering along the treacherous pavements, immensely tall and dark and absolutely improbable, in their woolly hats and down jackets and thick boots. A few brought babies with them: there have been seven births in the Sudanese community since 2002.

Sitting in the small, hot hall, warmed by an old-fashioned tile wood-burning stove, the Sudanese talked. From time to time, their mobile telephones, the absolutely necessary adjuncts to the refugee existence, as important here as on the streets of Cairo, rang. Heike Estolen, driving in from the airport, had spoken of standing on the border in Bosnia, watching refugees waiting to cross, their mobile telephones in their hands, making one last call before the battery ran out. It was not easy, the Sudanese said, one after the other, describing how they filled their time when not studying. The Finns were generous and always pleasant. The Dinkas were short of nothing. They liked their new gadgets and their television sets, and they liked feeling safe and knowing that their children were safe. But the language was so difficult, and they were not quite certain what they were doing in this dark northern city. Every one of them would have preferred Canada or the United States, had they been given a choice, and those with relatives already settled in North America are puzzled about why they have not been allowed to join them. Then they talked about their year's compulsory Finnish-language course, and how they wished they could learn English, for they still believe English is the only possible language of their future. They talked about not having understood about the restrictions on their papers: it will be at least eight years before they can become Finnish citizens, and until then they will not be allowed to travel abroad, not even briefly, not even to visit friends or relations. Alem, a man in his thirties, with deep tribal scars carved across his forehead, said that he had believed that he would be given the proper education, schooling and then university, that war had prevented him acquiring in Sudan. He spoke of education as something concrete, something that could be handed over, as a gift. The Finns have indeed given the Sudanese education, but it is not the education they dream about.

Later, at a church service in a classroom lent to them by the Lutheran church, sitting at desks in rows, their long legs folded awkwardly around the tables, the Sudanese sang revivalist hymns, the African beat loud in the utter silence of an Oulu Sunday afternoon, and they prayed, for the government of Finland, for one of their congregation soon to undergo an operation, for a newborn Dinka boy, and they prayed for peace to come to Sudan, so that, one day, they could go home.

And always, all the time that I spent with them in Oulu, the Sudanese talked about work. Work, their failure to find or have work, is a subject that never goes away. As they know well and as they tell each other every day, of the 250 refugees who were resettled in Oulu before them—Iraqis and Iranians, Bosnians and Somalis, Afghans and Burmese—only two have found work, and both of these are interpreters for social workers. Among the seventy-one Sudanese are teachers, electricians, nurses, farmers, and university students. Talking about their lives, they said that they had simply assumed that resettlement would bring with it education, and that with education would come work and a future. Now, it seemed, they would learn Finnish but not much else. They had never imagined, they said, never conceived it possible, that there might be a life without an occupation. "We watch television, we eat, we sleep," said Malish. "We visit people. And we sit. This is really useless for me. I had a dream. It was about how I would work, and learn things, and become someone. If I don't succeed in my dream, I don't know how my life will be. My dream is dead. I have nothing to look forward to. All of us talk about work and education. It is all we talk about. We eat and we sit and we talk about work." I asked some of the other men what they did to fill their days. "Actually," they said, using the word in a way particular to Africans speaking English, "actually, we do nothing."

Oulu has no work. It has employment for skilled information technology specialists, and it has a little work for men in the paper mill. Twelve percent of the workforce are unemployed, and levels of alcoholism are, as elsewhere in Finland, high. For the Dinkas, there are no jobs, and it is very unlikely that there ever will be any. One, perhaps even two, may find employment eventually as a cleaner or looking after old people, if their Finnish is judged good enough by the authorities. But for the engineers and the teachers, the nurses and the would-be university graduates, there is nothing.

So the Dinkas in Oulu wait, like the Palestinians in Shatila and the Liberians in Realmonte, for real life to begin, the dreamed-of life which, like Malish, they carried with them into exile. In the dream they have work and education and they know who they are. Having held tight to this dream during the transit years in Cairo, where it became a form of protection against an unacceptable present, they are trying to come to terms with the fact that Finland will never really provide it. Like Malish, they fear their dead dreams, and like Malish, they prefer to start dreaming again, to plan for the day when they will become Finnish citizens, with Finnish passports, and will be able to move on, to the life they hope for, in another country.

Yet even if Finland is now just another stage in a journey toward another future, the Dinkas in Oulu still worry about those friends and relations who have not passed the first hurdle. By the time I left Oulu, I had a list of names of those still in Cairo or Sudan and now in need of help, names that were not among those of the fifty-eight new Sudanese due to arrive in Finland very shortly as part of the continuing quota. The refugees brought these names to me one at a time, written on little scraps of paper. There were the younger brother and sister of Jeremiah, who has multiple sclerosis, and who joined him in Cairo from Sudan when his illness grew severe and who, not invited to accompany him to Finland, are now alone and on the streets in Egypt. There was Elizabeth Zacharia Arop and Simon Maderi Agei and Peter Dhykwan, all still in Cairo, all penniless, all with "Files Closed" many years ago. There was Amina's young son, eighteen-year-old Johannes Peter, waiting in Cairo to hear whether he will be allowed to join his mother in Oulu. At eighteen, he is no longer a dependent child. Talking to Amina, an imposing matronly woman in her early forties, whose pastor husband was killed in the fighting in Sudan, and who has brought with her to Oulu five young children, I thought again of the diaspora of the Palestinians. Amina's eldest son is still in Khartoum, having been, like Mary's son, forcibly conscripted into the army. She has a cousin in Cairo with five small children, whose husband and three brothers are all dead, and a niece in Australia. Her uncle is in America. When interviewed by UNHCR in Cairo, Amina said that she would be grateful to be sent anywhere she would find peace and safety for her children, so that they would not be attacked and abused. And she is grateful, she says, very grateful, for she has found both. But then she added: "Help is not just running away from death. In the end, that is not enough. Life has to have many different things." Sitting in the Lutheran church after the service, I asked Malish and Jeremiah, both of whom had talked with such passion about their education, whether there were books I could send them from England. Malish asked for Bertrand Russell's *History of Western Philosophy*, Jeremiah for Paul Burrell's book about Princess Diana.

• • •

IN THE NIGHT, when he cannot sleep, Maum thinks about his brothers, still in Rumbek, and wonders whether they are alive. He dreams often, dreams that turn into nightmares, and he wakes sad. As a small boy, the youngest in his family, he accompanied his eldest brother to watch over their cattle, and when he grew old enough, his brother taught him to mold little animals out of the black soil and to color them with ashes from the fire. The two boys, sitting while the cows grazed, made flocks of goats and herds of cattle, and figures of people, carrying spears, to watch over them. They preferred to make the animals they knew best, and seldom tried their hand at wildebeests or warthogs or even the lions who, from time to time, seized a cow and dragged its carcass off into the thicket. They were less frightened of the lions, who preferred killing cattle to attacking humans, than of the snakes, which were plentiful around Rumbek. Remembering the long vigils in the bush, Maum talks about the snake he most dreaded, over a yard long and very black and shiny. Its body, he says, was as thick as the thermos flask that sits between us as we talk; he describes the day a friend went down to the river to fish and was bitten as he moved through the long grass by the water's edge. But he has heard, from a cousin who was able to contact him one day from Khartoum, that there are fewer wild animals around Rumbek these days: the frequent gunfire from the civil war has frightened them away. It is when Maum talks about his childhood, when he describes, in careful detail, the daily events of a life that lasted until he and his family were forced to flee Rumbek in 1984, events that he recalls with precision and tenderness, that the immensity of the journey that he has made takes shape.

Maum was born in 1961, in a small square house with a thatched roof. His family had neither water nor electricity, Rumbek's one generator supplying just enough for the police station and the small hospital. He is not sure of the exact date of his birth, because births in Rumbek were registered casually, and it was often many months before anyone bothered to seek out the proper authorities and have them written down. His father was a farmer, with fields of wheat and cows, and the week that Maum and his sister were born, the family's second set of twins, he was killed in a tribal skirmish near the town. The absence of a father was a defining element in Maum's childhood. He was taught to miss him as one might miss a person one knows and loves. Because his grandfather had five wives, and his mother was one of eight brothers and sisters, Maum's boyhood passed in the midst of an enormous clan, in households that merged one into another, among children of all ages, all related by blood.

Though Maum finished nine years of school, it is his free time that he remembers most vividly, when he wandered around the surrounding countryside, fishing in the rivers with a spear, or a net left in the river overnight, trying to catch a dink, a fish with no bones apart from its backbone, the color of brown mud, considered by his mother the most digestible and delicious of all the river fishes. The boys in the family, Maum says, were not encouraged to hunt until they were fully grown, but he accompanied his elder brothers when they went out in search of antelope, taking with them long spears with metal tips. When he thinks about his childhood, Maum thinks about the seasons, blending mildly into each other, about the cattle grazing quietly in the bush, and about the days that he was sent into the market to sell a cow and buy new clothes for the family. Maum is very thin, with a wispy beard and two long pointed front teeth. There is a large gap where Khartoum's security forces knocked out a tooth. It was, he says, sitting on the family's new sofa in a bare room in northern Finland, a good life, except for not knowing his father; he can think of nothing in it that was bad. He was living with an uncle, studying, dreaming of a day when he might follow his cousins into a university education in some foreign city, when fighting came to Rumbek and he was forced to go north.

Mary's memories of her Rumbek childhood are less clear. One of eight children, she, too, helped watch her family's cows, and when she was free, she went with her friends to swim in the river that ran not far from their home. On weekends, when there was no school, she would walk the thirty-three miles to a village called Shomek, her father's village, where her grandparents still lived and where she helped pick olives. Mary loved her grandmother, and she was particularly fond of one of her brothers, who resembled her so closely that people took them for twins. She says little about her decision to become a dental nurse, or about her studies, or about her first husband and firstborn child and their deaths in a raid on Wau. Nor does she like to talk about the death of her much loved brother in the fighting, nor the loss of the second child, taken away by the government forces to serve as a child soldier. Of her marriage to Maum, Mary says that she chose him because he was a good boy with a good mind, and that despite the objections of his parents, who would have preferred a wife with no previous husband, they "entered into love" with each other.

When Mary and Maum and the four children reached Oulu from Cairo, changing planes in Helsinki, on March 17, 2003, there was still snow on the ground. Shinfig ran to touch it. Mary remembers the sense of shock, the way the cold made her catch her breath. In Cairo, she explains carefully, she had known cold indoors and out, on the few winter days when the evenings are cool. But there was no difference in the temperature, wherever you went, in or out. What struck her at once in Oulu was something she had not thought about: that inside the buildings it would be hot. Going from cold into heat, heat into cold, was something she had not expected.

·   ·   ·

THE FINNS ARE extremely conscious of the contradictions in which the resettled refugees live. They understand the need for work and occupation, and, in the offices in Helsinki where these things are discussed, they try to make generous provisions for language classes and further education of every kind. They worry that the refugees are not sufficiently prepared, so they give them pamphlets describing frostbite and how to deal with it; they are concerned about how Sudanese men, accustomed to being in control of their families, will adjust to a society as equal-minded and feminist as Finland. They foresee, too, future problems with resentment, when the Finns may grow angry at so much being given to people who now pay no taxes. Across the country, planners are trying to anticipate the racism now endemic in other parts of Europe, with publicity campaigns about the benefits brought by people from other cultures and societies. They worry, too, about these lives in limbo, about the way the refugees keep dreaming of what will happen next. "It is a wasted life," they say. "If you dream too much, you forget to concentrate on living." When, not long ago, a young Iranian, given his own apartment, living comfortably in another northern Finnish town, hanged himself, the authorities were shocked: "We thought that we had done so well."

It is in the second generation of resettled refugees that the authorities see real hope, the children whose bilingualism will ensure that they start their working lives equal in opportunity to their Finnish classmates. These young people will reach working age just when Finland's population tips heavily toward pensioners, the postwar boom generation grown to retirement, and jobs, particularly in the service industries, should be plentiful. In Helsinki I met Ekhias Osman, a Sudanese woman who has worked for the Finnish Refugee Council and for one of the municipalities most active in resettlement. Ekhias's story is different, in that she is not a refugee, but the Finns who work with her point to her experiences as a hopeful message for the future.

Ekhias has lived in Finland for fourteen years. She arrived in 1990 with her husband, who had a scholarship to study forestry at Helsinki University. It was November and almost completely dark. What she remembers is her sense of surprise at finding no leaves and no green trees. When her husband's degree was finished, he decided to stay on, to teach at the university, and Ekhias, who had brought two small children with her from Sudan, and arrived pregnant with a third, now had a fourth. There was no one for her to talk to, for she was the only Sudanese woman in the whole of Finland, and it took her five years to learn Finnish. She decided that she could cope perfectly well when the temperature was at 10 degrees below zero, but that what she really hated were the days when it sank to minus 20. There was also then nowhere to buy the spices she craved. Now, she says, everything is easy. In Helsinki at least twenty shops selling Middle Eastern and African food have opened in the last five years. She has many Finnish women friends. Her only regret is that she can find no way for her elderly mother to pay her a visit—the Finns will not grant her even a temporary tourist visa—so every two years, she takes the children and returns home to Sudan to see her. "I need to see my mother," she says. "And the children need their grandmother." Her husband is reluctant even to visit Sudan briefly, although he has learned no more than ten words of Finnish in his years at the unversity (he is able to teach in

English). Not long ago, to show her new friends something of her past life, Ekhias invited two Finnish women on a visit back to Khartoum.

For her children, Ekhias has no doubts about the rightness of their decision to stay. The eldest two are fluent in Finnish, Arabic, English, Swedish, and French. Their education has been excellent, and if the eldest, who is a boy, is currently talking about becoming a soccer player, the three girls have their minds already set on careers. The eldest, says Ekhias, is planning to be a pediatrician, the second a heart specialist. As for the youngest, she talks of entering the army or perhaps the police force; she enjoys the idea of being the only black woman soldier in the country. The girls are, as their mother says, affectionate and family-minded. They are also Muslim, which separates them from most of the new arrivals. It is only when talking about the future that Ekhias hesitates. The girls, already nearing the end of their secondary schooling, wonder what boy they will ever meet whom they might marry, and Ekhias has already begun to plan for the day when she will have to send them home to live with her mother to find husbands. What this spells, she knows, is the very arrangement that she most dreads: her family split across the world.

. . .

AT EVERY STAGE in the journey that led her ever farther from her first home, Mary shed possessions. Like most refugees, she has almost nothing from her past. But sitting at her table in Oulu, in the neat new flat with the sauna that she uses to air the children's outdoor clothes, I saw the photograph album that I had been shown when I first met her in Cairo. Its red-flowered plastic cover, with the inset silver heart and its photograph of a younger Mary, is a little more battered, but there inside were the portraits I remembered, of adults and children, babies and elderly men and women, in turbans and printed gowns and shawls of brilliant colors, many posed in photographers' studios, alone and in groups, serious, unsmiling, smartly dressed—so many of them, belonging to another time and another place. Turning the pages, telling me their names and who they were, Mary paused. This man, she said, is dead; this woman has fled to Khartoum; this couple has disappeared; this family is now in Cairo. It was as if nothing could ever be right again.

But Mary is not unhappy. She has accepted that it is unlikely that her Finnish will ever be good enough for her to work again as a dental nurse, because that would involve first the language, then seven years' retraining. She is in her forties and does not feel she has the time. But learning each day how to cope with new devices and contraptions, how to catch a bus to her Finnish lessons and make her way around the supermarkets, has brought her pleasure and laughter. She gives one of her long exclamations of disbelief and humor as she describes herself trying to work out the identity of electrical gadgets she has never seen and the contents of packets of food that look utterly foreign. She likes the way her children can bicycle along the bridle paths while she can be sure that they will come home safe. She is touched by the generosity and warmth of a Finnish family who have befriended them and who not long ago came to collect them in a car and drove them out to a farmhouse in the country, sending them home with a present of a Christmas tree and decorations to hang on its branches. Before that, she had only ever seen Christmas trees in pictures and wondered what they could be. And she talks with pride about the sports that the children have been learning at their schools and the delight they take in being taught to ski. Both she and Maum talk often to the children about Rumbek, about the house and land that they have never seen and the relations they have never met. Anwen, the only girl, is more curious than her brothers; she wants to know what it was really like. But Rumbek is a long way in the past now, and Mary does not dwell on those days; Shinfig's future, the safety of her daughter and her two small sons, are what concern her now.

Mary had brought doughnuts and large plates of cake for us to eat while the children watch a toboggan race on television. I find her quiet, almost subdued, though her smile is always affectionate. It is as if she has undergone a journey of a kind that can barely be comprehended, that has tested the very nature of adaptability. In the heat of the flat, with the dark and the cold of Oulu in winter kept out by heavy white curtains, the children go barefoot.

EPILOGUE

A Mode of Being

It becomes ever more urgent to develop a framework of thinking that makes the migrant central, not ancillary, to the historical process.... It might begin by regarding movement, not as an awkward interval between fixed points of departure and arrival, but as a mode of being in the world.

— PAUL CARTER, *LIVING IN A NEW COMMUNITY*

When Jeff Crisp joined UNHCR in 1987, "migration" was a dirty word. It was certainly not something that anyone was allowed to confuse with the legitimate claims of refugees forced to flee persecution. But at the beginning of the 1990s, he thinks, all this began to change. The end of the Cold War drove people abroad in search of work and better lives, and, almost overnight, international migration became a key topic in world politics. Commentators began to warn of uncontrollable floods of migrants, and the threat to national identity that all these culturally different and impoverished people might pose. As Crisp remembers it, it was at the Cairo Conference on Population and Development, in 1992, that UNHCR first presented papers about migration as a global issue that involved all people on the move, from asylum seekers to those in search of better lives. And it was in 1995 that the phrase "managed migration" found its way into the second edition of the *State of the World's Refugees*, and along with it the assumption that it was no longer right or possible to ignore migration as the crucial debate of the age, within which asylum occupied a particular corner. The pity, as Crisp and others like him see it, is that all this was not understood and addressed long ago. For managed migration may prove a large part of the solution to the problems that lie ahead.

Like internally displaced people, like refugees, there have always been migrants. Around the sixteenth century, people began to move, work, explore, and travel to find better lives. What no one quite anticipated was the emergence of new multicultural societies, nor the new patterns that migration has taken. The history of migration since World War II is one of unforeseen developments and unplanned consequences. No one, for instance, would have predicted that the remittances migrants send home would reach around $92 billion in 2003—virtually double what is spent on the entire global overseas development aid budget.* Globalization has produced not simply flows of goods, services, and capital, but a parallel flow of people and ideas.

According to UN statistics, only 175 million people—around 3 percent of the world population—are actually outside the countries of their birth at any one time, considerably more of them from the developed than from the developing world. What is more, the West needs them. The picture, say demographers, is now becoming clear. The populations of the developed world are aging, and fertility rates in some Western countries have fallen to as low as 1.2 children per woman. In the UK, for instance, though the so-called demographic deficit between the aging population and declining numbers of workers will not actually have an effect until 2020—later than its European neighbors—yet there are already labor shortages; the Na-

---

* In 2003, Sudan, for example, received $638 million in remittances and $225 million in aid.

tional Health Service would collapse without overseas staff. The West needs migrant workers.

The idea that migration must, somehow, be "managed" is now beyond doubt. All Western democracies have modulated their recent language to reflect this view. The worry is how to do it, given that September 11 increased the perception of a world under threat, and that even demographers are not able to predict precise labor needs. Even as the speed of change has challenged people's sense of identity across the Western World, necessary policy decisions to confront the new realities are judged as too unpopular, and public confidence has evaporated in the face of inefficient handling. The UN Secretary General, Kofi Annan, who is personally very interested in this issue and aware that the UN needs to be seen to act on such a crucial dimension of twenty-first-century politics, has set up a Global Commission on International Migration, though its budget is small and its life span short.

Within the EU there already exists a cross-border labor market for several million workers, and EU policy has been moving toward opening more doors to both skilled and unskilled migrants. But while those with advanced skills are perceived as necessary, there remain doubts about the numbers of unskilled workers the West will be able to absorb, particularly as current migrants are finding it harder to prosper economically than those who came before them. No one disputes that increased migration brings economic gains at a global level: the migrant moves from a place where he is less productive to a place where he is more productive. But migration works best when workers have skills different from the existing workforce, so that the new arrivals complement rather than replace those who are already there. The fear of brain drain—attracting skilled people away from where they are needed—is only one element in a debate that, say economists, has many still largely unexplored repercussions. The links between diasporas and development, they say, may prove promising.

Migration can only provide one answer to the needs of a future labor force, for migrants age too. People may also need to work longer and more productively, and to save more. In the UK there are plans to tap the 2.8 million men and women who are currently not working and who are older than fifty but not old enough to be eligible for government pensions. Across the EU, there are now new immigration programs, guest worker arrangements, and migrant quotas, drawn up both out of self-interest and in order to relieve pressure on overburdened asylum systems. There is also the suggestion, outlined not long ago by the economist Timothy Hatton of the University of Essex, that immigration and asylum could be integrated at EU level, by adopting a points system to include humanitarian points.

At the beginning of 1999, 500 people from different backgrounds, disciplines, and countries worked together in the Hague under the auspices of the Society for International Development to discuss the future of migration and refugee policy. Starting from a shared conviction that the present situation is no longer tolerable either for asylum seekers and migrants, or for the countries on which falls the burden of caring for them, and that the threats posed to stability and security are alarming, they produced a Declaration of the Hague in November 2002, a document with a more hopeful tone and outlook than many that have preceded it. A coherent and genuinely international migration policy, they argue, must go hand in hand with development policies and concerted programs to combat disease, poverty, and illiteracy; the root causes of forced displacement have to be tackled, such as the flow of arms, and the corporate sector, as well as government, must play its part in conflict resolution and postconflict reconstruction. The declaration comes at a good time: refugee numbers dropped by 10 percent to 9.7 million between 2003 and 2004, according to UNHCR, the lowest figure in a decade. In the past few years, more than 5 million people have gone home—to Afghanistan, Angola, Burundi, Iraq, and elsewhere.

Apart from the demographers' calculations and their uncertain predictions, more intangible questions arise. Why should something as arbitrary as where one is born determine where one is allowed to live?* Entrance restrictions, borders, and boundaries, often themselves accidents of history, stand as barriers to a more equal world, protecting the privileges of those who live in the least crowded, richest, and safest states. Against the moral claims of liberals, who argue that current restrictions on immigrants constitute a gross violation of human rights and who point out that it is ethically inconsistent to support the free movement of goods and services while restricting the free movement of people, come the counterclaims of the anti-immigration lobbies, arguing for the need to preserve by state boundaries the unique cultural communities of people who share common practices and understandings. To demand of a state that it show equal concern for those who live outside its boundaries is to ask it to pursue policies that may undermine the very institutions that provide social justice and cultural autonomy for those who live inside them. If to restrict entrance is to accept a world in which differences of citizenship correspond to differences in quality of life, then the arrival of large numbers of people can undermine the existing "provision of collective or public good" and profoundly alter the nature of a state. It is hard to halt entrance flows at just the right moment, before social disharmony breaks out. Once started, migration flows, with people following in one another's footsteps, are extremely hard to stop. By the same token, as migratory chains develop, so young people leave villages, thereby causing vast change in community life. And migration can only increase, say demographers, as high levels of insecurity and increasing disparity between rich and poor in so many parts of the world make families keen to send their children to safer and more stable economies.

In the mid-1970s the anthropologist Theodore Schwartz used the phrase "migrants of identity" to describe the search among young people in America for an identity they considered both "acceptable and authentic." Since then, much has been thought, debated, and written about the relationship between space and time in

---

*See Matthew Gibney, "Liberal Democratic States and Responsibilities to Refugees," *American Political Science Review*, vol. 93 (1999).

the construction of modern cultural identities. Wars, market forces, and environmental change all uproot people—not only refugees and migrants, but tourists, travelers, and businesspeople—and that movement can more and more be seen as the determining experience of the age. In the twenty-first century, "nonplaces," like waiting rooms, refugee camps, stations, airports, and hotels, have become temporary abodes. The idea of "home" is no longer that of a fixed and safe place, there to leave and return to, and which gives form to memory and anticipation. Rather it has become a more fluid idea, something to carry in one's head. Home, argues John Berger, is located in a set of routines, a repetition of habitual interactions, in styles of behavior and in dress, in memories and in myths, and in stories carried around in the head. "We dream in narrative," as Barbara Hardy famously observed, "day-dream in narrative, remember, anticipate, hope, despair, believe, doubt, plan, revise, criticise, construct, gossip, learn, hate and love by narrative." For Mamadu in Tel Aviv, Abdularam in Maryland, and Mary in London, whose original homes have disappeared into memory and for whom no return to a fixed place of the past is possible, these narratives, testimonies to their own histories, become a form of safety. As cultural anthropologists describe it, the modern age is an age of exile; displacement between worlds, existence between a lost past and a fluid present, present the most fitting metaphors for modern consciousness. In his condition of perpetual transit between so many different worlds, the modern traveler is at home in none, a "homeless mind" constantly subject to nostalgia for a past, fixed time when identity was rooted, safe, and communal.

. . .

AFTER THE WANNSEE Conference of January 20, 1942, and the launch of the Final Solution, Jewish refugees began to arrive in ever greater numbers to beg for asylum at Switzerland's western borders. Nearly all were turned back. Heinrich Rothmund, the head of the Swiss police, warned of the "menace to our spiritual identity if too many foreigners live here." Rothmund would later describe his twenty-year battle against the *enjuivement*, the "Jewification" of Switzerland. Regarding the decision to keep the frontiers closed, in the summer of 1942, Rothmund repeated a phrase that was much used in Switzerland during the late 1930s and early 1940s. "The boat," he said, "is full."

Even if the flows of migrants now trying to make their way to Western Europe, North America, and Australia were to be realistically addressed by an increase in working permits and a better understanding of labor needs, there are always going to be more people wanting to migrate than the developed states will be willing to take. Why they persist in such numbers given the increasingly restrictive policies is not altogether clear, beyond the fact that asylum seeker networks are growing and that smugglers are becoming ever more skilful. There will be migrants in search of better lives; there will be refugees, fleeing death and persecution; and there will be a huge gray area in the middle, growing all the time, where people move because of poverty, because they have been driven to the margins of life by ethnic tensions, or because a new dam has flooded their village. It is this gray area that makes UNHCR's position so difficult; the agency is bound on the one hand to insist that refugees are different from other migrants and deserve different treatment, without which their entire house of cards will collapse, while on the other it has to acknowledge that people move for many different reasons and need respect and rights. Migrants need protections, too.

Migration, as Gervais Appave at the International Organization for Migration in Geneva sees it, is the unfinished business of globalization. It is threatening because it challenges the last national defining characteristic: the ability of a country to say who comes in and who goes out. And it is threatening because by its very nature it is disorderly and unpredictable. While Australia has gone further than any other country in its efforts to make migration orderly, its draconian solutions are not possible on continents with many countries and many borders.

The paradoxes of the West are what make migration so uncertain. Western states are driven by the democratic will of their people, who are often hostile to refugees and migrants, but also by the rule of law, which makes excessive exclusion impossible. Since research for this book began, ever tighter restrictions on asylum are being debated throughout the EU, where recent elections reflect growing, but unfounded, fears that terrorists are using the asylum route to reach the West, while in the United States the many made homeless by the New Orleans hurricane have caused the very word "refugee" to take on new and confusing meanings. There is, as has been argued in many papers, speeches and articles, no panacea. There are things worth trying, from the speeding up and improving of the asylum process, to the spreading of more accurate and realistic information about true conditions in the West and the dangers and pitfalls that await immigrants, to the setting up of regular programs so that people can travel legitimately and not take the asylum route. But none can ever achieve enough, unless the root causes that send people abroad in the first place—poverty, violence, and instability—are addressed. Meanwhile, there is very little alternative but to follow the proposals of the Declaration of the Hague and to take steps to manage migration with clarity and imagination, while upholding the 1951 Convention, so that true refugees are treated humanely and with understanding. The whole refugee apparatus—rules, conventions, organizations—exists to offer substitute protection for people whose governments cannot or will not protect them. UNHCR's mission remains that of preserving asylum for those who need it and ensuring that those who are driven from their homes need not resort to clandestine means; it should not depart from its original mandate of protection by taking on tasks that others do better.

No one denies that it would be best if the situations that create the world's flow of refugees could be prevented. The diaspora Sudanese in Uganda, Ethiopia, Congo, Kenya, and Central Africa, and the diaspora Somalis in Yemen, the UK, the United States, and Djibouti, would rather not be there. But until that day comes, refugees will keep on moving, and governments have no alternative but to find policies that protect their borders but that are also humane and protect the rights of those who seek asylum. Some acts, like torture, are not negotiable; the prolonged detention of refugees, and particularly refugee children, comes close to torture. Protecting people who flee persecution is a responsibility all nation states must share if collective sovereignty is to have some moral worth.

And there is something more at stake. No one, in the end, wants to be a refugee. Exile is an unhappy state. Refugees seldom want to leave home, and when forced to do so, they dream of the day they can return. The best "durable solution" for any refugee is to go home, but to a home and a country that are safe; if that is impossible, the next best option is resettlement. It has to be accepted that some asylum seekers will never contribute anything to the West's economy: many will be too frail, too damaged, too inflexible to achieve a productive life. But to rail at that is to misunderstand the nature of asylum, because asylum in the end is not only about responsibility and interdependence but about morality; and because, in an age of globalization, it is simply not possible to ignore the world's dispossessed. How a state deals with its refugees should be a measure of its social and political health.

· · ·

BY E-MAIL, LETTER, and the occasional phone call, I was able to keep in touch with some of the Liberians I had met on my travels, just as I was able to follow the progress of Mary, the Ugandan girl who had fled to England after her long abduction by both rebels and government forces. In June 2003, Mary gave birth to a baby girl, and decided not to put her up for adoption. On appeal, she was first given four years to remain in the UK, and slowly, cautiously, she began to re-create her life—then just as she was settling down with friends and a possible college place in South London, she was "dispersed" by NASS to the twenty-fourth floor of a block of flats in Glasgow, with "forty-eight hours" notice. In Glasgow she knew no one; while she was out one day, her flat was broken into. Soon after, she received a letter from NASS. They had made a mistake: the UK was not willing to accept her as a refugee after all, on the grounds that she would be in no danger if she returned to Kampala. In the current ungenerous spirit that governs asylum decisions, Mary's fear and horror of return to a country in which she was repeatedly raped apparently no longer counts. While a new application is being prepared, she is moved, randomly, from flat to bed-sitter to hostel, with her baby and her few possessions, sometimes two or even three times a month. Her old terrors have returned.

The refugees I had no news of were those I had twice visited in Afghanistan, Jawad Wafa, the studious and solemn Hazaras teacher in Bamiyan, and the raisin farmers in the Shomali plain, Haji Kamal and Amir Jan. Afghanistan, largely forgotten by the West, without the money or the security promised by its allies, was again on the verge of anarchy. Poppies were now being cultivated in all thirty-four provinces, and opium production was said to account for over half of Afghanistan's GDP. The Taliban and the warlords were back in control of huge areas of the country.

As for the camps of West Africa, there were new reports of young women refugees resorting to prostitution in return for food and shelter. In Liberia, Charles Taylor, the president whose soldiers had driven the young Liberians into exile, had gone, but the country remains lawless. Of Fatima and her five surviving children, I could discover nothing. In the Mediterranean, rough seas continue to take the lives of asylum seekers who put out in leaky boats from the coasts of North Africa, hoping to find work and safety in Europe. And Madina, the young Russian woman geologist I had met in 2003 in Newcastle, had been sent to Italy, as she had feared, because it had been her first port of call on leaving Russia. After a year in Sezze Scalo, a cheerless railway town in Latina built by the fascists in the 1920s, on land reclaimed by Mussolini from the malarial Pontine marshes, where Horace once complained that he was kept awake at night by the croaking of innumerable frogs, her application for asylum was turned down on the grounds that it lacked credibility. She has filed an appeal, and been told that it may be more than a year before it is heard. The last time she saw her son Kolya, he was in a children's ward in a hospital in St. Petersburg, recovering from frostbite to his face and hands. When I went to Sezze Scalo to see Madina early in 2005, she was wearing an enormous, handsome, and very mothy mink coat, brought with her during her flight from Russia, and clung to on her many moves, to keep out the bitter winds that sweep down from the mountains across the plains.

In the spring of 2003, many of the young Liberians who had stayed in Cairo suddenly heard that they had been accepted for resettlement in the West. Their years of waiting, their powers of survival, their absolute determination not to give up had paid off. Their lives could now be split in two—the past, before Cairo, when they had lost everything and everyone once familiar and safe to them; and the future, when they would find an education and work and make families of their own. Cairo, a long, unhappy interlude, was the marking line. Canada offered a humanitarian visa to Kono, the thickset boy with the gap between his front teeth who had seen his mother raped and murdered, his father bayoneted, and the uncle and aunt who took him in killed while he was still a small boy; though Christian, Kono had tried to pass himself off as a Muslim at Al Azhar in return for somewhere to sleep. Hiding in different parts of the city since his escape, Kono had been growing ever more desperate; an Italian psychiatrist visiting Cairo found his level of depression was so acute that she was uncertain whether he would be able to pull out of it. Now, from Canada, came e-mails that made me think of the early Christian travelers. "Great thanks and appreciation to bro. Daniel," Kono wrote, soon after his arrival in Toronto. "He welcomed me like a motherly brother." Over the phone he told me about his own induction to the Canadian way of life. At the Canadian Embassy in Cairo, when he went for his second interview, not knowing whether they would accept him and hunched and mumbling as was his custom, an official had said to him: "When you are in Canada, you must stand up straight, pull your shoulders back, look people in the eye, and speak out loudly." She paused, then went on: "Welcome to Canada." Kono, used to making himself as inconspicuous as possible in a city in which to be black invited endless attacks, recalled the conversation with delight. "I suddenly understood," he said, "that I had possibilities again."

The other Liberians, one by one, were called for interviews at UNHCR and went off to new lives in different parts of America. "Hi. This is Mohamed, from Texas, sending you greetings," wrote the moon-faced young man who had watched his godmother's head kicked about like a soccer ball and who was now working as a garage mechanic in Austin. Abdularam, whose lack of back teeth had made his English so impenetrable, was sent to Maryland, where he was offered work as a caretaker in a laboratory working on animal experiments by day, and classes in accountancy and computer studies by night. "I haven't been engage in any social life," read his first e-mail, in the English particular to the Liberians. "As I have no friends. 2 days ago I met a Sierra Leonean guy in school and a Zambian guy. They are going to be my first friends." Abdula went to Iowa, to a factory making spare parts for cars; Bility, the good-looking boy in the brown woolly hat, who called all foreign women "ma'am," to Dallas; and Abudu, the tall, self-assured young man, who coped with the years of poverty and uncertainty by pretending they weren't happening, went to start his American life in Texas, but soon moved to Seattle, which he said he found more to his taste. Amadu had an American accent even before he got to America. Over the phone, their voices sounded light, buoyant.

At first anxious about being so far from one another, after the years of enforced and sometimes claustrophobic proximity, the Liberians kept in touch, obsessively, by mobile phone, ringing around the group two or three times every week. They still never talked about the past, nor did they talk about the present, beyond saying that they had a job and that life was easy—"life is not easy" was a sentence that each repeated again and again while in Cairo. What they talked about, between Dallas, Ohio, and Seattle, was the future. Across the huge distances that now separated them, talking often late into the night, they discussed night school and college entrance, law degrees and openings in business and management. It was as if their horizons had become so immense that there was nothing, now, that might not be possible. "All of us," Kono said to me with pride, "have a plan."

. . .

MARYLAND HAS A long tradition of resettling Liberians, many of whose ancestors today made the first journeys as freed slaves to colonize the new Liberia, land of the free, founded with U.S. help in 1822. Some four thousand Liberians live in the Baltimore area alone, and forty-six, resettled here from their places of flight and exile all over the world, arrived in 2004. Among these was Omar and his wife Maikan.

Omar was one of the eldest of the young men in Cairo. A contained, solemn figure, he worried about the others, helping those who did not get enough to eat, keeping an eye out for trouble and despair. He had been a teacher briefly before being imprisoned by Charles Taylor's soldiers in a warehouse in Monrovia and kept for a week without food or water, and he had fled to Cairo only after learning that he was to be detained again and this time probably executed. In Taylor's Liberia, there did not have to be a reason for the killings. When he first presented his case to UNHCR in Egypt, he was turned down, in the way that many asylum seekers are turned down, on grounds of insufficient evidence. It was only when his wife Maikan turned up in Cairo, having herself fled Monrovia after being raped by armed security men in front of her children, that their case was reconsidered jointly and then accepted. Unable to take the children with her as she fled from Liberia, Maikan had left them with her sister.

The couple arrived in Baltimore on a snowy afternoon in November 2003; just over a year later, on another snowy afternoon, I went to see them. Neither one of them had ever seen snow before reaching the United States. When they talked about that first moment of arrival, they stretched out their arms and showed how the snow settled on their hands, touched it, and felt it dissolve.

Maikan soon found work in a hotel, making more than $400 a week in wages and tips; Omar was given a job with a mail-sorting office. They have applied for their son and their daughter to join them; Omar has not seen his children for more than six years. When they talk to them on the telephone, the children often cry, such is their longing to reach the country that in their minds has come to represent not only reunion with their parents but the consumer goods—the bicycles, mobile phones, computer games—that have become symbols of the stability they have never known. In their gleaming flat, on an attractive housing estate on the outskirts of Baltimore, with its fitted white carpet and enormous fridge, there is a new television and video set and a computer, proof that life has again, after so many years of poverty, become predictable and prosperous.

Soon after they arrived, they were told about their rights: rights to education ᵃ⁻ ᵈ medical care, to food stamps and an allowance un- ork, to green cards and eventually to citizenship, and ₛ to have their children join them. Entitlement is heady to people who have lived for so long with no rights at all, on the casual charity of others, and the sense of being worth something again is what all the resettled refugees talk about. Maikan, who never spoke in Cairo, now cannot stop exclaiming over the new horizons in her life. "Being given things, just given them," she says. "I still find it impossible to believe. With our first food stamps I went into a supermarket and bought all the food that I had never seen and never eaten." Not that the threads that tie them to their childhoods are quite broken: Omar has long suffered from some kind of neuralgia in his jaw. It started when he was caring for the Liberians in Cairo, and it continues to mystify the American medical profession, who have sent him to see many specialists. Walking along in the snow, near his modern estate, Omar said, with an air of slight defiance, that he personally believed it was black magic, and that one of the young Liberians, in the edgy days in Cairo, when each watched the others for signs that they might be getting a better deal, had put a spell on him.

By some act of serendipity, for such neat pairings are not planned by the computer-driven process of selection and allocation, while homely Omar and Maikan were sent to orderly, slow-moving Baltimore, Ansu, the most canny and streetwise of the group, the young man whose step was almost jaunty even when in despair, was directed to New York. To understand Ansu's joy in his new surroundings, to comprehend the enormous luck and randomness of resettlement, one has to know something more of his past.

In the 1980s, Ansu's father, Siaka, owned a large coffee and cocoa, farm near the town of Bahn in Liberia's Nimba County, though he spent most of his time in Monrovia, where he was employed by the Ministry of the Interior. Ansu lived with his mother and six brothers and sisters in Bahn. They were Mandingos. The civil war reached Nimba in March 1990, when he was twelve. Charles Taylor's rebel forces, letting it be known that they intended to kill all Mandingos, the ethnic group with the largest number of educated and successful people, began rounding up and questioning everyone they could catch. Ansu escaped and hid in the bush, but was soon caught by the rebels and taken to a camp with other able-bodied boys and young men. Every day, the captives, tied to each other with rope, were led off to a diamond mine in a nearby swamp, and there, up to their waists in water, they dug for the diamonds with which the soldiers paid for their weapons. Boiled cassava leaves formed the basis of the prisoners' diet, and the boys often felt faint from hunger.

Because Ansu had grown up speaking not only Mandingo and English, but Gio, Jula, and Bambara as well, he was useful to the soldiers as an interpreter. After four months, he was taken one day deep into the forest to forage for food. Nonchalantly inching away from the others, he managed to untie the rope and escape, though he was shot in the leg as he ran off. Lame and in some pain, he reached Monrovia, where to his immense relief he found that his entire family had survived. Once his wound had healed he returned to school and completed his education, and though university was not available in Liberia, still in a state of prolonged civil war, he went to work in his father's office.

By now, Samuel Doe, the president favored by the United States was dead, and Charles Taylor had officially come to power, promising that there would be no further discrimination or witch hunts against Mandingos. Just the same, one morning in the late spring of 1998, after saying good-bye to his mother in the kitchen and driving with his father to work, Ansu was arrested by the security services and taken to the prison at Salt Beach. His father was arrested with him. Their arms were bound tightly behind their backs and they were tortured by men in black hoods. Ansu's feet were held over lit coals and burned. First, Siaka's fingers were slashed with a razor blade and then his head was plunged into a cauldron of hot melted rubber. When I went to see him in New York, seven years after this took place, Ansu described the scene: "When my father's head was pulled out of the cauldron, he couldn't see anything. He seemed to have gone blind. I begged the men to stop torturing him. One of them said: 'He has lost his eyesight? Okay. Now he will lose his soul.' Then he shot my father in the back of the head, and when he didn't die, but lay on the floor screaming with pain, they took a chainsaw and cut off his hands and feet." When the guards turned their attentions to Ansu, he fainted.

When he came to, his father's body had been taken away, and all that was left was a pool of blood. Eventually, helped by a guard who was a Mandingo himself, Ansu escaped. Hearing that his mother, as well as his brothers and sisters, had all been arrested, and had since disappeared, he accepted a friend's offer of a lift in a lorry to Guinea, and from there, in 1999, he accompanied another family friend, met in a refugee camp, to Cairo, to act as his driver in Alexandria. He was certain his family was now all dead. Left alone in 2001 when the friend died suddenly of a heart attack, Ansu joined the small band of Liberians in Cairo in search of refugee status and resettlement. A clever, good-looking boy, he appeared as a solitary, wary figure, who went to great lengths to avoid all talk of the past; to keep questions and concern at bay, he laughed, told jokes in the American voice that he had picked up from tourists in Alexandria. Sometimes he vanished for weeks on end; when he returned to the group, he brought back more jokes. In New York, looking back at that time when we met, he said: "I was thinking of committing suicide. No one could have stopped me. No one at all." Even then, his long passage of persecution and bad luck had not ended. Learning one day that one of his brothers was in fact alive and living in the United States he learned a week later that he had been killed in a car crash.

In the autumn of 2003, having by now spent almost two years penniless on the streets of Cairo, Ansu was informed that he was to be resettled in New York. His first weeks were very lonely. The city seemed too big, too frenetic. But then the parents of a young legal intern whom he had known in Cairo and who had recently lost their own son, befriended him, and then he started to feel better. Talking about himself, with charm and self-mockery and in the lilting cadences of West African English that stay long in the mind, Ansu often refers to himself by name. "And then," he says, "Ansu thought to himself: I'm a city boy. New York is the perfect place for me. I'm going to make it here."

At times, it seems that asylum seekers and refugees exist in a world almost exclusively governed by luck, good as well as bad. When Ansu's luck finally turned, it set in train a series of events so improbable that they belong better in fiction. Once he resolved to make the most of New York, he determined to make money in order to put himself through the college education the Liberian civil war had denied him. He found a first job as a restroom attendant, and a second as a cleaner, after advertising his services on the Web with the words: "I can make your house clean beyond all your expectations." People believed him, and he soon had enough saved to join the highly competitive two-week course as a Yellow Cab driver, emerging at the end of it as one of the few to get through on a first attempt.

Ansu's weekly contract with a cab company costs him $1,250, but as soon as that money has been paid each week, with something left over on which to live, he goes on to act as an interpreter for new West African arrivals. Not long ago he was invited to join a theater company staging shows to introduce New York children to foreign lands and foreign cultures. The children, who found his name hard to remember, christened him African Child. When Ansu reflects on the future, he toys with the idea of business or public relations, and sometimes, when he is feeling philosophical, he talks about joining the CIA, where he senses some of the unseen power that intrigues him about public life might lie.

Meanwhile, his life has again changed course. One morning, driving his Yellow Cab down Central Park West, he picked up an African passenger heading for the airport. From her clothes, a smart Western coat over a lapa, a tied cloth skirt worn by West African women, he thought she might be Guinean or even Liberian. She asked him, as many of his passengers do, where he came from. They fell to talking. It turned out that she was a businesswoman from Conakry in Guinea and that her name was Khalidatu. Idly, Ansu remarked that this was also his mother's name. As she paid her fare, his passenger gave him her card, saying that she worked with a Liberian woman also called Khalidatu, who traded in textiles across West Africa, and that Ansu might like to contact her, in case she might have news of other Liberians who had survived Charles Taylor's massacres.

Several attempts made to reach his passenger by phone failed, and Ansu lost the card on which her number was written. A few months later, cleaning out his room, the card fell out of a book. This time, his passenger answered and gave him a number to call. He dialed. A woman answered. He tells the story: "My heart stopped. I knew the voice. I said: 'Mom, it's me, Ansu.' There was silence. Then cries, laughter, screams. She couldn't believe it. I couldn't believe it." All that day, impervious to the Yellow Cab company's pleas that he pick up passengers, Ansu and his mother talked. She told him that she had managed to escape Monrovia with two of his sisters and one brother, and that she was now caring for them in a rented flat in Conakry, together with two orphaned nieces. Ansu suggested that he should immediately apply to have her join him in New York. (Resettlement allows for family reunification of a parent, a child, and a spouse). "Ansu," his mother told him, "I've got a boyfriend, I'm forty-nine, and I'm not going nowhere."

Ansu and Khalidatu now talk five to six times every week. "I started to get happy when I got hold of my mom," says Ansu. They talk as he ferries passengers up and down Manhattan, and as he walks home to his apartment in the Bronx, having parked his cab in the company garages; they talk late at night and early in the morning, as if to make up time for the six years they have lost. With the money that he sends her, $150 every two weeks, she has bought a plot of land in Conakry, and the foundations of a house have already been laid. But it is only when the roof is on that he will go to visit her, for by then he will have done what an eldest son should do, and that is care for his widowed mother and younger brothers and sisters. The thought that he is now in a position to do so gives him pleasure every day. But just as the Liberians do not talk to one another about their pasts, so his mother does not talk to him about what happened to her in the weeks that followed his and his father's arrest. He fears it was something terrible, and fears, too, that he might not have the strength to listen. "If I knew," he says, "maybe I wouldn't be able to drive." And so, in his baseball cap set at a boyish angle and his dark blue Ralph Lauren woolen jacket, bought with the first money he earned—clothes, like mobile phones, are crucial to Ansu's image of survival, just as they are crucial to all the young Liberians—he rides the city in his Yellow Cab, loving the early mornings when Central Park is full of mist. "African Child, I say to myself, you're a lucky guy. New York, where everyone says the F word, that's the place for Ansu."

•   •   •

THE FIRST TIME that I had bought glasses for Mamadu was late at night in a poor district of Cairo, where the shops stay open until after midnight and where a few generous-minded doctors and opticians see patients for free after their salaried working days. That was in the spring of 2002. Mamadu was then twenty-one, a thin, anxious, scholarly young Liberian, sole survivor of the massacre that had seen his parents and four younger brothers and sisters murdered in front of him. He was so shortsighted that the optician could not believe he was able to see his way across Cairo's frenetic streets. I then explained that Mamadu had spent six years in a refugee camp in Guinea before being helped by a family friend to come as an asylum seeker to Cairo. When he tried on his glasses, on that still, warm night, Mamadu marveled at a world he had until then perceived only as a blur.

The second time that I bought glasses for Mamadu, having at last tracked him down after more than a year of silence, during which I had feared that he might be dead, it was on a brilliantly sunny afternoon in January 2005. We were in a shopping mall in Tel Aviv, and the Israeli optician, like his Egyptian counterpart, could not believe that a boy so shortsighted could negotiate the hazards of everyday life without help. What I didn't tell him was that Mamadu had lost his first pair of glasses during his flight from Egypt across the Sinai, jostled and harried by the people traffickers to whom he had promised $3,000 for a one-way passage to Israel. It is through Mamadu's tale, and that of the other eleven young Liberians who fled to Egypt in 1999 and 2000, with their sequences of brutality and violence, fear and loss, hardship and poverty, that the other story of modern asylum and refugee life can be told, one in which luck can play so poignant and so harsh a part.

It was the arrest and torture of Amr in a police lockup on the outskirts of Cairo in the autumn of 2003, and his appearance in court with bruises on his face and neck and clearly fragile and confused, that had first unnerved the young Liberians. Not long afterward, Mustafa—the wiry, bookish boy who had been seven years old, and out fishing, when the rebels attacked his village in Liberia's Grand Capemount County and killed his parents and eleven brothers and sisters—was picked up and spent three weeks in a police cell in Cairo, blindfolded. Then Iziako was arrested after an argument with an Egyptian neighbor and deported. Hearing these stories, the young Liberians began to lose their nerve.

It was soon after all this that the departures had started. Though cautioned by others not to panic, the sense of fear, for some of them, became overwhelming. People traffickers are not hard to find in Cairo. In the last few years, a highly lucrative network of Africans and Egyptians, using the Bedouin nomads for the passage across the Sinai desert, has started trafficking groups of refugees from Egypt into Israel, following the routes traditionally used to smuggle drugs and arms. (In 2002, the Israeli paper *Ha'aretz* published the log of a border policeman who patrols the frontier. "July 22," it read, "3 bags of marijuana; July 24: 6 bags and 25 prostitutes; July 26: 10 prostitutes; 5 Africans; July 31: 4 Egyptians, 4 foreign workers, 1 woman.") In twos and threes, twelve of the young Liberians now agreed to pay middlemen for the traffickers $3,000 each for a passage to Tel Aviv, to be taken out of their wages on arrival. It was Mamadu, who had the easiest journey, who had the worst arrival.

Transported by car and truck, then put across the border on foot in only a pair of trousers and a T-shirt, with no documents, Mamadu had immediately found himself locked up by his smugglers in a bakery on the edges of Tel Aviv. He was awakened at four in the morning to start work, and kept working until seven at night. He was fed mostly bread and cakes. At night, he slept on a concrete floor with a single blanket. The dust and flour got into his lungs: he coughed. After a month, during which time he had not been allowed outside, the middleman for the smugglers, who was a Russian, moved him to a road-construction unit, giving him a uniform so that he would not be questioned by police. Together with a dozen other Africans, also paying off their smugglers, he was closely guarded, locked at night in a warehouse, and given food but no money. He was told that the fee would take eight months to work off: he counted the days, one by one. Allergic to some chemical in the machinery, he developed sores on his face, arms, and hands, which bled and became infected. These were the months I did not hear from him.

The smugglers' fee paid off, Mamadu joined the other smuggled Liberians from Cairo and applied to UNHCR in Israel for refugee status. Elsewhere, his case would probably have won recognition and resettlement in the United States or Canada. In Israel, the process is different. Though in theory a new immigration and refugee law, enforced by a special commission with the help and advice of UNHCR, regulates policy, in practice, as elsewhere in the world, asylum remains a murky area. Broadly, those who enter illegally from countries hostile to Israel, who are known as "infiltrators," are either quickly resettled in a willing third country or deported. Palestinian refugees have separate laws of their own. All the others—except for Liberia, Sierra Leone, Ivory Coast, and the Congo, which are "conflict" countries—are examined and either given refugee status or rejected. The nationals of the four current "conflict countries," providing they can prove that they are who they say they are, are given six-month visas, renewable until the moment when their country is declared "safe," when they are deported. Not long ago, Sierra Leone was declared "safe" and Sierra Leoneans are now on their way home. "The moment the weather looks better," an immigration lawyer said to me, "the Liberians will be on their way, too."

Mamadu and the other eleven Liberians live and work along the margins of Israeli life. They wash dishes in restaurants, clean lavatories, take the most dangerous and dirtiest of the construction jobs for wages that fall below the national level. After the government, worried about the failing economy and rising unemployment, embarked on a crackdown of illegal immigrants in 2002—said at their peak to number a quarter of a million, mainly African, Asian, and Eastern European, drawn by the demand for cheap labor in Israeli construction and agriculture—a new immigration police force was set up, which periodically carries out raids on poor neighborhoods. Most of these take place in the middle of the night, and those without papers are taken into detention and deported. All the Liberians have stories of being stopped, questioned, taken into custody. One day, coming back to the room he shared with another young African from his job washing up in a hotel, Mamadu was picked up by the police and handcuffed. When he asked to be allowed to urinate, the police refused; when he eventually did so in the police car, he was punched in the stomach.

Not one of the eleven young Liberians can forget that had they waited in Cairo, they would now be resettled in the United States or Canada. It haunts them. Mamadu, in particular, is tormented by all he senses that he has lost. In October 2004, while cleaning a house, he started to hear voices murmuring in his head. They told him that he was being watched, and they sounded angry. Sometimes, he told me when I saw him in January 2005, "I can hear people reading in my head. I shout abusive things. I see people laughing at me. I do believe people tried to use supernatural powers to destroy me." These episodes are followed by blinding headaches. "I am hungry for recovery," he said to me.

"Any time am out in the streets, I see angry faces," he wrote not long ago, in one of the many e-mails that followed my visit. "But am tired of living as such. I've always been running away from threats and intimidation. I am really tired." For the first time, he began to talk of going back to Liberia, to Monrovia, where as a nine-year-old boy he had heard his family being murdered in the road behind him.

SOURCES

Much—perhaps most—of the research in this book was performed in interviews with asylum seekers, refugees, and migrants in different parts of the world. Their stories form the heart of the book. Many have preferred not to be named, and for those I have invented new names; others were happy to be identified and I have accordingly done so. I also talked to many people who work and have worked with refugees.

The main human rights and refugee organizations issue regular reports, country profiles, press releases, and publications and have Web sites with up-to-date information about the countries and places I visited. I found the following particularly useful: Amnesty International, the *British Medical Journal*, the British Refugee Council, *The Economist*, the European Council on Refugees and Exile, *Forced Migration Review*, the Global Internally Displaced People project of the Norwegian Refugee Council, the UK Home Office, Human Rights Watch, Index on Censorship, the Information Centre about Asylum and Refugees, the International Rescue Committee, the Lawyers Committee for Human Rights, Opendemocracy, Refugees International, the Refugees Studies Centre, Reliefweb, the UN Commission on Human Rights, the UN High Commissioner for Refugees, U.S. State Department Country Reports, and the World Refugee Survey.

Chapter One: The Homeless and the Rightless

PAGE

36   Louis Henkin was a young: conversation with author, November 3, 2003.

38   No international organization: For an excellent overview of UNHCR's work, see Gil Loescher, *The UNHCR and World Politics: A Perilous Path* (Oxford: Oxford University Press, 2001). See also the newsletters of the International Council of Voluntary Organizations.

44   Ogata's interests: The following pages are based on interviews with UNHCR staff in February 2004.

46   The new millennium: See UNHCR, *The State of the World's Refugees*, 1995, 1997, 2000.

47   Not the least of Lubbers's challenges: See the publications of the Global IDP Project, Norwegian Refugee Council.

50   Among the boat people: conversation with Sally Verity-Smith, October 25, 2003.

52   Some $10 billion: See Web sites of UK Home Office (www.homeoffice.gov.uk) and UNHCR (www.unhcr.ch).

Chapter Two: Gli Extracomunitari

67   Lampedusa is popular: See David Gilmour, *The Last Leopard* (London: Quartet Books, 1988).

72   Europe's earliest migrants: See Raleigh Trevelyan, *The Companion Guide to Sicily* (London: Companion Guides, 1999).

73   At first, influxes: See Michael Pugh, *Europe's Boat People: Maritime Cooperation in the Mediterranean* (Challot Paper 41, July 2000).

73   With Silvio Berlusconi's election: See publications of the European Council on Refugees and Exiles. Also publications of the Commission for the Politics of Integration of Immigrants, Department of Social Affairs, Rome. Stefano Vincenzi, "Italy: A Newcomer with a Positive Attitude," *Journal of Refugee Studies*, vol. 13, no. 1 (2000). John Morrison and Beth Crosland, "The Trafficking and Smuggling of Refugees: The Endgame in European Asylum Policy?" UNHCR Working Paper No. 39 (April 2001).

Chapter Three: The Fence

94   It has become fashionable: See Philip Martin and Jonas Widgren, "International Migration: Facing the Challenge," *Population Bulletin*, vol. 57, no. 1 (2002). Amnesty International, "United States of America: Human Rights Concerns in the Border Region with Mexico" (1998).

99   And, of course, the routes: Wayne Cornelius, "Death at the Border: Efficacy and Unintended Consequences of U.S. Immigration Control Policy," *Population and Development Review*, vol. 27 (Dec. 2001). Also see Center for Comparative Immigration Studies, "Anti-immigration Vigilantes on the U.S.-Mexico Borderlands" (Oct. 2003), and "Policing the Border: U.S. Immigration Control Strategy" (Nov. 2003).

100 The migrants are not put off: Conversation with Nate Goetz, October 28, 2003. Also see reports in *Migration World*.

109 The detention of asylum seekers: See reports by Amnesty International, Human Rights Watch, Lawyers Committee for Human Rights.

Chapter Four: Fair Go

117 "Italians": For documents on early immigration, see Melbourne's Museum of Immigration.

125 It was under: "Not for Export" (Human Rights Watch briefing paper, Sept. 2002).

126 It came about: See the Web sites of the Australian Government Immigration Department (www.immi.gov.au) and the Refugee Council of Australia (www.refugeecouncil.org.au).

129 on August 24, 2001: David Marr and Marian Wilkinson, *Dark Victory* (Sydney: Allen & Unwin, 2003); see also Robert Manne and David Corlett, *Quarterly Essay 13: Sending Them Home* (Sydney: Pan Macmillan Australia, 2004) and Don McMaster, *Asylum Seekers: Australia's Response to Refugees* (Melbourne: Melbourne University Publishing, 2003).

132 It was about now: see Australia-Pacific Amnesty International, "Offending Human Dignity: The 'Pacific Solution' " (2002).

137 Woomera: See Tom Mann, *Desert Sorrow: Asylum Seekers at Woomera* (Sydney: Wakefield Press, 2003).

144 an alarming...picture: There are a great many papers and reports on this subject. See in particular, J. P. Wilson and B. Drozdele, eds., "The Politics of Asylum and Immigration Detention: Advocacy, Ethics and the Role of the Therapist" in John P. Wilson and Boris Drozdek, eds. *Broken Spirits: The Treatment of Asylum Seekers and Refugees with Post-Traumatic Stress Disorder.* (London: Brunner-Routledge, 2004). Also see Aamer Sultan and Kevin O'Sullivan, "Psychiatric Disturbances in Asylum Seekers Held in Long-Term Detention," *Medical Journal of Australia*, vol. 175 (2001).

Chapter Five: Newcastle and the Politics of Dispersal

164 In 2002, according to official figures: For up-to-date figures see the Web sites of the Home Office (www.homeoffice.gov.uk), the British Refugee Council (www.refugeecouncil.org.uk), and the Information Centre About Asylum and Refugees (ww.icar.org.uk).

168 In practice, people: See North of England Refugee Service, "A Transnational Network: Hearing the Voices of Refugees in Policy and Practice in the European Union" (2000).

173 None of this process: "What's the story?: Media Representation of Refugees and Asylum Seekers in the UK," Article XIX, 2003.

Chapter Six: Little Better than Cockroaches

190 In the autumn of 2002: Human Rights Watch, "Liberian Refugees in Guinea: Refoulement, Militarization of Camps and Other Protection Concerns"

(Nov. 2002). Also see Amnesty International, "Guinea and Sierra Leone: No Place of Refuge" (Oct. 2001).

196   Though the precise origins: For an excellent recent history of Liberia, see Stephen Ellis, *The Mask of Anarchy: The Destruction of Liberia and the Religious Dimension of an African Civil War* (London: C. Hurst, 1999).

209   UNHCR is at: See Tania Kaiser, "A Beneficiary-Based Evaluation of the UNHCR Program in Guinea" (UNHCR Working Paper, 2001) and Jeff Crisp, "No Solutions in Sight: The Problem of Protracted Refugee Situations in Africa" (UNHCR Working Paper, 2003).

214   No one really believes: See Robert F. Gorman, *Refugee Aid and Development* (London: Greenwood Press, 1993).

Chapter Seven: The Corridors of Memory

224   "blend of memory": Jabra Ibrahim Jabra, *A Bethlehem Boyhood* (Fayetteville, AR: Univ. of Arkansas Press, 1995).

225   there is no perimeter fence: For good accounts of the history of the Palestinians in Lebanon, see Rosemary Sayigh, *Too Many Enemies: The Palestinian Experiment in Lebanon* (London: Zed Books, 1994); D. Gilmour, *Dispossessed: The Ordeal of the Palestinians, 1917–80* (London: Sidgwick and Jackson, 1980); and Robert Fisk, *Pity the Nation: Lebanon at War* (London: Carlton Books, 1990). See also the archives of the International Committee of the Red Cross, and of the UN Relief and Works Agency.

230   As villages were deserted: Walid Khalidi, *All That Remains: The Palestinian Villages Occupied and Depopulated by Israel in 1948* (Washington, D.C.: Institute of Palestinian Studies, 1992).

231   "a black cave": Elias Khoury, *The Kingdom of Strangers* (Fayetteville, AR: Univ. of Arkansas Press, 1996).

242   The voice that has developed: Edward Said, *Reflections on Exile* (London: Granta Books, 2001), and *The Politics of Dispossession* (London: Pantheon, 1994).

243   "At one thirty": Mourid Barghouti, *I Saw Ramallah* (London: Bloomsbury, 2003).

247   "Basically": May Seikaly, *Al-Jana File on Palestinian Oral History*, The Arab Resource Centre, Beirut, 2002.

256   "All those who have been destined": Barghouti, op. cit.

Chapter Eight: The Illness of Exile

262   The literature of exile: See Paul Tabori, *The Anatomy of Exile* (London: Harrap, 1972).

265   Toward the end of the 1970s: For the literature on torture, see the publications of Amnesty International and the Medical Foundation for the Care of Victims of Torture.

272   Over the years: Jane Kramer, "Refugee," *The New Yorker*, Jan. 20, 2003.

Chapter Nine: Going Home

294   The Afghans know: See David Turton and Peter Marsden, "Taking Refugees for a Ride? The Politics of Refugee Returns to Afghanistan" (Afghanistan Research and Evaluation Unit, Dec. 2002).

296   The refugees did start: Amnesty International and Human Rights Watch have produced excellent reports on Afghanistan. See, in particular, Amnesty International, "Afghanistan: Out of Sight, Out of Mind: The Fate of the Afghan Returnees" (2003). See also reports of the British Agencies Afghanistan Group (BAAG); Michael Ignatieff, "Nation-Building Lite," *New York Times,* July 28, 2002; and Nicholas Stockton, "Strategic Coordination in Afghanistan," Afghanistan Research and Evaluation Unit, August 2002.

297   When . . . Robert Byron: Robert Byron, *The Road to Oxiana* (London: MacMillan, 1937).

301   In 1836: Sir Alexander Burnes, *Cabool: A Personal Narrative of a Journey to and Residence in That City,* 1836, 7 *and* 8 (London: J. Murray, 1842).

302   he remarked on the excellence: *The Baburnama Memoirs* (New York: Random House, 2002).

Chapter Ten: Dead Dreams

332   "So thick": Tété-Michel Kpomassie, *An African in Greenland* (New York, 2001). p. 10.

Epilogue: A Mode of Being

349   When Jeff Crisp: conversation with author, February 2002. See Jeff Crisp, "A New Asylum Paradigm? Globalization, Immigration and the Uncertain Future of the International Refugee Regime" (UNHCR Working Paper, Dec. 2003). See also Amnesty International, "Refugees: Human Rights Have No Borders" (1997).

352   At the beginning of 1999, five hundred people: Philip Rudge, conversation with author, March 15, 2004. See also Philip Rudge, "The Need for a More Focused Response: European Donor Policies Toward IDPs" (Washington, D.C.: The Brookings Institute, Jan. 2002).

352   Why should something: Matthew Gibney, conversation with author, October 2003.

353   In the mid-1970s: See Nigel Rapport and Andrew Dawson, eds., *Migrants of Identity: Perceptions of Home in a World of Movement* (Oxford: Berg Publishers, 1998).

355   Even if the flows: For a good overview, see Stephen Castles, "The International Politics of Forced Migration." In Leo Panitch and Colin Leys, eds.,

Fighting Identities: Race, Religion and Ethno-nationalism (London: The Socialist Register, 2002).

356   UNHCR's mission: Volker Turk, "UNHCR's Mission," *Refugee Survey Quarterly*, vol. 20 (2001).

ACKNOWLEDGMENTS

Lyndall Passerini, Frances D'Souza, Janet Powney, and my son, Daniel Swift, came with me on my journeys: I would never have traveled anywhere, and the book would not have been written, without them. I would like to thank them very much.

I particularly want to thank the following, who read different chapters and gave suggestions and advice: Anne Chisholm, Jeff Crisp, Beth Crosland, Michael Davie, William Hopkins, David Marr, Philip Rudge, and Kirteen Tait. I am also very grateful to the Society of Authors, for their grant from the Authors' Foundation.

This book would never have been started without the young Liberians in Cairo, and I owe them thanks for the many hours they spent talking to me about their lives. In Cairo, I would also like to thank Magda Ali, Fateh Azzam, Barbara Harrell-Bond, Sofi Elg, Enid Hill, Heba Kasseem, Mulki al-Sharmani, and Nachoua El Azhari, for her generous hospitality. Just as I would like to thank Diana Allen, Virginia Duigan, Gill and Robb Lodge, and Dawn Sparks for very kindly having me to stay on my travels, as well as the staff of the International Rescue Committee, Refugees International, Amnesty International, and UNHCR, who made my journeys in Guinea and Afghanistan possible. The archivists and librarians of the Refugee Studies Centre in Oxford, the London Library, the Medical Foundation for the Care of Victims of Torture, and the Refugee Council Archive at the University of East London were extremely helpful.

Many people talked to me for this book, helped me, drove me about, and showed me things. I am very grateful to them all. They are: Ghassan 'Abdallah, Leena-Kaisa Aberg, Eleanor Acer, Rafaelo Alarcon, Daniela D'Amico, Kathi Anderson, Gervase Apache, Paris Aristotle, Sister Bridget Arthur, Karim Atassi, Gian Luca Avanzato, Kenneth Bacon, Helen Bamber, Peer Baneke, Christina Bennett, Jean-Francois Berger, Paul Bergue, Deslie Billich, Tony Birch, Monica Bishop, Professor Geoffrey Blainey, Father Frank Brennan, Kielo Brewis, Sir Nigel Broomfield, Michelle Brown, Sandy Buchan, Julian Burnside, Sherman Carroll, Stephen Castles, Jean Chandler, Deirdre Clancy, Sister Claudette of the Sisters of Mercy, Rupert Colville, Marguerite Contat, Wayne Cornelius, Sarah Covington, Mark Cutts, Nomita Dave, David Deng, Damtew Dessalegue, Kate Durham, Jean-Francois Durieux, Ann Durst, Sue Emmott, Daniel Endres, Heike Estolen, Nabi Farahi, Erika Feller, Giovanni Fiannaca, Georgina Fletcher, Julian Fountain, Ana Liria-Franch, Joung-Ah Ghedini, Matthew Gibney, John Gibson, Brenda Goddard, Nate Goetz, Monica Gonzales, Guy Goodwin-Gill, Mariette Grange, Stefanie Grant, Aziz and Ayda Halimi, Luke Hardy, Ahmed Hawri, the late Arthur Helton, Anne Henderson, Katherine Henderson, Professor Louis Henkin, Taryn Higashi, Liz Hodgkin, Louis Hoffmann, Andrew Hogg, Christopher Horrocks, Bassam Jamil Hubaishi, Jurgen Humber, Linda Jaivin, Lucy Jones, Tania Kaiser, Maija Kajava, David Kapya, Rose Kasusky, Penny Kelly, Josephine Klein, Michelle Klein Solomon, Michael Korsinki, Kristina Kumpula, Margaret Ladner, David Lambo, Comfort Lamptey, Philippe Leclerc, Nick Leader, Eve Lester, Gil Loescher, Anne-Sophie Lois, Ruud Lubbers, Charles MacFadden, Ewen MacLeod, Dennis McNamara, Monique Malha, Robert Mann, Lucia Marghieri, Delphine Marie, Peter Marsden, Anne-Charlotte Martineau, Roberto Martinez, Pablo Mateu, Laura Maxwell, Peter Maxwell, Nicholas and Kerry Minchin, Robert Montgomery, John Morrison, David Murphy, Nancy Murray, Kathleen Newland, Clementine Nkweta Muna, Sayre Nyce, Pia Oberoi, Comfort Ofolabi, Grainne O'Hara, Patricia Omidian, Ekhlas Osman, Dr. Biagio Palumbo, Alison Parker, Mervyn Patterson, Dr. Michael Peel, David Petrasek, Charles Petrie, Margaret Piper, Michael Pugh, Ian Purves, Archi Pyati, Cesar Pastor Ortega, Ron Redmond, Rachel Reilly, Marianne Reiner, Ngareta Rossell, Aziz Royesh, Katherine Sainsbury, Eva Sallis, Angel Santa Ana, Rosemary Sayigh, Jason Scarpone, Ed van Schenkenberg, Col Mark Schnur, Nasir Shansab, John Shattuck, Zainab Sheik-Ali, Alanna Sherry, Ann-Charlotte Siren-Borrego, Russell Skelton, Malcom Smart, Elaine Smith, Dr. Thierno Maadjou Sow, John Spooner, Dr. Zachary Steele, Barry Stoyle, Tim Swett, Derek Summerfield, Larry Thompson, Robbie Thomson, Steve Tull, Volker Turk, Dr. Stuart Turner, David Turton, Amanda Vanstone, Susan Varga, Fulvio Vassalo, Sally Verity Smith, Andrew Wilder, Sara Wills, Arnold Zable, Monette Zard, and Abu, Ali, Hussein, and Mahmud Zeidan.

As always, I am most grateful for the help and encouragement of my agent, Clare Alexander, and my publishers and editors, Penny Hoare, Jennifer Barth, and Vanessa Mobley.

INDEX

Abdul (Afghan refugee), 307
Abdula (Liberian refugee), 5, 10, 23, 360
Abdularam (Liberian refugee), 5, 354, 360
Abdullai (Liberian refugee), 5
Aberg, Leena-Kaisa, 333
Aboriginals, 117, 119–20, 128–29, 141, 148–49
Abu (child refugee in Guinea), 10, 204–5
Abu Ghraib prison, 104
Abudu (Liberian refugee), 6, 360
Adrean (Liberian refugee), 64, 65–66, 80–81
Afghan refugees, 291–94, 301–4, 307
   Australia and, 122, 127, 129–33, 134–35, 151, 153
   resettled in Finland, 338
Afghanistan, 294–95, 310–11
   and heroin, 314, 358
   returnees and IDPS in, 292–94, 296–97, 303–20, 231–27, 352
   See also Al Qaeda; Kabul; mujahedeen; Shomali plain; Taliban
Africa
   AIDS in, 188, 206, 281
   IDPs in, 45, 48
   postcolonial turmoil, 40, 43
   UNHCR and, 40–41
African refugees, 1–27
   Italy and, 74, 79

Lebanon and, 224
Newcastle, England, and, 156–63, 169–79, 183–85
as percentage of world refugees, 188
as torture victims, 160
See also specific nationalities
Aga Khan, Prince Sadruddin, 40
Agei, Simon Maderi, 339–40
AIDS, 23, 48, 188, 206, 281
aid workers
   in Afghanistan, 321
   in Guinea, 203–6, 207–9, 213–14
   sexual exploitation scandal, 211–12
   targeting of, 207
Al Azhar (Islamic university in Cairo), 18
Al Hagh sect, 136
Al Qaeda, 291, 297
Alayarian, Aida, 275
Albanian refugees, 73, 74
Alem (Sudanese refugee), 339
Alex (Liberian refugee), 68–69
Algeria, 39
Algerian refugees, 168, 257–62, 278–81
Ali (Kurdish refugee), 170–72
All American Canal, 99
Allende, Salvador, 282
All That Remains (Khalidi), 230
Amal (Shiite militia), 238
American Friends Service Committee, 251

American University in Beirut, 234
American University in Cairo, 4, 14, 23
Amina (Sudanese refugee), 340
Amir (Afghan returnee), 316
Amira (Afghan social worker), 322, 325
Amnesty International, 111, 129, 148, 259, 260, 270
    conference on torture (1973), 269
Amr (Liberian refugee), 6, 17, 19–20, 23, 24, 25, 368
Anastasi, Father, 331
Angel Heights (home for asylum seekers), 179–83
Angela (Liberian refugee), 65
Angola, 43, 352
Angolan refugees, 159
Anja (Afghan widow), 322–25
Annan, Kofi, 186, 351
Ansu (Liberian refugee), 362–67
anti-communist refugees, 126
anti-immigration lobby, 50, 51, 97, 353
Appave, Gervais, 355
Arab world
    and the Palestinians, 238, 252, 255
    and the Zionists, 221, 229–31
Arafat, Yassir, 233
Arendt, Hannah, 33, 187
Argentina
    resettlement and, 334–35
Arizona-Mexico border, 98
Armenian refugees, 32, 275–76
Arop, Elizabeth Zacharia, 339–40
Ashcroft, John, 108
Ashmore Reef, 132
asylum seekers. *See* refugees and asylum seekers
Augusta, Sister, 124
Australia, 152
    Aboriginals, 117, 119–20, 128–29, 141, 148–49
    asylum requests in, 46n, 49
    child refugees and, 136–41
    detention camps in, 119–25 126–35, 136–41, 141–55
    hardening of refugee policy in, 118–35
    post–WW II refugees and, 36, 126

refugees and asylum seekers, 115–35, 136–55
    resettlement and, 11, 15, 333
Australian Department of Immigration, 147
Australian Department of Immigration and Multicultural and Indigenous Affairs, 124, 133
Australian Federal Court, 140
Australian High Court, 124, 138
Australian Human Rights and Equal Opportunity Commission, 140, 148
Australian Labor party, 125, 131
Australian Liberal party, 129
Australian Migration Act, 133
    Section 417, 138
Australian One Nation party, 129, 131, 135
Australian Refugee Review Tribunal, 124, 138, 140, 145
Austria, 37, 175, 176
Austro-Hungarian empire, 32
Awol, Anwen, 330–31, 335, 343
Awol, Majok, 330–31, 335, 343
Awol, Mary, 328–32, 335, 336, 343–47, 354
Awol, Maum, 328–32, 335, 340–43, 346
Awol, Nuomshett, 330–31, 335, 343
Awol, Shinfig, 330–31, 335, 343
Azerbaijan refugees, 180–83
Aziz (Afghan refugee), 301, 309–10

Babur, Moghul emperor, 302, 326
Bafalie, Khalidatou, 16
Bafalie, Mohamed, 16
Balad al Sheik (Palestinian village), 220–21, 224, 232, 233, 241
Balfour Declaration (1917), 229
Bali, 122
Balkans, 43
Bamber, Helen, 269–72, 274, 278, 280, 283
Bamiyan valley, Afghanistan, 315–20
    Buddhas, destruction of, 313, 315
Barghouti, 'Alaa, 243
Barghouti, Mounir, 243
Barghouti, Mourid, 31, 256
Baxter, Sir John Philip, 120

Baxter detention camp (Australia), 119–21, 123–25, 149
Beamish Museum, 184
Beazley, Jim, 131
Behnam (Mandaean refugee), 154–55
Beirut shelling of 1982, 236
Bellevue/NYU Program for Survivors of Torture, 110
Belsen concentration camp, 269
Benedict (Liberian refugee), 200–202
Ben-Gurion, David, 230–31
Benin resettlement and, 334–35
Benson, Ross, 175
Berger, John, 354
Berlin Wall, 43
Berlusconi, Silvio, 73
Bernadotte, Count Folke, 231
Bertrand (friend of Dialo in Newcastle), 156–63, 169
Bettelheim, Bruno, 264, 265
Biafra, Republic of, 42n
    crisis of 1967, 42
Bility (Liberian refugee), 17, 25, 360
Billich, Deslie, 149
Bishop, Monica, 156, 159–61, 162, 168, 184
"Bitaqit Hawia" (Darwish), 241
black economy, 9
Boabab organization, 163
boat people
    Australia and, 129–35
    Indochinese, 40
    Italy and African, 57–61, 62–72, 76–82
    Vietnamese, 50–51, 118
border(s)
    controls, rise of, 94
    cost of patrolling, 52
    ideal of world without, 94–95
    permeable, in West Africa, 191, 215
Bosnian refugees, 336, 338
Bossi, Umberto, 74
Bossi-Fini law (Italy, 2003), 74
Bourj el Shemali (Palestinian refugee camp), 245
Boutros-Ghali, Boutros, 44
Bowlby, John, 264, 275
"bracero" guest worker program, 95–96

Brahimi, Lakhdar, 296, 321
Brazil
    resettlement and, 334–35
Brennan, Father, 152, 153–54
Brewis, Kielo, 332
Britain. *See* Great Britain
British High Court, 167
British Home Office, 157, 164, 165, 168, 182, 183, 185, 273, 286
    safe countries list, 167
British Human Rights Act, 165, 167
British National Health Service, 274
British National party, 172–73, 184
British Press Complaints Commission, 175
British Refugee Council, 165
British Section, 55, 165
Bulgarian refugees, 32
Burgmann, Rev. E. H., 115
Burj al Barajinah (Palestinian refugee camp), 252
Burkino Faso, 198
    resettlement and, 334–35
Burmese refugees, 334, 338
Burnes, Lt. Col. Sir Alexander, 301–2
Burnside, Julian, 149, 151
Burrell, Paul, 340
Burundi
    as receiving country, 52
    refugees from, 4, 10–11, 352
Bush, George W., 11, 108
Byron, Robert, 297

Cairo, 5, 13
    African refugees in, 3–27, 359–67
    collapse of ideal of asylum in, 27
    human rights workers in, 26–27
    legal advice center in, 15
    UNHCR and, 9, 10–12, 15, 18, 23, 25, 27
Cairo Conference on Population and Development (1992), 349
California
    fence on border in, 91–94, 100–101
    migrants to, 83–90, 91–111
Cambodia, 43
Cambodian refugees, 40, 43

Canada
  border patrolling and, 52
  Palestinian refugees in, 250
  post–WW II refugees and, 36
  resettlement and, 11, 15, 25, 333,
    359–60
Canicatti, Sicily, 81–82
Capri, 66
Carey, Peter, 149
Carney, Terence, 156
Cartagena Declaration on Refugees
  (1984), 40
Carter, Paul, 349
Casa del Migrante, 83–86
Cavour, Count Camillo di, 76
Central America, 40
Centro di Permanenza Temporanea
  (CPTs), 75–76, 77
Chaldeans, 103–6
Chechen refugees, 181
Chechnya, 43, 181
children
  Afghan, 317
  Australian detention camps and,
    136–48, 152–55
  boy soldiers, 13–14, 47, 201, 203–6
  in Cairo, and schooling, 15–16, 23
  Convention of 1951 and, 110
  deaths of, and boat people, 137
  as guides for *coyotes*, 89–90
  Guinean camps and, 192, 195,
    200–206, 215, 217
  Liberian, 217–18
  Palestinian camps and, 244–49
  prison and detention centers and,
    136–48
  prostitution of, 50
  of refugees, 264–67
  separated from parents, 202–6
  translate for parents, 275
Chile
  resettlement and, 334–35
  torture in, 268–69, 282–84
Chilean Medical Association, 268–69
Chilean refugees, 282–84
Chilout, 149
China
  Great Wall, 94
Chinese migrants and refugees,
  92–93, 102, 117, 127

Christian (Guinean aid worker),
  203–6
Christmas Island, 129–30, 132
Cicero, 100
Claudette (Rwandan refugee),
  177–79
Claudette, Sister, 119–20, 124, 125
Clinton, Bill, 97–98
Cold War, 38, 42
Colombian torture victims, 268–69,
  272
Communism, "good" refugees and,
  37–38
Conakry, Guinea, 157, 187–88, 189,
  210–11
  transit center for children, 203–6
concentration camps, 141, 269–70
"conflict" countries, 370
Congo, 158, 356, 370
Congolese refugees, 159, 179
Congress of Royal Australian and
    New Zealand College of
    Psychiatrists, 146
Consortium for Asylum Support
    Services, 183–85
Conté, Lansana, 207–8
Convention on Transnational Crime,
    UN protocols of 2000, 50
Convention for the Rights of the
    Child, 152
Convention Relating to the Status of
    Refugees (1951), 5, 5n, 25,
    37–38, 53, 356
  Article 1, defines refugee and
    asylum seeker, 37–38
  Article 33, on *nonrefoulement*, 37
  Australia and, 127–28, 152
  Britain and, 161, 175–76
  Hocké and redefinition of refugee
    in line with OAU, 42
  Italy's reservation annulled, 73
  not externally supervised, 45
  number of countries signing, 52
  Protocol of 1967, 38
  questions about number valid
    refugees under, in 1980s, 49
  resettlement under, 333
  support for, while obstructing
    asylum seekers, 47
  unaccompanied minors and, 46–47

Coombs, Ann, 150
Cornelius, Wayne, 99, 100
Côte d'Ivoire, 200
Crisp, Jeff, 47, 101–2, 349–50
Cuban refugees, 108
Cyprus, 132
Czech refugees, 34

Daily Express (British newspaper), 116, 174, 175
Daily Mail (British newspaper), 174, 175
D'Amico, Daniela, 75
Daniel (Liberian refugee), 64, 80–81, 359
Dark Victory (Marr and Wilkinson), 135
Darwish, Mahmud, 241
Declaration of the Hague of 2002, 352, 356
de Gaulle, Charles, 187
Deir Yassin massacre, 230–31
Deng, David, 328–31
Deng, Francis, 47–48
Denmark, 176
    Palestinian refugees in, 250
deportations, 51
    Britain and, 167
    Greece and, 74
    Italy and, 74, 75
    U.S. and, 107
depression of 1930s, 33
detention
    Australia and, 119–25, 126–35, 136–55
    Britain and, 163
    Europe and, 42
    U.S. and, 109–11
development aid, 351
Dhykwan, Peter, 339–40
Dialo, Suleiman, 156–63, 169, 177, 215
Dinka people, 10, 328–32, 336–40
Djibouti
    Somalian refugees in, 356
documents, 11, 66, 126
Doe, Samuel, 17, 197–98, 363
Dolores (Mexican migrant), 88–90
Donzo (Liberian refugee), 13–14, 23
drug smuggling, 49, 74–75

D'Souza, Frances, 309
Dubai, 291–92
Dunant, Henri, 31–32
Dupree, Nancy, 313
"durable solutions," 25, 38
Durham, Kate, 151

Eastern Europe, 37–38
"economic migrant," 38, 40–42
    asylum seeker vs., 87–88
    effort to keep out, 51
    term enters jargon, 41
Economist, 175
ECOMOG, 198–99
education
    Afghanistan and, 299–300, 310
    Cairo and, 15–16, 23
    Finland and, 338, 339, 344
    Guinea and, 215
    Pakistan and, 301
    Palestinian refugees and, 249–51
Egypt
    Liberian asylum seekers in, 1–2, 3–27
    See also Cairo
    Ein el-Helweh (Palestinian refugee camp), 236, 243–44, 245–47, 249–50, 252, 253
Emaan (Afghan boat person), 134
Emam (Iranian refugee), 121, 123, 124
Eritrea, 43
Eritrean refugees, 4, 43, 168, 284–88
Estolen, Heike, 336, 337
Ethiopia, 43, 356
Ethiopian refugees, 4, 10, 41, 43, 168
ethnic cleansing, 43
Europe
    anti-immigration rhetoric in, 186
    asylum requests in, 41, 49
    refugee definition and, 37
European Convention on human rights British derogation from, 173
European Monitoring Centre on Racism and Xenophobia, 173
European Parliament, 186
European Union
    Afghanistan and, 322
    "economic migrants" and, 41–42, 49–50

European Union (*continued*)
  funding of UNHCR and, 45
  illegal entry as only option in, 50
  migration of labor and, 351–52
  refugees and migrants, hostility
    toward, 355–56
  Shatila camp and, 226
Evian Conference of 1938, 33–34, 117
Evin prison (Iran), 275, 276
exile, 262–67
  loneliness and trauma of, 110,
    264–67
  modern age of, 264–67
  post-traumatic stress disorder and,
    266–67

Fallah (Liberian refugee), 217–19
Farahi, Nabi, 306
Fatah (Palestinian political group),
    233–35, 244, 254
Fatima (Afghan boat person), 134
Fatima (Afghan displaced widow),
    322–25
Fatima (Liberian refugee), 192–96,
    215, 358
Fatima (Shatila vocational training
    center head), 249–50
Finland, resettlement in, 331, 332–47
Finnish Red Cross, 333
Finnish Refugee Council, 344
Flexner, Georgina, 183–85
Fofana (Liberian refugee), 24
Ford Foundation, 39
Foucault, Père Charles de, 260
France, 37, 262
  asylum seekers in, 164
Francesco, Father, 71–72
Franco, Francisco, 116
Fraser, Malcolm, 129
Freud, Sigmund, 264
Fugitive Pieces (Michaels), 266
Fumbe (Liberian refugee), 21, 26

Gagliano, Comandante Rino, 70, 71
Gateshead Muslim Society, 161
Gedaweh (Liberian refugee), 20–21,
    25–26
Gemayel, Bashir, 236
Genefke, Dr. Inge Kemp, 269
Geneva Convention of 1864, 32

Genghis Khan, 298, 302
genocide, 43, 44
  the Holocaust, 264–65, 268
  See also Rwanda
Germany
  Afghan refugees in, 294
  asylum seekers in, 164
  Palestinian refugees in, 240, 254
  UNHCR and, 37
  WW II and, 37
Ghanaian refugees, 80, 217
Ghazi (Palestinian refugee), 244–49,
    255
Gio people, 191, 197
Giuseppe, Father, 61, 64, 65, 77
Global Commission on International
    Migration, 351
Global IDP Database, 48
globalization, 94, 350
Goedhart, Gerrit Jan van Heuven,
    39–40
Goethe, 72
Gorton, John, 129
Great Britain
  Afghan refugees in, 294
  Algerian refugee in, 262
  appeals for asylum denied in,
    185–86
  asylum seekers in, 74, 156–63,
    169–86
  Australian policy as model, 176
  costs of asylum seekers in, 52n
  demographic deficit, 350–51
  Eritrean refugee in, 284–88
  Hadrian's wall, 94
  humanitarian protection in,
    175–76
  Jews to Palestine and, 34, 132
  media opposition, 173–75, 184
  number of refugees in, 164
  offshore centers and, 176
  and Palestine, 229–30
  Palestinian refugees in, 228–29,
    240–42, 245, 254
  Somalian refugees in, 356
  Ugandan refugees in, 357–58
  UNHCR and Convention and, 37,
    164
Green, Sir Andrew, 172–79
Grey, Earl, 160

Guantanamo Bay, "enemy combatants" in, 108
Guatemala, 105
Guékédou (Guinean refugee camp), 189, 205, 206–9
Guinea, 187–89
  aid workers in, 203–6, 207–9, 213–14
  camps scandal of 2001, 211–12
  cuts in spending for UNHCR in, 211
  as receiving country, 52, 188
  refugee camps in, 187–96, 199, 200–19, 367
  refugees from, 4, 156–63, 168, 217
  UNHCR and, 188–89, 192–93, 200, 201, 202–3, 205, 207, 209–15, 216
Guinean Red Cross, 202, 217
Gulf War, first, 252
Gypsies (Roma), 74, 175

Hadrian, 94
Haganah (Jewish underground organization), 220, 229, 230
Hague, William, 172–79
Haitian refugees, 109
Hakim, Abdul, 299
Halimi, Aziza (daughter of Zainab), 227
Halimi, Eyad (Palestinian refugee), 226
Halimi, Ghassam (son of Zainab), 226–27
Halimi, Hanan (granddaughter of Zainab), 240
Halimi, Marwan (son of Zainab), 226, 227–28
Halimi, Naifa (wife of Marwan), 226
Halimi, Rasmiyya (granddaughter of Zainab), 240
Halimi, Souha (daughter of Zainab), 239
Halimi, Tariq (son of Zainab), 224–25, 231–41
Halimi, Zainab (Palestinian refugee), 220–25, 226–28, 231, 232, 237, 238, 240–41
Hamas, 254

Hammarskjöld, Dag, 39
Hannan, Dr. Timothy, 138
Hanson, Pauline, 128–29
Happy (Liberian refugee), 62–63, 66, 81–82
Hardy, Barbara, 354
Harrell-Bond, Barbara, 5
Hartling, Poul, 40, 42
Hassan, Fakhri el, 232
Hatton, Timothy, 352
Hawke, Bob, 129
Hazaras (Afghan ethnic group), 298–301, 309–10, 313–16
Hema, Sister, 83–90
Henderson, Katherine, 156, 157, 161, 162, 164, 167, 168
Henkin, Louis, 36–37
High Commissioner for Refugees (League of Nations)
  created, 33–34
  See also United Nations High Commissioner for Refugees (UNHCR)
Hindu Kush mountains, 312–20
  poppies as crop, 314, 358
History of Western Philosophy (Russell), 340
Hocké, Jean-Pierre, 42–43, 46
Hoffman, Eva, 263
Holbrooke, Richard, 48
Holland, 254
Holocaust, 264–65, 268, 354
home, idea of, 321, 354
Horace, 358
Horowitz, M. J., 266
Howard, John, 129, 131–32, 133, 134, 135, 148, 153–54
Hubaishi, Bassam Jamil, 254
humanitarian movement, 32–33
"humanitarian pragmatism," 46–47
Human Rights Watch, 148, 190
human smugglers and traffickers, 20, 49–50, 368
  Australia and, 122–23, 127
  Britain and, 170
  identities recommended by, 166
  Indonesian, 124, 127, 154–55
  Italy and (*scafisti*), 60, 66, 67
  lack of protection for asylum seekers using, 50

human smugglers and traffickers (*continued*)
  Mexico and (*coyotes*), 84–85, 87, 89–90, 92, 98–99, 106
  Palestinian refugees and, 154
  revenues from, 68
  rise of, 67–68
  Tunisian, 66–67
Hungarian refugees, 34
Husein (son of Anja), 323
Hussein (Iranian refugee), 142
Hussein, Saddam, 103, 104, 121, 124, 127, 171, 197, 198
Hutu, 177, 271–72
  See also Claudette; Rwandan refugees

IDENT system, 97
Ignatieff, Michael, 148
Illegal Immigration Reform and Immigrant Responsibility Act (U.S., 1996), 100
Iman (Chaldean refugee), 105
"illegals," Australia and, 126–27
immigrants
  anti-immigration lobbies and, 51
  four categories of, in U.S., 107n
  need for, in Australia, 126
  See also refugees and asylum seekers; *and specific nationalities*
Immigration Act (UK, 1999), 168
Immigration Reform and Control Act (U.S., 1986), 96
Indonesia, 130–31
Interim Dispersal Measures (Britain, 2000), 167–72
"internally displaced" people (IDPs), 47–51
  defined, 47–48
  excluded from Convention, 38
  UNHCR and, 47–51
International Committee of the Red Cross, 32, 42, 251, 310–11
International Covenant on Political and Civil Rights, 152
International Office for Migration, 39
International Organization for Migration, 355
International Refugee Organization (IRO), 35–36, 39, 355

International Rescue Committee (IRC), 107, 202–3, 212
Iran
  Afghan refugees in, 294, 296, 299, 309, 314, 319, 322
  as receiving country, 52
Iranian refugees, 41
  Australia and, 121–25, 136–44
  Britain and, 163
  resettled in Finland, 338
  as torture victims, 275–77
Iraq
  war of 1990s, 43
  war of 2003 in, 170–72
Iraqi refugees, 41, 144
  Australia and, 122, 127
  Britain and, 170–72, 184
  Chaldeans, 103–6
  resettled in Finland, 336, 338
  returnees, 352
  torture victims, 272
Ireland, 175, 176
  resettlement and, 334–35
Islamic fundamentalists, 254
  See also Taliban
Israel, 220–25
  Lebanon invaded by, 246, 247–49, 253
  Liberian refugees in, 22–23, 25, 368–70
  Liberians charged with spying for, in Egypt, 6, 19
  Palestinian refugee camps and, 222–28, 232–34, 236–43
  See also Naqba; Occupied Territories
Israel Defense Forces, 221
Israeli Yishuv party, 229
Italian migrants, to Australia, 116–17
Italy, 72–76
  boat people in, 57–61, 62–72, 76–82
  emigration from, 73, 116–17
  and Jews, 74, 76
  migrants and, 73–74
  UNHCR and Convention and, 37
Italy-Albanian agreement, 70
Ivory Coast, 216, 370
  Guinea, crossing points to, 216

as receiving country, 52
refugees from, 4, 216–17
Izako (Liberian refugee), 14, 189,
209, 368

Jabra, Jabra Ibrahim, 224
Jahan, Shah, 326
Jaivin, Linda, 149
Jan, Amir, 307, 312, 358
Japan, 43, 49
Jeremiah (Sudanese refugee), 340
Jews
Australia and, 117
and the Holocaust, 264–65, 268,
354
Italy and, 74, 76
resettlement attempts, 33–34, 132
WW II and, 34–36, 354–55
Johannes Peter (Sudanese refugee),
340
John the Baptist, 121
Johnson, Prince, 197, 198
Jordan
Palestinian camps in, 223, 251,
255
Joy (Liberian refugee), 82

Kabineh (Liberian refugee), 17
Kabul, Afghanistan, 291, 295–99,
301–4, 308–12, 320–27
Kamal, Haji, 303–4, 306–7, 312, 358
Kanafani, Ghassan, 242
Kandahar, Afghanistan, 322
Kapya, David, 211
Karzai, Hamid, 296, 306
Keating, Paul, 125, 127, 129
Kelly, Penny, 149–50
Kenneally, Thomas, 149, 154
Kennedy, Edward, 40
Kenya, 356
Khalidatu (business woman), 366
Khalidatu (mother of Ansu), 366–67
Khalidi, Walid, 230
Khalil, George Naguib, 242
Khoury, Elias, 220, 231
Kissinger, Henry, 40
Kitoko, Gaby, 158–59, 162, 172–74,
176–79
Klein, Josephine, 274–75, 277
Koestler, Arthur, 270

Kolya (Azerbaijan refugee, Madina's
son), 181–82, 358
Kono (Liberian refugee), 17–18,
19–20, 23, 359–60
Konobah (Liberian refugee), 24
Korsinski, Michael, 278–81
Kosovo, 45
and torture, 272
Kou, Mayo, 329
Kpomassie, Tété-Michel, 332
Krahn people, 191
Kromah, Alhaji G. V., 18
Kromer, Mustafa, 18–19
Kuankan (Guinean refugee camp),
189–96, 201–2, 215–16
Kuchi nomads, 322
Kundera, Milan, 263
Kurdish refugees, 170–72
Finland and, 334
Italy and, 73
Lebanon and, 224
Kuwait
Palestinian refugee camps in, 223
Kuwaiti refugees, 168
Kyrgyzstan, 199

Lamine (Algerian refugee), 257–58,
267, 278–81, 288
Lampedusa, Giuseppe di, 57, 67
Lampedusa, Irene, 67
Lampedusa, Tomasso "the Leopard,"
67
Lampedusa island, 66–72
land mines, 302, 307, 315
Langa, Mandla, 257, 263–64
Laotian refugees, 40
League of Nations, 32–33
Lebanese Christian Falangists, 235,
247, 253
Lebanon
civil war in, 235–37
Israeli invasion of, 246, 247–49,
253
Palestinian refugees in, 222–28,
232–34, 236–56
Lega Nord, 74
Leonardo da Vinci (ship), 116
Leopard, The (Lampedusa), 57, 67
Letwin, Oliver, 173
Levi, Peter, 291, 326

Levi, Primo, 264
Lewis, Anthony, 108
Liberia, 9, 43, 196–200, 358, 361, 370
  civil wars, 198, 363
  Guinea, crossing points to, 216
  rebels raid Guinea refugee camps, 198–200
  as receiving country, 25, 52
Liberian refugees, 4
  as boat people in Sicily, 57–61, 62–72, 76–82
  Cairo and, 3–27
  flee Egypt into Israel, 19–21, 25–26
  Guinea and, 188–89, 191, 192–96, 199–200, 216, 217–19
  resettled in West, 359–67
  as torture victims, 20, 272, 364
Libya, 240
Light Garden of the Angel King, The (Levi), 291
Lindt, Auguste, 39
Liria-Franch, Ana, 25
Living In a New Community (Carter), 349
Loescher, Gil, 38, 251n
Logar, Afghanistan, 303, 312
Lola, Guinea, transit center, 217–18
Lubbers, Ruud, 45–46, 47, 48, 212
Luis (Chilean refugee), 282–84, 288
Luis, Father, 83, 84, 86–87
Luisa (Mexican migrant), 88–90
Lynch, Wayne, 137

Macedonian refugees, 168
McDonald, James G., 33
Madina (Azerbaijan refugee), 180–83, 358–59
Mafia, 60
Maghrebini, 74–75
Magyar refugees, 32
Mahfouz, Naguib, 242
Mahmada (Liberian refugee), 20–21, 25–26
Mahmoud (Palestinian refugee), 253
Mahmut (Palestinian refugee), 220–22, 227, 233
Maikan (Liberian refugee), 361–62
Maja (Liberian refugee), 218
Majid (Iranian refugee), 121, 123–24
Malaysia, 122

Malian refugees, 217
Malish (Sudanese refugee), 336–37, 338–40
Malta, 66
Mamadu (Liberian refugee), 21–23, 189, 215, 354, 367–71
"managed migration," 349–54, 356–57
Mandaeans, 121, 123–24, 154–55
Mandingo people, 13–14, 65, 191, 197
Manne, Robert, 149, 152, 153–54
Manoora (naval vessel), 133
Mano people, 197
Manus Island detention centers, 132, 134
Marr, David, 129, 135, 149
Marshall Plan, 36
Martelli, Claudio, 73
Mary (IRC teacher in Guinea), 212–13
Mary (Ugandan refugee), 281–82, 288, 357–58
Masood, General, 307, 309
Masoud (Iranian refugee), 121–22
Médecins Sans Frontières (MSF), 75, 192, 193, 305, 318, 325
medical care
  Afghanistan and, 325
  Palestinian refugees and, 254
  torture victims and, 268–69
Medical Foundation for the Care of Victims of Torture, 270–74, 272n, 278–81, 282, 287–88
Melbourne *Herald Sun*, 139
Mena (Iranian refugee), 142
Mende people, 7–8
Men in the Sun (Kanafani), 242
mental health
  Afghanistan and, 325
  detention of children and, 136–41, 141–48
  Guinea camps and, 215–16
  post-traumatic stress disorder and, 138–39, 147–48, 264–65
  torture victims and, 268–69, 273
  self-mutilation, 151
  See also suicide
Mercy (Liberian refugee), 62–63, 64–65, 66, 74, 78
Mexicali canal, 87–88

Mexican migrants, 83–90, 91–111
Mexican-U.S. border
  history of migration across,
    95–101
  fence, 91–94, 100–101, 132
  people smuggled into, 84–85, 87,
    89–90, 92, 98–99, 106
Micciche, Calogero, 75
Michaels, Anne, 266
"migrants"
  defined by Article I of
    Convention, 37–38
  need for protection, 355–56
  percent of world's population as,
    94–95
  prosecution of, in U.S., 100
  See also refugees and asylum
    seekers
"migrants of identity," 353–54
migration, 354–57
  changing attitudes toward, 97–98,
    99–100, 355–56
  globalization and, 94, 350
Migration Watch UK, 172–79
Mira (Afghan returnee), 316–17
Misericordia (Italian ambulance
  service), 64–65, 77
Mo (Afghan returnee), 308, 327
Mobaraka, Bibi (wife of emperor
  Babur), 326
Mohamed (Liberian refugee), 10, 16,
  198, 215, 360
Mohamed (Sudanese refugee),
  168–69
Moldova, 199
Moroccan refugees, 74
Morteza (Iranian refugee), 141–44,
  148, 154
Moscat, Dr., 66
Mozambique, 43
Mugabe, Robert, 169–70
mujahedeen, 292–93, 303, 304, 323
Mussolini, Benito, 358
Mustafa (husband to Salima), 323

Nabokov, Vladimir, 262
Naked Dead, The (Langa), 257
Namibia, 43
Nansen, Fridtjof, 32–33
Napolitano Bill (Italy, 1998), 73

Naqba (uprooting of Palestinians of
  1948), 220–25, 228–31, 241–42,
  245, 251
Nasir (Afghan returnee), 292–94,
  305–6, 307, 320
Nasser, Gamal, 235
National Asylum Support Agency
  (NASS), 168, 169, 170, 357–58
National Temperance Hospital
  (Britain), 270
National Union of Journalists
  (Britain), 175
Nauru detention center, 132, 133,
  134, 150–51, 153
Newcastle, England
  asylum seekers in, 156–63, 169–79,
    183–85
  Byker area, 169–70, 172–74,
    176–70
New River, 99
New York Review of Books, 108
New Zealand, 133
  resettlement and, 333
Niemöller, Martin, 108
Nigeria, 42n
Nigerian refugees, 74, 102, 217
Nigerois refugees, 217
North American Free Trade
  Agreement (NAFTA), 99
North Korean refugees, 172
North of England Refuge Service, 156
Northern Alliance (Afghanistan), 307
Norway, 130–31, 175, 333
Norwegian Refugee Council, 48
Nsamba (Congolese refugee), 179
Nzerekore, Guinea, 189–90, 211

Occupied Territories, 241, 248, 251
Ogata, Sadako, 43–45
Omar (Liberian refugee), 361–62
Operation Blockade, 98
Operation Foxbat, 100
Operation Gatekeeper, 93, 98
Operation Hold the Line, 98
Operation Jaguar, 100
Operation Relex, 133, 135
Operation Safeguard, 98
Operation Thunderbird, 100
Operation Wetback, 97n
opium growers, 313

Organization for African Unity (OAU), 40, 42
Organization for Economic Co-operation and Development, 175
Organization Guinéenne des Droits de l'Homme, 188
Ortega, Cesar, 211
Osman, Ekhias, 344
Ottoman empire, 32
Oulu, Finland, 335–40

Pacific Solution, 132–33, 135, 150, 151, 153–54
Pakistan, 52
    Afghan refugees in, 294, 296, 299–301, 303–4, 309, 314, 322
Pakistani refugees, 168
Palapa (boat), 129–30
Palestine
    Jews and, 34, 132, 221
    partition of, 229–31
    WW II and, 34, 132
    See also Naqba; Occupied Territories
Palestine Liberation Organization (PLO), 225, 233, 234–35, 248
    Arab Muslim's and, 238–39
Palestinian Authority, 253–54
Palestinian refugees, 220–28, 232–34, 236–56, 370
    Arab Muslim's and, 238–39
    education available to, 253–54
    not included in 1951 Convention, 38, 251n
    number of, 242n, 244, 251
    "right of return," 223–25, 223n, 231
    work available to, 253
    UNRWA and, 227, 243, 246, 251n
Palestinian state, 230–31
Palumbo, Dr., 76–79
Papua New Guinea, 132
Passerini, Lyndall, 15
Peace of Westphalia (1648), 32
Pedro (Mexican migrant), 88–90
Peel, Dr. Michael, 278
Permanent Temporary Centers. *See* Centro di Permanenza Temporanea

Peter (Liberian refugee), 194, 200, 215
Physicians for Human Rights, 110
Pinochet, General, 282
Polish refugees, 34
Port Augusta detention center (Australia), 119, 120, 149
Port Hedland detention camp (Australia), 142
post-traumatic stress disorder, 138–39, 147–48, 264–65
    torture victims and, 273
Potsdam conference, 34
Professional Alliance for the Health of Asylum Seekers and Their Children, 141
prostitution, 49–50
    migrants in Italy, 74

Qaddafi, Col. Muammar, 68
Qassam, Shaykh Izz al-Din al-, 224

racism, 74, 128–29, 172–79
Ranch Rescue, 100
Rania (Chaldean refugee), 105
rape, 8, 43, 245
    and AIDS, 23
    of refugees by aid workers, 212
    survivors of, 266, 271, 272, 281–82
Red Cross movement, 32
"refugee," definition and granting of status of, 37–38, 42
    Australia and, 129–30
    Convention of 1951 and, 41
    OAU and, 42
    unaccompanied minors and, 110–11
    West and, 52
refugee camps, 42
    Australia and, 119–25, 126–35, 136–55
    developing world and, 40, 213–15
    as destructive places, 214–15
    difficulty raising money for, 52
    Europe and, at end of WW II, 38
    Guinea and, 189–96, 205–19
    Hocké attempts to end long-term, 42
    Palestinian refugees in 222–28, 232–34, 236–43
    See also specific camps

Refugee Convention. *See* Convention Relating to the Status of Refugees of 1951

refugees and asylum seekers
  African, in Cairo, 3–27
  as "agents of development," 210
  arrests and torture of, 258–59, 268–78, 280, 281–84, 364
  asylum policy crisis and, 49–50
  boat people, 40, 50–51, 118, 129–35
  boat people, in Sicily, 57–61, 62–72, 76–82
  boat people, in Australia, 115–35, 136–55
  change in policy toward, in Australia, 119–20, 125
  children and unaccompanied minors, 46–47, 110–11, 264–67
  children of, and parental trauma, 110–11
  cost of handing, in UK, 52n
  cross from Mexico to U.S., 83–90, 91–111
  defined by UNHCR and Convention of 1951, 37–38, 40, 41, 42
  denied asylum, in Britain, 167–68
  deportations of, 51
  detention of, in Australia, 119–25, 126–35, 136–55
  detention of, in U.S., 109–11
  difficulties of, in Britain, 167–68, 171–73
  dispersal of, in Britain, 156–63, 167–79
  extraordinary journeys of, 105–6
  families and women with children, 15
  finances of, 14
  funding and coordination issues, 49
  future of policy on, 352–53, 355–56
  global attitudes on, 355–56
  "good" vs. "bad," 37–38, 41, 117, 134
  history of Geneva Convention and UNHCR and, 36–39
  hostility towards, 50, 51, 97, 353
  human rights workers and, 26–27
  idea of "home" and, 321
  IDPs and, 38, 47–51
  language problems, 157, 161, 168, 261–62, 274, 336–37
  legal hurdles and, in U.S., 107–9
  local community and, in Britain, 169
  media opposition to, 173–75, 184
  mortality rates of, 70–71
  pain of exile and past traumas of, 264–67
  Palestinian diaspora, 220–25, 228–31, 241–42, 245, 251
  political reaction to, 117–19, 132–33, 135, 150, 151, 153–54, 172–73, 184
  post-traumatic stress and, 273
  post-WW II in Europe, 34–36
  as returnees, in Afghanistan, 292–94
  repatriation, 43–44
  resettlement of, in Finland, 331, 332–47
  resettlement of, in West, 360–63
  self-mutilation, 151
  suicide of, 13, 137, 138, 139, 142–43, 156–86, 249, 364–65
  top ten receiving countries, 52
  torture and rape victims as, 8, 23, 43, 258–59, 266, 268–78, 280, 281–84, 356–57
  under the age of 18, 46–47
  whites-only policy, of Australia, 128–29
  See also children; torture victims; unaccompanied minors; *and specific receiving countries and nationalities*

Refugee Therapy Center, 277–78
Reith, Peter, 135
relief
  first UNHCR and, 39
  protection issue vs., 40–41
resettlement
  asylum vs., 331–32
  Finland and, 331, 332–47
Reyes, Silvestre, 97–98
Rhodesian refugees, 41
"right of return," 223–25, 223n, 231
Rinnan, Arne, 130–31, 135n
Roland (Liberian refugee), 62–63, 64–65, 66, 74, 78

Romanian refugees, 32, 34, 169
Roosevelt, Franklin D., 33
Roses and Thorns (Khalil), 242
Rothmund, Heinrich, 354–55
Rousseau, Jean Jacques, 31
Ruddock, Phillip, 129–30, 131, 133, 135, 138, 139, 140, 147, 148
Rural Australians for Refugees, 150–51
Rusk, Dean, 37
Russell, Bertrand, 340
Russia
    and Chechen refugees, 181
    See also Soviet Union
Russian refugees
    Britain and, 180–83
    Finland and, 331
    revolution of 1917 and, 32–33
    WW I and, 32
    WW II and, 34
Rwanda
    genocide in, 43, 44, 298
Rwandan refugees, 4, 10–11, 159, 177–79
    as torture victims, 271–72

Sabra (Palestinian refugee camp), 236–37
Saeed (Iranian refugee), 136–41
Said, Edward, 222, 242, 251, 262–63
St. Petersburg, 181–83
Salaam (Chaldean refugee), 104–6
Salem (Iranian refugee), 121–25
Salima (Afghan widow), 322–25
Salimov (Chechen refugees), 181
Sallis, Eva, 149
Saloh, Hassan Omar, 171
Salvo, Francesco di, 65
San Biagio Platani
    Liberians in, 76–77
San Diego, California
    border with Tijuana, 91–93, 96–101, 132
    Chaldean Iraqis in, 105–6
Santa Ana, Angel, 96
Sargon the Akkadian, 103
Satta, Alya, 134
Satta, Kawthar, 134
Satta, Ronkayya, 134
Saudi Arabia, 253
Save the Children Fund, 318

Sayigh, Rosemary, 239
Scarpone, Jason, 214
SCCPI (situation of chronic conflict and political instability), 308
Schnyder, Félix, 39, 40
Schwartz, Theodore, 353
Sciortino, Nene, 57–61
Sciortino, Vera, 57–61
Seikaly, May, 247
Sekou (boy soldier from Sierra Leone), 203–6
Selassie, Haile, 10
self-mutilation, 151
Senegalese refugees, 66
Sennacherib of Mesopotamia, 103
September 11, 2001 (9/11), 49, 101, 107, 351
sexual exploitation, 211–12
Sharon, Ariel, 19
Shatila (Palestinian refugee camp), 222–28, 232–34, 236, 244, 252
    conditions in, 225–26
    population of, 225
    shelling and attacks on, 236
Shayan (Iranian refugee), 136–41, 148, 154
Sherif, Musa, 3–10, 20, 23, 215
Sherif, Zainab (wife of Musa), 8, 9
Shikaki, Khalil, 230, 255
Shinfig (Sudanese refugee), 328–32
Shomali plain, 301–3, 312
Shubnam (Iranian refugee), 137, 139
Siaka (Liberian refugee), 363–64
Sicilia, La (Italian newspaper), 61
Sicily, 57, 72
    Liberian boat people in, 57–61, 62–72, 76–82
Sierra Leone, 200, 370
    as receiving country, 52
    refugees from, 4, 10, 43, 168, 188–89, 191, 206–9
SIEV-X (boat), 134
Silove, Derrick, 144
Siren-Borrego, Ann-Charlotte, 334
Sisalem, Aladdin, 153
Slovakia, 199
Smith, Adam, 83
Smith, Elaine, 150–51
Society for International Development, 352

Somali refugees, 10, 43, 168, 176, 333–34, 336, 338, 356
Somalia, 41, 298
Sophie (Liberian nurse), 216
South African refugees, 164
South American refugees, 74
Southern Illinois Trauma Center, 209
sovereignty issue, 38, 44
Soviet Union
    Afghanistan and, 294, 303–4
    IRO and, 35–36
    post-WW II refugees and, 35–36
    See also Russia
Sow, Dr. Thierno Maadjou, 188
Spain, 64, 262
Spanish Civil War, 115, 270
Spanish refugees, 116
Sri Lankan refugees, 41, 102, 172, 184
    as torture victims, 272
Stalin, Joseph, 35–36
State of the World's Refugees, 350
Statute of Rome, 152
Steel, Dr. Zachary, 144–48
Stern Gang, 230
Stoltenberg, Thorvald, 43
Straw, Jack, 175–76
Sudan, 285
    civil war, 4
    lost boys, 4
    Palestinian refugees in, 255
    remittances and, 350n
Sudanese refugees, 4, 10, 14–15, 168–69, 328–32, 356
    resettled in Finland, 331, 336–47
Sudan People's Liberation Army, 329
suicide, 364–65
    in Britain, 156–86
    in Cairo, 13
    detainees and, 137, 138, 139, 142–43
    in Finland, 343
    Holocaust survivors and, 264, 265
    See also mental health
Sultan, Dr. Aamer, 144, 146
Summerfield, Dr. Derek, 273
Sun (British newspaper), 174, 175
Sunday Times (British newspaper), 175
Sundous (Afghan boat person), 134
Surinam, 102
"suspect aliens," in U.S., 108

Sweden, 74, 175, 240, 333
Swiss People's party, 174
Switzerland, 174
    anti-Semitism and, 354–55
Sydney *Daily Telegraph,* 139
Syria
    Lebanon and, 236
    Palestinian refugee camps in, 223, 251, 255
Syrian refugees, in Lebanon, 225

Taliban, 127, 291, 293, 294, 295, 301, 302, 304, 305, 306–7, 313–20, 323, 358
    Bamiyan valley Buddhas, destruction of, 313, 315
Tamburlaine, 302
Tampa (tanker), 130–32, 135n, 150
Tampering with Asylum (Brennan), 152
Tanzania
    as receiving country, 52, 176
Taraki, Nur Mohamed, 294
Taylor, Charles, 8, 13, 14, 19, 20, 189, 190, 198–200, 358, 361, 363
Tesfay (Eritrean refugee), 284–88
Thai refugees, 102
Tiberius, emperor of Byzantium, 67
Tijuana, Mexico, 91–93
    migrant workers, refuges for, 83–90
Times of London, 248, 252, 276
Tocqueville, Alexis de, 73
torture victims, 18–20, 258–59, 268–78, 280, 281–84, 287–88, 356–57
    Afghanistan and, 294–95
    Algeria and, 278–81
    "climate of disbelief" and, 270
    Liberia and, 364
    Sudan and, 329
    Turkey and, 269, 272
Touré, Sékou, 187–88
trauma
    leading to exile, 278–81
    See also post-traumatic stress disorder; rape; torture victims
Treaty of Vienna (1815), 32
Tunisia, 68
Tunisian refugees, 66–67, 74

Turkey, 66
  massacres of Armenians, 32
  people smuggling and, 69
  refugees from, 168
  torture victims and, 269, 272
Turkish Kurds, 102
  Britain and, 170–72
Tutsi, 271–72
Tyrant's Novel, The (Kenneally), 154

Uganda, 356
Ugandan refugees, 281–82
Ukraine, 199
Ukrainian refugees, 34
unaccompanied minors, 46
  detention of, in U.S., 110–11
  Vietnamese boat people and, 50–51
unemployment, 46
UNICEF, 318
United Kingdom (UK). *See* Great
    Britain
United Nations
  Afghan returnees and, 292–94,
    296–97, 303–27, 352
  Australian detention and, 148
  refugees and, post-WW II, 350
  West African conflicts and, 198
UN Convention Against Torture,
    268
UN Convention on the Rights of the
    Child (1989), 110
UN General Assembly
  Resolution 194 ("right of return"),
    223–25, 223n, 231
  Palestine, partition of, 229–31
United Nations High Commissioner
    for Refugees (UNHCR), 5n,
    36–39, 39–45
  Afghan returnees and, 292–94,
    303–27, 352
  asylum seekers in Cairo and, 9,
    10–12, 15, 18, 23, 25, 27
  attitudes toward refugees and,
    174–75
  budget and funding of, 45–46, 52,
    321
  definition of refugees and, 37–38,
    40
  detention of asylum seekers and,
    109, 132–33, 148

"economic migrants" and, 41
  founding and history of, 38–45
  in Guinea, 188–89, 192–93, 200,
    201, 202–3, 205, 207, 209–15,
    216
  IDPs and, 38, 47–51
  internal affairs of nations and, 38
  long-term camps in Guinea and,
    188–89
  and the media, 175
  migration and, 349–54
  misconduct in, 211
  Palapa and, 129–30
  Palestinian refugees and, 38, 242n,
    251–54
  refugee status, refusal of, 328–32
  relief vs. protection and, 45–51
  report of 2003 on camps, 242n
  resettlement and, in Australia, 126
  Sierra Leone and, 200
  Vietnamese boat people and,
    50–51
UN Relief and Rehabilitation
    Administration (UNRRA),
    34–35, 38
UN Relief and Works Agency
    (UNRWA), 226
United States
  Afghan refugees in, 294
  anti-immigration lobby, 51
  asylum requests in, 46n
  child refugees and, 110
  detention in, 109–11
  guest workers in, 95–96
  history of immigration into, 95–96
  immigrants, categories of, 107n
  legal hurdles in, post–9/11, 101,
    107–9
  Liberia and, 197–99
  Liberian refugees in, 360–67
  Mexican border and, 84–85, 87,
    89–90, 92, 98–99, 106
  nationalities crossing into, 95, 101–6
  number of asylum seekers in, 11,
    46n
  Palestinian refugees and, 231, 250
  post-WW II refugees and, 34–35,
    36
  resettlement and, 6, 11, 15, 23, 24,
    25, 333

Somalian refugees in, 356
unaccompanied minors and, 110–11
UNHCR and, 39, 49
U.S. Border Patrol, 84–85, 86, 91–92
U.S. Congress, 108
U.S. Department of Health and Human Services (HHS), 110
U.S. House of Representatives Committee on Foreign Affairs, 268
U.S. Immigration and Naturalization Service (INS), 97
U.S. Office of Refugee Resettlement, 110
U.S. State Department, 36
Universal Declaration of Human Rights (1948), 35, 152
USA Patriot Act, 108

Vanstone, Amanda, 124, 135, 147
Varga, Susan, 150
Vietnamese refugees, 40, 50–51, 127
in Finland, 332
vigilantes
in Guinea, 207–8
U.S.-Mexico border and, 99–100
Villawood detention center (Australia), 137–39, 140, 143, 144, 154–55
Virgil, 262
visas, 50, 140
Voltaire, 31

Wafa, Jawad, 299–301, 307, 314, 319, 358
Wannsee Conference (1942), 354–55
wars and civil conflict
casualties from, 43
See also specific conflicts
West
asylum policies in, 43, 49
image of, in refugees in Egypt, 12
migration and, 355–56
See also Europe; *and specific nations*
West African Economic Community, 188

White, T. W., 117
White Australia policy, 117–19
Whitlam, Gough, 118, 129
Why Am I Here? (Amnesty International report, 2003), 111
Wiesel, Elie, 3
Wilder, Andrew, 311
Wilhelmensen, Wilhelm, 130
Wilkinson, Marian, 135
women
Afghanistan and, 308, 322–25
as rape survivors, 8, 43, 245, 266, 271, 272, 281–82
trafficking of, 49–50
See also prostitution; rape
Woomera detention center (Australia), 120, 123, 136–37, 142–43, 149
work, availability of
Britain and, 171, 172, 180
Egypt and, 9
Finland and, 338–39
Italy and, 73–74
World Food Programme (WFP), 193–94, 309
World Health Organization (WHO), 260
World War I, 32
World War II, 264, 350
displaced person and, 34–36, 117–18

Yalta conference, 34
Yemen
as receiving country, 52, 356
Youhana (Iranian refugee), 121, 123–24
Yugoslav refugees, 44, 73, 74

Zable, Arnold, 149
Zahra (Afghan boat person), 134
Zahra (Iranian refugee), 136–41
Zimbabwean refugees, 159, 168, 169–70, 172, 184
as torture victims, 272
Zionists, 221, 229–31
"zones of protection" proposal, 176